Practical C++

Practical C++

Mark A. Terribile

McGraw-Hill, Inc.
New York San Francisco Washington, D.C. Auckland Bogotá
Caracas Lisbon London Madrid Mexico City Milan
Montreal New Delhi San Juan Singapore
Sydney Tokyo Toronto

Library of Congress Cataloging-in-Publication Data

Terribile, Mark A.
Practical C++ / Mark A. Terribile.
p. cm. — (UNIX/C series)
Includes index.
ISBN 0-07-063738-5
1. C++ (Computer program language) I. Title. II. Series.
QA76.73.C153T47 1993
005.13'3—dc20 93-28661
CIP

2 3 4 5 6 7 8 9 0 DOH/DOH 9 9 8 7 6 5 4

ISBN 0-07-063738-5

The sponsoring editor for this book was Jeanne Glasser, the editing supervisor was Christine H. Furry, and the production supervisor was Donald Schmidt. This book was set in Century Schoolbook by North Market Street Graphics.

Printed and bound by R. R. Donnelley & Sons Company.

This book is printed on acid-free paper.

To Nanny and Poppy

Contents

Preface

This book is addressed first to the professional programmer who wants to take the step from C to C++, and who wants not only to write C++ but to write it well. For those who must make the step from some other procedural language to C++, or who want to brush up on C first, refer to App. A, “A Summary of C.”

The text presents alternately the need for a C++ feature, its syntax and semantics, its proper use, and the design of programs around it, more or less feature by feature. Some of the design issues may seem either trivial or opaque until you try to put them into practice. C++ is a language for large projects, and its organizing principles extend well back into design and analysis. Those topics are far too large to cover in this volume, but the continuity between them and actual C++ code-writing can only be covered here.

Certain C++ idioms are useful or essential to the effective and safe use of C++. So far as these are known to the author, they are included with the language features they buttress. The set grows with use; the author already has some candidates to add to the chapter on templates. (Some believe that this is a fundamental weakness of C++; on the contrary, it indicates that C++ is both rich and general, and that it rewards experience and expertise—like any good tool.)

Each chapter of this book ends with a brief, section-by-section summary, which provides a quick reference and a guide to the main text. The text includes references forward and backward to feature interactions described in other chapters. Appendix D relates keywords and symbols to the syntax constructs that use them, and summarizes those constructs.

The main text assumes knowledge of C. C runs almost everywhere on nearly every computing platform, and it is worth knowing for its own sake. There are many fine books (and some not-so-fine) on C and C programming, and App. A, Secs. A.1, A.2, and A.3 of this text introduce the major concepts of C. They are neither a complete reference manual nor an implementor’s guide to C.

Nor is this text an implementor's guide to C++. The author estimates the increment in knowledge, skill, and experience from an expert user of C++ to a competent C++ implementor as the equivalent of a 4-year degree in a 'hard' science. Ron Guilmette, a member of the ANSI/ISO committee, has suggested that this estimate is conservative. (Ron is well known to readers of the netnews newsgroups on C and C++.)

The ANSI/ISO standards committee (ANSI x3j16, ISO WG22) labors steadily at their task. Even with the inevitable organizational inertia, they are making real progress on an immense job. C++ is a large language, and in spite of everyone's best efforts it is breaking new ground. The standard is officially scheduled for 1996, but that date may be optimistic.

Much of the committee's day-to-day discussion is carried out by electronic mail, allowing issues to be raised and considered between meetings. The author's machine has 15 *megabytes* of archived electronic mail produced in this effort as of December 1992. The many pounds of paper documents produced reflect thousands of hours of hard and careful thought, as well as the viewpoints and needs of dozens of user and vendor communities. Most of the key committee members are backed by their employers. All deserve the support of the C++ community.

Many thanks to all the people I've worked with over the years, and don't be surprised if you see some of your influence in my ideas and approaches.

Mark A. Terribile

Introduction

C++ is an extension of the C programming language. It shares C's simple, effective control structure, and much of C's "flavor." Programs can be written to compile and run identically under both C++ and ANSI C. Nevertheless, C++ is a very different language from C. C++'s type system directly supports both programmer-defined types and Object-Oriented programming. C++ can be a much safer and more productive language than C when its advanced facilities are used well.

Whether C++ is or is not an Object-Oriented Programming Language (OOPL) is still debated, both because C++ supports many styles of programming and because many people consider OOP to be 'what Smalltalk does' or 'what CLOS does' or 'what *<insert favorite language>* does.' This is unfair and misleading; many of those languages are used for different purposes than C++ and ought to have a different 'look and feel.'

Object-Oriented techniques promise to make programmers and software engineers more effective. Learning and using C++ is not the same as designing Object-Oriented software. Nor does skill in one imply skill in the other. Without sound methods for designing and detailing Object-Oriented systems, C++ can give only limited benefits. Programming in C++ increases the obligations of analysts, architects, and designers by requiring that analytical discoveries be recorded, architecture be formulated, and design decisions be *made* instead of being allowed to 'happen.' And if C++ is to be used successfully, the analysis and design must accommodate the facilities that C++ provides.

Right now this may be the weakest link in the use of C++. Thinking in O-O terms and C++ terms is easier than communicating what you have thought, or committing it to paper (or to CASE databases) for the benefit of the programmer.

C++ has another side. Like C, it allows code to be written 'close to the machine.' Such code can be encapsulated safely using the type system. It can also be used to support the type system, replacing tradeoffs made by the compiler and run-time designer with decisions more suited to the situation at hand. Such 'low-level' issues demand a different kind of thinking than Object-Oriented analysis and design. A C++ expert must be able to consider both the broad concepts and the mechanics, and probable effects of each upon the other.

Both the mechanics and the C++ way of thinking about programming quickly become second nature as you use them. You will soon find yourself reluctant to go back to plain old C. But you must use the C++ approach. Please try the examples in the text. And use C++ for your work as soon as you can. Even if your first efforts go little beyond ANSI C, you will have taken the first step.

That first step is important. There is a long way to go. Not until Chap. 6 do we introduce inheritance and virtualization, by which C++ provides Object-Oriented Programming. The delay is needed not because inheritance and virtualization require all the material in Chaps. 2 through 5, but because once we start on inheritance and virtualization there will be no time for storage management, conversions, and operator overloading.

No matter what the order in which we examine the parts of C++, we must defer some aspects of some features until we examine other features which work with them. And we must state rules and examine their exceptions later. We will try to warn when we do this, and to provide forward references in the text.

Versions of C++

C++ has seen several major revisions since gaining public attention. With the anticipated publication of the ANSI/ISO standard, it will have reached maturity. That standard is not due until 1995 or 1996, and may be delayed further as each parcel of new ground is trod over and over to ensure that it has been completely covered. Until the ANSI/ISO dialect is universally available, programmers must know how to use earlier versions. Until all the programs written for earlier versions have been rewritten, programmers must be able to deal with 'historical code' whose language is no longer current and supported. The worst incompatibilities are between versions before AT&T Release 2.0 and Release 2.0 and later. Release 2.1 added a few genuine incompatibilities and several enhancements. Release 3.0 added several important enhancements (most notably Templates). (On this scale, ANSI C++ will probably correspond roughly to Release 5.0.)

Because of the rapid growth of the C++ community, most programmers will find 'pre-2.0' code a primordial myth. This book mentions those differences in passing, rather than in detail.

These releases are AT&T's definitions of C++. Other major vendors include Project GNU of the Free Software Foundation, Zortech, Borland, Microsoft, Liant, and Hewlett-Packard. Most vendors' major releases have corresponded closely to an AT&T release. The release *numbers* do not necessarily correspond; one vendor's "3.0" might correspond to AT&T's Release 2.1; another's "2.0" might be more advanced than AT&T's Release 3.0.

Here are some tests by which you can guess to which AT&T release your compiler most nearly corresponds:

- Pre-2.0 releases with release numbers like 1.1, 1.2, and 1.2E will fail to compile

```
class A {} ; class B {} ;
class C : public A, public B {};
```

- 'Beta 2.0' releases will compile the previous code, perhaps warning about classes without members, but should not compile

  ```
  class A { void f() const; };
  ```

  Beta 2.0 releases were not widely distributed.

- 'Real' C++ Release 2.0 and later releases should compile both of the previous examples.

- C++ Release 2.1 and later should compile the preceding examples, as well as

  ```
  class C { typedef int I; }; C::I i;
  ```

- C++ Release 3.0 compiles the following:

  ```
  template< class W >
  class   A
    : public W
  { };
  ```

- C++ releases that compile the following are more advanced than Release 3.0:

  ```
  void
  throwint( int i )
  {
          throw i;
  }
  ```

Chapter

1

Classes, Functions, and Objects

Overview

Chapter 1 presents enough C++ to write small programs and to learn to recognize C++ constructs at sight. It assumes mastery of C and presents some of the basic differences between C++ programming and C programming. (The programmer whose C is not strong should begin with Appendix A.) The major features presented in Chap. 1 are function prototypes (for type safety) and classes and member functions (for data abstraction). Both must become familiar at a glance. For function prototypes, learning to recognize and code prototypes is probably harder than understanding their semantic ramifications: prototypes do not change the fundamental processes of programming. Classes and member functions do. They require mastery of an unfamiliar syntax and unfamiliar semantics as well as a profound shift in how we think about programming.

Chapter 1 introduces a number of other changes, small but pervasive. We must examine some properties of C that are old but not widely understood before presenting the corresponding properties of C++. And we will examine some principles of C++ programming.

1.1 Basic Changes, Part I

These changes are simple and can be understood in isolation, though some have important ramifications to other C++ features.

1.1.1 New comment format

C++ allows both the C-style comment:

```
/* begins a comment, which is ended by */
```

and a comment style borrowed from C's predecessor, B:

```
// begins a comment, which ends at the end of the line.
```

Each type of comment can hide the other:

```
/* begins a comment
(//) which ends here=> */

// Begins a comment which /* ends here =>(\n)
```

Because C++ often uses the local C preprocessor, and because C preprocessors don't recognize the // comment, the interaction between the two types of comments is not always reliable. It is unwise to use the // comment in text which the preprocessor will substitute.

```
#define HO "Fritter my wig!" // Answer to any loud cry
```

This is seldom a problem: in C++ the compiler does much work that C entrusts to the preprocessor. As ANSI/ISO-compliant C++ compilers become available, the problem will disappear. Even as of this writing, some C preprocessors have been modified to accept the // comment when invoked with an appropriate flag.

1.1.2 An underscore warning

C++ and C allow the underscore ('_') in identifiers (variable, function, and type names). ANSI C restricts identifiers with a leading underscore; such identifiers may be introduced (defined) by the compiler or compiler-provided library only. ANSI/ISO C++ also imposes this restriction.

In addition, C++ identifiers may not contain two adjacent underscores anywhere within them. This restriction protects an implementation trick used by some compilers for overloaded function names (Chap. 4, Sec. 4.3). Pre-ANSI/ISO compilers may allow the doubled underscore, but enough compilers use the trick that portable code should avoid doubled underscores, except when the symbols are defined by a library that is provided with the compiler.

1.1.3 Unsigned and long integer constants, signed chars

C++ and ANSI C support type suffixes for integral constants. The letters `u`, `U`, `l`, and `L` may be suffixed to an integral constant to indicate that the constant's type is to be modified by `unsigned` or `long`. `U` or `u` and `L` or `l` may be combined in either order.

```
25u      // Unsigned 25
1000L    // 1000, long
4096UL   // 4096, unsigned and long
0LU      // Zero, unsigned and long
```

Because the lowercase 'ell' can be mistaken for the numeral 'one', it is usually better practice to use `L`.

C++ adopts the ANSI rules for signed and unsigned chars. Both signed and unsigned are supported; an unadorned char is the 'natural' character on the machine at hand. Prior to Release 2.0, signed chars may not be supported. C++ processors which generate C code should not depend upon the underlying C compiler for the behavior of signed chars, but some do.

ANSI C and ANSI/ISO C++ permit an implementation to support an extended precision type called `long double`.

```
long double need_lotsa_precision;
```

An implementation may treat `long double` as `double`.

Floating point constants may be explicitly marked `float` or `long double`. A floating constant may be suffixed by `f` or `F` to indicate a `float` constant, or by `l` or `L` to indicate a `long double` constant. (Again, the lowercase 'ell' should usually be avoided.)

```
1.2     // double
1e-3f   // Floating
0.01L   // Long double
```

1.1.4 Introduction to basic streams output

To get any work done, we must know a little about output. Instead of standard I/O (stdio), C++ uses *streams*.

```
#include <iostream.h>

int
main()
{
      cout << "Hello, World.\n";       // Does the obvious ...

      cout << "Hello, " << "Bold New C++ "
              << "World. \n";          // Also works ...

      return 0;      // Don't forget a proper return from
                     // main()!
}
```

Stream I/O requires `<iostream.h>` instead of `<stdio.h>`. Stdio can be used, but it is not idiomatic C++ and shouldn't be mixed with streams. Prior to Release 2.0, it won't work with streams; in Release 2.0 and beyond, mixed streams and stdio will work, but one or the other may become very inefficient.* See also Sec. 1.8.2 for changes that ANSI/ISO C++ may bring.

`cout` is an object of type `ostream`.† `ostream` is a "class type" programmed with some formidable capabilities. We meet classes in this chapter, and most of this book is about them. For now, `cout` is an object (like a variable or an instance of a `struct`), with all the properties of an object. For instance, it has an address that can be assigned to a pointer, and the pointer can be dereferenced to access the object:

```
ostream* outp = &cout;

*outp << "Hi, Mom!\n" ;
```

(These examples are legal *only* because of the declarations in the header `<iostream>`. Without it, C++ can generate a barrage of precise error messages that are helpful if you know what `<iostream>` must provide.

The exact declaration of `cout` in `<iostream.h>`, and of a pointer to it, depends on the release of C++. The stream I/O package has been redesigned several times, and the ANSI/ISO committee is working on a "once and for all" definition.

Besides `cout`, which routes characters to the program's standard output, there is `cerr`, which routes characters to the program's standard error output (diagnostic output).

```
if( ! ( cout << msg << "\n" ) )
{
        cerr << "Cannot write to standard output!\n"
                << msg << "\n";
        fail( Ghastly );
}
```

The test in the `if ()` is legal, too, for reasons we will address in Chap. 10. It will fail if the output operation somehow fails.

---

* Prior to Release 2.0, instead of including `<iostream.h>`, you must include `<stream.h>`. Some later compilers will also allow you to include `<stream.h>`. On some it works properly (but may lack advanced capabilities); on others it works poorly or not at all.

† Actually, it's not quite that simple. `cout` isn't *exactly* of type `ostream`, but can be used as though it is. The full story must await Chaps. 6, 7, and 10.

Other things besides character strings can be "inserted into the output stream":

```
int i;
for( i = 1 ; i <= 50 ; i++ )
{
        cout << "Page " << i << " begins with line "
                << ( i * 56 - 55 ) << "\n" ;
}
```

We parenthesize arithmetic expressions inside stream insertion (output) expressions; we may not need to. Even though it has been redefined in `iostream.h`, the `<<` (left shift operator or stream *inserter*) retains its ordinary precedence in an expression. The precedence of the C and C++ shift operators is low enough that parentheses aren't usually needed,* but extra parentheses do no harm beyond cluttering the page. They seem justified here.

There is an analogous facility for input using `>>` overloaded as an *extractor:*

```
int i;
cin >> i ;        // cin is a predefined istream, or input
                  // stream.
cout << "You picked ... " << i << " (ta-da!)\n" ;
```

Because accepting input involves parsing input (an interesting problem of its own), we'll defer it as much as possible until Chap. 10, which deals with the stream I/O system.

Prior to C++ Release 2.0, don't try to output a single-quoted character constant; it will be treated as an integer:

```
cout << '\n' ;  // is the same as cout << 10
                // before Release 2.0
```

If you need to put out a single `char` before Release 2.0, you can write:

```
char one_c = '\n' ;

        ... ...

cout.put( one_c );
```

We'll soon see how this odd expression statement is legal C++.

---

* Recall that the shift operaters have a precedence just below binary + and – and just above >, >=, <, and <=.

Using << (left shift) operator to perform output requires giving it a new meaning. Using it for character strings (pointer to char), for integers, and for single characters requires giving it several new meanings. This is called *overloading*. We will meet overloading in Chap. 2, and will study it in detail in Chaps. 4 and 5.

The << operator, in this context, is called the "insertion" operator because it inserts characters into the output stream. "This context" is defined not by C++, but by the contents of `<iostream.h>`. The stream I/O system, including the insertion operator, is programmed *in C++ itself,* using general-purpose language features available to any C++ program, and depending ultimately on function calls to native I/O on the "Operating System At Hand."

Declaring and defining the stream I/O system requires just about every advanced programming capability in C++; we will finally study it in detail in Chap. 10.

Using streams requires at most a suspension of disbelief: Yes, that is legal C++ (when `<iostream.h>`'s declarations are included) and even has a useful meaning.

Stream I/O provides a good example of how class types should be written: It is useful without knowledge of the type's internals. The type uses whatever capabilities will provide a simple-to-use interface. (Stream I/O has some sophisticated features, but it is very useful without using them.) Whether a type should overload operators in "interesting" ways depends on how the type will be used.

1.1.5 Review: declaration versus definition

C and C++ allow data and functions to be *declared* and *defined.* The distinction between the two is crucial.

When a function is declared, its type is given:

```
int no_args_fn();
```

When it is defined, its body is given:

```
int no_args_fn()
{
        reset_args();
        return set_arg_count( 0 );
}
```

When a datum is declared, its type is given, but storage is not reserved, nor is an initial value provided:

```
extern int arg_count;
extern char** arg_list;
```

When a datum is defined, its type is given, storage is reserved, and an initial value may be provided:

```
int arg_count = 0;
char** arg_list;
```

Only external or "static external" data are separately declared and defined; all other data are declared and defined in one step.* When a definition for an external datum occurs without an initializer, ANSI C labels it "tentative" and allows subsequent definitions, the last of which may have an initializer. C++ allows just one definition.

1.1.6 Function declarations and prototypes

In C++ (and ANSI C) a function's type includes not only the type of the value it returns, but also the types of all of its arguments. *A function's* signature *is the list of the types of each of its arguments, taken in order. A function's* type *is its return type combined with its signature.* Note that the function's signature does not include its return type. In this, C++ differs from Ada.

In C++, a function must be declared before use. A function's declaration includes its signature. C++ (and ANSI C) have a new syntax for function definitions and declarations. This format is called a *function prototype.* (See Fig. 1.1.)

C assumes the type of an undeclared function is "function returning `int`." C++ does not. In C++, *all* functions must be declared before use, or the program will not compile.

A function's definition can serve as its declaration, but it is better practice to write declarations and place them where they are each written once and seen by everything that may need them. Usually this means placing them in headers.†

Function prototypes do more than provide the function's type. They allow the compiler to insert conversions in function calls:

```
double sin( double );    // Declaration(prototype)
 ... ...
const sin0 = sin( 0 );   // Call
```

In Classic C this call is a serious error. In ANSI C, the conversion of the argument will be done properly so long as there is a prototype vis-

* For `static extern` ANSI C says '`extern` with internal linkage'.

† Whether a "header" is represented as a "file" is an issue that belongs to the environment and the implementation; all that C and C++ require is that the environment can associate a unit of source code (or its equivalent) with the name of the header.

```
In old C:          int    f(); |◄────── The type of f is (int) ()
                   ... ... ... ...
                   int
                   f( x,   y )
                   int     x;
                   char   *y;
                   {
                            ... ... ... ...
                   }
```

```
In ANSI C and C++: int f( int, char* ); |◄────── The type of f is
                   ... ... ... ...                (int)( int, char* )
                   int
                   f ( int x, char* y )
                   {
                            ... ... ... ...
                   }
```

Figure 1.1

ible before the function call ('in scope'). In C++ there must be a prototype in scope.

Arguments to C++ functions are not widened: floats are passed as floats, shorts as shorts, and chars as chars. (Nor are arguments widened in ANSI C when the function has a prototype in scope.)

Descriptive *dummy names* may be given in a function prototype:

```
int f( int, char* );              // These two are
int f( int size, char* data );    // equivalent.
```

Dummy argument names can describe the calling sequence of a function, especially one that is not obvious:

```
double sin( double );    // Obvious

double pow( double, double );     // Not obvious
double pow( double arg, double exp );    // Obvious
```

There is an important difference between C++ prototypes and ANSI C prototypes. The declaration:

```
int f();
```

informs C++ that `f` is a function of no arguments returning int. It informs ANSI C that `f` is an *unprototyped* function (a function that is declared in the old way and whose signature is unknown) returning `int`.

Both C++ and ANSI C recognize

```
int f( void );
```

as a prototype for "function 'f' of no arguments returning integer." This form is recommended only for code which must remain compatible with ANSI C.

Since `main()` is a function, it must have a signature. C++ allows the implementation to define the signatures that may be used, but requires that the implementation support at least these two:

```
int main( int, char** );

int main();      // In ANSI C:  int main( void );
```

ANSI C also accepts these prototypes for `main()`. In some environments, there may be additional arguments (e.g., pointers to 'environment variable' strings.)

C++ begins a "program execution" at `main()`, just as C does. Chapter 2 explains how some code can be executed before `main()` to initialize static and external objects, and after `main()` to finish their work and dismantle them in an orderly way.

Because of the extra work surrounding the startup and cleanup of `main()`, C++ does not permit `main ()` to be called from within the program; it is no longer an ordinary function. (A C program may call its `main()` explicitly.)

Because C++ has a more complete understanding than C of types and of the properties of types, type-related compiler warnings should be considered errors unless they are shown to be a compiler bug.

1.1.7 Initialization versus assignment

Assignment and initialization are different operations. In C the distinction is usually moot and they are often confused, especially for automatic variables. C makes little distinction between

```
int i;
for ( i = 1 ; i <= 50 ; i++ )
{
        cout << "Page " << i << " begins with line "
                << ( i * 56 - 55 ) << "\n" ;
}
```

and

```
int i = 1;
for ( ; i <= 50 ; i++ )
{
        cout << "Page " << i << " begins with line "
                << ( i * 56 - 55 ) << "\n" ;
}
```

In C++, the distinction between assignment and initialization is crucial. The distinction affects all of C++'s "data abstraction" facilities, and much besides.

The semantics of parameter passing rest on the distinction between initialization and assignment. The standard for C states that the value of the actual parameter is converted to the type of the formal parameter as though an assignment were taking place.*

When a function is called in C++, the values of the actual parameters *initialize* the corresponding formal parameters, which are otherwise ordinary automatic variables. The value in the return statement's expression initializes the function call expression that invoked the function.

```
int f( int, int );

    ... ...

                    //  In C++:
    x = f( 1, 2 );  // The expression on the RHS is
                    // initialized by the expression in the
                    // return statement within the call of f(),
                    // and that RHS value is assigned to x.
    ... ...

int
f( int arg1, int arg2 ) // When the call above is made,
                        // arg1 is initialized with 1 ,
                        // and arg2 with 2 .
{
    return arg1 + arg2;    // For the call above, the
}                          // function call expression
                           // is initialized with 3 .
```

1.1.8 Declaration and initialization in C++

In C++, certain variables must be initialized in their declarations. To compute values for their initializers, statements may have to be executed before their declarations. To permit this, C++ declarations are considered statements and may be mixed freely with other statements. The object declared is in scope from the end of the declaration until the end of the smallest enclosing scope (function body or { }—enclosed compound statement).

---

* ISO/IEC *International Standard 9899:1990(E)*, section 6.7.1.

```
#include <iostream.h>
        ... ...
int sumfun( int );
  ... ...
int tot;

int i;
for( i = 0, tot = 0 ; i < 50 ; i++ )
        tot += sumfun( i );

/*
 *      Note that the declaration follows the
 *      executable statements.
 */
ostream* osp = tot > 0 ? &cout : &cerr;

*osp << "For 50 " << tot << "\n";
```

What about something like this?

```
while( something-- > 0 )
        int c;
```

The scope of this declaration is the declaration itself; the object declared as `c` cannot be visible to any other statements. This is forbidden before C++ Release 3.0. In Release 3.0 and ANSI/ISO C++, the compiler treats the code as if it were written as:

```
while( something-- > 0 )
{
        int c;
}
```

The same rule is applied to the inner statements of `for(;;)`, `if`, `if/else`, and `do/while` statements.

It is bad practice to declare a variable before it is needed, to declare a variable without initializing it (unless this cannot be avoided), or to declare a variable in a larger scope than necessary.

In C, pointer declarations are commonly written with whitespace to the left of the `*`:

```
double *xp;
```

In C++, it is standard practice to declare pointers with the whitespace to the *right* of the `*`:

```
double* xp;
```

Be careful!

```
double* xp, yp;
```

is read as

```
double *xp, yp;
```

Only xp is covered by the pointer declaration. To avoid this pitfall, you should *declare only one object or function per declaration.*

1.1.9 Objects and values, r-values and l-values

We have mentioned *objects* several times. The notion of an object is hidden deeply in the definition of C, along with the notion of the value and the distinction between rvalues and lvalues. These belong to the model of computation implicit in C and C++.

An *object* is a *region of memory with a type.* A value is harder to define, though we know it when we see it. In fact, a value is what we see when we look at an expression; it is what the expression *evaluates to,* what it "becomes" or "means" when it takes effect.

A value can be an object with a name (a variable or constant); it can also be the unnamed result of a computation. The latter objects are transient or *temporary.* They are named neither by a program symbol nor by an address, but only by the computation that produced them.

Values can be divided into lvalues and rvalues.* An lvalue is the value that identifies an object. It is the value that permits an assignment to the object. (Internally, an lvalue is represented by an address or a register number.) An rvalue is any value, whether it identifies an object or just the memory state that an object represents. (Think of "left-hand-side value" and "right-hand-side value," the values needed on the left and right sides of an assignment.)

1.1.10 Initialization of arrays by string literals

C and C++ permit an array to be initialized by a string literal:

```
char legal_in_C_and_Cplusplus[ 5 ] = "char";

char legal_in_C_only[ 4 ] = "char";
```

* Pronounced as "ell—value" and "aar—value," respectively.

In C, if there is not enough room for the null character which terminates the string, it is ignored. In C++, it is an error: the character array must provide enough room for the null character.

1.2 Extensions to the Type Structure

These changes to the C type structure are essential to C++.

1.2.1 Consts

(Consts have been adopted by ANSI C.)

In C++, any object may be declared constant:

```
const int Lines_per_page = 66;
int const Pages_per_ream = 500; //  const int  and
                                //  int const  are
                                //  the same.
double const Pi = 3.14159265359;
```

A constant cannot be changed:

```
Lines_per_page++;       // Illegal!
```

A constant *must* be initialized when it is defined:

```
const char* iron_duke = "Wellington";      // Points to
                                           //   const char
char* const work = &scratch[ next_free ]; // Pointer is const
```

`const`'ness does not affect whether a value is an lvalue. An lvalue that specifies a `const` is a *nonmodifiable lvalue,* and the lvalue of a non-`const` is a *modifiable lvalue.* (That "nonmodifiable lvalue" is an oxymoron is irrelevant.)

Arguments are initialized local variables and may be `const`:

```
int strcmp( const char*, const char* ); // Promises not
                                        // to change
                                        // the strings it
                                        // examines ...
void fixated( char* const, char* const ); // Promises not
                                          // to move the
                                          // pointers it's
                                          // been passed ...
```

In C++, preprocessor `#define`'s are rarely used except to control preprocessor `#if`'s.* Consts can be type-checked by the compiler and the compiler can provide lvalues for them, so they are full citizens, not just stand-ins.

The keyword `const` is considered to be a "type specifier" in C++ and a "type qualifier" in ANSI C. By any name, using it properly in complicated declarations takes practice.

```
const char* beef = "Wellington";
```

`beef` is a pointer to a (`char` that is `const`).

```
char const* beef = "Wellington";
```

`beef` is a pointer to a (`const` that is a `char`).

(These two examples mean the same thing.)

The declaration must always be read from the name declared outward. Because the 'const' and 'char' may come in either order, the '*' must be placed completely to the right of them. If the '*' appears to the left of a 'const' qualifier, it separates the qualifier from anything further to the left:

```
char* const beef = "Wellington";
```

`beef` is a `const` that is a (pointer to a `char`).

With practice, this becomes automatic: the `const` is placed (usually) to the left of a type name for the thing pointed to, but always to the right of a `*` for the pointer itself. `const` and an adjacent type name go together; `const` seperated from a type name by the `*` refers to a different level of indirection (degree of reference).

This is clearer if we write the `const` *after* the type name (see Fig. 1.2).

C++ (and ANSI C) try to enforce the meaning of `const`. C++ will not allow a `const` to be changed by assignment or other operation.

```
#include <iostream.h>

        ... ...
        const ostream* os = &cout;

        cout << "Who's a const?\n";     // Ok.
        *os << "I'm a const!\n";        // Illegal!
```

---

* In versions of C++ prior to Release 3.0, the preprocessor is sometimes used to simulate templates (Chap. 8). This usage is advanced, exotic, and error-prone, so it is not used lightly.

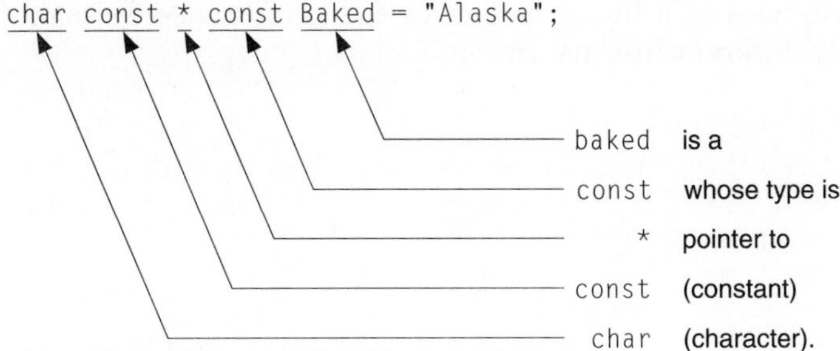

Figure 1.2

The declaration of os as a pointer-to-const declares that we will point to things with it only to examine them, not to change them. It is legal to change cout by inserting characters, but not when accessing it by a pointer-to-const. When **(pointer-to-const)* is evaluated, the resulting lvalue is nonmodifiable.

Nor can a pointer-to-const accidentally be made into a pointer-to-non-const; C++ will refuse to assign a const X* to an X*, or to initialize an X* by a const X*. However, a pointer-to-const may be explicitly cast into a pointer-to-non-const. Such casts should be used very carefully lest they conceal a bug. Program designs which call for casting away const should be avoided unless they have a very high payoff per such cast written. The ANSI/ISO committee is considering two changes: a special cast syntax for 'casting away const' (Chap. 3, Sec. 3.4.2) and 'never-const' (Chaps. 3, Sec. 3.1.4.5) for struct, union, and class) members that are not const even though the object to which they belong is.

In one case, C++ allows a const to be treated as a non-const.

```
char* Im_NOT_a_const_star = "(but I SHOULD be!)" ;
```

A double-quoted string ("literal") should be treated as a pointer-to-const-char except in the most machine-dependent and controlled circumstances. Neither C++ nor ANSI C define the result of an attempt to alter such a string.

This loophole provides compatibility with some very old code. It does not apply to array initializations:

```
char curs_com[] = "\033]Pxx;Pyyc";
```

In this case, the string notation is merely a shorthand for:

```
char curs_com[] ={ '\033', ']', 'P', 'x', 'x',
                   ';', 'P', 'y', 'y', 'c', '\0', };
```

Different instances of a literal in source code may reuse the same storage. So may different literals. In

```
const char* first_lit =
"These are the times that try men's souls."
... ...
const char* second_lit =
"These are the times that try men's souls."
```

first_lit and second_lit may have the same value. And if we add

```
const char* third_lit = "try men's souls.";
```

third_lit may point into the string at which first_lit points.

The behavior of a program that attempts to modify a literal a string is undefined.

1.2.2 Extents and consts

If consts are to be used instead of #define's, they should be no more expensive than #define's. Yet we must be able to declare any object const, and to use it in any way that does not alter it. These requirements conflict. They can be resolved if we accept some side effects: Although a const will always have the same rvalue, it will not always represent the same lvalue.

To see why, we must understand the *extent* of an object. The extent of an object describes when and how storage is allocated for the object, and when it is released. There are four extents:

- *Program* or *external extent* contains external variables.
- *File* (or 'translation unit') *extent* contains external static variables.
- *Local extent* is the extent of a function body or block (compound statement).
- *Dynamic extent* is the extent of dynamically allocated memory.

An external variable is an lvalue that is known by a single name throughout the program. This is called *external linkage.* The lifetime of an external variable is the lifetime of the program.

The lifetime of external static variables is still the lifetime of the program, but a given lvalue is known only within one translation unit (a source file and the headers it includes). This is called *internal linkage.*

Objects in local extent are created and deleted with a local scope.

Objects in dynamic extent have no names and are not managed by the compiler. They are deleted only when explicitly deleted by the program.

Because C++ may be separately compiled, anything that is managed entirely by the compiler and linker must have file extent and internal linkage. *A top-level const is given file extent by default* and may be defined and initialized in headers. To give a top-level const program extent, declare it `extern` in any header in which it appears and withhold the initializer. Define it in just one program file by writing both the extern and the initializer.

If the `const`'s lvalue is needed, the compiler must create an object to provide the lvalue; otherwise the compiler is free to provide only an rvalue. (For example, a `const int` may only exist when it is added, pushed onto a stack of function call arguments, or written into an addressing mode). If an object is created, it has file extent and there may be one created per source file.

In ANSI C, a const has program extent and external linkage by default. In either C++ or ANSI C, the programmer may explicitly select either file extent or program extent for an external `const` by specifying it as `static` or `extern`, respectively.

1.2.3 Volatile

Recall that "`const`" is considered to be a "type qualifier" or "type specifier." There is another such qualifier or specifier. It is `volatile`. It is introduced in ANSI C and adopted by C++.

An object is declared *volatile* as a warning to the compiler that something which the compiler cannot detect (e.g., hardware access to memory or to an address space shared between processes or threads) may modify or use the object, and that the compiler must avoid aggressive optimization of that variable.

A pointer-to-volatile indicates to the compiler that dereferencing the pointer will yield an lvalue that names as a volatile object.

1.2.4 References

In C and C++, 'pointer-to-`X`' is a type which can be used to name an `X`, and 'function-returning-`X`' can also be used to provide an `X`; likewise for 'array-of-`X`.'

C++ supports another type-that-can-name-an-`X`. It is the *reference.* Pointers are declared with a `*`; references are declared with an `&`. Pointer operations are *explicit;* reference operations are always *implicit.*

A reference is *used* as a variable but *initialized* with (hidden) pointer semantics:

```
int i = 0;
int& ir = i; // This is an INITIALIZATION of
             // reference-to-int ir by int i .
```

`ir` is now a synonym for `i`, and `&ir == &i`.

```
ir = 5; // Now i == 5 and ir == 5 .
```

Using the reference is fully equivalent to naming the variable:

```
#include <iostream.h>
        ... ...
int
main()
{
        cout << "Hello ";
        ostream& output = cout;

        output << "Brave New C++ ";

        cout << "World\n";

        return 0;
}
```

When necessary, a hidden temporary will be created:

```
const int& needs_temp = a + b;     // The compiler will create
                                   //   int hidden_temp = a + b;
                                   //   int& needs_temp =
hidden_temp;
```

A reference may not be initialized by `*(` *null pointer* `)` or any equivalent expression:

```
int* ip = 0;
int& ir = *ip;  // Illegal!
```

If you need to be able to represent a ‘null’ case, use a pointer or a `const` pointer.

A reference may be used as an argument type or as a return type; these are just the most common uses of references. Here’s an offbeat but perfectly legal example:

```
#include <iostream.h>
        ... ...
/*
 *      Insert will hide <<
 */
ostream& insert( ostream&, const char* );
```

```
int
main()
{
        insert( cout, "Hello, " );
        insert( insert( cout, "Brave new " ),
                              "C++ World!" ) << "\n";
        return 0;
}

ostream&
insert( ostream& o, const char* message )
{
        o << message;
        return o;
}
```

This is even wilder and woolier than it seems. `insert()` undoes the careful work of the authors of the `ostream` class, who thoughtfully hid those nested function calls under the `<<` operator!

Stream I/O depends heavily on returning objects passed by reference. Consider:

```
cout << "Hello, " << "Brave New " << "C++ World\n" ;
```

This associates as

```
(    ( cout << "Hello, " )
                << "Brave New " )
                        << "C++ World\n" ;
```

where each of the parenthesized expressions returns a reference to the `ostream` into which it inserted the characters.

References may be used as parameters in more prosaic ways.

```
#include <iostream.h>
        ... ...
ostream&
pad( ostream& o, int i )
{
        while( i-- > 0 )
               o << " ";
        return o;
}
        ... ...
        tabpos( cout, 16 ) << "Hello, Central.\n";
```

This issues 16 spaces, followed by “Hello, Central.” and a newline.

A simple swap function can be implemented with references:

```
void
swap( int& x, int& y )
{
        int temp = x;
        x = y;
        y = temp;
}
    ... ...
        int     i = 1;
        int     j = 30;

        swap( i, j );        // Leaves i == 30 and j == 1
```

`const` reference parameters are often used to pass large objects. They are as cheap as call-by-reference and nearly as safe as call-by-value. (For small objects such as ints and chars, call-by-value may be cheaper.) And safety is assured only so long as code is not malicious and does not typecast with reckless abandon. C++ is error-resistant, not proof against malice or wantoness.

`const` reference parameters protect against some unexpected errors.

```
void takes_ref( const double& );
        ... ...
double dubadubdub = ... ... ;

takes_ref( dubadubdub );

takes_ref( needs_temp + 3 ); // double ftemp =
                             //        needs_temp + 3;
                             // takes_ref( ftemp );
takes_ref( 4 );           // takes_ref( (double) 4 );
```

For the second and third calls to be legal, `takes_ref()` must accept a reference-to-`const`. This guards against making a change to a temporary, believing the change to be permanent. (Prior to Release 2.1, compilers may warn of the possible error but are not required to; and prior to Release 2.0, they probably will not warn of it.)

It is an error to return a reference to an object whose local extent is the scope of the function: the object won't be there after the function returns.

```
Uvw&
abc( Uvw obj, Uvw& ref )
{
        Uvw automatic;
```

```
… …
            return obj; // <== Wrong: obj is local .
… …
            return automatic; // <== Wrong: automatic
                              //     is local .
… …
            return ref;// <== Legal: ref is a
                       //     reference to an object
                       //     that was passed in.
```

A C++ compiler should issue a warning against obvious violations of this rule; detecting all violations would require dataflow tracing and, potentially, solving the Halting Problem.*

Unless you actually mean to alter an object passed by reference, pass it—that is to say, accept it—as a reference-to-`const`.

The proper and thorough use of `const` is called *const correctness.* Const correctness removes many bugs before they are written, and a program that is not const correct is suspect on that fact alone.

Before C++ Release 2.0, the checking of const was spotty, and headers and libraries were not const correct. One release did not accept this simple code sequence:

```
const char* hello_world = "Hello, World\n";

cout << hello_world ;
```

because the `<<` operator was written to accept `char*` on the RHS, and not `const char*`. This has long been fixed, although some compiler vendors have had more recent trouble with consts in some of their headers.

If a given function could accept a `const` and does not, your callers are faced with three bad choices:

- Don't use `const`, even when it's appropriate and would make the code safer.
- Use `const`, and make a non-`const` copy to pass to the function.
- Use `const`, and explicitly cast a pointer-to-`const` into a pointer-to-non-`const`.

The first choice may make the caller's code bigger and slower, and much less safe. Worse, callers may have to demand a non-`const` from *their* caller. The const correctness violations ripple outward from their source through the whole program, a process called *const poisoning.*

---

* The basic proof that not all problems have an algorithmic solution. It contains within it a contradiction not unlike "This statement is false," (the Epimenides Paradox).

The third choice holds a grave danger: if ever your function is changed to deliberately change its arguments, there will be no compiler warning of the code passing a `const` to you in the guise of a non-`const`. The second choice (restoring const correctness as soon as possible) may be expensive but is often the best.

Const correctness quickly becomes a habit.

The experienced C programmer may wonder if references are not a step backward. Isn't call-by-value one of the advantages of C?

Call-by-value wards off a whole family of programming errors, but prototyping and the const correctness give even stronger protection. Embedding the decision to call by value or by reference in the call*ed* function makes code more malleable by reducing the number of places that must be changed if ever the decision must be changed.

Initializing a reference with the name and lvalue of the object (rather than an explict pointer) allows the same expression to be passed either call-by-reference or call-by-value. This uniformity improves maintainability. It is also necessary for C++'s overloading (Chaps. 4 and 5).

So long as the compiler will object if a compiler-generated temporary would be passed as a non-const, C++'s reference arguments are even safer than unprototyped call-by-value.

1.2.5 Consts and safety in programming

In C, brace-enclosed blocks are sometimes written just to limit the scope of variables that are needed for only a few lines of a computation. This assures the reader that the variables are used nowhere else and affect nothing else. Of course, this is possible only if the variables *are* needed nowhere else and *do* affect nothing else. This is often true because good practice calls for using each variable for exactly one purpose. (And limiting the range of register variables can help some compilers reuse the registers, removing any incentive to reuse the variables.)

Sometimes a variable must be set in just one place in a lengthy computation and used throughout it. To assure the reader that the variable is used for just one purpose (and frustrate the misplaced sense of economy for which a maintainance programmer might reuse it), a variable can be made `const`, declaring it when its value is computed. This too is good practice.

A (non-`const`) variable is more flexible than a `const`. That flexibility brings uncertainty. Does this have the value it had a few steps ago? Does this still mean what I think it does? The privilege of changing the variable has a price. If the datum must be changed, the price is reasonable. If the datum need never change, if the code section does not need write access to the datum, then the price is too high.

In C++, it is easy to declare a datum `const`; it is easy to declare a pointer or reference to `const`. `const`s and const correctness are powerful measures for program correctness. And when we introduce overloading (Chaps. 4 and 5), it may even be possible to use a less expensive version of a function where a `const` is involved.

1.2.6 Composing consts, pointers, and references

When writing types, `const` is prefixed or postfixed to the type name, and `*` and `&` are postfixed. This causes no end of confusion.

```
const char* constant_chars;
char* const constant_pointer = "Must be initialized";
char* const& ref_to_constant_pointer = constant_pointer;
```

Read the declarations from the name declared outwards:

```
int x;                  //  x     names an int
int const xc;           //  xc    is const and names an int
int* xp;                //  xp    names a pointer-to-int
int* const xcp;         //  xcp   is const and names a
                        //                  pointer-to-int
int const* xpc;         //  xpc names a pointer-to-const-int
int const* const xcpc; //  xcpc is const and names a
                        //                  pointer-to-const-int
```

When `const` and a type name occur together, the `const` is commonly written first, as an adjective is written before a noun in English:

```
const int* const xcpc;
```

References work in about the same way, except that they are always 'constant' and so no such qualifier occurs after the `&`:

```
int& xr;              // xr   names a reference-to-int
int const& xrc;       // xrc  names a reference-to-const-int
int& const xcr;       // Illegal!
```

And `volatile` works the same way `const` does:

```
int volatile xv;      // xv   is  volatile  and names an  int
int volatile* xpv;    // xpv  names a pointer-to-volatile-int
int const* volatile xvpc; // xvpc  is  const  and names a
                      //         pointer-to-volatile-int
int volatile& xrv;    // xrv  names a reference-to-volatile-int
```

Practice and experience help, just as with

```
int* x[ 4 ];     // x is an array-4 of pointer-to-int
int (*x)[ 4 ];   // x is a pointer to array-4 of int
```

1.3 The Wheels Problem—C with Prototypes Version

To illustrate the change from the sequential programming, C way of thinking to the object-based, C++ way we will change an idiomatic C program step-by-step into an idiomatic C++ program, using C++ features as we cover them. We begin with an ANSI C version.

The problem to be programmed is this: we have some number of sets of string fragments. In each set, the fragments may have different lengths, from zero to arbitrarily long. Each set represents a position in the result string, and the result string is created by catenating one fragment from the first set, one from the second, and so on. We wish to enumerate all the possible result strings, extracting them one at a time from a generating mechanism. (This rules out recursion until we learn some object-based techniques.)

We will use an 'odometer' algorithm. Each set is represented by a 'wheel,' and each string fragment occupies one side on the wheel. We step though the output set by cycling the wheels as though they were the wheels of an odometer. To extract a result string, we read off the fragment from the front of each wheel. To step to the next result string, we advance the last wheel to the next side. If it has gone full circle, we advance the previous wheel, checking again if it has gone full circle, and so on. When the first wheel has gone full circle, we have extracted all the result strings.

Thus, if we have three wheels, and they have three, five, and two sides, respectively, and if the values of the sides are

Wheel 1	Wheel 2	Wheel 3
"the"	"water"	"spout"
"one"	"earth"	"ball"
"no"	"air"	
	"fire"	
	"thunder"	

then the first seven calls to the code implementing the algorithm would produce these strings:

the water spout

the water ball

the earth spout
the earth ball
the air spout
the air ball
the fire spout

Here it is, using the 'ANSI C part' of C++.

```
/*
 *      An 'odometer' algorithm for generating all
 *      combinations of 1 string  where there are M wheels
 *      and N-sum-M positions on each wheel.
 *
 *      Include prototypes for malloc() and free() ...
 */
#include <stdlib.h>

/*
 *      This is one wheel of the 'odometer.'  It has a pointer
 *      to an array of char*, each of which points to one side,
 *      and it has a pointer which indicates the 'front.'  The
 *      array of char* must be terminated by a null pointer.
 *      The wheel has gone full circle when the 'next' pointer
 *      points at the null.  The pointer must then be reset.
 */
struct  wheel
{
        const char** sides;
        const char** next;
};

/*
 *      We manage the set of wheels here; we have a pointer
 *      to an array of wheels and a count of wheels.
 */
int n_wheels;
struct wheel* wheels;

/*
 *      init_wheels() begins initializing the system by
 *      allocating space for an array of  n  wheels.
 */
void
init_wheels( int n )
{
        n_wheels = n;
```

```
        wheels = (wheel*) malloc( n_wheels
                                * sizeof( struct wheel ) );
}

/*
 *      To initialize a wheel, set up our own array of pointers
 *      so that we don't rely on our caller's array.  We'll
 *      continue to rely on their copies of the strings.
 *
 *      This must be called for each wheel.
 */
void
init_a_wheel( int wheel_no, const char** strings )
{
        /*
         *      Find out how many strings we have, and
         *      allocate our pointer array.
         */
        const char** s = strings;
        while( *s++ )           // Skip past the null ...
                { }

        /*
         *      Get a handy pointer to our wheel, and
         *      allocate the memory.
         */
        struct w* = &wheels[ wheel_no ];
        w->sides = (const char**) malloc(
                                sizeof ( const char* )
                                        * ( s - strings ) );

        /*
         *      Copy the pointer over and set the 'next'
         *      pointer at the beginning, and we've
         *      initialized a wheel.
         */
        for( s = strings, w->next = w->sides ;
                                        w->next++ = s++ ; )
                { }

        w->next = w->sides;
}

/*
 *      'Read off' the strings now displayed on the front of
 *      the wheels.  Return true for success, 0 for abject
 *      failure. (Typically due to incomplete initialization.)
 *
```

```
 *      Our callers should know how long the big string can
 *      get, having given us all the pieces.
 */
int
read_wheels( char* to )
{
        /*
         *      Are we set up?
         */
        if( ! wheels
         || ! *wheels[ 0 ].next )
                return 0;

        /*
         *      Read off each wheel in turn.
         */
        struct wheel* w = wheels;
        for( ; *w ; w++ )
        {
                register const char* s = w->next;
                while( *s )
                        *to++ = *s++;
        }

        *to = 0;

        return 1;
}

/*
 *      The algorithm to advance the wheels.  Starting with
 *      the last wheel, advance that wheel.  If it has gone
 *      completely around, set it back to the beginning and
 *      do the next one, otherwise return indicating 'more
 *      to do.'  If that *next* wheel has reached the end,
 *      advance *it* ...  If the last wheel has gone
 *      around, there's no more left to do.
 */
int
advance_wheels()
{
        int wh_no = n_wheels - 1;

        register struct wheel* w = &wheels[ wh_no ];
        for( ; wh_no >= 0 ; wh_no--, w-- )
        {
                if( *++w->next )
                        return 1;
```

```
            w->next = w->sides;
        }
        return 0;
    }
```

1.4 Classes I: Rationale

The *class* is the feature which most distinguishes C++ from C. Programming with classes is very different from programming with functions.

1.4.1 Scope as an organizing principle

The region of a program in which a given variable or function name (a 'symbol') can be used ('is visible') is called its *scope*. A scope is established by a function, module, block, or other structuring mechanism that divides or organizes the program's code. Scope also expresses the lifetime of the activity that the source code represents (e.g., function call or execution of a block). If there are several copies of that 'activity,' there may be several copies of the scope, which, depending on the programming language, do or do not share some or all of the types, functions, and data visible in the scope.

Programming languages support a variety of scoping mechanisms. Some languages (e.g., Pascal) support hierarchical scopes nested indefinitely. Others (e.g., C) support a 'static external' (file) scope. Others support a scope per 'module' or 'package.'

Each of these has weaknesses. External and static scopes cannot be replicated. If you need a second instance of a 'module,' you must create a new copy of the module's code. Or you may keep the per-instance data ('instance variables') in a record which the the module's callers pass as a parameter to the module's functions on each call. The module is then called a type manager.

Languages that support true modules support multiple copies of a module scope, but some give each module its own thread of execution, providing data abstraction through concurrent programming.

Under indefinitely nested scope ('true block structure'), routines can only share data with their ancestors and descendents. They cannot share data with their peers without involving their ancestors, so true data-hiding modules are impossible. Nor can they share functions privately. And mutual recursion in true block structure requires local variables to be accessed through *access links* or a *display*. This is a solved problem, but the solution has a price (Aho, Sethi, and Ullman, 1986).

Data structuring mechanisms in most languages (COBOL and some "data languages" excluded) build data structures or records up as aggregates of data of existing types, and permit arbitrary instances of a structure or record. Nevertheless, the scopes of data instances conform to the structure of the program's code; the structure of code in no way conforms to the program's data. Even data organized into structures or records are subordinate to the scope of the program's code structure.

One of the first rules of program design is: 'Structure the program around the data.'* But code structuring mechanisms divide a body of code, and do not support the structuring of code around data.

1.4.2 One example: HeapSort

The standard implementation of HeapSort requires at least one internal function, and perhaps two. Here's a possible implementation in a C-like syntax. Because of the internal functions, it is not C. (For an explanation of HeapSort, see App. B, Sec. B.1.)

The internal procedures are hard to avoid. We could use file scope and store the variables for the Heap in a struct, passing the struct's address to each HeapSort function. This would make the HeapSorter a 'type manager module' and the structure for a Heap an 'instance record':

```
/*
 *      Turn the Heap into a sorted array.
 */
for( h->end = h->size - 1 ; ; )
{
        exchange( h, 0, h->end );

        if( --h->end <= 0 )
                break;

        sift( h, h->start, h->end );
}
```

On a segmented machine,† a 'near' pointer can address 64K rapidly. A 'far' pointer can address the entire process space, but at one-quarter to one-twentieth the speed. A large internal sort can be speeded up by sorting small heaps and merging them. The merge can also be carried out with the aid of a heap. To handle multiple heap instances, the program must be in the form of a type manager with instance records.

---

* An excellent exposition can be found in chapter 4 of *The Elements of Programming Style* (Kernighan and Plauger, 1978).

† Appendix E summarizes extensions commonly made to C and C++ to deal with segmented machines.

```
void
heapsort( int size, Object array )
{
     int start, end;

     if( size <= 1 )
               return;
     /*
      *      Turn the unsorted array into a Heap.
      */
     start = size / 2 - 1 ;
     do
     {
             sift(start, size );          <-- sift() is called here.
     } while ( start-- != 0 )

     /*
      *      Turn the Heap into a sorted array.
      */
     for ( end = size - 1 ; ; )
     {
             exchange( 0, end );          <-- exchange() is called here.

             if ( --end <= 0 )
                     break;

             sift( start, end );          <-- sift() is also called here.
     }
                                          sift() is an internal function.
                                          It needs heapsort()'s internal data.
     /*
      *      Here's the sift operation.  The s_end parameter
      *      is the first position beyond the end of the Heap.
      */
     sift( int s_start, int s_end )
     {
             int next;
             for( ; ; s_start = next)
             {
                     int left = s_start * 2 + 1;
                     int right = left + 1;

                     if( left >= s_end )
                             break;

                     if( right >= s_end
                      || array[ left ] > array[ right ] )
                             next = left;
                     else
                             next = right;

                     if ( array[ s_start ] >= array[ next ] )
                             break;

                     exchange( s_start, next );   <-- exchange() is also called in sift().
             }
     }

     exchange( int one, int two )
     {
             Object t = array[ one ];
             array[ one ] = array[ two ];     <-- exchange() is also an internal function.
             array[ two ] = t;
     }
}
```

Figure 1.3

As the merge process extracts an item from the merging heap, it draws a replacement from one of the other heaps and sifts it into place in the merging heap. The heap which provided the record must be sifted again to restore it to a heap. Thus, internal operations must be callable across HeapSort instance boundaries, but the management of individual heaps should not be compromised by these extramural relationships.

This problem will be simplified by a language feature which can manage the relationships between the instance record types and the functions which operate on them, and between function invocations and the instance records to which the invocations apply.

C++ expresses and represents these relationships with a family of types called *class types* or *classes.* All of C++'s advanced programming facilities are based on class types.

1.5 Classes II: Classes and Members

A type manager module must explicitly maintain the relationship between a function managing a type and the instance of the type to which an invocation of the function belongs.

In C++ this relationship can be managed implicitly using a family of types called *classes.*

1.5.1 Introduction

C++'s `class` is a generalization of the C `struct`. C++ gives both `structs` and `classes` the additional capabilities, but with some minor differences, which we will note as we go along.

A class is declared thus:

```
class  C1
{
        int member_one;               // Member data--each  C1 will
        char* member_two;             // have a member_one and a
        ... ...                       // member_two and ...
};      // <= Don't forget the semicolon!
```

The name (tag) of the class (or struct) becomes a type name, just as if a typedef had been written:

```
class  C1
{
        int member_one;
        char* member_two;
        C1* another_C1; // Pointer to another C1
};
```

```
... ...
C1 c1;     // Declare an object of type (class) C1 .
C1* c1p;   // Declare a pointer to an object of type C1 .
```

A class member has a name and type (`int member_one`, `char* member_two`). In addition, members of a class or struct have a full or 'qualified' name and type, which include the class to which the member belongs. The qualified name or type is created by prepending the class name and the 'qualification' or *scope resolution* operator to the member name or type:

```
class  B        // full (qualified) full (qualified)
{               //      name:             type:
  public:
        int a;   //      B::a              (int B::)
        int b;   //      B::b              (int B::)
        int c;   //      B::c              (int B::)
        B* next_B;    // B::next_B         (B* B::)
};
```

Note that `B::a` consists of three separate tokens, `B`, `::`, and `a`, just as `b.a` consists of the three tokens `b`, `.`, and `a`. An expression such as `b.a` selects an instance of member `B::a` from an instance of `class B` (or `struct B`, if `B` is a `struct`). An expression such as `B::a` identifies the class and member, rather than the instance. And an expression such as `int B::` identifies the type of an `int` that is a member of `B`. What's that `public:` for? We'll examine it in Sec. 1.5.3.

1.5.2 Member functions and class scope

This section is extremely important. *You must master this material before going any further.*

> *From here forward, nearly everything we do will involve member functions and class scope. If the syntax and semantics of member function definitions and member function calls are not second nature to you by the end of this section, you will have great difficulty with everything that follows.*

1.5.2.1 Structs, classes, and members. A C `struct` groups related data within the program into a single aggregate, and allows arbitrarily many instances of that aggregate.

Like the C `struct`, the C++ `class` is an aggregate whose instances (may) contain data. Unlike the C `struct`, the C++ `struct` or `class` defines a scope within which functions and types, as well as data, may be declared. The member declarations which appear in the `class` or struct header (the type declaration) are the declarations for the class's or struct's scope, and functions which are declared in that scope are called *member functions.*

Each object (instance) of a class has its own instance of the class scope, with an instance of each data member of the class.

An ordinary (nonmember) function lies within global scope. A member function lies within the scope of its class, which in turn lies within global scope. Thus, *a member function can access the members of the class by name,* just as it accesses external and local variables.

Member functions are *declared* within the class declaration:

```
class C
{
        int a;          // Member data  C::a
        C* next_C;      // Member data  C::next_C

        int f( int );   // Member function  C::f( int )
        C* get( C* );   // Member function  C::get( C* )
};
```

Member functions are *defined* at the top level (in external/file scope) using their qualified names:

```
/*
 *      This is a definition of  C::get( C* )
 */
C*
C::get( C* arg )
{
        ... ...
}
```

(Exceptions to this rule are presented in Chap. 2.) Typically, the class declaration will be placed in a header ('.h') file, and the member functions in code ('.C') files.*

From this point forward, most of the functions and function calls we write explicitly will be member function calls. Where the function calls are implicit, the fraction will be somewhat lower, but still more than half.

1.5.2.2 Calling member functions. A member function's scope lies within its class's lexical scope. But there are as many instances of that

* On some systems, notably MS-DOS, these are ".hxx" and ".cxx" or ".hpp" and ".cpp".

scope as there are objects of the class. Which instance of the class scope is used? How is it specified?

```
class D
{
  public:
        int retrieve();             // int D::retrieve();
        void store( int );          // void D::store( int );

        int a;                      // int D::a;
};
    ... ...
void
D::store( int new_a )
{
        a = new_a;          // D::a = new_a;
}
```

A member function is called on behalf of an object (instance) of the member's class. The object is specified with the *object.member* notation:

```
D d1;
d1.store( 1 ); // Call  D::store( int ) on behalf of  d1 .
               //       Here, the "a" visible in
               //       D::store()  is  d1.a :
               //               d1.D::a = 1;

D d2;
d2.store( 50 ); // Call D::store( int ) on behalf of d2 .
                //      And here, the "a" visible in
                //      D::store()  is  d2.a :
                //              d2.D::a = 50;
```

Pointers to class and struct objects work just as they do for member data:

```
D* dp = &d2;
dp->store( 50 );          // Identical to  d2.store ( 50 );
```

Within a class's scope, that class's members can be written as though they were ordinary variables. When a qualified name appears, it usually means something special (see Chap. 2, Sec. 2.6 and Chap. 6, Sec. 6.3).

To call a member function you must have either an object of the class, a nonnull pointer to object of the class, or a properly initialized reference to object of the class.*

---

* There are exceptions for certain members; see Chap. 2, Sec. 2.1 (on constructors) and Sec. 2.6.2 (on static members).

Besides member data, other member functions of the class may also be called without naming the object:

```
class   E
{
        ... ...
        E* ee1( E* );
        E* ee2();
        E* ee3();
        E* ee4( E*, E* );
        ... ...
};
        ... ...

E*
E::ee1( E* ep )
{
        return ee2() ->ee4( ee3(), ep->ee3() );
}

        E eccles;
        E ethelred;

        eccles.f1( &ethelred );
```

This example is a little complicated. `E::ee1()` is called on behalf of `eccles` with `ðelred` as a parameter. Then

1. `E::ee2()` is called on behalf of `eccles`, and it returns an `E*`.
2. *a.* `E::ee3()` is called on behalf of `eccles`, and
   b. again on behalf of `ethelred` (pointed at by `ep`), each time returning an `E*`.
   (The order of calls in 2*a* and 2*b* is determined by the implementation.)
3. `E::ee4()` is called on behalf of the object named by the pointer returned in (1) with the pointers returned in (2) as arguments, and the call returns an `E*`.
4. `E::ee1()` returns with the value returned in item 3.

1.5.2.3 The `this` pointer. In the previous example, let's say that `E::ee1()`, called on behalf of `eccles`, wants to call `E::ee4()`, passing as one of the arguments to `E::ee4()` *a pointer to* `eccles` *itself:*

```
E*
E::ee1( E* ep )
{
        return ee2()->ee4( ???, ep->ee3() );
}
```

Within each member function, there is a pointer called `this` predefined to point to the object on behalf of which it is called:

```
E*
E::ee1 ( E* ep )
{
        //  The compiler defines an
        //  E* const this =  the E on whose
        //  behalf E::ee1 ()
        //  has been called

        return ee2 ()->ee4 ( this, ep->ee3 () );
}
```

`this` is a C++ keyword and may not be declared or redefined. The `this` pointer is similar to the "self" reference in some other Object-Oriented programming languages.

1.5.2.4 Const member functions. Like an object of a built-in type, a class object may be declared const. Such an object may not be changed, even by its members. Only member functions which are pledged not to change it may be called on its behalf. Such member functions are called *const member functions.*

```
class   Scherbattsky
{
  public:
        int count() const;    // Const member function
        int countess();       // NOT a const member function
        ... ...
        int leo;
};

int
Scherbattsky::count() const
{
        ... ...
```

C++ ensures, to the extent it can, that the `const` member function will honor its pledge and treat this as a pointer-to-`const`.

A `const` member function may not change any members of its object nor call any but `const` member functions on its object's behalf or on behalf of any of its members, nor pass the address of the object or any of its members to anything that might change it.

```
Scherbattsky sch;
const Scherbattsky const_sch = sch;        // const_sch MUST
                                            // be initialized!

sch.count();     // Legal -- sch isn't a const, and
                 // count () is
sch.countess();  // Legal -- neither sch nor countess
                 // is a const
const_sch.count();   // Legal -- object and member are
                     // both const
const_sch.countess();    // Illegal -- the object is const,
                         // but the member function isn't.
const_sch.leo = 0;       // Illegal -- the members of a const
                         // object are const.
```

`const` member functions are not supported by C++ before Release 2.0.

(Chapter 3, Sec. 3.1.4.5 discusses a proposal before the ANSI/ISO committee whereby some members of a `const` class object would not be `const`.)

1.5.3 Visibility of class scope: public and private

How much of a class's scope is visible to the outside world? Ideally, only those member functions which the outside world is meant to use. In C++, the members of a class may each be made either *public* (visible outside the class) or *private* (visible only within the class scope).

Public and private sections are marked in the class declaration by *access specifiers* written in the style of labels. A class begins with a private section:

```
class C
{         // <== The compiler provides a
          //       "private:" here .
  public:       // But we start off with public stuff.
           ... ...//     stuff here is public ...

  private:      // and now go private ...
           ... ...//     stuff here is private ...

  public:       // public again ...
           ... ...//     stuff here is public ...

  private:      // and then private ...
           ... ...//     stuff here is private ...
};
```

Only public members of C can be invoked or examined by the outside world. Only code with access to C's class scope can use C's private members.

Very early versions of C++ supported only the `public` keyword. Everything before it was private, everything after it public.

1.5.4 Classes, structs, and unions

Here is one difference between the class and the struct:

```
class   C
{       // <== The compiler supplies
        //      a "private:" here.
        ... ...
};

struct S
{       // <== The compiler supplies
        //      a "public:" here.
        ... ...
};
```

A C++ class is just like a C++ struct, except that the class begins private and the struct begins public.

C++ is defined so that, as far as possible, code that is legal in both C++ and C has the same meaning. A legal C structure declaration has exactly the same meaning in C++ as in C, so you can still write

```
struct  S
{
        ... ...
};

        struct S s;       // <== The "struct" keyword is
                          //     optional; we could also
                          //     write just S s;
```

(Because of changes in C leading up to the ANSI standard and C++, versions of C++ prior to Release 3.0 have some additional, subtle incompatibilities which vary with the version. And there are a few constructs whose meaning does change in C++.)

Classes and structs can have member data and functions, and their members can be public or private. What about unions? With some exceptions, unions can have member functions and their members may be public or private. (See Chap. 2, Sec. 2.7.3 for the exceptions.)

1.5.5 Public, private, and memory layout

In C, the members of a struct must be laid out in memory in the order in which they are declared in the structure declaration. In C++, this holds for a struct or class with one important exception: wherever a public or private label appears, the compiler is free to alter the order. Between two access control labels (with no other access control labels intervening), the compiler must respect the order in which the declarations are written. (In Chap. 6, Sec. 6.2.3, another access declaration is introduced; this rule applies equally to that declaration.) (This rule is introduced in C++ Release 3.0.)

1.5.6 Using class scope to organize programs, I

Classes are a powerful tool for organizing programs. To use them well, we must learn to think about programming in a different way.

A class's member functions belong to and represent the class. Invoking a member function commands the class object as a whole to perform some operation on itself or to provide some information. Operations on class objects should be invoked through member functions. There are exceptions, most of which fall into known categories.

The operations that a class will support should be designed when the class is designed. It is not enough to provide operations; they must be the right operations. The right operations are those which match the class's assigned role or duty. Unless the class's role or duty is well defined, it will not be possible to find the set of the 'right operations' for a class to provide.

Organizing a program into classes therefore requires defining roles which must be filled within the program and which, when filled, allow the program to function. *The types which fill these roles must model the problem and customize C++ to it.*

These class types may deal with the problem domain's basic natural types, whatever they are. They may deal with the program's process or procedure organization, with the interpreting of arguments to the program or the parsing of an input stream, or with the particulars of some algorithm, or with other essentials of a problem or a programmed solution.

To organize a C++ program into classes, the problem must be understood in terms of the roles which the types will play. To get the full benefits of C++, the only "application" function unrelated to the class structure should be `main()`. This is not an absolute rule, but exceptions should have good reason. (Some nonmember functions may be needed to fulfill certain C++ semantic and syntactic rules; these are still associated with certain classes. Others are associated with built-in types, e.g., `double abs( double )` and `size_t strlen( const char* )`).

The process of identifying the problem-domain roles for a given problem is *analysis* (for C++, Object Oriented Analysis or OOA). Determining how the players will look and what their lines are, and listing their supporting cast is *design* (for C++, Object Oriented Design or OOD). OOA and OOD are more than writing class member names on index cards, just as programming is more than writing functional decompositions and data flow diagrams. Both are young disciplines and both must be learned in order to write large C++ programs.

Classes also change a program's likely use of `extern` variables. Variables in class scope are more persistant than those in their member functions, so any variable which might be declared `static` in a member function's local scope is a candidate data member. A static variable in the function occurs once per program, a member variable in the object, once per object. The latter is usually what we really want. (Members can provide the former behavior as well; see Chap. 2, Sec. 2.6.2.)

A function which needs static data may be made into a class with a member function. What if you someday want several copies of "it," operating independently? Calling the member function may seem less convenient than calling the external function. The difference is small and the calls can be made to look alike. (See Chap. 5, Sec. 5.1.2.)

Class scope may also include the definition of classes, structs, unions, typedefs, and enums. In Release 2.1 and later, these are wholly local to the class scope. Prior to Release 2.1, the typenames are "promoted" to external scope, but enumerators remain in class scope.

We will pick this thread up again in Sec. 1.8.1.

1.6 Wheels with Classes

We can begin to transmute the Wheels program into idiomatic C++. (This is only the first step. We have a long way to go!)

```
class   Wheel
{
  public:
        void init( const char** );
        int advance();
        int copyout( char* ) const;
        void cleanup();
  private:
        const char** sides;
        const char** next;
};

class   Wheel_set
{
```

```
    public:
        void init( int );
        void wh_init( int, const char** );
        int copy( char* );
        int advance();
        void cleanup();
    private:
        int n_wheels;
        Wheel* wheels;
};

void* malloc( long );

void
Wheel::init( const char** strings )
{
        if( ! strings )
                sides = next = 0;

        const char** s = strings;
        while( *s++ ) // Loop past the null ...
                { }

        sides = (const char**) malloc( sizeof( const char* )
                                        * ( s - strings ) );
        for( s = strings, next = sides ;
                       *next++ = *s++ ; )
                { }

        next = sides;
}

int
Wheel::advance()
{
        if( *++next )
                return 0;

        next = sides;
        return 1;
}

int
Wheel::copyout( char* to ) const
{
        for ( const char* s = *next ; *s ; s++, to++ )
                *to = *s;
```

```
        return s - side;
}

/*
 *  Needs a null-terminated list of strings ... the strings
 *  we will use pointers to, but we'll create our own list.
 */
void
Wheel_set::wh_init( int wh_no, const char** strings )
{
        if ( wh_no < n_wheels )
                wheels [ wh_no ].init( strings );
}

void
Wheel_set::init( int n )
{
        n_wheels = n;
        wheels = (wheel*) malloc( n_wheels
                                * sizeof( struct wheel )  );

        for ( int i = 0 ; i < n_wheels ; i++ )
                wheels[ i ].init( 0 );
}

int
Wheel_set::copy( char* to )
{
        if( ! wheels
         || ! *wheels[ 0 ].next )
                return 0;

        for( register Wheel w = wheels ; *w ; w++ )
        {
                to += w->copy_out( to );
        }
        *to = '\0';

        return 1;
}

/*
 *  The heart of the algorithm: starting with the last wheel,
 *  advance the wheel.  If it's gone around, set it back to
 *  the beginning and do the next one, otherwise return indi-
 *  -cating that we have more to do.  If the last wheel we
 *  advance has gone around, there's no more left to do.
```

```
*/
int
Wheel_set::advance()
{
        int wh_no = n_wheels - 1;

        register wheel* w = &wheels[ wh_no ];
        for( ; wh_no >= 0 ; wh_no--, w-- )
        {
                if( ! w.advance () )
                        return 1;
        }
        return 0;
}

void
Wheel::cleanup()
{
        if( sides )
                free( sides );
}

void
Wheel_set::cleanup()
{
        for( int i = 0 ; i < n_wheels ; i++ )
                wheels[ i ].cleanup;

        free( wheels );
}
```

We have made some functional changes as we begin to convert the code into the C++ idiom. Besides a type for the individual Wheel we have a type for the 'wheel set' (or rotor machine, or whatever we decide to call it).

We have added member functions to handle the initializations, cleanup functions, and some safety checking. When an object is initialized but its subsidiary objects are not yet allocated, we ensure that the pointers are zeroed, and we check before attempting to clean up an object that the memory was actually allocated. We are paying more attention to the *state* of the object.

This adds complexity in the types that implement the operations. C++ can state some of the complexity more simply. We also have function calls where before there was inline code. C++ can avoid the function call overhead while retaining the function call semantics (Chap. 2, Sec. 2.4.4).

We have not addressed interactions between allocating memory, initializing objects, and suddenly treating a chunk of memory as an object. We consider these issues in Chaps. 3 and 5.

In Chaps. 4 and 5 we will see notational conveniences that C++ can provide.

Treating the entire set of wheels as a type unto itself allows us to create an arbitrary number of `Wheel_set`s in whatever scope is appropriate. The data and function names supporting the `Wheel_set` and `Wheel` are removed from the global name space. We are assured that nothing else tinkers with the (previously external) wheel data and that we have before us all the code that uses those particular data. Most important, it is the set of wheels, not the individual wheel, that provides a result, and so the set should be represented as a type.

1.7 Classes, Data Abstraction, and Objects

By associating a scope and member functions with an object, we have gained a scope that is tied to the lifetime of the object and that can be entered arbitrarily many times by invoking member functions, a scope of which there are as many copies as objects, a scope which can be partially or completely hidden even from the code which 'owns' the objects and in whose scope they lie.

By making data private and providing member functions which will use the data members of the class, we define the data in terms of the operations or transactions in which it participates, and which represent it.

Data Abstraction in C++ is accomplished by organizing data into classes and organizing the operations on the data into transactions performed by member functions. Data members are made private to prevent unauthorized operations on them.

Typically, a class exists either to represent some specific concept (a file which can be opened, read, written, and closed) or to perform a specific job (accept data as provided, process it, and parcel it out upon request).

Public data members are rare in C++. They generally violate the concepts around which C++'s advanced programming capabilities are built. They have some legitimate uses. For instance, they can can describe an external interface:

```
struct _86Regs
{
        union { unsigned int x; struct _86pair a; } a;
        union { unsigned int x; struct _86pair b; } b;
        union { unsigned int x; struct _86pair c; } c;
        union { unsigned int x; struct _86pair d; } d;
```

```
    int intdos();
};
```

A function which returns parsed data (e.g., 'name-value' pairs) can use a struct with public members to pass the data back to its caller. ('To present for use the data it has parsed.') Such a struct is a simple *transaction record.* And if it is not simple, it is probably better to make it into a class whose data are private.

We now give a new definition of an Object. Recall that in C an object is a region of memory with a type.

C++ also uses this definition *at the level of the language's semantics.* A higher-level definition is possible, and may be helpful when programming in C++:

> An Object has State Information and supports certain Operations that are defined by (or that define) its type.

At the machine level, we have a region of memory; at the design level, we have State information. At the language level, we have a type; that type is defined by the operations it supports.

Aristotle considered matter and form the essences of existence: a thing that exists is matter arranged according to some form (Material and Formal Causes, see also Chap. 3, Sec. 3.9). This parallels our definition of an Object: Memory corresponds to Matter (Substance) and Type (defined by an Object's operations) to Form.

1.8 Some Matters of Practice

Programs built of classes do not just happen; they are designed. Effective design considers many factors, many issues, so that the components of the design work effectively and efficiently together.

1.8.1 Using class scope to organize programs, II

A well-known title in Computer Science declares that 'Algorithms + Data Structures = Programs' (Wirth, 1975), and that programs decompose into algorithms and data structures. We have begun to divide up programming along a different boundary. 'Objects + X = Programs.' What do we insert for the *X?* What do we call the collective use of types by which larger operations are composed?

The cooperative relationships whereby objects work together in systems of objects and systems of objects interact in programs are called *mechanisms.*

Types designed for relatively close cooperation define mechanisms between them. Consider the `Wheel_set` and the `Wheel`. In such cases, the mechanism is represented by (and hidden behind) the class which presents the service which the mechanism provides.

The more closely a type is coupled to mechanism, the less general it will be. Where the interaction is simply the use by one class of another's 'ordinary' and generally available services (e.g., the arithmetic operations provided by a Complex Number* class), the mechanism uses the class but does not own it. Only when the service is specific to the operation does the class belong to the mechanism.

A type that is especially designed to support a mechanism and that is closely coupled to it should document its role in the mechanism, preferably by stating its role and refering to the description of the mechanism. If the type is the main locus of the mechanism, the mechanism may be documented with the type.

Identifying the services needed by the program and creating mechanisms to provide them are functions of (Object Oriented) Analysis and (Object Oriented) Design.

As a starting point for analysis, ask what built-in types you would provide in a language written for the given problem. Nroff and troff (Kernighan, Lesk, and Ossanna, 1978) have text, positions, sizes, and fonts for their types; the UNIX Operating System shell talks of files, strings, and programs that succeed and fail; COBOL talks of fixed-width text and numeric data. As a starting point for design, ask what sort of types would make your problem trivial, or at least very simple. Then identify the mechanisms needed to support the operations you need, and decide how to divide those mechanisms between types.

The first step will tend to produce types close to the program's data storage needs; the second, types close to the program's process management needs.

These steps will cover only the smallest and simplest programs. For others, sound OOA and OOD techniques must be studied and used.

1.8.1.1 The roles of classes. In Sec. 1.5.6 we wrote, "To organize a C++ program into classes, the problem must be understood in terms of the roles which the types will play." Identifying the roles means identifying mechanisms, since the mechanisms and the roles define each other. Some mechanisms may be specified by the requirements which the program must meet; most will be selected in the Analysis of the problem and Design of the solution.

---

* Appendix B contains a brief introduction to complex numbers.

Here are some of the many roles which classes can play:

- A class can represent a small datum of some general-purpose type. For scientific and engineering programs, a 'complex' number* is a general-purpose type. It can be represented by two floating-point numbers and a variety of stock operations can be provided for it.

  For most programs, a string type would be a 'small, general purpose type.' `string` requires more internal management than `complex` does; it will probably use a dynamically allocated buffer, and so it is a step more complicated than `complex`.†

- A class object can provide access to another object while keeping track of it. Classes can manage and hide reference counts, releasing the pointed-to object when all references are gone. Such a 'handle' class can also store information about the object it manages, or about how the object has been used.

- A class object can store information about the state of a 'real' object or process it represents. Sometimes the sequence of states is strongly sequential (which step of a recipe, which cycle of a dishwasher). Sometimes the sequence of states is not sequential, but is strongly sequenced (a finite-state machine). Sometimes the states are not sequenced at all. (Is a file open? Closed? In the middle of writing? Is there a lock on a record or a range of keys?) The member functions of such a class can and should manage the transitions from state to state, and all the actions that the transitions entail.

- A class object can represent data with structure (a sparse array, a mapping of strings to strings) or data with much structure and effort hidden (access to a file or to an RDBMS, or to an "array" stored outside the program's address space).

- A class object can manage a program's "plant," embodying the program's major data structures and relationships and the operations they support. In this role, member functions work better than type-manager modules because the class object's member functions have the object's member data in scope and do not need complicated and error-prone addressing expressions.

- A class object can perform a program's "middle management," group-

---

* Complex numbers are supported by FORTRAN, PL/I, and other languages meant for scientific and engineering use. For a brief introduction to complex numbers, see App. B.

† The ANSI/ISO committee is considering a string type, or family of types, for the standard library. It will probably be accepted, but it may not be well-tuned to all needs.

definition in the namespaces of the compound statements in which it is nested, in the function's namespace, in the class's namespace, and finally in the external namespace.

Namespace Management creates additional, named namespaces within external scope. Names of all sorts (objects, functions, types, templates, and nested namespaces) may be defined in a named namespace (a *Namespace*). Individual names from a Namespace may be accessed by scope qualification (Sec. 1.5.1). Namespaces may be given aliases. A name from a Namespace may be imported directly into the current scope. And a Namespace may be added to the list of namespaces that are searched for names seen in the current scope.

Namespace Management uses two new keywords, `namespace` and `using`.

Namespace Management affects Inheritance relationships (Chap. 6, Sec. 6.2.3.4.).

1.9.2 Creating, naming, and renaming namespaces. A Namespace is declared by its first *namespace declaration:*

```
namespace Montserrats_Magnificent_Matrices
{
        class   Matrix
                    ... ...
}
```

Here `Matrix` is a class name within the Namespace:

```
Montserrats_Magnificent_Matrices::Matrix
```

A given Namespace may have many declarations. Each one adds to the Namespace:

```
namespace Montserrats_Magnificent_Matrices
{
        Matrix::Matrix( ... ... )
                    ... ...
        Matrix::Matrix()
                    ... ...
}
    ... ...
namespace Montserrats_Magnificent_Matrices
{
        const Matrix::Matrix&
        operator+ ( const Matrix&, const Matrix& )
                    ... ...
```

```
        const Matrix::Matrix&
        operator* ( const Matrix&, const Matrix& )
                ... ...
}

/*
 *      A Namespace declaration may be empty.  Were this the
 *      first declaration with this name, it would just
 *      introduce the name.
 */
namespace Montserrats_Magnificent_Matrices { }
```

This is called *distributed specification* of the Namespace.

A Namespace's name must not conflict with any other name (object, function, type, template name, or enumerator) in the global scope. A conflict in local scope may be resolved by qualifying the Namespace name.

A Namespace whose name expresses its vendor's trademark will probably not clash with Namespaces from other vendors. This is intended. It will also lead to long, awkward names. If every mention of this Namespace must contain "Montserrats_Magnificent_Matrices" the program will be difficult to write using ordinary 80-column terminals and printers.

Worse, each code fragment that uses matrices may have to name Magnificent Montserrat, making it costly to switch to the compatible library from Fantastic Francesca.

C++ allows Namespaces to be renamed:

```
namespace MatLib = Montserrats_Magnificent_Matrices ;
```

Now the rest of the program can name `MatLib`, which is bound at one place to `Montserrats_Magnificent_Matrices.`

If even `MatLib` is too long for a function studded with explicit references to the Namespace, it can be renamed again:

```
namespace ML = MatLib;
```

1.9.3 Using a namespace. Within a Namespace, the Namespace's names are accessible just as though they were external. The Namespace is searched just before the external namespace.

```
namespace NS
{
        int f();
}
```

```
int f();

Namespace NS
{
        int callit()
        {
              return f();  //  It is  NS::f()  that is invoked,
                           //  not  ::f() .
        }
}
```

From without the Namespace, there are three ways that the Namespace's names can be accessed:

- They can be explicitly named (e.g., `NS::f()`).
- They can be imported into the namespace of the current scope by a *using definition.*
- They can be made accessible by a *using declaration.*

1.9.3.1 Importing a name with the `using` definition. The `using` *definition* specifies that a name from a Namespace is to be aliased into the current scope:

```
namespace Horologic
{
        Timestruct f();
        ... ...
}

int f();

void
hours()
{
   using Horologic::f() ;    // Makes  f()  a local alias for
     ... ...                 //  Horologic::f() .
   int i = f();              // Uses Horologic::f() , whose return
                             // type is probably incompatible with
                             // initialization of  int .
}
```

1.9.3.2 Opening a namespace for general use. The `using` *declaration* puts a Namespace in the list of namespaces to be searched, just ahead of the global (external) namespace.

```
namespace Horologic
{
```

```
        Timestruct f();
        ... ...
        Moonstruck g();
          ... ...
}

int f();

void
hours()
{
       using Horologic;      // Puts Horologic in the search path
         ... ...             // for names in this scope.
        int i = f();         // Uses Horologic::f() , whose return
                             // type is probably incompatible with
                             // initialization of int .

        g();                 // Calls Horologic::g() .
}
```

We've shown `using` definitions and declarations in various local scopes. They may also be written in file (external) scope.

1.9.4 Resolving conflicts between `using` declarations. Names from one Namespace can conflict with names from another:

```
namespace Pasta
{
          ... ...
        class  Wagon_wheels
                ... ...


          ... ...
}

namespace Chandeliers
{
          ... ...
        class  Wagon_wheels
                ... ...

          ... ...
}

using Pasta;
using Chandeliers;

Wagon_wheels roundup;   // ?? ? Pasta or Chandelier ? ??
```

Both Pasta and Chandeliers define Wagon_wheels. Namespaces do not take precedence over each other, so this is ambiguous.

We can avoid the ambiguity by qualifying Wagon_wheels explicitly, thereby bypassing the name search:

```
using Pasta;
using Chandeliers;

Pasta::Wagon_wheels roundup;
```

If one of the two Namespaces (say, Pasta) contributes most of the Namespace-based names, the using declaration for the other Namespace can be replaced by using definitions for the few names needed:

```
using Pasta;                           // using declaration
using Chandeliers::ir_intensity;       // using definition
using Chandeliers::visible_intensity;   //    "       "
using Chandeliers::surface_heat_flow;   //    "       "

Wagon_wheels roundup;    // Pasta is searched; Chandeliers is not .
```

1.9.5 Do as I do: a stdlib namespace. The ANSI/ISO committee believes that the C++ standard library should be subject to Name Management. If it acts on this belief, there will probably be two versions of each standard library header: the 'real' header containing a Namespace declaration which holds the various library declarations, and a 'compatibility' header containing an #include for the real header and a using declaration to make the whole Namespace visible. The real header may abandon the ".h" while the compatibility header retains it, per Sec. 1.8.2.

1.10 Summary

Section 1.1.1 C++ introduces a new type of comment:

```
// New comment, which comments out  */  and  /*
/*
 * And the old format comments out the  //  (see
 * what I mean?)
 */
```

Some C++ processors use old preprocessors and the new comment cannot be used in #includes (App. A, Sec. A.3.1.2.2).

Section 1.1.2 C++ adopts ANSI C's rules for unsigned and long constant suffixes (u, U, l, L) and for signedness of chars (signed char, `unsigned char`, and `char` which is signed or unsigned depending on the compiler) (See Sec. 1.1.3). For signedness and overloading, see Chap. 3, Sec. 3.4.3 and Chap. 4, Sec. 4.1.2.

Section 1.1.3 C++'s basic character input-output mechanism is the stream which can be set up for input, output, or both (Chap. 10, Sec. 10.2). Stream I/O looks approximately like the following:

```
#include <stream.h>
    ... ...
    cout << "Hello, World.\n"
            << "Pick a number: " ;
    int i;
    cin >> i ;      // cin is a predefined istream, or input stream.
    cout << "You picked ... " << i << " (ta-da!)\n" ;
```

For overloading the I/O operators, see Chap. 4, Sec. 4.4.7 (overloading) and Chap. 10 on stream mechanics.

Section 1.1.4 C++ enforces the multiple-declaration, one-definition rule (ODR) strictly (C does not). For initialization rules, see Sec. 1.1.7 and Chap. 2.

Section 1.1.6 C++ requires that functions be *prototyped.* A prototype declares the function and its argument types, which constitute its *signature:*

```
/*
 *      Type is int ( int, char*, int, int )
 *      Signature is ( int, char*, int, int )
 */
int somefun( int, char*, int, int );
```

In C++, the function `main` is distinguished and may not be called from within the program.

Section 1.1.7 Initialization and assignment are different operations and obey different rules. See Sec. 1.2.1 (consts), Sec. 1.2.4 (references), Chap. 2, Sec. 2.1.2 (constructors), Sec. 2.1.5 (default initialization), Sec. 2.1.6 (member initializers), and Sec. 2.1.13 (dynamic initialization).

Section 1.1.8 An object is a region of memory with a type, or a State Memory with Operations defined upon it. Reconciling the two definitions is a core challenge when programming in C++. Objects have values. One value they share with their copies (rvalue), another is a property of the individual instance of the object (lvalue).

Section 1.1.8 In C++, when a string literal is used to initialize an array, the array must have room for the trailing null character; C does not require this.

Section 1.2.1 C++ supports constants objects of all types. These are qualified in their declaration by `const` and must be initialized. Special rules apply to `const` objects and pointers-to-`const` (*const correctness*).

Section 1.2.2 C++ uses `consts` instead of `#defines`, and changes the default visibility and linkage of external consts to file scope. See also Chap. 2, Sec. 2.3.5 on enums.

Section 1.2.3 C++ supports `volatile` as well as `const`. `volatile` indicates that something which the compiler cannot see may change the object, and that the compiler must limit optimization of evaluation of the object.

Sections 1.2.4, 1.2.5, 1.2.6 References provide alias names to existing objects. They are *implicit* indirection. References provide reference and const reference parameters. See Chap. 2, Sec. 2.1.3 ("Copy Constructors") and Chap. 4, Sec. 4.4 ("Operator Overloading").

Section 1.4 Class types organize code and scope around data. See Secs. 1.6, 1.8.1, and Chaps. 2 (Sec. 2.8.3) and 3 (Secs. 3.9, 3.10) on using and designing with classes.

Sections 1.5.1, 1.5.2 Classes have member functions as well as member data. Member functions are called from (on behalf of) a class object, and see that instance of the object in their scope. (See Fig. 1.4)

For `public` and `private` see Sec. 1.5.4.

Section 1.5.4 Class members may be *public* (accessible inside and outside the class) or *private* (accessible only inside the class). They may also be *protected.* (See Chap. 6, Sec. 6.2.3.2.)

Section 1.5.5 Classes, structs, and unions have similarities and dissimilarities. Classes and structs are more alike to each other than to unions. All support member functions.

Section 1.8 Classes are the organizing principle of C++ programs. They have to be organized in source and header files, and those must

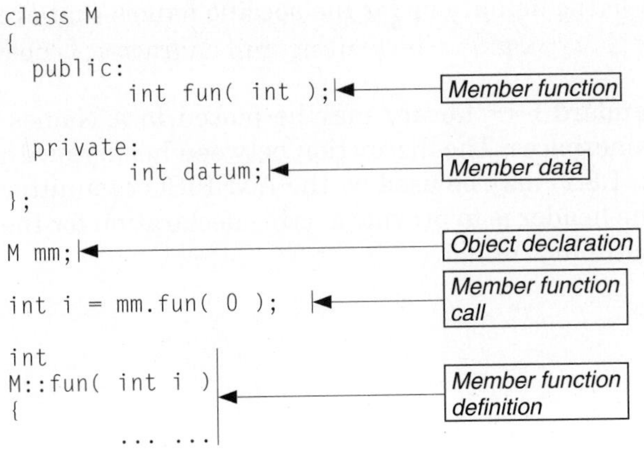

```
class M
{
  public:
        int fun( int );     <-- Member function

  private:
        int datum;          <-- Member data
};

M mm;                       <-- Object declaration

int i = mm.fun( 0 );        <-- Member function call

int
M::fun( int i )             <-- Member function definition
{
        ... ...
```

Figure 1.4

be compiled. The source code organization should reflect the program's organization; compilation is generally similar to the compilation of C. See Chap. 8, Sec. 8.4 for special compilation considerations in programs using advanced C++ features.

Section 1.9.1 Each scope in a C++ program has an associated namespace. Namespace Management creates additional, named Namespaces. These lie just within external scope, or just within each other (when one is nested within the other). Namespace Management uses the keywords `namespace` and `using`.

Section 1.9.2 Declaring a Namespace declares its name. The same name may be used in multiple Namespace declarations; they are all taken together to provide the contents of the Namespace (*distributed specification*). A Namespace may be renamed to provide a shorter name or to decouple a program from a particular library implementation.

Section 1.9.3 The contents of a Namespace are visible within that Namespace. Code anywhere can access names in the Namespace by qualifying the name with the Namespace name.

Sections 1.9.3.1, 1.9.3.2 A name from a Namespace can be given an alias in the current scope by a *using definition*. A Namespace can be added to the namespaces to be searched for names with a *using declaration*.

Section 1.9.4 Ambiguities created by multiple `using` declarations can be resolved by explicitly qualifying the names or by replacing one of the `using` declarations by `using` definitions for the specific names that are needed.

Section 1.9.5 The standard C++ library may be placed in a Namespace, or in several Namespaces. The distinction between headers with and without ".h" (Sec. 1.8.2) may be used by the ANSI/ISO committee to indicate whether the header is to provide a `using` declaration for the Namespace (for compatibility) or not.

Chapter

2

Managing Classes, Enhancing Functions

Overview

In Chap. 1 we examined two groups of changes from C to C++. The first was a collection of important oddments; the second, the class with its scope, member data, and member functions. Now we study a vital aspect of C++'s class types: the creation and destruction of class objects. We also meet enhancements to C's rules for functions, more oddments, and some indispensable specialties.

This chapter will leave us with a more consistent—but not at all complete—understanding of C++, class types, and their use. We create a loose end by introducing overloading. It will take all of Chaps. 4 and 5 to ravel that thread.

2.1 Classes III: Constructors and Destructors

The lifetime of a class object's member data begins before the first use or access of those members, and ends after the last use or access of those members. Constructors and destructors manage these extremes of a class object's lifetime.

2.1.1 Modules, monitors, and the class scope lifetime

Classes are user-defined types whose instances are objects with operations defined on them and a clear distinction between what is externally visible (public) and what is not (private). A class object has its own scope, persisting from one member function call to the next, from creation to destruction of the object. An activity can be split across member function calls by using the object's data members as the activity's variables.

Classes support many programming models. For example, a class whose member functions have no local variables can behave like a procedure with multiple entry points. Although a class does not own the thread of execution which enters and leaves its scope, when the thread is within the object's scope it acts on behalf of the class.

The lifetime of a class object's member data begins sometimes before the first member function call or public access, and ends sometime after the last member function call or public access. We must be able to program these extremes of a class object's lifetime.

```
class  Args
{
  public:
        // Set up the arg list ...
        void init( int arg_count, char** arg_list );
        int more();
        void next();
        istream* open( open_mode read_write ); // An istream
                                                // is for input
                                                // ...
        // Close the last open stream and reset ...
        void release();

  private:
        ... ...
};

int
main( int argc, char** argv )
{
        Args a;

        // ... ... ... ... It's not safe to use a here ...
        a.init( argc, argv );    // <== Until it's initialized
                                 //     here ...
        for( ; a.more() ; a.next() )
        {
                istream* input = a.open();
                if( *input )
                        process( input );
        }
        // Any resources that a took for itself are
        // tied up, any pending work incomplete ...
        a.release();      // <== ... until the explicit call
                          //     that finishes it up.
}
```

The 'Abstract Data Type' (ADT) represented by `Args` is incomplete unless it can guarantee that the work of an `Args` is properly started and properly finished. So long as an instance of `Args` must be set up and cleaned by the code which creates it, `Args` is neither a complete type nor a safe programming abstraction.

2.1.2 Introduction to constructors and destructors

To manage the creation and destruction of class objects, C++ has special member functions called *constructors* and *destructors*. Constructors control the initialization of a class's instances; destructors control the dismantling of those instances. If a class has a constructor, the constructor *will* be called to initialize an object of the class when that object is created. If the class has a destructor, the destructor *will* be called to dismantle an object of the class when that object is destroyed.

Constructors and destructors are invoked automatically, ensuring that setup and cleanup are not forgotten, entail what they may. Operations in constructors and destructors are securely under control of the author of the class. They also allow the lifetime of an object to be used as a programming tool.

For class `XYZ`:

Constructors are named `XYZ::XYZ()`

Destructors are named `XYZ::~XYZ()`

Constructors may take arguments; destructors may not. Constructors and destructors have no return value. It is an error to declare a return type, or to try to return a value.*

```
class   Fido
{
  public:
          void Fido();     // Illegal
          void ~Fido();    // Illegal
}

class   Ruff
{
 public:
          Ruff();             // Correct
          ~Ruff();            // Correct
}
```

* G++, the GNU version of C++, allows destructors to have return types and return values.

```
                Krazee kr( "brubulububullaboolllaaabroo" );

                abort();        // <= Abnormal exit!!!

                // kr.~Krazee() is NOT called.
            }

        // Neither is rhyme.~Sane() .
    }
```

None of the objects created by the callers and callers of callers, right back to main, will be destroyed properly, nor will static or extern object destructors be called. (For abnormal termination that causes destructors to be properly invoked, see Chap. 9, "Exceptions.")

What happens when objects must depend upon each other?

For local and file scope (definitions within blocks and static external definitions), C++ enforces some consistency. Objects in local or file scope will be created in their order of definition (not declaration) and before the execution of any functions (member or nonmember) in that file ('compilation unit') (except other constructors and functions invoked by constructors). They will be destroyed in the opposite order after the last execution of any such functions.

```
extern Z_of_y z_thing;          // extern declaration; does not
                                //   initialize  z_thing .

X x_thing( z_thing );           // Created first, destroyed last.
  ... ...                       // It can safely store the ADDRESS
                                //   of z_thing , but it cannot
                                //   safely _use_z_thing .

Y_of_x y_thing( x_thing );
  ... ...

Z_of_y z_thing( y_thing );      // Created last, destroyed first.
```

A constructor for `x_thing` might call a member function of `z_thing`. C++ does not defend against this, so constructors and destructors must avoid unnecessary accesses to static or external objects and calls to functions which might cause such accesses. (The ANSI/ISO committee is looking for possible improvements in this area, but it is a difficult problem.)

For objects of dynamic extent (dynamically allocated objects) the programmer must ensure that objects may remain as long as they can be referenced. (See Chap. 3.)

What happens when the objects have external scope? In Release 2.0 and beyond, objects of external or file extent will be initialized from top to bottom *relative to objects within the same compilation unit* (source code file). The order of initialization relative to objects in other compilation units is not defined.

Within each compilation unit, the objects will be destroyed in the reverse of the order in which they were created.

Thus, if file `a.C` defines external objects `a_1`, `a_2`, and `a_3` (in that order) and file `b.C` defines external objects `b_1`, `b_2`, and `b_3`, and these two files are compiled and their object codes linked into a program, the Objects may be created in any of these orders:

```
a_1, a_2, a_3, b_1, b_2, b_3
```

or

```
b_1, b_2, b_3, a_1, a_2, a_3
```

or

```
a_1, b_1, a_2, b_2, a_3, b_3
```

Other orders are legal as well, so long as the order of objects within each file is respected. In practice, the orderings in the first two lines are the most probable.

When C++'s consistency controls on initialization are not strong enough, special measures can ensure that the objects are created and have not been destroyed. See Sec. 2.1.13.

Because all objects are ultimately destroyed, linked data structures must be kept consistent or else properly dismantled before the program exits.

The guaranteed order of creation and destruction for file scope objects was introduced in C++ Release 2.0.

2.1.3 Copy constructors

Passing an argument to a function and returning a value from a function are initializations.

```
class   Mogul
{
  public:
        Mogul( int, int );
            ... ...
};
    ... ...
const Mogul
mage( Mogul midge )
{
        ... ...
```

```
        return midge;
}
        ... ...
        Mogul margin( 0, 5 );
        Mogul marlin = mage( margin );
```

margin is initialized by Mogul::Mogul(int, int) . But how does margin initialize mage(Mogul)'s parameter midge? And how does the return of the value of midge initialize the RHS expression in the declaration of marlin? And how is marlin initialized by the value of that expression?

Since Mogul has a constructor, a constructor initializes a Mogul. But the constructor defined for Mogul is Mogul::Mogul(int, int) .

The answer to the dilemma has three parts. First, these initializations need a particular constructor. Second, a class may have more than one constructor. Third, C++ provides some constructors automatically.

The constructor that initializes a Mogul by a Mogul is

```
Mogul::Mogul( const Mogul& )
```

This is called a *copy constructor.* The copy constructor for class X is X::X(const X&) (i.e., the signature for the copy constructor for class X is (X&)).

If Mogul lacks a Mogul::Mogul(const Mogul&) but has a Mogul::Mogul(Mogul&), C++ will use it wherever it is legal. In this example, the declaration of margin would be legal, and so is the function call to mage. The declaration of marlin would not be legal because the return of mage(Mogul) is const and cannot be used as a non-const Mogul.

In C++ Release 2.1 and beyond, constructors with default arguments (Sec. 2.4.1) can also be used as copy constructors so long as they can be called with a copy constructor's signature.

If a copy constructor is unavailable (e.g., if it is private and we do not have access to its class's scope) we cannot pass objects of that class into functions, nor can we call a function that returns a value of that class.*

2.1.4 The overloading of constructors

Mogul must have two constructors, each with a different signature. Both are named Mogul::Mogul. A function name for which there are

* C++ releases before Release 2.0 did not enforce this uniformly, but the rule was always there.

two versions, distinguished by their signatures, is said to be *overloaded.* Constructor overloading is a simple case of a very rich and very general facility whose description takes all of Chaps. 4 and 5.

Constructor overloading allows multiple ways of initializing a class's objects. Without it, few classes could use constructors. Any class used as a parameter or return type would be excluded. You could either have the copy constructor and pass parameters of the class (how would the first object be initialized?) or have a noncopy constructor and not pass or return objects of the class.

When there are several overloads of a constructor, C++ will select the one (if any) which best matches the arguments provided. *Best match* will be defined at length in Chap. 4, but C++ easily distinguishes between a copy constructor and a constructor of no arguments, between either of those and a constructor of two or more arguments, and between a copy constructor and a constructor that accepts a built-in type (e.g., `int`, `double*`) or an enumerated type.

```
class   Widget
{
        ... ...
        Widget::Widget();
        Widget::Widget( int );
};

Widget::Widget()        // Initialize with no arg ...
{
        ... ...
}

Widget::Widget( int i ) // Initialize using an int ...
{
        ... ...
}

        Widget x1;                  // Uses Widget::Widget()
        Widget x2( 30 );            // Uses Widget::Widget( int )
```

2.1.5 Default initialization

A class object's members are themselves objects that are initialized when the class object is initialized. Often, they can receive 'default' initialization, the initialization they would have as 'uninitialized' nonmembers:

```
class   Got_no_constructor
{
  public:
```

```
        int counter;
        Got_no_constructor* left;
        Got_no_constructor* right;
};

Got_no_constructor in_program_extent;

void
a_func()
{
        Got_no_constructor in_local_extent;
}
```

in_program_extent and in_local_extent are default-initialized. Got_no_constructor's members are initialized like nonmembers written in the same place as its parent object. Here the members of in_program_extent will be initialized to integer 0 (for Got_no_constructor::counter) and the null pointer (for left and and right). in_local_extent's members are 'initialized' with whatever their memory contains when they are created.

```
class   Have_a_constructor
{
  public:
        Have_a_constructor();

        int counter;
        Have_a_constructor* left;
        Have_a_constructor* right;
};

Have_a_constructor::Have_a_constructor()
{
        counter = 0;
        left = 0;
        right = 0;
}

Have_a_constructor constr_in_program_extent;

void
b_func()
{
        Have_a_constructor constr_in_local_extent;
}
```

Have_a_constructor has a constructor of no arguments. This is called a *default constructor* and is invoked to initialize constr_in_program_ extent and constr_in_local_extent.Have_a_constructor::Have_a_constructor() *assigns* zero to each of its members. It does not initialize them. C++ will reject this:

```
class   Have_a_const
{
  public:
        Have_a_const( int max_n );

        const int limit;
        int counter;
        Have_a_const* left;
        Have_a_const* right;
};

Have_a_const::Have_a_const( int a_lim )
{
        limit = a_lim;  // ILLEGAL: limit is a  const
        counter = 0;
        left = 0;
        right = 0;
}
```

This constructor is illegal. A constructor may no more *assign* to a const than may any other function. It must *initialize* the const.

2.1.6 Member initialization

Have_a_const::limit belongs to a Have_a_const object and it's created *before* the body of the constructor. Code in the constructor body is too late to initialize it; it already exists.

There is a special syntax for initializing member data. (See Fig. 2.1.) The members and initializers are listed before the constructor body in a *member initializer list.* As explained in Chap. 6, Sec. 6.2.4, it's also called a *base initializer list.* This example initializes Have_a_const::limit by the argument a_lim, Have_a_const::counter by integer zero, and Have_a_const::left and Have_a_const::right by (Have_a_const*) zero.

The member initializer list can initialize reference members, const members of all sorts, members whose constructors take several arguments or none at all (leave the argument parens empty) and any other nonstatic members.*

---

* Prior to C++ Release 2.0, some compilers had trouble with intializing const and reference members of any type.

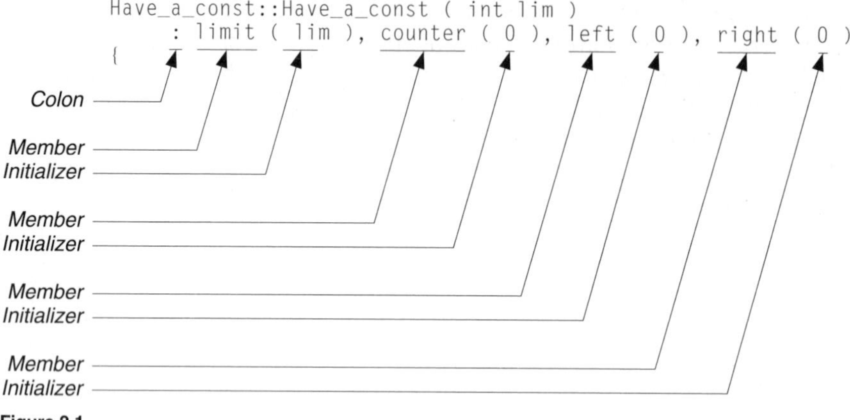

Figure 2.1

```
class Inner
{
  public:
        Inner( int, const char*, int );
          ... ...
};

class Outer
{
  public:
        Outer( int, const char*, Inner&, Inner& );
          ... ...
  private:
       Inner in_1;       // This may be initialized in the list
       const Inner in_2; // Const and references MUST

       Inner& other_1;   // be initialized in the member
       Inner& other_2;   // initializer list.
};

Outer::Outer( int a, const char* nm, Inner& lhs, Inner& rhs )
  : other_1( lhs ), other_2( rhs ),
    in_1( a, nm, 0 ), in_2( a, nm, 1 )
{ }
```

The initializations are performed *in the order in which the members are declared in the class header*, not *the order in which the initializers are written in the constructor*. (Here, `in_1` and `in_2` will be initialized first, then `other_1` and `other_2`.) This ensures that the member objects can reliably be destroyed in the reverse order, no matter how the initializers are written in different (overloaded) constructors.

Because member objects are created in order of their declaration and destroyed in the reverse order, objects that depend upon each other must be properly ordered in the class header:

```
class   Five_of_Em
{
  public:
        Five_of_Em( Em* list_of_em );
        ... ...
  private:
        Em& first;
        Em& second;
        Em& third;
        Em& fourth;
        Em& fifth;
};
    ... ...
Five_of_Em::Five_of_Em( Em* list_of_em )
  : first( *lots_of_em ), second( *first->next ),
    third( *second->next ), fourth( * third->next ),
    fifth( *fourth->next )
{ }
```

If the Em&s were declared in another order, this code would be illegal. Assuming the list is five long may be unwise, of course.

```
Em nil; // An lvalue to use in place of a null pointer.

Five_of_Em::Five_of_Em( Em* list_of_em )
  : first( lots_of_em ? *lots_of_em : nil ),
    second( first->next ? *first->next : nil ),
    third( second->next ? *second->next : nil ),
    fourth( third->next ? *third->next : nil ),
    fifth( fourth->next ? *fourth->next : nil )
{ }
```

2.1.7 Memberwise constructors provided automatically

For each class, C++ can provide two constructors automatically. If no constructor is written for a class, C++ will try to provide a default initialization for that class's objects. That default may require a (hidden) constructor. If a copy constructor is needed and none is written, C++ will attempt to create one for the class, even if there are other constructors.

A constructor provided automatically performs member-by-member or *memberwise* initialization. For each data member of the class object, in the order of their declaration, C++ tries to find an appropriate initialization for that member.*

If the data member is of a built-in type, it will be initialized appropriately for that type, with default initialization if the constructor is a default constructor, or value copy if the constructor is a copy constructor. *Const and reference members cannot receive default initialization, and C++ will reject a declaration for a class with const or reference members, but without constructors.*

If the data member is of a class type and there is an appropriate (default or copy) constructor available, that constructor will be used. Otherwise, this procedure will be applied recursively to create a default or copy constructor.†

An extant copy constructor may be unavailable, e.g., it may be private. And if `X::X( const X& )` is not defined, `X::X( X& )` may be used as a copy constructor if the actual initializer is not `const`. If both are defined, C++ will use the first for `const` parameters and the second for non-`const`, in accordance with the rules in Chap. 4, Sec. 4.1.3.

These rules apply to structs as well as to classes.

Consider:

```
class   alpha
{
  public:
        alpha beta( alpha numeric );
        const alpha* gamma( const alpha& ) const;
        void delta( int );
        int theta() const;

  private:
        int sigma;
        char* tau;
        aleph null;  // There exists a public
                     // aleph::aleph()
        eta pi;      // but no constructors for eta .
        alpha* omega;
};

        alpha particle;
```

* Releases of C++ prior to C++ Release 2.0 supported not memberwise initialization but bit-by-bit copy. This was a serious flaw. If the member depended upon a copy constructor to maintain integrity (e.g., by reference or resource count) the constructor would be bypassed when creating the object in which the member was embedded.

† Some early releases (before Release 2.0) would not create a copy constructor automatically if there was another constructor.

Applying the rules given at the start of this section,

1. `particle.sigma` and `particle.tau` are initialized by integer zero and pointer null, respectively and in that order.
2. `aleph::aleph()` is called on behalf of `particle.null`.
3. `particle.pi` is initialized according to the same rules we are applying to `particle`.
4. `particle.omega` is initialized with pointer null.

Consider also:

```
alpha particle;
... ...

particle = particle.beta( particle );
```

In calling `particle.alpha::beta( alpha numeric )`, how is numeric constructed within `alpha::beta ()`?

1. `numeric.sigma` and `numeric.tau` are initialized with the values of `particle.sigma` and `particle.tau`, respectively and in that order.
2. `aleph::aleph( particle.null )` is called on behalf of `numeric.null`.
3. `numeric.pi` is initialized according to the same rules we are applying to `numeric`, using as its initializer `particle.pi`.
4. `numeric.omega` is initialized with the value of `particle.omega`.

2.1.8 When C++ can't be trusted (to provide constructors)

For certain classes C++ will generate copy constructors that are almost certainly wrong.

If initializing a class object involves managing resources or establishing or adjusting of linkages of any kind, the copy constructor provided by C++ is almost certainly wrong and will probably result in disaster when the program executes.

This does not apply if all the 'action' takes place within members whose copy constructors work properly. Only for the class that is actually responsible for the correct interactions between data structures and creation structures will the memberwise rules generate a bad constructor.

Looking at it another way: If there is a relationship between this object or its members and an outside object, this object 'means something' to that other object by its existence. If there are linkages between the members of this object, the existence of the object means that those linkages are needed and permitted. If an object needs resources, its existence represents a relationship between the object and those resources. If the object means something by its very existence, a memberwise constructor will not describe everything that must be done when creating the object any more than a memberwise destructor describes everything that must be done when dismantling it.

Objects of a type which represents only an rvalue and which is represented entirely by rvalues (e.g., a complex number) can usually use the automatically provided constructors. But for an object that represents an rvalue but is represented with linkages (e.g., a `String` class with its dynamically allocated character array), memberwise construction and destruction will not manage the relationship properly, and the copy constructor provided by C++ will not be correct.

2.1.9 Programming with lifetimes

An object's lifetime is bracketed by the execution of its constructor (if any) and destructor (if any). Constructors and destructors must work from wherever they are called and must be programmed to work reliably without undue side effects, independent of unreliable external conditions. Object creation and destruction semantics pervade C++, which relies on types to manage themselves.

That a declaration invokes 'real' user code can be unsettling, that the end of a lexical scope can invoke user code even more so. And, that code can be invoked before and after `main()` may lead to a crisis of C/C++ faith. It can also mean deliverance, as the `Args` example showed. Stream I/O's buffering facilities depend upon destructors to clear the buffers.

Counted references and access objects are possible. An object (say, a database) can be invoked through a member function that returns an object that gives access to the first object. The "access object" may also store state information. When it is created, the database allocates resources for this 'port,' and when it is destroyed, the database is notified and releases whatever resources were needed for it (e.g., locking table records).

The destruction of an object can hide arbitrary complexity, including the destruction of linked objects. Here's an offbeat example:

```
#include <iostream>
#include <stdlib>
class FATAL
{
 public:
      FATAL( ostream& o ) { out = o; };
      ~FATAL() { out << flush;    // flush is a special object
```

```
                        ::abort(); };      // which forces the stream
                                           // to be flushed.
            ostream& s() { return *out; };
      private:
            ostream* out;
    };
            … …

            if( … … )    // OMIGOSH!
            {
                    FATAL rip( cerr );
                    … … Lots of analysis … …
                    rip.s() << … …;
                    … … Lots more analysis … …
                    rip.s() << … …;
            }               // <== And abort()  is invoked here.
```

2.1.10 Equivalent initializer syntaxes

Given a class `String` with `String::String( const char* )`, the following forms are identical:

```
String st = "Fillet of a fenny snake";

String st( "Fillet of a fenny snake" );

String st = String( "Fillet of a fenny snake" );
```

The first two are the forms that we've seen before: the assignment syntax for initialization and the constructor-of-one-argument syntax. The third form is 'value builder' syntax, and the reason for it is found in Chap. 3, Sec. 3.3.

If `String` also has `String::String( int, const char* )`, these two are identical:

```
String st( 50, "In the cauldron boil and bake" );

String st = String( 50, "In the cauldron boil and bake" );
```

With more than one argument, the assignment syntax cannot be used.

2.1.11 Typedefs and class names with constructors and destructors

Consider

```
class   Alas
{
        ...
```

The initialization of `i_am_extern` is a normal C initialization and is handled as C would handle it: the compiler puts linker information in the object code that fills `i_am_extern`'s memory location with `33` before program execution begins. This is called *static initialization.*

In contrast, initializing `j_is_extern`, `k_has_file_scope`, and `hc` must be done at run time, just after the start of program execution. This is *dynamic initialization.* All static initialization is completed before dynamic initialization begins. *Program extent and file extent objects that are to receive dynamic initialization are first given default, static initialization.*

A compiler can implement dynamic initialization by creating a 'constructor' for each file. This 'file constructor' performs initializations like those of `j_is_extern` and `k_has_file_scope`, and calls `hc.Has_a_constructor()`. The linker (or a postlinker) can arrange that all the file constructors will be invoked once by either the run-time start-up or the generated `main()`. (This is just one way to implement dynamic initialization.)

There is no way to determine in what relative order objects in different files should be initialized, so C++ leaves the order indeterminate. The order in which objects from different source files are dynamically initialized may change from compile to compile and even (in theory) from run to run. The ANSI/ISO committee on standardizing C++ is examining several proposals that would allow the order of initialization to be specified, but no satisfactory proposal has emerged as of June 1993.

An external object which must be initialized before an external object in another source file cannot depend on dynamic initialization. There are schemes that can be made to work. One is used by C++'s stream I/O and (in outline) it works like this: There are several types of streams, related by inheritance (Chap. 6) which allows them to be used more or less interchangeably. One type is a 'with_assign' stream, which can be 'assigned' another stream. The assigned-to stream becomes, in effect, an alias for the stream on the RHS of the assignment.

`cin`, `cout` and `cerr` are with-assign streams. With-assign streams are static-initialized to an empty, unusable state. To set them up for use, there is a class named `Iostream_init`. `Iostream_init` has a static data member (a data member shared by all instances of the class and given program extent—see Sec. 2.6.2) that is static-initialized to zero.

When an `Iostream_init` is created, it increments that static member. If the member's value is already greater than one, the I/O system is already initialized and the `Iostream_init` does nothing. If that static member's value is one, this `Iostream_init` is the first `Iostream_init`, so it creates the 'real' I/O streams and assigns them to the with-assign streams. When an `Iostream_init` is destroyed, it decrements the static member. If the member has gone to zero, it's the last `Iostream_init`, and it flushes and closes the I/O streams.

The headers for the I/O stream system declare static (file scope) instances of the `Iostream_init`. Every compilation unit (source file) which includes `stream.h` as its first header is assured that the I/O system will be initialized before any constructors that might use it are executed.

2.2 Wheels with Constructors and Destructors

Now that we have constructors and destructors, we can improve the Wheels example. We can't quite go the whole way just yet because we don't know how to make constructors and destructors work with dynamic allocation yet. Here's what we can do:

```
class   Wheel_set
{
  public:
        Wheel_set( int );
        ~Wheel_set();
        void wh_init( int, const char** );
        int copy( char* );
        int advance();
  private:
        int n_wheels;
        Wheel* wheels;
};
 ... ...
Wheel_set::Wheel_set( int n )
{
        n_wheels = n;
        wheels = (wheel*) malloc( n_wheels
                        * sizeof( struct wheel ) );
        for( int i = 0 ; i < n_wheels ; i++ )
                wheels[ i ].init( 0 );
}

Wheel_set::~Wheel_set()
{
        for( int i = 1 ; i < n_wheels ; i++ )
                wheels[ i ].cleanup();

        free( wheels );
}
```

```
        r.a.p.h = Set_cursor_position;
        r.c.x = 0;
        r.d.p.h = y;
        r.d.p.l = x;

        r.int86( BIOS_Video_Driver );
```

Notice that we must write the three qualifiers to name a half register, and two to name a full register. Using C++'s *anonymous union,* we can write a better interface.

```
/*
 *      A register pair has a low and a high register.
 */
struct i86pair
{
        unsigned char l;
        unsigned char h;
};

/*
 *      A register may be either a 16 bit register or a pair.
 */
struct  i86Regs
{
        union { unsigned int ax; struct i86pair a; };
        union { unsigned int bx; struct i86pair b; };
        union { unsigned int cx; struct i86pair c; };
        union { unsigned int dx; struct i86pair d; };
        ... ...
};
```

The unions that are members of this struct have no names; they are *anonymous.* The names of members of an anonymous union (`ax`, `a`, etc.) are accessible as members of the enclosing class or struct (`i86Regs`). Anonymous unions may also be written with file scope ('external static'). All their members must be public, since their namespace is transparent to their surroundings.

```
/*
 *      Put the cursor at( x, y ) .  ...
 */
i86Regs r;

r.a.h = Set_cursor_position;
r.cx = 0;
r.d.h = y;
r.d.l = x;
r.int86( BIOS_Video_Driver );
```

This is better. There is no extra qualifer (p). We still have to write the half and full registers differently, but with only two qualifiers in the worst case.

Here C++, a higher-higher-level language, provides a cleaner interface to a low-level machine manager. If C++ refused to work at low levels as well as high levels, the improved higher-level interface couldn't be programmed in C++. Cleaning the mess means dirtying your hands so that when you do clean them, they stay clean.

2.3.5 Enums are fixed

C and C++ support an enumerated type:

```
enum Color { Red, Blue, Green, Transparent = -1 };

Color foreground;
Color background;
```

In both C and C++, the enumerated type is an integral type for which the enumeration names the valid constant values.

In 'Classic' (pre-ANSI) C, it is an error to use an enumerated type value as the control expression in a switch. ANSI C allows it. C++ supports it; if 'most but not all' the possible values are named in cases, a warning may be generated.

enums have another important use. Recall that #defines are deprecated. There are some places where a const is not constant enough: in array size declarators, for the expression in a case label, and as the initializer for an enum. For these places, an *enumerator* (the name of one of the values of an enum) may be used instead. Anonymous enums are permitted:

```
/*
 *      'Red', 'Blue', 'Green', 'Transparent',  'Foreground',
 *      and 'Background' are enumerators belonging to
 *      anonymous enums.
 */
enum { Red, Blue, Green, Transparent = -1 };
enum { Foreground = 0, Background = 10 };
      ... ...
setcolor( Foreground, Red );
```

The values assigned are

```
Red == 0;
Blue == 1;
Green == 2;
Transparent == -1;
```

An anonymous `enum` may not be used to declare variables.

An `enum` written within a class belongs to that class's scope. See Sec. 2.6.3. `enums` can be used within classes to provide true compile-time constants.

You will sometimes see an enumerator `Me` of an enumeration `E` described in language documentation as `E::Me`. *This is a notational device only; it is* not *legal C++ code.* See Sec. 2.6.3.

An `enum` may be freely converted into any integral type large enough to hold all its values. This will generally be `unsigned` unless negative enumerators have been defined (in which case `int` will be used) or unless enumerators too large have been defined, in which case signed or unsigned `long` will be used. (Prior to ANSI/ISO C++, enumerators were generally represented by signed integral types.)

Conversion of integral types to enumerated types is permitted by cast.

2.3.6 Enums may become first-class types

The `enum` suggests a type which represents '1 out of *N*' aspects of the problem being programmed. C's `enum` was often used otherwise, and C++'s `enum` is expected to follow suit. They are used as general-purpose constants, as 1-of-*N* indicators, and as bitfield/bitflags that can be OR'd together. When coding an `enum`, you should specify what it represents, and under which of these (or other) cases it falls.

In the July 1992 meeting in Toronto, the ANSI/ISO C++ standards committee considered what happens when built-in arithmetic and bitwise operators are applied to enumerated types. Based on the discussion and on minutes of the subsequent November and March meetings, the following changes appear likely for ANSI/ISO C++:

- When both operands of an arithmetic or bitwise operator are enums of the same type, the result will be of that type.
- In consequence, an enum variable may legally take on values other than those of the enumerators written for that type.

Look for these changes in July or November of 1993.

2.3.7 Block versus compound statement

In C,

- an open brace, followed by
- zero or more declarations, followed by
- zero or more statements, followed by
- a close brace

is variously called either a compound statement or a block. In C++, a distinction is sometimes made: a compound statement that contains a declaration or a block is called a *block*.

```
/*
 *       A compound statement.
 */
{
        x++;
        cout << "hic\n";
}

/*
 *       A block.
 */
{
        int eye = i;

        while( zark ( eye-- ) )
                {}   // But this is a compound statement ...
}
```

This terminology is not part of the definition of C++, but it is used in discussing the language.

2.3.8 goto, constructors, and scope

By making an object's lifetime extend from well-defined construction to well-defined destruction and allowing an object's lifetime to be tied to a scope, C++ creates interactions between 'ill-conditioned' jumps and declarations. Consider this code fragment:

```
{
        Goodest baddest;

        if( bogus )
                goto hither;     // Illegal!

        if( bogartus )
                goto thither;    // Ok.

        Bestest worstest( 1, 3, 5 );

  hither:
        cout << "Sick?" << endl ;
}

thither:
```

The first `goto` would transfer into the scope of `worstest`. This is not allowed, since it would bypass the initialization of `worstest`.

The second `goto` skips the scope of `worstest` entirely. It does *leave* the scope of `baddest`, but that is legal. A `goto` may leave the scope of a variable (or const or array); the destructor will simply be called during the execution of the `goto`.

This restriction also applies to `switch()` statements. This, for example, is illegal in C++:

```
switch( n )
{
  case 1:
        ...
        break;

        {
                int miomaio;

  case 2:       // This  case  is a label within the scope
                // of  miomaio  .
                ...
        }
}
```

Would anyone write such a thing? See Duff's Device in App. B (Sec. B.3) (which can be written as legal C++).

2.3.9 Alternate spellings for national character sets

Certain national character sets (most notably the Danish 7-bit set) lack some of the characters needed for C++ operators. In ANSI C, *trigraphs* were provided (App. A, Sec. A.1.1.3). These proved to be less than ideal. To make C++ more useful around the world (and to promote harmony in international standards bodies), the ANSI/ISO C++ committee adopted a set of 'alternate spellings' for various tokens. These become new tokens, and in some cases, new reserved words, in ANSI/ISO C++.

These are the alternate spellings and the symbols for which they substitute:

Alternate spelling	Primary spelling
<%	{
%>	}
<:	[
:>	]

Alternate spelling	Primary spelling
`and`	`&&`
`or`	`||`
`not`	`!`
`bitand`	`&`
`bitor`	`|`
`xor`	`^`
`compl`	`~`
`and_eq`	`&=`
`or_eq`	`|=`
`xor_eq`	`^=`
`not_eq`	`!=`
`%%`	`#` (For the preprocessor only)
`%%%%`	`##` (For the preprocessor only)

There will also be alternate spellings for >, >=, <, <=, ==, and !=. These are the subject of heated debate.

Unlike trigraphs, these alternate spellings are not recognized inside quoted character constants or string literals.

At this date (June 1993), it is still possible, though very unlikely, that the standards committee will repent of this change.

2.4 Enhancements in the Calling of Functions

C++ has several extensions to make functions and their calls more maintainable, more convenient, and more affordable.

2.4.1 Default arguments

C++ allows arguments to have default values ('default arguments'):

```
void f( int x, int y, int z = 909 );    // 909 is the default
                                         //   value for z .

... ...

f( 1, 2, 7 );
f( 2, 2);       // Equivalent to f( 2, 2, 909 );
```

Only trailing arguments may be defaulted.

```
void g( int x = 0, int y = 0 ); // Two optional args ...
g( , 10 );                 // ILLEGAL--only trailing args
                           // may default.
```

Functions (especially member functions) often have both prototypes and definitions. The default argument can be written in only one place, and should be written where it will be seen by everything that needs to see it, generally in the prototype that appears in a header file. In the compilation unit (source file and headers it includes) in which the function definition appears, the default argument must appear before the definition. For member functions, the declaration of the function in the class header will usually be the first declaration of the function, and is almost always the correct place to put the default argument values.

Some inline functions (Sec. 2.4.4) may be used before their definition is seen. In this case, the default argument must appear on the first declaration or definition.

When a constructor's arguments all default, the object is declared without constructor arguments or constructor argument list:

```
class   Merlon
{
  public:
        Merlon( int = 0 );
        ... ...
};

        Merlon merl( 17 );
        Merlon cren;      // All arguments default on
                          // Merlon::Merlon
```

Default arguments can be used to enhance an existing program:

```
void Zt::dump();          // Print the object on cerr .
```

We can add a new capability without rewriting all the calls to `Zt::dump()`:

```
void Zt::dump( ostream& dumpout = cerr );
```

Existing calls of `Zt::dump()` will use `cerr`, but other calls can default to `cerr` or name any output stream. The callers of `Zt::dump()` must be recompiled, but not rewritten.

C++ supports many such kinds of source-code-preserving enhancement. In general, changes to class definitions or function prototypes require the users of the class or the callers of the function to be recompiled, but most enhancements to properly written C++ programs can be made without changing the source code that uses the class. (This helps to define 'properly written.')

2.4.2 Unused arguments

Remember that a function's type includes the types of its arguments. So does the type of a pointer-to-function:

```
char f( char* from );     // Let's invoke this function
                          //   through pointers ...

char(*fp1) ( char* ) = &f;
char(*fp2) (char*, int ) = &f; // Type violation !!
```

If you want to invoke function `f()` through `*fp2`. `f()` must be declared to take arguments `char*` and `int`.

```
char f( char* p, int n );
char(*fp2) ( char*, int ) = &f; // Legal now ...
```

Unfortunately, if argument `n` is unused in `f()`, the compiler may—and should—issue a warning. C++ allows us to declare that an argument will be unused, by omitting the argument name in the function definition:

```
char
f( char* from, int )      // The second argument will be
{                         //   accepted but not used.

        ... ...

char(*fp2) (char*, int ) = &f; // Ok: both are
                               // char(*) ( char*, int )
```

This is useful for functions that are to be called out of tables. It's also vital to the OOP mechanisms that C++ provides, and which stand in relation to tables of functions as classes stand to type manager modules and explicit instance records (Chap. 6).

2.4.3 Unknown arguments

Even in C++, functions that are used like `printf()` are sometimes needed. These require lists of unspecified arguments, which C++ and ANSI C declare with the ellipsis:

```
int typesetf( char*, ... );

void whazzit( void*, ... );
```

(The last comma in the argument list may be omitted.) There must always be one prototyped argument.

These are strongly discouraged because type checking and certain type semantics must be suspended. Moreover, the function's definition must be either machine-dependent or else must use a clumsy mechanism called `stdargs`, described in App. A, Sec. A.1.

When an object of a type with a constructor is passed via the ellipsis, the type system cannot ensure that it is properly copied. In C++ Release 2.0 the issue was addressed by prohibiting such arguments. In C++ Release 2.1 and later the object is copied bit-for-bit. In other words, the object is not copied; its representation is copied. If the object has linkages, resource counts, etc., it is the responsibility of the called function to somehow make things right. And, when the object has the property called *virtual multiple inheritance* (Chap. 7, Sec. 7.2), it has internal linkages created by the compiler. Bit-for-bit copy is an inadequate solution.

Arguments passed through the ellipsis are subject to the C rules for widening of `float` to `double`, and of `char`, `short`, `unsigned char`, `unsigned short`, bitfields, and `enums` to `signed` or `unsigned int`.

2.4.4 Inline functions

Data abstraction requires that a class's member data be hidden from the outside world. Even simple data should be read and set through member functions. But calls to very small functions can take more time than the operations in the functions, and can be very costly if done often.

In C, when data abstraction is simulated by type managers small 'functions' are coded as preprocessor macros (e.g., `getchar()`). But preprocessor macros don't have access to a class's private members, nor can they check prototypes and insert conversions. Instead, C++ provides *inline functions.* A C++ function may be declared `inline`. The compiler will expand the function inline if it is possible, in the compiler's sole judgment, to do so. Inline functions have the full support of C++'s type system and are full-fledged functions in almost every way. In particular, parameters to an inline function are evaluated once and once only, no matter how often the argument variables appear in the body of the function. Parameters may be passed by value or reference. And it's legal to take the address of a function whether it is inline or not. But nonstatic inline functions may not access static data members of a class (Sec. 2.6.2).

Inline functions have file (compilation unit) scope; if they are useful to multiple source files, they must appear in headers, usually in the header files with the class declarations. And if the compiler must create out-of-line copies of the function, there may be one per source file which uses it. (The compiler must create an out-of-line copy of a function if a pointer to an inline function is taken, either explicitly or implicity, in support of C++'s OOP facilities—see Chap. 6).

More sophisticated C++ compilers try to prevent this, and some offer manual control over which compilation is responsible for creating out-of-line copies. In general, these work the same way as the 'vtable' creation controls (Chap. 6, Sec. 6.5).

The best candidates for inlining are functions which set or get a data member or which reformat their arguments and call one or two other functions. Constructors and destructors are often poor candidates for inlining because they can carry a lot of hidden baggage if their class uses C++'s OOP facilities (Chap. 6). Among nonmember and static member functions, the best candidates for inlining are those that are just a few expressions long, or that provide a short, heavily used computation. Such inlines often resemble FORTRAN's arithmetic statement functions.

It is rarely worth inlining a function with more than three or four expressions, and sometimes even that is unprofitable. There are exceptions. Sometimes functions are written for clarity instead of code sharing. Declaring these inline may make sense even if they are large. The compiler is free to ignore the request to inline the function. (Functions that contain loops or multiple returns or `goto`s are less likely to be inlined, but this depends on the compiler at hand.)

There are two ways to declare a function inline. A member function may be made inline by writing it within the class declaration:

```
class Coccoran
{
        Rackstraw me;
        ... ...
  public:
        Rackstraw& iam() { return me; }
        ... ...
};
```

When C++ reads the class header, it considers inline functions written in the header as both declarations and definitions. It processes them as declarations where they are seen and processes them as definitions at the end of the class header. This means that an inline member function body may use members that are declared either before or after it.

When writing a class or struct in local scope (within a function), the class is only known in that scope. It is unknown in external scope and cannot be used to qualify member names, so ordinary member functions may not be written. Local classes can have inline member functions, although a given implementation of C++ may place restrictions on them.

A friend function (Chap. 3, Sec. 3.6) may also be written inline in the header of the class that declares it a friend.

If a function really needs these types, and if they really should be internal, they can be moved into the class of which the function is a member. If the function is not a member, a class can be created to represent the function's 'mission' and the function made a static member. Then the local classes are moved out into the new class.

Any function, member or not, can be made inline by declaring it inline in its first prototype (or all its prototypes) and its definition.

```
inline int apply( a_class&, b_class& );
        ... ...

inline int
apply( a_class& hither, b_class& yon )
{
        return hither.somefunc( yon );
}
```

This form too has file extent and should be placed in a header.

One problem with inlines declared in class headers is that mutual dependencies between classes may occur. If class `A` is declared before class `B`, and member functions of `A` use `B`, they cannot be written inline in the class header. They can be written inline later, so long as care is taken to ensure that all the declarations they need will be available when their header is `#include`'d.

Mutual dependencies are messy, and one seasoned contributor to the netnews C++ newsgroup, Bob Martin of RCM Consulting, has argued on netnews that they should be avoided in inline functions if at all possible; this seems a sound practice.

When will the compiler refuse to expand a function inline? This is compiler-dependent. AT&T compilers have refused to inline functions that are 'very large,' that contain a loop, or that have multiple returns (unless the flow control follows certain limited patterns). Other compilers use other criteria, including size, complexity, and certain constructs which are difficult or expensive to expand inline.

There is a bug in some early AT&T C++ compilers. Certain if-else statements, when written inline, generate semantic errors from the C compiler used to generate code. In these statements, the statements in the if-part and the then-part are expression statements and have different types:

```
int     f();
void    v();
... ...
if( cond )
        f();
else
        v();
```

This code fragment won't generate the problem, but it is typical of those that do. The problem has been observed when the second expression statement is a `delete` (see Chap. 3).

Long lists of inlines can slow compilation or compete with type information, etc., for a compiler's physical and virtual memory. Nevertheless, inlines are an important tool and should be used as needed. Short inlines in class headers can make a program clearer, especially if those inlines do nothing but return or store member variables. Longer inlines in the header usually do the opposite.

2.5 Wheels with Inlines

We can now make inline some of the little functions in the `Wheels` example. This will buy back most or all of the efficiency lost to the access control in member functions.

It's common to squeeze lines out of functions that are written in the class header to keep the header short.

```
class   Wheel
{
  public:
        void init( const char** );
        int advance()
        {       if( *++next ) return 0;
                else { next = sides;
                        return 1; }
        };
        int copyout( char* );
        void cleanup() { if( sides ) free( sides ); };

  private:
        const char** sides;
        const char** next;
};
```

This is as much as we can write inline. It's important: `Wheel::advance()` will be called often. `Wheel_set::advance()` and `Wheel::copyout()` would be candidates for inlining. They contain loops, but one

Accessing a data member this way violates data abstraction. Fortunately, C++ also supports *static member functions.* A static member function has no pointer, but it does have access to the private part of its class's scope and other static members of that class are visible to it. It may be invoked either on behalf of an object or with the class name and qualification operator.

```
class   Flugelhorn
{
  public:
        static int census();
        ... ...
        static int n_flugelhorn;
        ... ...
};

Flugelhorn f;

int
Flugelhorn::census()                // Flugelhorn::census() does
{                                   // not see any of Flugelhorn's
        return n_flugelhorn;        // members EXCEPT the static
}                                   // member n_flugelhorn.

        int how_many = Flugelhorn::census();

        Flugelhorn tootler;
        how_many = tootler.census();
```

Static members may also be used for internal 'helper' functions that are needed for the class's job, but that don't actually work in the class's name scope. For instance, a hash function used by a class's member functions is a good candidate for a static member function; so are functions that belong to a class's subject area (e.g., a typography class might include public static member functions to convert between inches, picas, points, etc.).

Static member functions are also valuable for computations which must be performed in order to initialize data members:

```
class   Cooked_stats
{
  public:
        Cooked_stats( const raw_stats& );
        ... ...
  private:
```

```
        const int n_samples;
        const float mean;
        const float sum_sq;
        const float std_dev;
        ... ...
        static float compute_mean( const raw_stats& );
        static float compute_sum_sq( const raw_stats& );
        static float compute_std_dev( int n_samp,
                        float sum_of_sqrs, float mean_sq );
};

Cooked_stats::Cooked_stats( const raw_stats& rs )
  : n_samples( rs.n_samples ),
    mean( compute_mean( rs ) ),
    sum_sq( compute_sum_sq( rs ) ),
    std_dev( compute_std_dev( n_samples, sum_of_sq,
                                    mean * mean ) )
{
        ... ...
}
```

The `compute_`*XXX*`()` functions almost certainly contain loops and could not be written as expressions in the member initializer list.

Static member functions were introduced with C++ Release 2.0. Until then, they were faked with member functions that used only static member variables. These were called on behalf of the 'object' named by a null pointer. This is disallowed in current releases.

2.6.3 Nested classes and types and local classes

So far we have examined classes, structs, and unions defined at the top level (i.e., in file scope), and enums defined at the top level and in class scope. Types of all sorts may be written within local and class scope. Certain rules and restrictions apply.

Before Release 2.1, handling of nested types was incomplete and erratic. Classes could be written in local scope and class scope, but they were 'promoted' to the smallest enclosing local or file scope. In Release 2.0, enums were also promoted, but their enumerators were not! And so on.

From C++ Release 2.1 forward, types and type names obey the general scoping rules of C++, with some restrictions and special handling.

2.6.3.1 Nesting types within scopes. Enums obey the scoping and visibility rules simply. So do most `typedef`s, those which do not contain an actual class, struct, or union header.

A type defined within a class may be referenced outside that class (subject to the access control rules) by qualifying it:

```
class   Has_an_enum
{
  public:
        enum Is_an_enum { en_1, en_2, en_3 };
        ... ...
  private:
        enum Nuther_enum { ne_1, ne_2, ne_3 };
          ... ...
};

        Has_an_enum::Is_an_enum inner_enum =
                          Has_an_enum::en_1;

        /* Illegal! Nuther_enum is private. */
        Has_an_enum::Nuther_enum inner_enum =
                           Has_an_enum::ne_1;
```

Classes, structs, and unions defined in local (function) scope have special restrictions. They may not have static members of any kind and all of their member functions must be inline functions defined in the class header. A C++ implementation is free to impose severe restrictions on what functions will actually be compiled inline (Sec. 2.4.4). Within a class scope, a member `plugh` will hide a variable of the same name in the enclosing scope. There is no way to get at that hidden name.

2.6.3.2 Forward declaration of nested classes (ANSI/ISO C++). Nesting classes can control namespace pollution and is important when the classes are actually *class templates* (Chap. 8). Nested classes can become excessively long and excessively 'deep' across the page.

The ANSI/ISO committee has accepted a proposal by Tony Hansen to permit nested classes (and structs and unions) to be *forward declared.* The new type name is established within the parent class's scope. Then the new type's definition is provided after the parent class's definition is complete:

```
class   Outer
{
          ... ...
        class Inner;     // Outer::Inner  is declared
                         // inside Outer .
          ... ...
};
```

```
class   Outer::Inner    // Then Outer::Inner  is defined
                        // outside  Outer.
{
        ... ...
};
```

Since the size of `Outer::Inner` is not known before the end of `Outer`'s declaration, `Outer` cannot have an `Outer::Inner` as a member. Nor can functions written in the class header of `Outer` use the members of `Outer::Inner`.

2.6.3.3 What lexical nesting means. When classes (and structs and unions) are defined within class (or struct or union . . .) scope, they belong to the outer class's namespace. *These inner types have no special access to the enclosing class scope.* They are subject to the outer class's public/private mechanisms. In addition, *objects of the class are* not *presumed to lie within an object of the enclosing type.*

```
class Outer
{
  public:
        class Pub_inner
        {
          public:
                void pub_in_fun();

          private:
                void priv_in_fun();
        };
        int public_mem() const;

        Outer();

  private:
        class Priv_inner
        {
          public:
                void pub_in_fun();

          private:
                void priv_in_fun();
        };

        int private_mem() const;
        Outer( int, int, const Outer& );
};
```

Outer::Pub_inner and Outer::Priv_inner have access only to Outer's public part:

```
void
Outer::Pub_inner::pub_in_fun()
{
        Outer ou;
        Outer ou_x( 0, 0, ou );

        ou_x.private_mem();     // Illegal!
          ... ...
}

void
Outer::Priv_inner::pub_in_fun()
{
        Outer ou;
        Outer ou_x( 0, 0, ou );

        ou_x.public_mem();      // Ok
          ... ...
}
```

Outer has access to the public parts of its nested classes:

```
int
Outer::private_member() const
{
        Pub_inner pb;       // Outer::Pub_inner belongs to
                            //   Outer's scope ...
        pb.pub_in_fun();// OK.
        pb.priv_in_fun();   // Illegal:  priv_in_fun() is
                            //   private to  Outer::Pub_inner

        Priv_inner pv; // Outer::Priv_inner belongs to
                            //   Outer's scope ...
        pv.pub_in_fun();    // OK.
        pv.priv_in_fun();   // Illegal:  priv_in_fun() is
                            //   private to  Outer::Pub_inner
};
```

Things outside of Outer have access to the types in Outer's public parts:

```
void
j_random_func()
{
```

```
        Outer::Pub_inner opin;  // Legal: Outer::Pub_inner
                                //   is public.
        Outer::Priv_inner opin; // Illegal: Outer::Priv_inner
                                //   is private.
}
```

Here an object of a class nested within Outer has been created in a context not nested within Outer's scope. When we accessed Outer::public_mem() in Outer::Priv_inner::pub_in_fun(), we did so on behalf of an object ou_x local to that function. Since there is no guarantee that an instance of a nested class lies within an instance of its 'parent' class, the nested class does not lie within the the parent class's scope.

In releases of C++ from Release 2.0 through Release 3.1 there is an exception to this rule.

For functions written inline within the header of a (nested) class, static members of the enclosing classes may be accessed without qualification. (These inline functions include *friend* functions as well as member functions. See Sec. 3.6.)

```
class Wrap
{
  public:
        static int gift();
        static int plastic();
        struct   Per
        {
                int diem() const
                {   return gift();  };  // No Wrap:: needed
                                        // when the member is
                                        // written here.
                int centum() const;
        };
};

int
Wrap::Per::centum() const
{
        return Wrap::plastic();     //  Wrap::  is needed
                                    //  when the member is
                                    //  written outside the
                                    //  class header.
}
```

This oddity was introduced to comply with the familiar visibility rules of lexically nested scopes. It turns out that this greatly complicates the rules that specify the order in which the namespaces of various scopes are searched for a given name. Long discussion with many examples convinced the ANSI/ISO committee that there is no way to 'get this right.' Every solution results in 'surprises,' including surprises that are legal interpretations and don't generate a compiler error message. This feature will be removed from ANSI/ISO C++.

2.6.3.4 Nesting to preserve the global namespace. The value of enums nested in classes for providing local constant names and enumerations should be obvious. The value of classes nested in classes may be less obvious.

In a large system, nesting classes by subsystem can prevent namespace collisions. Where one type acts as an 'assistant' to another (e.g., a class X needs a linked list-of-X class, a class Y needs a linked-list-of-Y class, etc.), nesting the assistant classes in their principals can reduce the clutter of types and typenames. When a group of types implements a single behavior presented in a single interface (e.g., an indexed or linked structure which masquerades as an array or associative file) nesting all but the type which offers the services can encapsulate an entire mechanism.

Nesting classes to create 'modules' with single interfaces becomes more important as templates (Chap. 8) achieve widespread use (C++ Release 3.0 and later).

2.6.3.5 Namespace discipline. C++ is a difficult language to parse. Some constructs require almost arbitrary lookahead in the lexical analyzer and others need extra covert cooperation between the lexical analyzer and the parser. Nested types superadd problems of their own: that typenames are scoped and can be qualified like member names. The grammar (parser specification) must know whether an identifier is a type name or an ordinary identifier. This is a solved problem in C (for typedef names), but in C++ an identifier may revert from a type name to an ordinary name after a ')', and after either a *::* or a *typename::* the lexical analyzer must assess the next identifier in a different scope. It's legal to use `Outer` (earlier) and its nested classes; thus:

```
void
john_doe()
{
        Outer::Pub_inner opi;           //  Pub_inner is a
                                        //    type name.
        struct Toper
        {
                Toper( const char* n ) : name( n ) {};
                const char* const name;
```

```
        };

        Toper Pub_inner( "john_doe" );  //  Pub_inner is an
                                        //    ordinary
                                        //    identifier.
}
```

There is a proposal before the ANSI/ISO C++ committee that would require that the meaning of a member or nested type declaration not change if the member and nested type declarations are rearranged (ignoring the effects on access control—public and private). It would forbid such code as this:

```
class   Bee
{
 public:
        int     bop;  //  bop  is first a member object ...
        ...

        class   bop   //  ...then a type name.
        {
                ...stuff...
        };
};
```

Here, if the declaration of the inner class is moved to the top of the outer class declaration, the code becomes illegal (`bop` is a type name, and cannot be used as a member name).

This rule will probably be adopted. Even if it is not, declarations such as this one seem to detract more than they add from a program.

2.6.3.6 Other namespace issues: incomplete types versus lexical nesting. Mixing incomplete and complete types of the same name with nesting of class types also leads to some surprises. Under the rules presently favored by the ANSI/ISO committee, an incomplete type can be completed in a nested scope:

```
class   Complete
{
  public:
        ...stuff...
  private:
        ...stuff...
};

class   Incomplete;
```

```
class   Nestee
{
  public:
        class   Complete        // Declares Nestee::Complete
        {
          public:
                ...other stuff...
          private:
                ...other stuff...
        };

        class   Incomplete      // Defines ::Incomplete !!
        {
          public:
                ...bewildered stuff...
          private:
                ...bewildered stuff...
        };

};

class   Incomplete     //Illegal!  ::Incomplete was completed
{                      //   -->inside<--  Nestee .
  public:
        ...real stuff...
  private:
        ...real stuff...
};
```

So many issues arise when trying to define how namespace lookup should be performed, especially when Inheritance is involved, that it is unlikely that all surprises will ever be banished. What is important is that surprises occur infrequently, and that they are detected and reported.

2.7 Classes IV

Six 'specialty' items remain in the capabilities and specification of a class. Two (friends and forward declarations) we will defer until after the objects-and-values issues that provide the bulk of Chap. 3. One, Inheritance, takes all of Chaps. 6 and 7. Here we examine pointers-to-member, array initialization, and C++ enhancements to unions.

2.7.1 Pointer-to-member

A pointer to an object points to or *selects* one object from the program's memory space. An array index selects one object from an array of uniform objects. Neither can select a member from a class's namespace. For this, C++ provides the *pointer-to-member.* The type of a pointer-to-member includes both the class and the type of the member identified by the pointer.

Recall that the full type of a class member includes the class:

```
int Xy::zzy;
void Xy::f();
```

Pointers-to-member are declared and used with an arcane, if consistent, syntax:

```
int Xy::* mem_p;            //  mem_p is a pointer-to-int-
                            //  member-of-Xy( int Xy::* ).

mem_p = &Xy::zzy;           //  We can take the address of an
                            //  int Xy:: .

void(Xy::* memf_p)() ;    //  mem_fp is a pointer-to-member-
                            //  function-of-Xy-returning-void .
                            //  (Before Release 2.0, it must be
                            //  declared as(*Xy:: memf_p)() .)

memf_p = &Xy::f;            //  And we take the address of a
                            //  void Xy::() .
```

Then we can write:

```
Xy plugh;

plugh.*mem_p++;        //  Dereference  ::*  with  .*  .
(plugh.*memf_p) ();
```

Pointer-to-class-object with pointer-to-member (`->*`) works too.

```
Xy *plover = &plugh;

plover->*mem_p--;      //  Pointer with pointer-to-member
                       //  ( * ::* ) is dereferenced as a
                       //  unit with ->*
(plover->*memf_p) ();
```

C++ considers `::*`, `.*` and `->*` each to be a single token and a single operator. Some pre-Release 2.0 implementations mistokenize expressions involving pointer-to-pointer-to-member. The compiler tries to treat `.*` and `->*` as two operators each, rather than as single operator.

Parenthesising the expressions fully will guide the parsing and lexical lookahead correctly.

Pointer-to-member may be applied to structs and unions as well as to classes. A member function may return a pointer-to-member pointing to a private member.

Pointer-to-member is especially useful for 'composing' an object with an operation or 'property.' A pointer-to-object can talk about which object you are selecting; the pointer-to-member can talk about which operation you are selecting.

```
switch ( op->arity() )
{
 case UNARY:
        ( lh_op->*( op->func() ) ) ( 0 );
        break;

 case BINARY:
        ( lh_op->*( op->func() ) ) ( rh_op );
        break;

        ... ...
}
```

The 'extra' parentheses shown are needed. Member pointer selection has a relatively low precedence (below the unary operators) and associates left-to-right. Parenthesize pointer-to-member expressions that also contain . , `->`, array indexing, function calls, or `sizeof`.

Because member names are implicitly prefixed by `this->` when they appear in member functions, you might expect that we could omit `this->` when we write `this->*xyz`. We cannot. **pointer_to_member* is not the same as *member.*

Pointer-to-member has some limitations. `void*` is not guaranteed to be large enough to hold a pointer-to-member, nor are the effects of conversions between `void*` and pointer-to-member defined.

Pointer-to-member and address-of-member do not support static members. An attempt to take the address-of-member for a static member results in a pointer to the type of the object, not a pointer-to-member.

```
&classtype::staticmember;    // The result has the type
                             // of  staticmember  with no
                             // class and no membership.
```

Pointer-to-member may not be used to identify an array element within a member array:

```
struct Node
{
        enum { N_child = 5 };
        Node* children[ N_child ];
        ......
};

        /*
         *   This doesn't work.  Pointer-to-Node*-member-of-Node
         *   (the declaration) is fine.  The initial value is not.
         *   The address of an element of a member array is not a
         *   pointer-to-member and is not even legal.
         */
        Node* Node::* child_p = &Node::children[ 0 ];
```

There are no references-to-member.

2.7.2 Arrays of class objects and other aggregates

When classes with constructors are used as array elements, their objects must be initialized. Several syntaxes are supported, and unlike C arrays, *they may all be used for either external or local arrays.* (Member arrays may not be explicitly initialized, except for static member arrays, which are initialized externally. See Sec. 2.6.2.)

If a class or struct has neither constructors nor private members and does not use any of C++'s OOP facilities (Chap. 6), it is an *aggregate.* Aggregates are also called Plain Old Data Structures (*PODS*). They are initialized as in C:

```
class   Element
{
  public:
        int number;
        int n_isotopes;
        char* name;
        char* abbrev;
};

Element hydrogen
{
        1, 3, "hydrogen", "H",
};

Element element_tab[ 110 ]
={
        { 1, 3, "hydrogen", "H", },
```

```
                Value val;

                Subtree left;
                Subtree right;

                short imbalance; // height of left - height of right
        };
        friend struct Node;         // Sec.3.6, Gives Node access to
                                    // AVL_tree's private members

  public:
        ... ... member function declarations ... ...

  private:
        ... ... member function declarations ... ...

          Subtree root;
};

void
AVL_tree::Subtree::balancer( AVL_tree::Node* just_inserted )
{
        Val v = just_inserted->value();

        /*
         *      Descend adjusting the balances as we go.
         */
        for( AVL_tree::Subtree* stp = this ;
                                stp->node != just_inserted ; )
        {
                if( v < stp->node->value() )
                {
                        stp->node->shift_left() ;
                        stp = &stp->node->left;
                }
                else
                {
                        stp->node->shift_right() ;
                        stp = &stp->node->right;
                }
        }

        /*
         *      The change might have left us balanced ...
         */
        if( node->imbalance == 0 )
                return;

        /*
         *      If both imbalances are in the same direction, use
         *      a single rotation, otherwise a double.
         */
```

```
        if( v > node->value() )
        {
                AVL_tree::Node* second = node->right;

                if( second )
                        node = second->imbalance < 0 ?
                                        rotate1_left( node ) :
                                        rotate2_left( node ) ;
        }
        else
        {
                AVL_tree::Node* second = node->left;

                if( second )
                        node = second->imbalance > 0 ?
                                        rotate1_right( node ) :
                                        rotate2_right( node ) ;
        }
}
```

Conclusion? Although data structures are good candidates for 'semantic centers,' and for being treated as objects, the declared `struct` we normally use to implement the data structure does not always represent the actual semantic center.

We will pick this topic up again in Chap. 3, Sec. 3.9, and in Chap. 8, Sec. 8.3.5 we will see a method for designing a class-and-object version of a linked data structure.

2.8.4 As designs evolve

As a design evolves, the boundaries of classes will shift. The better the analysis process that preceeded design, the less the change that will be experienced. But as the responsibility for something is moved from class to class, three different kinds of change occur.

First, the classes' roles in the overall program (external semantics) will change. Second, the various mechanisms in which the classes participate will change. And third, the internal representation and operation of the classes will change.

To understand the change in the design, we must understand all three types of change it implies.

2.9 Summary

Sections 2.1.1, 2.1.2 A class object's member data exists from the creation of the object to its destruction. *Constructors* and *destructors* are special functions which are used to initialize and clean up class objects.

For a class
are named
given in th

Sections 2.1
signature c
used to pas
class X. A c
their signa

Section 2.1.
initialize a
be initializ
present. Se
structor. Se

Section 2.1.
there is a
structors fo

Sections 2.1
structors in
are danger
(derived cla

Section 2.1.
object enab

Section 2.1.
of a traditi

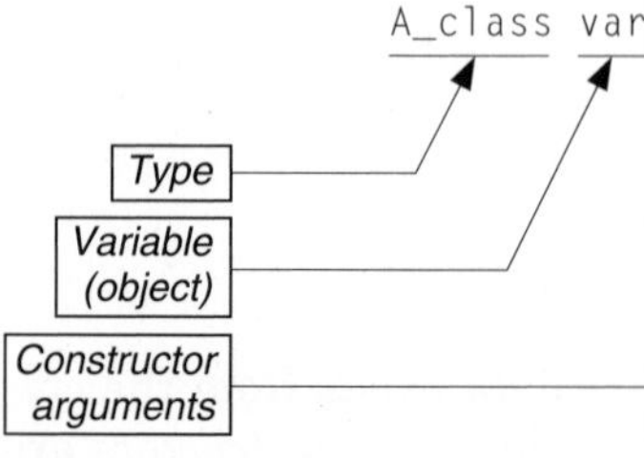

Figure 2.2

punning'). C++ needs type-correct allocation of objects so that constructors and destructors can be invoked consistently.

3.1.1 `new` and `delete` for built-in types

C++ manages free store with the type-secure operators `new` and `delete`. `new` returns a pointer to an object of the correct type:

```
int* ip = new int;  // Initializes ip with the
                    // address of a new int.
... ...         //  OR
ip = new int;       // Assigns the address of
                    // a new int to ip.
... ...         //  OR
return new int;     // Returns an int* pointing
                    // to a new int.
```

`delete` destroys and deallocates the object. It returns `void` :

```
delete ip;     // Release the object at which  ip  points.
```

Deleting an object that was not allocated by `new` is a ghastly error that can cause addressing violations, infinite loops, random pointer writes, and general misery. Deleting an object twice is also a ghastly error with the same consequences. With luck, the damage will be evident immediately. Otherwise the program may be haunted for years by irreproducible problems.

The null pointer points at no object, and C++ explicitly treats a `delete` through a null pointer as a harmless no-op. If the pointer is not a `const`, C++ may null it or otherwise alter it.

Good practice includes:

- Deleting an object using the same pointer that was assigned or initialized by the value returned by `new` when the object was allocated.
- Using different pointers to identify memory which will and will not have to be `delete`'d.
- Ensuring that a pointer which will be used for a delete will always contain either a valid, `delete`'-able pointer or null, from the point of its creation to the point of its destruction. A delete should be followed immediately by either a statement that gives the argument of the delete a valid value, or by a statement which nulls the argument of the delete, or by the end of the scope of the variable that was the argument of the delete.

Some versions of C++ prohibit a `delete` on a `const` pointer. ANSI/ISO C++ will permit it.

It is *not* legal to delete an object through a pointer-to-const. A pointer-to-const may not be used to modify the object at which it points. Returning the object to free store changes what may be done with the object and is assumed to sooner or later cause modification of the object.

A special syntax is used to allocate and deallocate arrays. To allocate an array of five `int`s:

```
int* ip = new int [ 5 ] ;
```

To allocate an array of `n_ptr` pointer-to-long:

```
long** lpp = new long* [ n_ptr ] ;
```

(`n_ptr` must be a `size_t` (in AN/I/ISO C++) or an `int` (in older versions), or convertible into that type.)

To delete an array,

```
delete [] ip;

delete [] lpp;
```

In Release 2.0, the length of the array must be given in the brackets:

```
delete [ 5 ] ip;         // In Release 2.0
delete [ n_ptr ] lpp;    // In Release 2.0
```

Compilers for C++ Release 2.1 and some later releases will accept the length in the brackets, but will ignore it. ANSI/ISO compilers do not have to accept it, but some may do so for compatibility.

If the brackets are omitted, subtle errors may result. Destructors for class types (Sec. 3.1.2) may not be properly called, and the wrong delete operator may be used (when delete is overloaded—Chap. 5, Sec. 5.5.5).

In Release 2.0, the types and abstractions that keep track of the allocated array length should be designed for reliability:

```
class   String
{
 public:
        String::String ( const char* init )
          : len ( 1 + strlen ( init ) ),  // + 1 for the null
            space ( len ),
            chars ( new char [ len ] )
        {
```

```
            if ( chars )                        // new returns null
                strcpy ( chars, init );         //  if it cannot
                                                //  find space to
                                                //  allocate.
        };
            ... ...
    private:
        short len;          // How long is the string?
        short space;        // How much space was allocated?
        char* chars;        // The actual allocated space.
            ... ...
};
```

3.1.2 New, delete, and class types: part I

`new` and `delete` may be used for classes and structs as well as for built-in types. Class and struct types may have constructors and destructors, which `new` and `delete` will invoke at the appropriate time. Constructor arguments are written in the `new` expression:

```
X* xp = new X;          // Uses X::X() if there is one.

X* xq = new X(
    "The Quick Brown Fox ...." ); // Uses X::X( const char* )
                                  // or X::X( char* )
  ... ...
delete xp;          // Invokes X::~X()
delete xq;          // Invokes X::~X()
```

Arrays may be allocated so long as no constructor arguments are needed. (Prior to Release 2.1, constructors with default arguments were not allowed.)

```
xp = new X[ X_Len ];  // Needs X::X() in Release 2.0 and
                      // before; in Release 2.1 and ANSI
      ... ...         // C++, can use X::X( int = 0 ) , etc.
      ... ...
delete [] xp; // In Release 2.0:  delete [ X_Len ] xp;
```

The constructor is called first for the zeroeth element of the array, then for the first, and so forth. Destructors are called in the reverse order.

C++ cannot, in general, check whether the pointer in a `delete` expression points at an object or at an array of objects. If the square brackets are improperly omitted—or improperly written—bad things are likely to happen. Disciplined handling of the pointers will prevent many errors. If allocated memory is tracked by types (e.g., 'handles') whose semantics define allocation and release, so much the better.

If the constructor needed by an invocation of `new` is unavailable (perhaps because it is private), that invocation is illegal; if the destructor exists but is unavailable, an invocation of `delete` is illegal.

3.1.3 Memory exhaustion

A program that allocates memory may run out of memory. C++'s `new` operator tries several actions when this happens.

First, it examines an external pointer-to-function which is declared thus:

```
void (*new_handler)();
```

If this pointer is null, the `new` operator returns a null pointer, skipping whatever initialization that an allocated object would have received.

In C++ releases through Release 3.1, `new_handler` is initialized to 0.

If `new_handler` is nonnull, the function it addresses is invoked. That function may or may not return. If it does not return, the program is terminated; if it does return, `new` begins looking for space again. To prevent infinite regress if space still cannot be found, the first action of a function invoked through `new_handler` should be to change this pointer.

In ANSI/ISO C++, the initial value of `new_handler` is a pointer to a function that *throws an exception* representing the out-of-space condition (`xalloc`). If this exception is not *caught,* the program will terminate. If it is caught, the code which catches it can arrange to abandon or retry the operation. (Exceptions are discussed in Chap. 9.)

The new-handler function should not do anything that could result in an attempt to call `new`. It must not manipulate a `String` type that allocates memory, for example. And it should not attempt to send output to a stream that has received no output; the stream might attempt to allocate a buffer. (This includes `cerr`.)

To make manipulation of `new_handler` a bit less grimy, there is a functional interface:

```
typedef void (*PF_v)();

extern PF_v set_new_handler( PF_v );
```

`set_new_handler ()` returns the old value of `new_handler`. This allows the handler to be stacked and restored after some section of code is executed.

---

* In some versions of C++, this may be spelled `_new_handler`. ANSI/ISO may use this spelling because the name is defined by the language, library, and environment.

This is a good use for a 'store and restore' class:

```
class   Re_Store_NH
{
  public:
        Re_Store_NH( PF_v handler )
          : old( ::set_new_handler( handler ) )
        { };

        ~Re_Store_NH ()
        { ::set_new_handler( old ); };
  private:
        const PF_v old;
};

            ... ...
        {
                void section_3_recover();
                Re_Store_NH( section_3_recover );

                ... stuff with new and delete ...

                // Re_Store_NH is going out of scope ...
        }
```

A 'store-and-restore' class protects against interruption of the program by exceptions; if an exception unwinds the stack of function invocations, the class's destructor is called to restore the `new_handler` (and thus to restore the program's external state). (See Chap. 9, Sec. 9.5.) The store-and-restore class also ensures that the program's state will be restored when the function that created it returns, by whatever path.

Such store-and-restore classes (or 'stacking' classes) are good candidates for definition by template (Chap. 8).

3.1.4 Managing free store safely

The `new` and `delete` operators do not just allocate memory; they create and destroy objects. Memory is drawn from free store, a type is imposed upon it, and the pointer is returned by `new`, an object is given to `delete`, its type is stripped away, and its memory reverts to the free store heap.

This is good for most uses, but some applications need finer control over the memory in which objects will be built. C++ allows the programmer to take as much responsibility as the job requires (Chap. 5, Sec. 5.5). The added responsibility carries added risk as more of the free store management is custom-programmed. 'Manager' classes should be used to encapsulate free store operations; templates (Chap. 8) may also help.

C++ does not have garbage collection. Memory which is lost remains lost. 'Conservative' allocator-garbage collector systems are possible (see Boehm and Weiser, 1988). These require overloading the `new` operators. The program's architecture and design must state clearly what code is responsible for allocating, tracking, and releasing memory, and when. (This doesn't mean painstaking comments in executable code, but a clear exposition of data structures and the principles on which they are organized.)

Some useful techniques:

- When allocating into networks of linked objects, make their constructors link them together, be sure of which links are responsible for tracking the memory, and arrange to have objects destroyed in their 'parents" destructors when those links are severed.
- What cannot be pushed into a constructor should be done by management member functions and by using 'handle' objects in place of simple pointers. This is especially important in the newer versions of C++ that support exceptions and exception handling (Chap. 9, Sec. 9.5).
- Debug any replacement `new` and `delete` operators early, stress test to ensure that memory isn't lost inside them, and build in debugging capabilities so that they can help to debug the code that uses them.

3.1.4.1 Explicit handle objects. More general than the string class is a "handle" class which allocates space when created and releases it when deleted. In a handle, only one length need be stored and both length and space pointer can be made const. ('Handle' is used here in a generic sense. Various environments and operating systems have objects which they call Handles; these are another story.)

```
/*
 *      Buf is a handle for a char array.
 */
class   Buf
{
  public:
        Buf( int sz );
        ~Buf();
        const char* p() const { return area; };
        int len() const { return size; };
```

```
  private:
        const int size;
        char* const area;
};
Buf::Buf( int sz )
  : size( sz ), area( new char* [ sz ] )
{ }

Buf::~Buf ()
{
        delete [] area;
        /*
         *      In Release 2.0, use
         *              delete [ size ] area;
         *      instead.
         */
}
Buf b( 40 );

#include <string.h>

          ... ...
        strcpy( b.p(), "Hello, World!\n" );    //  b is
                                       // converted to  char*

        cout.put( b.p()[ i ] );
```

Buf ties the allocation of memory to a lifetime which can be controlled by declaring a Buf[e4] object.

The awkward construction b.p()[i] can be improved; the member function p() can be replaced by operator char*() (Sec. 3.3.5), allowing us to write simply b[i] . (In fact, this is the form we would prefer.)

(For AT&T C++, this example won't work before Release 2.0; the member initializer list will be mishandled by a compiler bug. This class does not handle memory exhaustion; see Sec. 3.1.3 and Chap. 9.)

Buf handles only char. In C++ Release 3.0 and later releases through ANSI/ISO C++, it can be extended to arbitrary types using *templates* (Chap. 8). The template version has the advantage that it can handle (almost) arbitrary types with one definition. Its disadvantage is that the classes in question may have to accomodate the template's facilities for initialization parameters.

3.1.4.2 Controlled pointers. Buf provides temporary storage. It can be modified to provide 'tentative allocation' instead. Under tentative allocation, the handle still allocates the array (or object) for which it is responsible, but something else may take responsibility for that array later. If so, the handle no longer manages the array's deletion.

We must make Buf's member data non-const and add a member function:

```
char*
Buf::take()
{
        char* val = area;

        area = 0;
        size = 0;

        return val;
}
```

A call to Buf::take() returns the address of the space stored, and relinquishes Buf's ownership of the space. For general use we ought to add some kind of safety check:

```
/*
 *      Buf is a handle for a char array.
 */
class   Buf
{
  public:
        Buf( int sz );
        ~Buf();
        char* p() const
        { if( ! area )
          {  … announce ghastly error …
          }
            return area;
        }
        int len() { return size; };

        char* take();

  private:
        int size;
        char* area;
};
```

What action can we take in Buf::operator char*() when we are asked to return a pointer and the pointer is null (either the allocation failed or we've given up the pointer)? We can return the null pointer and let things run their course. We could return an error (perhaps Buf should have an error-handling facility of some sort?). We could cause an `abort()` or trigger a warning message. (These things should probably be done by an out-of-line member function.) Or we might 'throw an exception' (Chap. 9).

3.1.4.3 Smart pointers. The basic mechanism of `Buf` can be used to implement pointers that count references, copy-on-write, and so forth. Reference counts and copy-on-write require that the 'real' object, the pointed-to object, contain the reference count. There should be private functions to examine it, increment it, and decrement it. When we examine operator conversions (Sec. 3.3.5) and the rules for overloading (Chap. 4, Sec. 4.1), we will see that C++ can often distinguish between a conversion that needs an `X*` and one that only needs a `const X*`. For the latter, no action need be taken; for the former if the 'real' object beneath the pointer is shared, this 'pointer' must be given its own copy and the reference counts adjusted appropriately.

There are endless variations on this theme; many of them are invisible to the code that uses the types. Most depend for that transparency on the overloading of special operators (Chap. 5, Sec. 5.3). Many or most are candidates for implementation by template (Chap. 8).

3.1.4.4 Replacing `alloca()` . Some implementations of C provide a function called `alloca()` . `char* alloca( int )` returns a pointer to space which will be released when the current function returns. It generally does so by manipulating the function's stack frame (activation record) and returning a pointer to the space it has 'borrowed.' The space will automatically be freed on function return. Not all machines implement their C activation records as stack frames. Not all stack frames can be adjusted in this way without destroying the integrity of the activation record.

Unfortunately, some very useful programs use `alloca()`, including many available at no cost in source code under various 'use it but don't sell it or claim it' licenses.

It's easy to create an allocator which can provide pointers to arbitrary space (allocated as `char`) and which keeps track of the space that it has allocated, releasing it when the allocator is destroyed. In Chap. 5, Sec. 5.5 we'll see the 'proper' way to integrate such space management with C++'s free store management, but for built-in types the techniques from `Buf` are sufficient.

3.1.4.5 Hiding A Class's constness: `~const` or `mutable`. The traditional, C meaning of `const` is *bitwise const.* The bit pattern that represents the object must not change in a `const` object, and must not be changed through a pointer-to-`const` or reference-to-`const`.

But when the 'Object' represented by that memory includes a pointer, and the pointer does *not* point to a `const` object or memory, a `const` declaration does not suffice to make the 'Object' `const`:

```
class   Name
{
  public:
        Name () : mymem( new char( 16 ) )
        { if( mymem ) mymem[ 0 ] = '/0' ; };

        ~Name() { delete [] mymem; };

        ... ...
        const Name& assign( const char* a ) const
        {       strncpy( mymem, a, 16 );
                return *this;
        };

  private:
        char* const mymem;
};

        ... ...
        const Name naem;

        naem.assign( "ShortName" );
```

The various `const`s cannot prevent the `Name::assign()` function from writing into the memory pointed at by `naem->mymem` . It's up to the class author to make `const` meaningful by the proper use of `const` member functions.

The opposite problem can occur: an object that is constant in concept might not actually be a bitwise `const`. In pre-ANSI/ISO versions of C++, a member function can cast its `this` to a non-`const`:

```
int
Class_that_has_a::hard_computation () const
{
        if ( is_cached )
                return cached_value;

        Class_that_has_a* fake_this =           // Cast away the
                (Class_that_has_a*) this;       //   const  of
                                                //   this .
        fake_this->cached_value = do_hard_computation();
        fake_this->is_cached = 1;

        return cached_value;
}
```

The ANSI/ISO committee is considering a better way. The feature is still uncertain as of March 1993; it might not be adopted, but it is backed by most of the Extensions Working Group. It is called `~const` ('never-const'), and it may end up being called `mutable`.

A never-const member remains non-const even in a const object:

```
class   Class_that_has_a
{
  public:
        int hard_computation () const;
   ... ...
  private:
   ... ...
        int cached_value ~const;  //  Even in a  const
 // or perhaps                    //  Class_that_has_a
 // int cached_value mutable;
        int is_cached ~const;     //  these two members will
                                  //  _not_ be const.
};
```

With these members declared never-const, they can be changed even when they are addressed (implicitly) by a pointer-to-`const`.

```
int
Class_that_has_a::hard_computation () const
{
        /*
         *      This is legal even though  this  is a
         *      pointer-to-const.  The un-const functions
         *      are never const, even in a const object.
         */
        if( ! is_cached )
        {
                cached_value = do_hard_computation();
                is_cached = 1;
        }

        return cached_value;
}
```

Never-const allows the internal organization or representation of an object to be updated—including any free store it may manage—during an operation that is 'conceptually' read-only.

Even if never-const is adopted, there are two reservations. First, the syntax adopted by the ANSI/ISO committee might differ from this. Second, it probably will not be extended to pointer-to-member (Chap. 2, Sec. 2.7.1).

3.1.5 Programming resources and relationships

The guaranteed initialization and destruction provided by constructors and destructors can be used to ensure that resources are released when no longer needed, and that linked data structures are maintained properly. These are all cases of programming Relationships: there are Relationships between this object and some resource, or between this object and some other object, that must be maintained.

The general issue of the programming of Relationships is vital to Object-Oriented (or Object-Based) programming. Most texts on Object Orientation treat the analysis of Relationships reasonably well; few give the programming of Relationships any consideration.

There are several steps in analysis and design for the programming of relationships:

1. The Relationships must be identified.
2. The Rules which the Relationships must obey must be identified. These 'rules' are based on the Relationships themselves: a one-to-one relationship requires that one object be created along with another; a one-or-zero-to-one allows an object to be created and linked with another that already exists; etc. Phrases like 'one-to-one' describe the *cardinality* of the relationship (that is, the number of each kind of Object or entity participating in it).
3. The Rules for the Relationships must be restated as Policies: When this object is created, that one must be created; when this object is created, that resource must be obtained; when this object is created, it must be given the address of another object.
4. Responsibilities for the Policies must be assigned to member functions (principally constructors and destructors) of the various classes involved. Sometimes extra member functions should be created to help manage the linkages between the objects, and sometimes extra 'data structure' objects must be created (especially for 'many-to' and 'to-many' relationships).

Such critical steps should be spelled out explicitly. Most design methods ('methodologies') don't. The first two steps properly belong to Design and the last to Detailing (Sec. 3.10.2). Restating the Rules as Policies might be considered either Design or Detailing.

3.2 Examples

3.2.1 The `FATAL` class

We can dynamically allocate a `FATAL` class (Chap. 2, Sec. 2.1.9). We can take advantage of how `delete`'ing a null pointer has no effect. And we can use a reference instead of a pointer for the output stream now that we know how to initialize it.

```
#include <stdlib.h>

class   FATAL
{
  public:
        FATAL ( ostream& o ) : out ( o ) {};
        ~FATAL() { out << flush;  //  flush  is a special object
                   ::abort (); }; // which will force the stream
                                  // to be flushed.  (See Sec.
                                  // 10.4.6)
        ostream& s() { return out; };
  private:
        ostream& out;
};
          ... ...
        FATAL* fp = 0;
        ... ...

        if( ... ... ) // OMIGOSH #1
        {
                fp = new FATAL( cout );
        }
        ... ...

        if( ... ... ) // OMIGOSH #2
        {
                if( !fp )
                        fp = new FATAL( cout );
        }
        ... ...
        if( ... ... ) // OMIGOSH #3
        {
                if( !fp )
                        fp = new FATAL( cout );
        }
        ... ...

        delete fp;      // Only aborts the program if one of the
                        // OMIGOSHes was hit.
```

Notice the mechanism: we are now concerned with another lifetime, the lifetime from the creation of a FATAL to its deletion by means of the FATAL*. We can package that lifetime as well, this time in a LETHAL.

```
class   LETHAL
{
  public:
        LETHAL( ostream& o ) : out( o ), f( 0 ) {};
        ~LETHAL() { delete f; };

        ostream& s () { if( !f ) f = new FATAL( out );
                              return f->s ();
                        }
  private:
        FATAL* f;
        ostream& out;
};
  … …

void
summfunct()
{
        … …

        LETHAL omigosh ( cout );

        … …

        for ( … ; … ; … )
        {
                … …

                if ( … … ) // GREAT BIG OMIGOSH
                        omigosh.s() << … …;

                … …
        }
        … …

}       //  If and only if at least one of those calls to
        //  omigosh.s() was made, the program will abort
        //  here.
```

3.2.2 Allocating the wheels

Recall the Wheels example from Chap. 2, Secs. 2.2 and 2.5: a Wheel_set names a group of Wheels, allocates them, and arranges for their initialization.

We now know how to allocate the wheels dynamically:

```
class   Wheel
{
  public:
        Wheel( const char** );
        ~Wheel() { delete sides; };
        int advance()
        {       if( *++next ) return 0;
                else { next = sides;
                        return 1; }
        };
        int copyout( char* to ) const;
  private:
        const char** sides;
        const char** next;
};

class   Wheel_set
{
  public:
        Wheel_set( int );
        ~Wheel_set();
        void wh_init( int, const char** );
        int copy( char* ) const;
        int advance();

  private:
        int n_wheels;
        Wheel** wheels; // Note that this is an array of POINTERS
};

Wheel::Wheel( const char** strings )
{
        const char** s = strings;
        while( *s++ )  // Loop past the null ...
                { }

        sides = new char* [ s - strings ];

        for ( s = strings, next = sides ; *next++ = *s++ ; )
                { }

        next = sides;
}

Wheel_set::Wheel_set( int n )
  : n_wheels( n ), wheels( new Wheel* [ n_wheels ] )
{
        for( int i = 0 ; i < n_wheels ; i++ )
```

```
                wheels[ i ] = 0;
}

Wheel_set::~Wheel_set()
{
        for( int i = 0 ; i < n_wheels ; i++ )
                delete wheels[ i ];
        delete [] wheels;
}

void
Wheel_set::wh_init( int i, const char** sides )
{
        if( i > n_wheels )
                return;

        delete wheels[ i ];     // Just in case ...
        wheels[ i ] = new Wheel( sides );
}
```

Each `Wheel` is created in the `Wheel_set`'s initialization function, which creates the `Wheel` using the `new` operator and a constructor argument. In the old version, we allocated memory for all the `Wheel`s at once and built each `Wheel` in place. That is uglier and more error-prone. There is a way to do it in C++ within the type system, but it exposes the programmer to some extra risks, and should not be used without good reason (see Chap. 5, Secs. 5.5.5 through 5.5.9).

3.2.3 Linking the Wheels

The `Wheel/Wheel_set` system needs to know the number of `Wheel`s in advance. This opens an opportunity for a mistake. With dynamic allocation and linked structures, the size of the `Wheel_set` can be set by the number of `Wheel`s actually given to the `Wheel_set`.

```
class   Wheel
{
 public:
        Wheel( const char** sds, Wheel* next_w = 0 )
          : sides( sds ),
            next( sides ),
            next_wheel( next_w )
        { };

        /*
         *      There's a recursive call in the destructor;
         *      C++ will have to create an out-of-line copy.
```

```
         */
        ~Wheel() { delete next_wheel; };

        /*
         *     We advance the wheel set by advancing this wheel;
         *     if it has rolled over, we look for another; if
         *     there is none, or if IT, when advanced, declares
         *     that we have wrapped around, then the whose set has
         *     wrapped around.
         *     advance () also will require an out-of-line copy
         *     to support a recursive call--or else some fancy
         *     tail-recursion elimination.
         */
        int advance()
        {       return  advance_me()
                    &&  ( ! next_wheel
                       || next_wheel->advance() );
        };

        int copy_rev( char* ) const;
  private:
        int advance_me() { if ( *++next ) { return 0; }
                           else { next = sides;
                                  return 1; } };

        int copyout( char* ) const;
        const char** sides;
        const char** next;
        Wheel* next_wheel;
};
```

The Wheels are added one by one to the linked list in which they are stored. Each call to `Wheel_set::add_wheel()` provides the parameters for initializing one new Wheel.

```
class   Wheel_set
{
  public:
        /*
         *      In this version, we needn't know ahead
         *      of time how many wheels we will have.

         */
        Wheel_set() : wheels( 0 ) { };
        ~Wheel_set() { delete wheels; };

        /*
         *      add_wheel() replaces the old wh_init()
         */
```

```
        void add_wheel( const char** sides )
        {       wheels = new Wheel( sides, wheels ); };

        int copy( char* to ) const
        {       return wheels ? wheels->copy_rev( to )
                              : 0 ;
        };

        int advance()
        {       return wheels ? ! wheels->advance ()
                                  : 0 ;
        };

  private:
        /*
         *      And here's the linked list of wheels.
         */
        Wheel* wheels;
};

int
Wheel::copy_rev( char* to ) const
{
        int st = next_wheel ?
                           next_wheel->copy_rev( to )
                         : 0;

        st += copyout ( &to[ st ] );

        to[ st ] = '\0';

        return st;
}

int
Wheel::copyout( char* to ) const
{
        for( const char* s = *next ; *to++ = *s++ ; )
                { }

        return s - *next - 1;
}
```

We have advanced from coding algorithms embedded in data types to are building objects and telling the compiler how to implement them.

When the rotor machine must be advanced, C++ can do the first wheel without activating the recursion, and without actually making the function call. Whether a given compiler does this depends on the compiler.

3.3 Values, Constructors, and Conversions

Values are the 'contents' of objects. Values come into existence with their objects. A constructor can be used to create an object in order to create its value. *Conversions* are given a value of one type and create a corresponding value of another type. Some constructors can serve as conversions.

3.3.1 Initializers and value builders

Recall that given `String::String ( const char* )` we can write

```
String s1 = "Katie Casey was baseball mad," ;

String s2( "had the fever and had it bad;" );

String s3 = String( "Just to root for the home town crew," );
```

All three invoke `String::String ( const char* )`.

`s1` is initialized using the 'assignment initialization' or direct initialization syntax. `s2` is initialized using constructor argument syntax. `s3` is initialized using 'value builder' syntax.

A value builder is a constructor invoked as a function call; it returns the object constructed. This object has no name and has local extent, so it is a temporary to be destroyed (by destructor, if there is one) silently when it can no longer be used (Sec. 3.3.6).

When it is used in an initialization such as this, there is no need for the temporary; the variable being declared can be initialized directly. But value builders can be used in arbitrary expressions.

The term 'value builder' is not part of the standard C++ terminology. There is no official term for a constructor invocation as an expression; this seems as good as any.

A default (no-argument) constructor (or a constructor with all arguments defaulted) is invoked as a function of no arguments; given `String::String()` and `Fan casey( String )`, we can write

```
casey( String() );
```

Thus, given `String::String ( int, const char* )` and given `Fan casey( String )`, we can write

```
{
        casey( String( 50, "ev'ry sou--  Katie blew." ) );
        casey( String( 50, "On a Saturday her young beau" ) );
        casey( String() );
        ... ...
        /*
         *  C++ must at this point destroy the return value
         *  object (Fan) and value-builder-created-String
         *  created by each of the casey( String( ... ) )
         *
         *  The appropriate destructors will be called to
         *  do the job.
         */
}
```

Now, imagine we have an `int Fan::isit()` . What happens if we write the code below?

```
if(   Fan( String( "called to see if she'd like" ) ).isit ()
  ||  Fan( String( "to go/To see a show" ) ).isit ()
   && Fan( String( "but Miss Katie said 'no,' " ) ).isit () )
      ... ...
```

Operators && and || short-circuit. The expressions on the RHS of either may never be evaluated, and value builders on their RHS may never create their return objects. An object that is not created cannot be destroyed.

A C++ compiler should generate code to destroy the right objects at the right times. Historically, compilers from several vendors have rejected this construct as "not implemented." More modern compilers seem to handle it properly.

3.3.2 Value builders in function call and return

When we write

```
X yzzy = X( y, z );
```

only the one constructor named in the value builder need be called, even though it appears that we have written both a value builder operation (the RHS) and a copy constructor operation (the initialization). What if we use a value builder as a function argument or return value?

```
/*
 *      Assume  Shivermi::Shivermi( int, int )
 *      and     Shivermi::Shivermi( const Shivermi& )
 */
```

```
int f( const Shivermi& );
int g( const Shivermi& );

void shakes( Shivermi );

Shivermi
timbers( Shivermi w )
{
        int i = f( w );
        int j = g( w );

        return Shivermi( i, j );
}
      ... ...

        shakes( timbers( Shivermi( 0, 7 ) ) );  // <= Look here ...
```

The value builder `Shivermi( 0, 7 )` creates a temporary which is used to initialize win `timbers()`. Likewise, `timbers()` uses a value builder to create a temporary which is returned, intializing the expression involving `timbers`, and that is used to initialize the argument to `shakes()`.

C++ is free to 'optimise away' such intermediate temporary objects. A smart compiler can use the inner value builder to initialize `timber()`'s parameter variable directly, and even use the value builder in the return expression in `timber` to initialize the parameter variable of `shakes()`. If the copy constructors have side effects (logging, resource consumption, prints to standard error), the optimizations can be detected, but they remain legal.

Whether or not the copy constructor is actually used, it must be accessible to code which passes or returns objects of its class. `Shivermi::Shivermi( const Shivermi& )` must be accessible (e.g., public) or this code is illegal, regardless of whether the constructor is actually used.

Before C++ Release 2.0, the accessibility of the copy constructor (or other implicitly invoked constructor) was not always checked properly. Also, before Release 2.0, the default copy constructor was a bitwise, not memberwise, copy, and therefore dangerous (Chap. 2, Sec. 2.1.7).

3.3.3 Constructors as conversions

When a constructor with a single argument is used as a value builder it is, in effect, a conversion:

```
Zark zed;
         ... ...

zed = Zark( "syzygy" );
```

Not only does it act like a conversion when called explicitly; C++ treats it as a conversion in all respects. *A single argument constructor becomes an* implicit *conversion.* C++ adds the conversion represented by a single-argument constructor to the set of conversions it can invoke automatically.

In the previous example, we could just as well write

```
zed = (Zark) "syzygy" ; // Explicit conversion
```

or

```
zed = "syzygy" ;        // Implicit conversion
```

3.3.4 Conversions in casts and functional form

The rules for conversions are symmetric. These are equivalent:

```
f2 = (int) f1;
f2 = int( f1 );
```

For any unadorned type (a type written without `*`, `&`, `[]`, `()`, and without qualifiers such as `long` or `unsigned`), a cast may be written as a conversion in functional form.

The 'unadorned' requirement means that these are *not* equivalent:

```
ptr_to_int = (int*) ptr_to_void;
ptr_to_int = int* ( ptr_to_void );          // Illegal!
```

The restriction is not on the type itself, but on how the type is written:

```
typedef int* Int_star;

ptr_to_int = (Int_star) ptr_to_void;
ptr_to_int = Int_star( ptr_to_void );    // Quite legal.
```

Where both types are class types, certain ambiguities can break the symmetry between these two forms (Chap. 5, Sec. 5.3.5).

3.3.5 Member operator conversion functions

A constructor-as-conversion specifies how to convert either a built-in or user-defined type *to* a class type. It is also possible to convert *from* a class type to any of these types.

Such a conversion is a member function with a special name:

```
class   Rotation
{
  public:
```

```
        /*
         *      Return the angle in degrees ...
         */
        operator double() const;
        ... ...

Rotation::operator double() const
{
        ... ...
```

`operator` is a C++ keyword. The return type is not written; it's part of the member function's name.

The name of the member function is `operator double`; likewise, we can write `operator int`, `operator char*`, etc. A member operator conversion takes no arguments and should usually be `const`, unless creating the new (converted value) object changes the original object.

Apart from its name and the ability of C++ to insert it as an implicit conversion, a member operator conversion is an ordinary member function. It may be invoked explicitly by a cast or functional conversion, or even by name.

```
Rotation turn( ... ... );

cout << (double) turn << "\n" ;
cout << double( turn ) << "\n" ;
cout << turn.operator double() << "\n" ;
```

All three of these are synonymous (except in the presence of certain ambiguities; see Sec. 3.4.5, Chap. 4, Sec. 4.1.4, and Chap. 5, Sec. 5.3.5).

What about conversion to 'adorned' types?

```
class   Won_too_many
{
  public:
      operator const char* () const;              // Ok
      operator const Won_a_few& () const;         // Ok
      operator Won_to_free_Thor (*)( void* )() const; // NO GOOD!
        ... ...
```

The last is a conversion to pointer to function-accepting-a-`void*`-argument-and-returning-a-`Won_to_free_Thor`. It's too complicated. The rule is that you may have

1. An unadorned type name, possibly preceded by `const` or `volatile` or both.
2. (1) followed by any number of 'pointer-op' clauses. A pointer-op clause is one of `*`, `&`, and *Classname*`::*`, possibly followed by `const` or

volatile or both. There may be at most one & and it must head the last clause.

In other words, given a type with a simple name, you can have a conversion to it or to a reference to it or pointer or pointer-to-pointer or ... or pointer-to-member or ... to it, with consts and volatiles scattered throughout.

If you need a conversion operator to a pointer-to-function or pointer-to-array, you must use a typedef to provide an unadorned name for the type. (This is good practice anyway for complicated types.) Since typedef creates a synonym for a type, not a new type, using a typedef doesn't interfere with later use of the type.

Compiler releases before C++ Release 2.0 may not be able to handle member conversion to const types.

Conversion to a built-in type can be used for 'status testing':

```
class   Parse_stat
{
  public:
        enum Stat { SUCCESS, FAIL, INCOMPLETE };

        operator const void* () const
        {       return stat == SUCCESS ? (const void*) this
                                       : 0 ;
        };
          ... ...
  private:
        Stat stat;
          ... ...
};
  ... ...

        Parse_stat ps;
              ... ...

        if( ps )
                ... ...
```

Parse_stat::operator void* () const can return either null or (const void*) this, which is a handy nonnull pointer which we can use to indicate success. We use const so that this is treated as a pointer-to-const and the function return is not a type violation.

3.3.6 Lifetime and semantics of temporaries

(As of March 1993, the ANSI/ISO committee is still deliberating this issue.)

There is a general rule for creating and destroying objects that belong to scopes: No object shall outlive an object that was created before it. All of the rules for declared objects uphold this rule, and temporaries are held to it as well, so far as is possible.

There are plenty of implementation choices within this rule. For instance, the temporary object may be destroyed at the end of the expression in which it is embedded:

```
returns_temp();          // Temporary object is destroyed.
```

This approach is favored by authors of compilers and libraries for high-powered numerical codes because it provides certain opportunities for optimization, allowing the codes to be vectorized more easily, with a large performance improvement.

Others are concerned about code like this:

```
String s1 = … … ;
String s2 = … … ;

String concat( const String&, const String& );

const char* cp = concat( s1, s2 );

if( strcmp( cp, "something or other" ) )
{
        … …
```

This code will work only if the temporary returned from `concat()` lingers until the end of the scope in which `cp` is declared.

These represent the probable limits of behavior in a pre-ANSI/ISO C++ compiler, and the probable limits of how the ANSI/ISO committee will decide this issue.

If the value is used explicitly to initialize a reference, the temporary *must* be kept until the end of the smallest enclosing scope:

```
String s1 = … … ;
String s2 = … … ;

String concat( const String&, const String& );

String& sr = concat( s1, s2 );
```

In such code, the lifetime of the temporary will be the lifetime of the reference.

A related issue is the whether temporaries are always `const`. Temporaries created by conversions that are inserted automatically in function calls cannot be used for a non-`const` reference parameters (Sec. 3.4.4). But what about other temporaries?

```
concat( s1, s2 ) = String( "Little lambs eat ivy." );
```

If `concat()` actually returns a `String`, the assignment ought to be legal (according to the rules which govern assignment—see Chap. 4, Sec. 4.5). Nor is this code so ridiculous; if the function were instead `Sparse_array::index( int )`, it could return a linked object which accepted the 'assignment' and stored the value in the sparse array. There are C++ programmers and library designers (including the author) who would like to do this.

If, on the other hand, the temporary is `const`, this code fails:

```
… … = concat( concat( s1, s2 ).mk_ucase (),
                          "Little lambs" );
```

Until the ANSI/ISO committee rules on the issue, none of these constructs (except the initialization of the reference in its declaration) is portable, and no code can rely on any of them.

3.4 Programming with Conversions

Most programming languages support type conversion. Which (if any) conversions should be implicit or automatic has been debated since mixed-mode was first allowed in FORTRAN. C++ allows a set of types to support 'mixed mode' operations by conversions and overloading.

3.4.1 The place of conversions in C++

C++ adds user-defined conversions automatically to the compiler's list of possible implicit conversions.

Classes encapsulate; class objects are values. With explicit and implicit conversions, C++'s object values can act like values in an algebraic language such as FORTRAN. A conversion creates a new value; it is also creates a new object. This does not involve OOP, but it does involve the class's constructors and destructors.

A successful C++ type may need to support the traditional algebraic language notion of a value (rvalue), the data abstraction notion of an encapsulated, user-programmed type, and the OOP notion of an object (lvalue).

Programming conversions requires good judgment and discretion, which in turn require an understanding of How Things Work. *That* requires some practice. Without it, you can accidentally concoct 'Type Goulash,' a potion more toxic than Preprocessor Pudding or Pointer Stew.

3.4.2 Three semantics of conversions

(The information in this section is based on the minutes of the November 1992 meeting of the ANSI/ISO C++ committee, on the documents prepared for that meeting, and on the sessions of the July 1992 meeting of that committee. It is incomplete and partly speculative.)

Classic C views conversions indiscriminately: you get what you ask for almost without interference from the type system. ANSI C is somewhat stricter. Certain conversions are 'good' and will be performed without special instruction; others are 'bad' and require an explicit cast.

ANSI/ISO C++ will probably make a stronger distinction between these conversions, even introducing a different, and preferred, syntax for them.

The essence of conversion is that, for a given value of one type, a corresponding value of another type is produced. There are three kinds of conversions:

- *Conversions that request an 'equivalent' value in a different representation.* Conversions beween `int` and `float` fall into this category. So do most conversions involving user-defined types. So, by the definition of C and C++, do conversions between integral types of various widths and signednesses (including the various `char` types). Conversions in this group are 'good.' Included are conversions from other pointer types to `void*`.
- *Conversions that demand that a bit pattern be reevaluated without sanction of the type system.* Conversion of `double*` to `unsigned long*` falls into this category. So do conversions from `void*` to pointers to other types (although the type system actually defines how these must behave). Conversions in this group are 'bad' (for the purposes of this discussion).

  Conversions of this kind are sometimes termed *coercions.*
- *Conversions that require run-time checks to determine into which category they fall.*

The first two kinds of conversion are familiar from C; the third is new. Although the full story requires all of Chaps. 6 and 7, its salient issues are these:

- C++ can sometimes allow an object of one type to be interpreted as an object of another type while retaining type correctness. Thus, some pointer and reference conversions are 'good' and are grouped with the value-interpreting conversions. (There may actually be run-time 'magic' involved—for instance, changing the value of a pointer in the 'conversion.')

- In some cases, C++ cannot determine at compile time if a conversion on pointers or references is 'good' (within the scope of the type system) or 'bad' (outside the assurances of the type system). If the information will be available at run-time, the conversion belongs to the third group. (Whether the information will or will not be available is known at compile time.)

The conversions which interest us now are those in the first group, those which are deemed 'good.'

In Chap. 4, Sec. 4.1.5 we will begin to examine why we need to distinguish between the three groups of conversions.

It is very likely that ANSI/ISO C++ will provide three new ways of writing conversions, one for each group. The syntax proposed is borrowed from templates (Chap. 8) and introduces three new reserved words:

```
double d = 4.501;

// Reserved word: static_cast

int i = static_cast< int >( d );     // Convert within the type system.

// Reserved word: reinterpret_cast

int* ip = reinterpret_cast< int* >( &d ); // Contravene the type system.

Base_class_see_ch_6* bp = … … ;         // Can the object
Class_with_virtuals_ditto* cvp;         //    pointed at by bp
                                        //    also legally be
// Reserved word: dynamic_cast

cvp = dynamic_cast< Class_with_virtuals_ditto* >( bp ); // pointed at
if( cvp )                                               //  by cvp?  If
      … …                                               //  so, convert
                                                        //  the pointer;
                                                        //  if not,
                                                        // return null.
```

If the proposal is adopted, it will probably use this syntax. Using the angle brackets this way introduces plenty of ambiguities in parsing and lexical analysis, but the problem already exists with templates.

There is also a fourth special conversion: `const_cast`, to be used to make `const` things non-`const`.

The conversions discussed in the following sections all are of the first kind, the `static_cast`, with semantics of value converted to value within the type system.

```
    ... ...
class   Blue_fish
{
  public:
        int fishy;

        Blue_fish( const Sun_fish& );
    ... ...
void
tried_and_true( Blue_fish& bw )
{
        bw.fishy++;
}
    ... ...

        Sun_fish o_f;

        tried_and_true( o_f ); // Illegal as of Release 2.1.
                               // Before Release 2.1, uses
                               // Blue_fish ( o_f ) , and so
                               // of.fishy is not ++'d
```

If a function needs a non-const `X&`, and the expression provided for the argument is a `const X`, the implicit conversion is forbidden. (Explicit, deliberate conversion is permitted.)

In Chap. 4, Sec. 4.4 we will see that overloaded operators obey the same rules for argument matching. A type that is to support arithmetic or mixed-mode patterns of use should neither use non-const reference arguments, nor encourage their use. A type whose design encourages non-const reference arguments shouldn't try to support mixed-mode arithmetic operation. (This does not apply to assignment (Chap. 4, Sec. 4.5).)

If the type must support both modification of reference arguments and mixed-mode operations, it may need two layers, an upper layer seen by the type's user and a lower layer to do the real work, with linkages, back linkages, and reference counts.

3.4.5 Keeping implicit conversions under control

Implicit conversions can cause nasty surprises when they are invoked unexpectedly. Here are some rules for avoiding trouble.

First, do not write unneeded conversions. Operator member conversions are more dangerous than constructors, but both can cause trouble.

```
class   My_thing
{
```

```
    public:
            My_thing();
            My_thing( const char* );
            ... ...
    };

    void dosomething( const My_thing& );
        ... ...

            My_thing mine;
            dosomething( "mine" );  // OOPS!! dosomething (
                                    //      My_thing ( "mine" ) )
```

Sooner or later, most C++ programmers get bitten by this one.

To reduce the danger, reduce the set of possible conversions from class to class, and from class group to class group. A constructor `String ::String( const char* )` is reasonable; a default conversion from `Something_with_a_name` to `String` is asking for trouble.

There are two ways to prevent a constructor from being used as a default conversion. First, the signature of the constructor can be changed by adding at least one nondefaulting trailing argument. (It can be unused.) Second, the convert-from class can be changed by adding an operator conversion that would be identical to the constructor. This will prevent the implicit conversion by introducing an ambiguity.

If a conversion can be implemented by both constructor and conversion operator, it cannot be invoked implicitly. Such a conversion can be invoked explicity as a cast, and will result in a call to the member operator. There is no way to force a constructor conversion. (In very early versions of C++, this was not well-specified. The explicit rule was introduced around the time of C++ Release 2.0. And yes, it appears that ANSI/ISO C++ will keep it.)

Operator member function conversions should be used only (1) at most once per class to convert to a built-in type, and (2) to convert to a simpler type in a 'family.' If `Short_rational` is a 'simpler' type than `Arb_rational`, `Arb_rational` should be responsible for conversions between them. These would be `Arb_rational::Arb_Rational ( const Short_Rational& )` and `Arb_rational::operator Short_rational () const`.

Mutual conversions should also usually be avoided, except where the types are truly 'arithmetic' (their rvalues matter, their lvalues do not) and there are multiple types, each for a different representation of some data (e.g., `Short_rational` and `Fixed_decimal`). If the types are coequal, the conversions should be by constructor.

There is an excellent paper on this topic in the *Proceedings of the 1988 USENIX C++ Conference* (Murray, 1988). It does not mention two-step conversions because their existence wasn't described officially until C++ Release 2.0. (They could occur in previous releases when the built-in type was an integral type.)

3.5 Wheels: A Quick Visit with Value Builders

Let's define the constructor for the Wheelset thus:

```
class   Wheel_init
{
  public:
        Wheel_init( const char* const*, const Wheel_init& );
        Wheel_init( const char* const* );
        ... ...
        operator Wheel* ();
        ... ...
};

class   Wheel_set
{
  public:
        Wheel_set( Wheel_init& w ) : wheels( w ) {};
        ... ...
};
```

where a Wheel can be initialized from a Wheel_init. Then we could create a rotor machine with this declaration:

```
/*
 *      Assume that the c_ss's are const char* const *'s,
 *      appropriately set up.
 */
Wheel_set rotors( Wheel_init( c_ss_1,
        Wheel_init( c_ss_2, Wheel_init( c_ss_3,
        Wheel_init( c_ss_4, Wheel_init( c_ss_5,
        Wheel_init( c_ss_6, Wheel_init( c_ss_7,
        Wheel_init( c_ss_8 )   ) )  ) )  ) )  )  );
```

"Great LISPing PrettyPrinters!" This is messy C++, but it can be made to work and it is a plausible use.

3.6 Friendship

Part of a class's scope will be private, inaccessible from without the class's scope. The public/private distinction does not recognize 'cooperating' code and cannot grant it special privileges, even if the program's logical structure calls for them. And parts of a class's capabilities may be better written outside the class scope, either because they do not always need to be compiled in (e.g., I/O) or because C++'s semantics make a nonmember function better than a member function in a certain context (for examples, see Chap. 4, Sec. 4.4.4).

3.6.1 Introduction to friends

A class may declare *friends*. A *friend function* is not a member of this class (though it may be a member of another class). A class's friend functions have complete access to the class's scope. A *friend class* is another class whose member functions are all granted friendship by the first class.

```
class   A
{
        friend void f( int );      // One function is a friend.
        friend class B;            // The whole class is
        ... ...                    // a friend.
  private:
        int x;
        ... ...
};

class   B
{
  public:
        int a_x( const A& a   ) const
        { return a.x };     // <== Legal; B is a friend of A
};

void
f( int x )
{
        A a;
        a.x = x;     // Legal: f() is a friend of A .
}
```

Recall that in Chap. 2, Sec. 2.8.2 we needed to give a nested class access to its surrounding class. Friendship provides that access:

```
class   Cat
{
  public:
        void catfun ();
  ... ...
```

```
    private:
            /*
             *      Kitten helps to implement Cat, and must see
             *      the internal structure of Cat.
             */
            class   Kitten
            {
             public:
                    void kitfun();
              ... ...
            };
            friend class Kitten;
      ... ...
};
```

3.6.2 Friend members, forward class declarations

A member of one class may be a friend of another:

```
class   U
{
        friend void W::boojum( U& ) const;
    ... ...
```

For this to be legal, C++ must recognize `W` as a class name. But if the declaration for `class W` lies above this, then so do the declarations of `W`'s members:

```
class   W
{
        void boojum( U& ) const;
    ... ...
```

For *this* declaration to be legal, `U` must be recognized as the name of a type. It can't be, because the declaration of `U` now follows the declaration of `W`.

A *forward class declaration* introduces a class name without the class body:

```
class U;

class   W
{
        ... ...
        void boojum( U& ) const;   // void W::boojum( U& )
        ... ...
};
```

```
class   U
{
        friend void W::boojum( U& ) const;
        ... ...
```

The return type and argument declarations *must* be present, since the argument types are a part of the function's type and since there may be overloads on the member function name.

It is legal to write a forward declaration for a 'class' Xyz and to later declare Xyz as a struct, or vice versa. union may not be confused with class or struct in this way.

Two classes can be mutual friends, but they cannot both extend friendship to each other's member functions individually:

```
class Tweedle_dee;
class Tweedle_dum;

class   Tweedle_dee
{
        //   This next declaration is illegal, since the
        //   class header for  Tweedle_dum  has not yet
        //   been seen.
        friend char Tweedle_dum::dumfun( int ) const;

        int deefun( char ) const;
    ... ...
};

class   Tweedle_dum
{
        //   And this next declaration WOULD be illegal if
        //   we were to put  Tweedle_dum  in front of
        //   Tweedle_dee .
        friend charTweedle_dee::deefun ( int ) const;

        int dumfun( char ) const;
    ... ...
};
```

A nonmember friend function may be inlined by writing it in the header of a class which grants it friendship:

```
class   Toad
{
        static int stoat;
```

```
        friend Animal& badger( ... ... )
        {       ... ...
                stoat = 0;        // Toad::stoat = 0;
                ... ...
        };

        friend Animal& old_badger( ... ... );
        ... ...
};
```

A friend written in the class header obeys the same scope rules as a member written in the class header: static members of the enclosing class are visible without ::-qualification.*

Outside the class header, it obeys the scope rules of an ordinary function:

```
Animal&
old_badger ( ... ... )
{       ... ...
        Toad::stoat = 0;   // Toad::stoat , NOT just  stoat .
        ... ...
}
```

Of course, a nonmember function written inline in a class header must appear once and only once, in one header, and the particular class header must be visible wherever the function is needed.

3.6.3 Cooperating classes, cooperative pitfalls

Operator overloading (Chaps. 4 and 5) favors friend functions over members for many purposes. There are other legitimate uses of friends, and many questionable uses.

C++ magnifies both weaknesses and strengths in software design, design methods, and management. Poor architecture, poor design, and poor management can all create artificial needs for intimate interaction between 'modules.' Refusing to make incremental changes in architecture or design as a problem matures, allowing too little time for analysis and design, and intransigence by Module Tsars can all keep a program from accomodating the problem's needs.

Removing these obstacles takes enlightened management, good development methods, and teamwork across organization boundaries.

---

* See the note at the end of Chap. 2, Sec. 2.6.3.2.

Conway's Law states that a system reflects the lines of communication of the organization that designs it (Conway, 1968). 'If five groups work on a compiler, they will produce a five-phase compiler.' This means that the organization must be structured according to the solution to be implemented, and, ideally, according to the problem to be solved. It must, at all hazards, remain flexible enough to adjust as the understanding of the problem improves. Management must be educated to the technical structure of the project and adjust to it as it changes.

Section 3.10.2 provides one breakdown of 'phases' in software development.

3.6.4 Private constructors and classes

Constructors, like other member functions, may be private. A class whose constructors are all private is a *private class*. A private class must have either a friend or a public static member function. Without one of these, there is nothing which can create the first object of that class.

Private classes have important roles as cooperating classes. A relational database class `Relation` might grant access to itself by providing a `Relation::Access` object linked to itself. Read and write operations on the relation are performed by the public members of the `Relation::Access` object (much like operations on a file are written as operations on the open file handles, descriptors, control blocks, etc.). When the access object is destroyed, the `Relation` is informed; it can release resources, clear tables, etc.

3.6.5 Delegating capabilities separately

Some languages provide more precise control over friendship than C++, allowing a class to grant access to its members individually. This is important for large types that present complicated interfaces to multiple mechanisms. This can be simulated by access classes, each providing access to a particular set of capabilities.

```
class   Factotum
{
  public:
        class   Cook
        {
                friend class Kitchen;
                static int cook( Factotum& f,
                                const Kitchen& k, char c )
                {       return f.cook( k, c );  )
        };
        friend class Cook;
```

```
                                 // It doesn't work; this
int B::x( A::some_func () );     // declaration gets an error
                                 // message asserting that A::
                                 // somefunc() is private. So it
                                 // is, but this initialization
                                 // really occurs in the class
                                 // scope of B, which is a friend
                                 // of A.
```

The current draft of the ANSI/ISO working paper is explicit; the initialization takes place in the scope of `B` and has all the access rights due a member of `B`.

3.6.8 "Optional extra" classes

A class should be portable between environments. In particular, it should limit itself, as far as possible, to facilities available in all environments. Obviously, an interface to a GUI environment will depend upon that environment. But application classes in the program should try to be independent of the environment.

Because C and C++ can be supported in 'nonhosted' environments (environments in which there is no ordinary operating system or in which the operating system cannot be approached in the usual way), even ordinary I/O should not be built directly into such general-purpose classes.

Environment-dependent operations such as I/O should be implemented in friends instead, and the classes should be coded so that the 'core' class can be linked into a program without necessarily linking in the 'I/O option' class.

In general, the core class cannot make any calls to the option class(es). If there are inline functions in the headers, and if they are controlled by reliable conditional compilation (`#if`/`#endif`, App. C, Sec. 1.3.1), calls may appear there. It's important that they not be compiled into any functions which appear in a precompiled library unless there is some mechanism for providing alternate versions of the libraries. Nor may they be `virtual` (Chap. 6, Sec. 6.4). (The mechanics of this are necessarily environment-dependent.) Member data must not be conditionally compiled.

Consider an I/O friend for a string class:

In String.h

```
class   String
{
        friend class String_IO;
```

```
    ... ...
};
#if Stream_IO_included
# include <String_IO.h>
#endif

    In String_IO.h

class   String_IO
{
  public:
        static ostream& put( ostream& o, const String& str )
        { return o << str.chars ; };
};
```

How do we invoke the I/O operations? As we have written the class, we must write something like this:

```
String s;
... ...
String_IO::put( cout, s ) << "\n" ;
```

This works, but it's clumsy. We can interpose a nonmember, also written in `String_IO.h`:

```
inline ostream&
put( ostream& o, const String& str )
{
        return String_IO::put( o, str );
};
```

Why not just make this function a friend of `String`? Because there is a chance that in some environment the presence of the function name in the class header will cause the I/O function to be linked into the executable even if it is nowhere called. Why not use conditional compilation to leave it present or absent? It clutters the class header and it doesn't really belong there.

There's another reason. Output of something like a string is a fairly simple operation. Input is harder, and may require multiple functions and data objects shared between functions. Then the `String_IO` input function, and all its helper functions, become nonstatic members, and the data they share are made members of `String_IO`. Then the nonmember input function can create an instance of `String_IO`.

Why should the ultimate interface to a class's clients be a nonmember function? The reason will become apparent in Chap. 4, Sec. 4.4.4.

3.7 Wheels and private classes

If we use the linked `Wheels` approach of Sec. 3.2.3, the `Wheel` class can be made private and the `Wheel_set` can be made a friend of `Wheel`. The `Wheel_set` manages the `Wheel` objects; the outside world never touches them.

Alternatively, we can make the `Wheel` class internal and private to `Wheel_set` and leave their member functions public. `Wheel` helps to implement `Wheel_set`, and represents its internal structure.

Both of these provide simple, self-contained interfaces to the Odometer Algorithm. Compare them with the original version in Chap. 1.

3.8 Generators

3.8.1 Wheels as a generator

A *generator* is an object that can be invoked repeatedly to produce a sequence of values. (Think of a random number generator.) A generator encapsulates some kind of state sequence, upon which the output sequence depends, and is a classical tool of Object-Orientation.

The `Wheel_set` object, when packaged as described in Sec. 3.7, is a generator. It's possible to think of an input stream as a generator, if its 'internal state' is stretched to include the entire source (e.g., file) of characters.

3.8.2 Generators and 'source of control'

A program's clarity may be improved by changing the 'source of control' (or 'top level' or *control locus*). Object Orientation provides a locus for data, a strategic place to hold state information that is needed from time to time. Placing such information in a generator allows the control of iteration to be separated from the state information that yields the sequence of values. The generator can be kept in a different function, or even passed by reference between several functions.

Consider a recursive descent parsing system. Each node in the parser tree accepts a token, interprets it appropriately, and returns some indication of whether the parse has completed, has failed, or is continuing.

In this structure, a token must be passed from the top level down to whatever recursively defined part of the tree is ready to accept a token:

```
Token tokenize ( istream& );

for( Syntax parser ; ; )
{
        Parse_status ps =
                parser.parse( tokenize ( prog_input ) );
```

```
        switch( ps.stat () )
        {
          case Continuing:
                continue;

          case Error:
                ps.err();
                /* Fall-Through */
          case Accepted:
                return parser;
        }
}
```

A token generated by `tokenize()` may be passed down through many levels of the recursive `Syntax::parse()`, and return values must be passed back up all the way to the top for each token. This is easy to specify, but expensive and inflexible. It's also error-prone when coding.

What happens if we redesign `Syntax::parse()` as `Syntax::parse( iostream& )` and pass it the `prog_input` stream, allowing it to call the tokenizer? This allows the tokenizer to be called at the level that needs it. But it embeds the interface between the tokenizer and the input stream into many pieces of code.

It would be better to turn the tokenizer into a generator:

```
Tokenizert ( prog_input );
Syntax parser;

Parse_status ps = parser.parse( t );

switch( ps.stat () )
{
 case Continuing:
        ps.incomplete();
        /* Fall-Through */

 case Error:
        ps.err();
        /* Fall-Through */

 case Accepted:
        return parser;
}
```

The `Tokenizer` is now a generator whose state includes the whole source of characters. It manages its own state and its own interface to the input stream and can implement whatever lookahead is needed. `Syntax::parse()` contains the control loop. No function calls are spent passing tokens into the syntax tree and the tokenizer can be passed by reference to whatever needs it. The tokens it yields are available where they are needed, not attached to a single loop. And the tokenizer is burdened by neither the iterating control structure nor scattered data and data access.

In many applications, generators can be used instead of coroutines, threads, or tasks. They are a weaker mechanism, and an easier mechanism to design and debug. They allow the locus of control to be moved using only the function call and member function call disciplines. Moreover, generator objects can be copied freely and their state saved or duplicated. This cannot be done in all coroutine, thread, or task environments.

3.9 The Relationship Between Code and Documentation: How Code Can and Cannot Explain Itself

In *The Elements of Programming Style* (Kernighan and Plauger, 1978), Kernighan and Plauger argued that whatever *can* be stated clearly in expressions, statements, and declarations should be. Comments must cover what's left. (Fifteen years old, burdened with examples in FORTRAN 66 and PL/1, this book remains the best text on programming as a communication art. It no longer covers the whole field, but what it covers, it covers with brilliant style and irresistable force.)

3.9.1 The limits of procedural languages: *how, what, why*

Structured Programming is our best coding discipline. What is its virtue? There are two incompatible theories. Structured Programming's virtue may be that it simplifies formal proofs on the code. Or it may be that it organizes problems so that people can better understand them.

Formal proofs of code are rare, but a programmer can grasp what structured code says with neither analysis nor proof. I claim that Structured Programming is a recipe for writing code to a human audience, and that it reveals certain relationships in the code.

A program is a system of cause and effect. Causes are Posterior or Prior (or Material or Formal; see Chap. 1, Sec. 1.7). "Why is it so warm in here?" "Because I turned the thermostat up." The change to the thermostat came before the warmth; it is the *prior* cause. "Why did you do that?" "Because I wanted to be warm." The desired warmth came after the changed thermostat; it is the *posterior* or *final* cause of the action.*

* Since prior causes *effect* change, they are also called *efficient* causes; posterior (final) causes are also called *ends,* and should not be confused with the *ultimate* cause.

We program to meet requirements (posterior causes); statements in the program are their effects. To debug we study effects and seek their prior causes in statements. Maintenance programmers trace links from effects back to final causes. Mathematical proofs on code deal only with prior causes; the human reader needs both. Mathematical proofs can assure us that the code meets spec, not that it answers the need.

Code must tell us *What, Why* and *How. What* does this code do? *Why* does it do it? *How* does it do it?

We may also ask "*When* is something done? *Where* is it done?" These are correlatives of What and How. To find Where an action is performed, determine What each code unit does. To find When an action occurs, determine How each code unit works and at which step it takes that action.

The Why (final cause) of a code unit may come from either the program's requirements ("The specs say 'delete the file if -a is set' ") or from other parts of the program. *A* Why *from the specifications must be given in comments. A* Why *from within the program is best made clear in the code itself, lest commentary and code someday conflict.*

Structured Programming uses two structures, *Governs* and *Invokes,* to unmask cause and effect by organizing the flow of control.

Structured loops and branches (basic flow constructs) are *Governs* structures: this code governs whether and how often that code takes effect. A code block is activated as a unit in response to a single prior cause and, presumably, to meet a single final cause. Governs gathers Why and What into a single, traceable hierarchy.

(In COBOL, a labeled paragraph can either be entered from the top or executed remotely using the PERFORM verb. It has long been recognized that a paragraph should be entered from the top or else PERFORMed, but not both. It should either be invoked or be allowed to govern—but not both.)

Invokes is the function/procedure call. It encases control flow causality. In it a well-defined Why and What coincide. The Invokes creates a named unit of code. The What of all the steps within must answer a single purpose, their Why. That Why is the What of the invocation of the named unit. "What are we doing?" "Computing the absolute value." "Why?" "Because we were asked." "By whom?" *"polyroot()."* To *polyroot(),* the absolute value computation is a What that is part of How *polyroot()* satisfies its final cause.

How is usually clear from the What of a code unit and of its parts. The division of cause and effect by the Governs structure makes code tractable, given two conditions. First, the expressions and statements must be clear: the What of each must be obvious. Second, the problem must be solved directly. A recondite algorithm (e.g., heapsort, hash-ing,* FFT†) must be commented on outline and subgoals to fill in the How of the outer structure and the Why of the inner.

The Governs and Invokes hierarchies provide strong focal points for named actions (subroutines/functions) and weaker foci to link chains of decisions through many cause-effect stages (Governed and Governing units). The Why and its corresponding What are grouped together in levels, exposing each Why.

Neither Governs nor Invokes addresses the cause and effect transmitted through a program's data.

3.9.2 What C++ and object-based programming add

Structured Programming provides causal links for flow control, but not for data. The What and Why links are broken when code communicates by data.

Communication by data requires reader and writer to agree arbitrarily on the data's meaning. For data used locally, the agreement is obvious. We name local variables *i, j,* and *k* ignoring the data's representation, which we comment only if it is recondite. Local data that are commented are described once, not separately at each use. And all code communicating by it is visible at once, so the agreement is visible.

Long-range data are thoughtfully named, and nonobvious uses are described separately at each use of the data. The actions of code upon the data are described, obvious or not. The agreement of reader and writer is carefully fostered.

We hide the difficulties of long-range data behind functions that name actions (What and Why) instead of data encodings. Long ago, we invented subroutines with built-in return, removing state jump tables, jump variables, and ALTER statements.‡ And we limit the places from which long-range data are visible to narrow the Where from which an action may be taken.

The problems of Representation include not only the ability of a Representation to store information and to yield it up on retrieval, but also the expression of cause-effect relationships between the code that stores the information and the code that retrieves it, between the Representation and the program's intended purpose.

---

* A technique for searching for records by keys, 'obvious' to practitioners of that art, and covered in most 'basic algorithm' texts, such as Knuth's *The Art of Computer Programming* (Volume III), as well as in some compiler texts.

† A numerical signal processing algorithm for Fast computation of the Fourier Transform, which describes a signal as a sum of pure circular (sine wave) signals at specific frequencies.

‡ COBOL's ALTER statement permits a program to change the targets of its GOTO statements as it executes.

Data Abstraction and the Object model are strongly centered around data, limiting the data's visibility and keeping its meaning local. Named member functions give callers a cause-effect link from the What of the invocation (the data's Use) instead of from the data's representation. They sidestep data's inability to communicate cause and effect.

3.9.3 Toward malleable software

A malleable material can be hammered into arbitrary shapes without fracturing. A material that is not malleable is 'brittle.' A brittle material fractures under blows that will deform and reshape a malleable material.

Software is known as a brittle medium. True, we can hammer it into any shape we want, but when it gets to that shape it's often riddled with flaws.

Brittle software is expensive. Reusing Version *N* as the foundation of Version *N* + 1 requires hammering version *N* into version *N* + 1. The result must work reliably, and often doesn't.

How do we make software malleable? Let's say we have a problem statement P_1 and a development method M which leads us to a solution:

$$S_{M1} = S_M (P_1)$$

where S_{M1} is the best solution (program) that method M can give for the problem statement P_1. And let's say that method M is our best method. (We're only interested in the best way.)

Once we have S_{M1} out the door to our customers, we are given P'_1, an incremental modification of P_1, from which we are to produce S'_{M1}. Since P'_1 is an incremental modification away from P_1, we might write

$$\frac{|P'_1 - P_1|}{|P_1|} << 1$$

(where $|X|$ means 'the magnitude of X'). In words, the changes in the problem statement P'_1 are tiny compared with P_1 itself. If we were to apply our best method to get S'_{M1}, we would get

$$S'_{M1} = S_M (P'_1)$$

This S'_{M1} is the best solution possible for P'_1.

Applying method M takes time. It will often be quicker to modify the solution S_{M1} directly to get S'_{M1}. If we chose this speedy route, we get

$$S'_{M1} = S'_M (P_1)$$

S'_{M1} in this case will be the best S' possible under method M_1 if and only if

$$S'_{M1} = S'_M(P_1) = S_M(P'_1)$$

In words, we would like the result of tinkering with the solution to be the same as the result of reengineering the solution from the modified problem statement. Otherwise, it is not our best solution (engineering the solution by method M gives us that).

Schedules dictate that the 'best' solution is the quickest one. A product that is late to market may lose all chance of recovering its development costs. There are two ways for the best solution to be the fastest. First, the tinkered solution might be identical to the reengineered solution. Second, the process of reengineering the solution might be speeded up so that it is as fast as tinkering.

If the changes that turned problem statement P_1 into P'_1 were properly done, they are the simplest, or nearly the simplest, and most fundamental changes possible. In the general case we will expect the changes to the solution to be at least as large as the changes to the problem:

$$\frac{|S'_1 - S_1|}{|S_1|} \geqslant \frac{|P'_1 - P_1|}{|P_1|}$$

Common experience is much worse; a minor change in the problem statement often causes large changes in the solution program:

$$\frac{|S'_1 - S_1|}{|S_1|} >> \frac{|P'_1 - P_1|}{|P_1|}$$

Why is this? I claim that the principle reason is a discrepency in the *structure of semantics.* The problem calls for certain behaviors on certain inputs according to certain semantics. Those problem semantics have an inherent underlying organization. The solution provides certain behaviors on certain inputs according to certain semantics, which also have an underlying organization. The organization of the semantics of the problem and of the solution are not necessarily the same—but they should be. If they are, every design issue stated in one place in the problem statement would be embodied in exactly one place in the program—the program would have no unnecessary coupling. Related elements in the problem would be related in the solution—the program would be perfectly coherent.

If the semantic structure of S_{M1} differs slightly from the that of P_1, then the semantic structure of the tinkered solution will probably differ more from that of the original solution. After multiple releases, it will become harder and harder to change the program because whatever relationship originally existed between the problem and the program has been violated over and over.

This 'incongruence of semantic structure' between the best problem statement and the best solution program is the major obstacle to malleability, and it grows worse with time. There are two escapes. One is to make malleability of the program irrelevant: make method M so fast that it is quicker to produce $S_{M1}(P'_1)$ than it is to produce $S'_{M1}(P_1)$. This is an elusive goal, but it has been met for compilation of a higher-level-language to assembler or binary.

The other solution is to make the semantic structure of the solution program agree with the semantic structure of the problem statement in P_1 and S_1 and to maintain that agreement (*congruence*) through P'_1 and S'_1, P''_1 and S''_1, P'''_1 and S'''_1, etc. If we can do this, method M becomes a matter of translating literally the language of the problem into the language of the solution. Method M is very fast *and* is the means to the 'tweaked' solution.

Object Orientation asserts that the way to have our cake is to eat it. This ideal situation is possible, or nearly so, if we can model the problem in the same terms as we design and code the solution. Object Orientation allows this.

We must understand the basic elements of semantic organization. These are the semantic system, or *domain* and the semantic center (or *locus*), which is the Object.

We'll pick up this thread again in Chap. 5, Sec. 5.6

3.10 Engineering and Objects

Software engineering, applied to C++, must concern itself with Object-based and Object-Oriented techniques, and those techniques must not neglect the basic rules of good practice.

3.10.1 Good practice is good practice still

Some textbooks, in order to illustrate Object-Oriented Programming, Design, or Analysis, overlook good software engineering practice. In practice, good practice is essential.

In designing a network of Object Types to model an application, we come sooner or later to a 'basic' type. "The height and width of the display window will be float." They may be `float` when the program runs on this display system on this hardware platform, but a sound program declares them all as, say, `Display_len`, which the display module typedefs as `float`. Programs with demanding numerical properties may have a series of typedefs, e.g., `Float_6`, `Float_12`, `Float_16`, `Float_22`, and `Float_20_Xrange`. The types for the application's types are typedef'd in terms of these. On platforms without a distinct `long double`, the last two may be simulated by class types with the attendant cost. With operator overloading (Chaps. 4 and 5), the source code which uses the types need not change when the implementations of the types change.

Consider a problem in which data must be transmitted over a link of some sort. The link is 7 bits wide, which suffices for text, but binary data must be encoded. Some OO techniques—and Structured techniques as well—would suggest that such data be passed through an `Encoder` of some sort. But a better solution would be to pass *all* data for the link through a 'Link Adaptor,' which, for 7-bit ASCII data, would pass the data through unencoded (a 'null' adaptor). The data link and the link adaptor should then be packaged as an arbitrary-width link. Then someone studying code which transmits ASCII text would understand the user requirements of the data link. And when video images must be transmitted, the model will suggest a place to put the image compression algorithms.

Some OO-Analysis techniques suggest that a type like the null adaptor, which just passes through the call to another type, should be eliminated. This makes sense for a type that originates in the Problem and that is discovered by Analysis. But it can't be applied to a type that originates in the program's Architecture.

The Architecture or Model of the system must provide organizing concepts and principles to guide those who implement, understand, and extend the system. It must model not only this particular problem, but part of the Subject to which the particular problem belongs. *Object Orientation is a means to better Architecture, not a substitute for Architecture.*

A brief caution is in order on the word 'architecture.' Everyone who has ever used it uses it differently. In this text, it means *the relationship among parts and whole that give the parts their meaning in the context of the whole.*

3.10.2 Object-oriented software engineering phases

The phases to which Object Orientation lends itself are Analysis, Synthesis (or Modeling, or Architecture), Design, Detailing, and Programming:

1. Analysis *recognizes* and *characterizes* the parts of the real or as-yet-hypothetical system which the program must emulate and *describes* the relationships between these parts.
2. Synthesis identifies the *concepts* and *underlying structure* of the Problem and the *Problem's Subject* area and *organizes* the components in an Architecture or *Model.*

The Architecture defines the roles to be filled by Application and Subject Domain types. For each type, the existence and roles of the other types defines (1) the obligations of that type within the system, (2) the resources available to it to fulfill those obligation, and (3) the contribution that type makes to the operation of the system as a whole.

To do this, the architecture may need to introduce other types, either for grouping (modules) or as placeholders to make the network of relationships more regular, or as separators to reduce unnecessary coupling.

3. Design determines *how each component will fulfill the role given it by Architecture.* It may also address nonarchitectural requirements, such as performance requirements that are met by local (intratype) measures rather than by global (intertype) measures (as when running time is dominated by an algorithm whose control lies within a single type).

Design may also introduce types, either to share code, or to fill roles needed by another type for its nonarchitectural requirements, or to partition a type's role into components (which may introduce architectural issues *within* a type).

4. Detailing (often called Detail Design) is specifying the code that will implement the design. Consistant Detailing is essential. Without it, a function called in one line may demand a pointer to an object, a function in the next, a name to identify the same object, and in the next a reference to the object. A Detailing Plan should spell out how various classes and objects of those classes are to be identified in various parts of the system, and whatever else is necessary to ensure that the parts work smoothly together.

5. Coding *implements* the Detailed Design.*

These phases might not be completely sequential. Analysis and Synthesis often run side by side. And in the design of a component, it may be discovered that the component is still too complex to be implemented without further analysis, synthesis, and design. Ideally, the situation will be recognized before the design phase; if it is not recognized before coding, there may be a serious problem.

The better the development method is at asking the right questions and recording the answers, the less backtracking from Design into Analysis will need to be done.

---

* Notice that the traditional user of 'Detailed Design' means a design which has been worked out to the level of details; here we mean a design which has been subjected to the process of Detailing. The final meaning is the same, but we make 'Detail' into a verb to dignify the activity with a name of its own.

Note that these phases can be carried out directly only when the model that results from one is suitable as the input to the next. Object Orientation preserves the overall model from analysis right through to coding.

We'll refine this further in Chap. 5, Sec. 5.6.3.

3.10.3 Software engineering phases and types

A type in a program may originate in any of the program's engineering phases.

The analysis phase provides the *problem-domain* (or *application-domain*) types. (In an engineering problem, there are physical quantities like forces, torques, and speeds, some of which may be represented by a complex number type.) It also provides some *subject-domain* types (the complex number type itself, which belongs to large parts of engineering math, not to any specific problem.)

The synthesis phase distinguishes the problem-domain types from subject-domain types. It also can introduce *architecture* or *model domain* types, which help to organize the program (as by filling out an empty space in a layered architecture).

The design phase provides types specific to the *representations* of other types and to the *interactions* between other types (e.g., a transaction record or a multiparameter aggregate), and to those 'management' characteristics that are important to the design (e.g., fast free-store management in a speed-critical program, types specific to 'interesting' algorithms such as Chap. 1's *Heapsorter*).

Detailing introduces types necessary to implement other types, and in particular, types that provide interfaces for other types.

The programming phase provides types that aid the implementation. These can be types that manage data or implement algorithms which are not specified by the design. They can be types that provide interfaces or wrappers not specified by the design. They can be types needed to provide other types with desired semantics.

Much of the literature on Object-Oriented techniques concentrates on problem-domain types, neglecting or even deprecating types that are introduced to meet the needs of phases besides analysis. But the other phases must be done well and they will almost invariably result in the introduction of types.

The later phases may also change types from non-Object to Object. For instance, Analysis may determine that some Object has an attribute (a non-Object member) that represents a color. But Design might juxtapose two parts of the model provided by Analysis and discover that Color is a composite value containing values of red, blue, and green (or hue, lightness, and saturation, or cyan, magenta, yellow, and black, or whatever). In systems where the colors can be represented by names or constants, it might be better to represent colors as enums or small indices in Objects that have color and perform the color-to-component mapping in one place. But if colors can be entered, invented, or synthesized on the fly, this won't do and Color will have to become an Object, in Design if not in Analysis.

The documentation for a type should indicate in a straightforward way from which domain or design phase it comes. For problem-domain and subject-domain types, the requirement or principle represented should be indicated. For model-domain types, the part of the model should be indicated. For design-phase types, the requirement (if there is a requirement) and purpose of the type should be indicated. For programming-phase types, the purpose or service provided and beneficiary types should be indicated. This has been neglected in many parts of the Object-Oriented literature.

3.10.4 Roles of types and characteristics of types

There are butchers and bakers and candlestick makers; there are librarians and lawyers and barkers and bricklayers. They wear different clothes, exercise different skills, and use different tools, and their jobs just *look* different.

Types too can have different roles, and types in different roles may look quite different. Moreover, a type's role may be determined during different design phases. A type which provides a user interface (problem-domain) may be implemented with the services of a type which manages tables of strings (design or program phase).

Most problem- and subject-domain types, and some model-domain and design-phase types perform one of these roles:

- Representing problem-domain components ('the real or as-yet-hypothetical system to be emulated')
- Representing subject-domain features or rules (e.g., engineering may use complex arithmetic, financial applications project monetary value backwards and forwards through time)
- Organizing processes or procedures
- Implementing a process or procedure
- Representing a transaction between problem-domain types
- Management (representation) of data relevant to the problem domain or the Model

Most other model-domain and design phase types perform one of these roles:

- Representing the mechanisms whereby information is presented to or accepted from human users
- Representing the state, or representing or recognizing the status of processes, procedures, or transactions
- Implementing services which the design uses to meet certain requirements (e.g., fast free store for some types)

Roles often played by detailing-phase and coding-phase types include:

- Implementing services which are not tied directly to requirements
- Managing internal data for types from the design and programming phases
- Providing interfaces, either as wrappers or as transaction or parameter records (representations) for interactions between types or by helping to provide special semantics for other types

Note the frequency of the words 'represent' and 'representation.' Dealing with representations is the Data Abstraction portion of Object Orientation.

3.10.5 Notes on Object-Oriented argot

Here are C++ translations for some terms from the lexicon of Object-Orientation.

Services provided by an Object are creation, deletion, allocation, initialization, and cleanup, and making certain state information available. In C++, this means constructors, destructors, `new` and `delete`, and member functions that simply return the value of a data member, and possibly computations performed by static member functions. Also, resource or object allocation by static member functions might be called a service.

Messages accepted by an Object are all other requests which the Object recognizes. In C++, this means all other member functions.

Contracts correspond to member function interfaces for public or friend use. Each contract has a certain responsibility to its callers, and a certain role in the mechanism it is designed to support. Interfaces that are not designed into specific mechanisms can more resemble prospectuses than contracts. A contract usually does not correspond to a single member function (method), but to a group of related member functions. A class can have one contract (ideal) or many.

Polymorphism is the ability to send a request to an object without knowing the object's exact type. C++ provides polymorphism through

Inheritance and Virtualization (Chap. 6). Some programming languages use their polymorphic facilities to provide composition as well.

Composition is the ability to assemble types according to a pattern with parameters or inserted types. C++ provides composition by *templates* (Chap. 8).

3.11 Summary

Section 3.1.1 C++ requires type-correct dynamic allocation by means of the `new` and `delete` operators. See also Chap. 5, Sec. 5.5 (overloading `new` and `delete`) and Chap. 6, Sec. 6.4.7 (`new` and `delete` with inheritance and virtualization).

Section 3.1.2 For class types, type-correct dynamic allocation and deallocation include invocation of constructors and destructors, and the syntax needed to pass arguments to the constructor.

Section 3.1.3 Memory is a finite resource and can be exhausted. C++ provides a 'hook' to gain control on exhaustion. See Chap. 9 for another approach.

Section 3.1.4 Keeping track of allocated memory is a perennial programming problem. It can often be solved by using nondynamic objects and their lifetimes to manage units of dynamically allocated memory.

Section 3.1.4.5 When an object is implemented by other objects to which it points, and especially when those objects involve dynamically allocated memory, there are 'const' operations which in fact need to change internals of the object; likewise, there are operations which would be legal by the bitwise criterion for const-ness, but which make no sense for an object declared 'const.' The latter can be managed by the proper use of 'const' member functions. The former may receive help from a language feature under consideration by the ANSI/ISO committee: 'Never-const' or 'un-const':

```
class   Inconstant
{
  public:
      ... ...
  private:
          int cached_value ~const;        // This syntax is NOT
                                          // final.
          int is_cached ~const;
};
```

Section 3.3.1 Constructors can be used to create unnamed values in expressions. These are called *value builders,* and their syntax is borrowed from constructors and function calls.

Section 3.3.2 Value builders can often be used in ways that help the compiler avoid making intermediate copies of objects.

Sections 3.2.3, 3.2.4 Value builders with one argument act as type conversions and C++ treats them as such, allowing them as either explicit or implicit conversions.

Section 3.2.5 Operator member conversions allow class types to be converted to other class types and to built-in types.

Section 3.4.1 Conversions are important to rvalue semantics (see Chap. 6, Sec. 6.3.3 for lvalue conversions) and classes may be designed to serve their users by either lvalue or rvalue semantics or both.

Section 3.4.2 Conversions can work within the type system (true conversions) or controvene it (type coercions). ANSI/ISO C++ will probably have different syntaxes for conversions, coercions, and runtime-checked conversions (which only come into play with types that are polymorphic).

Section 3.4.3 C++ can invoke conversions automatically. C++ will try so hard and no harder to find a sequence of conversions for a given time. C++ divides conversions into several types, which C++ will use according to certain rules.

Section 3.4.4 Non-const reference arguments must not require conversions (except for the lvalue conversions of Chap. 6, Sec. 6.3.3).

Section 3.4.5 Implicit conversions can create unmanageable chaos. There are rules whose application can prevent this.

Section 3.6.1 A class can grant access to its entire scope to a single function or to all member functions of a class. These classes are *friends* of the class granting access.

Section 3.6.2 The declarations required for friendship often require class names to be introduced as type names before the class declarations. The *forward class declaration* does this. Either `class` or `struct` may be used to forward-declare either a struct or a class; union must be used to forward-declare a union.

Sections 3.6.4, 3.6.5, 3.6.6 A class can depend upon its friends for creation and other vital functionality. Such a class can have no interaction beyond what its friends allow it. Where one class implements another or represents another, these dependent (*private*) classes can express the problem or the program's architecture. Combined with nested classes (Chap. 2, Sec. 2.6.3), private classes can also give a class multiple interfaces, each accessible only to certain classes.

Section 3.6.7 A friend class cannot call upon a private function to initialize its static members. (Early releases only.)

Section 3.6.8 A friend class can provide features that should not be compiled into the core class, for whatever reason.

Section 3.8 An OO construction called the *generator* can encapsulate state information, allowing the locus of control in some programs to be moved to modules other than the 'obvious' module under top-down design.

Section 3.9 A program that is under control is one whose cause-effect relationships are known. Structured programming organizes causal relationships in flow control and flow locality. Data Abstraction and Object-Based programming create data-centered loci and manifest the causal relationships surrounding program data.

Section 3.10 When learning OO techniques, other good practice must be retained. The Object relationships found during analysis are only some of the relationships that must be programmed in a real system.

Chapter 4

Principles of Overloading

Overview

Overloading, and especially operator overloading, is reckoned a wild and lawless territory. In C++, this reputation is undeserved. C++ overloading is powerful and its effects far-reaching, but it can be used safely and can even safeguard (see Chap. 2, Sec. 2.1.4 on constructors). Operator overloading can impose order on types suited to it, and maintain order when a native type is displaced by a custom-bred class type.

4.1 Introduction

C++ supports *overloading*. An "overloaded function name" is a function name that represents several functions in the same scope. (If two different classes both have member functions named `memfun()`, they do not constitute an overload because they are in different scopes and different 'name spaces.')

4.1.1 Where and why

When an overloaded function name is used, its context determines which function is meant. *Context* here means the function signature (Chap. 1, Sec. 1.1.6), which can be determined from the function call, or (if the function's address is taken) from the type of the pointer-to-function which is assigned or initialized from the name.

```
int snark( const char* );          // 3 prototypes for
int snark( int, int = 0 );         //   snark() declare three
double snark( double, int = 0 );// overloads of  snark() .
```

```
snark( "forks and hope" );      // snark( const char* )
snark( 1279 );                  // snark( int, int = 0)

int(*fn_di)( double, int )
                = snark;        // snark( double, int )
```

The different overloads have different return values, but the return values are not part of the signature (Chap. 1, Sec. 1.1.6) and cannot be used to discriminate between overloads:

```
void snark( double );    // Conflicts with
                         // double snark( double, int = 0 )
                         //   which can be called with only
                         //   the double arg.
```

C++ permits overloading of member and nonmember functions. It permits overloading of most of the built-in operators, *when their operands include class, struct, union, or enum types.*

(Overloading on enums is added in ANSI C++; it is not part of C++ Release 3.0 or C++ Release 3.1.)

Prior to C++ Release 2.0, nonmember function names to be overloaded had to be declared with the overload keyword. The keyword was required both because overloading was deemed dangerous and to simplify the implementation (Sec. 4.3.1, "Name Encoding"). It turned out that overloading is safe as C++ now defines it and that the attempt to escape "name mangling" was not. (Stroustrup, 1988.)

In Release 2.0, all nonmember function names may be overloaded and overload declarations are ignored. overload will be recognized as a keyword in ANSI C++ if it appears anywhere in an overload declaration; otherwise, it may be used as an ordinary identifier.

Operator overloading cannot change the built-in meaning of C++ operators, nor change their precedence, nor introduce new operators. It *can* define a type Complex such that we can write

```
class   Complex
{
        ... ... // Something in here defines a  "+"
        ... ... // for class  Complex
};
    ... ...

        Complex c1 = Complex( 1, 0 );
        Complex c2 = Complex( 0, 1 );

        Complex c3 = c1 + c2;
```

Operator overloading can allow objects of a named type to be used like built-in arithmetic types. Whether the name is a user-defined type or a `typedef` to an `int`, the type's users write the same arithmetic operators. If a built-in type is later replaced by a class type, the type's definition must be changed, but the code using the type need only be recompiled. (This works well but not perfectly; for special cases see Sec. 4.4.5.)

When operators like + are applied to built-in types alone they are not considered overloads. They obey C's rules on type promotion and conversion, not C++'s rules on overloading.

Overloading of both functions and operators remains a potential source of errors; it could conceivably provide malicious code with one more place to hide.

4.1.2 Types overloading can distinguish (signatures)

Overload resolution involves conversions, which may be needed to match a function signature to the types written in a call. Conversions in function matches were introduced in Chap. 3, Sec. 3.4, so the basics of this section may seem familiar.

C++ divides conversions into four groups.

1. *Trivial conversions.* These conversions are often 'unavoidable'; they are needed to meet C and C++ semantics. They do not affect the selection of an overload match, but a given conversion may be illegal, making the selected match illegal. (`T` stands for any type.) Any number may be applied in one step.

```
T          <==> T&
T          <==> T&
T[]         ==> T*
T( argtypes ) ==> (T*) ( argtypes )
T           ==> const T
T           ==> volatile T
T*          ==> const T*
T*          ==> volatile T*
```

2. *Promotions.* Promotion, or widening, is the conversion from a type with a representation and a width to a type with the same representation but a possibly greater width (e.g., `short int` to `long int`). Promotion from `float` to `double` is allowed, and from an `unsigned` type to a wider `unsigned` type. Conversions between `signed` and `unsigned` are not promotions.

3. *Other built-in conversions.* These are conversions between arithmetic types with different representations (signed, unsigned, floating point), from any pointer-to-object to `void*` or from `void*` to any pointer-

to-object (C++ will not insert this implicitly), and the conversions required by Inheritance and Virtualization (Chap. 6):

Derived& to *Base&* and *Derived** to *Base** and their inverses (which C++ will not insert implicitly).

4. User-defined conversions. Conversions by constructor or member conversion operator.

Built-in conversions for built-in types around built-in operators are the 'usual arithmetic conversions' of ANSI C*:

1. If either operand is `long double`, the other is converted to `long double`, and the result is `long double`.
2. Otherwise, if either is `double`, the other is converted to `double`, and the result is `double`.
3. Otherwise, if either is `float`, the other is converted to `float`, and the result is `float`.
4. Otherwise, `char`s (signed and unsigned), `short int`s, enumeration values, and bitfields are converted to `int` if `int` can hold their values, or to `unsigned int` if `int` cannot. (These are *integral promotions.*) Then
   a. If either operand is `unsigned long`, the other is converted to `unsigned long`, and the result is `unsigned long`.
   b. Otherwise, if one operand is a `long int` and the other an `unsigned int`, they are both converted to `long int` if `long int` can hold all the values of an `unsigned int`; otherwise, they are both converted to `unsigned long`. The type of the result is the type to which the operands are converted.
   c. Otherwise, if either operand is `long`, the other is converted to `long`, and the result is `long`.
   d. Otherwise, if either operand is `unsigned`, the other is converted to `unsigned`, and the result is `unsigned`.
   e. Otherwise, both operands are `int` and the result is `int`.

These are the ANSI C++ rules. They preserve value first, then signedness. Because they depend on whether a `long` is wider than an unsigned `int`, they can give different results on machines with different widths for the built-in types. And there is no guarantee that an integer can be represented exactly in floating point. A 64-bit `long` (supported on some machines) can take on values that a 64-bit `double` cannot.

---

* Early versions of C++ (1.0, 1.1, 1.2, 1.2E) used the pre-ANSI rules for the usual arithmetic conversions. The major difference is that under pre-ANSI rules, unsigned was never converted to signed.

4.1.3 The matching of arguments

When C++ encounters a function call with *N* arguments, it considers all visible function overloads of that name. It identifies the overloads eligible to be called with *N* arguments (including those using default arguments). Then it determines which of the eligible overloads can match the arguments provided, and attempts to find a 'best' match. To be a best match, an overload must

- Equal or better every other eligible overload's match on every argument.
- Better every other eligible overload's match on at least one argument (not necessarily the same for each).

How is one match better than another? Some matches need conversions inserted, others don't. Some conversions are considered closer matches than others. And some matches are allowed only as a last resort.

If an overload's argument can be matched to the actual argument by several conversions, one better than the others, the better one will be taken as the overload's candidate. If there are two or more 'equally good' conversions, and any could be the best, the match is ambiguous and the overload cannot match the actual call.

For example:

```
int f( float, long );
int f( double, unsigned );
```

No conversion at all is a better match than promotion, and promotion a better match than a signed-unsigned change (the full rules follow in Sec. 4.1.4).

```
f( 1, 1 );      // Call: f( int, int )
```

The choices to match an overload to the call are

```
f( int=>float, int=>long )
f( int=>double, int=>unsigned )
```

The first overload provides a better match on the second argument, and an equally good match on the first argument.

```
f( 0U, 1 );      // Call: f( unsigned, int )
```

The first overload provides a better match on the second argument and an equally good match on the first.

```
f( 1.0F, 0 );    // Call: f( float, int )
```

The first overload provides better matches on both arguments.

```
f( 1.0, 0 );     // Call: f( double, int )
```

The first overload provides a better match on the second argument but the second overload provides a better match on the first argument. The call is ambiguous.

Overload matching has been one of the most troublesome parts of C++ and some current compilers are too quick to declare an ambiguity. Be warned.

The compiler must see all the relevant prototypes before an overloaded call in order to properly resolve that overload. *Header files must be designed carefully to ensure that all relevant overload prototypes are visible wherever they are needed.*

One common trap involves user-defined conversions:

```
class   Xebec
{
  public:
        operator const char*() const;
        ... ...
};

void frange( const char* );

/*
 *      Oops! We SHOULD have
 *
 *              void frange( const Xebec& );
 *
 *      but it's in a header we forgot to include . . .
 */
        ... ...

        Xebec xeb;

        frange( xeb );  //  We WANTED to call frange( const
                        //  Xebec& ). We GOT frange( const
                        //  char* ) using the conversion.
```

Code with a mistake like this might produce correct results but run slowly as the more expensive version of `frange()` performs needless lookups. Or it might not work at all.

Similar problems arise from unintended constructor conversions (Chap. 3, Sec. 3.4.5).

4.1.4 Overload matching and type conversions

The 'closeness' of a match involving conversions depends on the conversions needed. There are five levels of closeness in ANSI/ISO C++. The matching algorithms have changed with time; this one was introduced in Release 2.0 and modified for Release 2.1. Release 3.0 uses the same rules as Release 2.1.

Besides the five 'major' levels of closeness, there are distinctions within each level. These 'fine levels' depend upon `const` and `volatile`: a match which does not involve converting non-`const` to `const` or vice versa is better than one which does; likewise for volatile. In some cases, the conversion needed will make the call illegal; see Chap. 1, Sec. 1.2.4. *Even if the conversion makes the best match illegal, it remains the best match; the whole call becomes illegal.*

Nonstatic member functions have an additional 'fine level' degree of closeness. If two overloads of a member function have the same arguments, but one is declared `const` and the other is not, the `const` version will be called on behalf of const objects, and then non-`const` version on behalf of non-const objects:

```
class   Clepe
{
  public:
        ... ...
        const char* yclept( const char* );
        const char* yclept( const char* ) const;
        ... ...
};
        Clepe uther;
        const Clepe arthur;

        uther.yclept( "Pendragon" );     // Uses const char*
                                         // Clepe::yclept
                                         //  ( const char* )

        arthur.yclept( "Pendragon" );    // Uses const char*
                                         // Clepe::yclept
                                         //  ( const char* )
```

The `const`/non-`const` distinction is made when the types involved are pointers or references; the distinction is between what is pointed at or referred to, not to the parameter itself. These signatures in these two pairs of calls cannot be distinguished on const'ness:

```
void f( int );          // In both of these calls, the int
void f( const int );    // parameter is copied, so there is
                        // no difference to the callING
                        // function.
```

```
int g( char* );            // And in both of these calls, the
int g( char* const );      // pointer parameter is copied, so
                           // there is no difference to the
                           // callING function.
```

Recall the four grades of conversion: trivial, promotion, other built-in, and user-defined (Sec. 4.1.2). The five grades of match, in order from best to worst, are

- Match using no conversions or using trivial conversions
- Match using promotions or promotions and trivial conversions
- Match using other built-in conversions, including those introduced by Inheritance (Chap. 6, Secs. 6.2, 6.3), and possibly trivial conversions
- Match using user-defined conversions, and possibly built-in conversions, and possibly trivial conversions (a user-defined conversion alone is not better than a user-defined conversion with a built-in conversion; they have the same closeness)
- Match using the ellipsis

There are some constraints on the conversions that will be tried. Except for trivial conversions, there may be at most one user-defined conversion and one built-in conversion or promotion; no longer sequence will be tried. And if the best match is illegal, so is the function call.

Prior to Release 2.0, C++ did not distinguish between int and char in overloading. (This affected the I/O stream library; see Chap. 1, Sec. 1.1.4. Also, in C++, `sizeof( 'a' )` is 1 because a `char` constant is truly a `char`; in C it is `sizeof(` *int* `)` because a char constant is promoted to type `int`.)

The use of the ellipsis is discouraged; see Chap. 2, Sec. 2.4.3.

The overload matching sequence is modified when function templates that may match the overload are available (Chap. 8, Sec. 8.2.6).

4.1.5 Explicit conversions for ambiguity resolution

When the compiler cannot find an unambiguous match, or cannot find any match at all given its rules for conversion, a function call is still possible; just write the conversions explicitly:

```
void gonkulate( unsigned );
void gonkulate( double );

gonkulate( 'c' );         // No good--no conversion from char
                          // to ???
```

```
gonkulate( (unsigned) 'c' );      // Perfectly legal--but
                                  // dangerous.
```

The second call to `gonkulate()` is legal, but dangerous. Consider this code, which has just two changes from the previous code (not counting the removal of the ambiguous call):

```
void gonkulate( unsigned* );
void gonkulate( double );

gonkulate( (unsigned*) 'c' );    // Perfectly legal--and lethal.
```

In attempting to write a conversion that falls within the type system, we may accidentally write one that contravenes it. This case is contrived; in Chaps. 6 and 7 we will see cases much less contrived.

In Chap. 3, Sec. 3.4.2 we examined three semantics of conversion and stated that ANSI/ISO C++ will probably contain a different syntax for each. When that happens, write disambiguating conversions (and other conversions to help the type system) using the syntax that instructs the type system (`static_cast`) rather than the one that contravenes it (`reinterpret_cast`). Until then, be very careful of such conversions.

4.1.6 Differences in older versions of C++

The ability of C++ to distinguish between overloads on the basis of const or volatile was introduced in Release 2.0, whose definition is the first to fully support those distinctions.

In Release 2.0, the fifth grade of conversion match, a match with user-defined conversions, is divided into two grades: those that do not require the creation of a temporary and those that do. This is hard for the user to recognize and Release 2.1 through ANSI/ISO C++ deem illegal those matches which create a temporary for a non-const.

Before Release 2.0, the rules for matching were more vague, taking first an exact match, then any match with a built-in conversion, and finally a match involving user-defined conversions. Matches involving promotions were considered exact matches. Matches using both built-in and user-defined conversions were considered less close than matches with user-defined conversions alone.

4.2 Overloading Functions

Nonmember functions may be overloaded.

4.2.1 Nonmember function overloads

Prior to Release 2.0, all nonmember functions and operators which are to be overloaded must be declared with the `overload` keyword before use.

```
overload double sqrt( double );
overload Complex sqrt( Complex );
overload Fixed_10_4 sqrt( Fixed_10_4 );
```

This was required for two reasons. First, overloading was considered dangerous enough to require declaration. Experience has shown that within C++'s rules, overloading does not carry any exceptional danger. This came as a pleasant surprise.

Second, it was expected that the overload declarations would make it easier to link programs with overloading. This was found to be a grievous error; what is actually needed is a way to declare that a particular overload of a name is not presented as an overload to the linker. This is done with the "foriegn language linkage" declaration.

4.2.2 Foreign language linkage

Overloading requires that extra information be passed to the linker so that the linker can distinguish between the various overloads (Sec. 4.3). With current linkers, which have hardly advanced in the past quarter-century, this precludes any of the overloads being linked under its own name. For instance, if we overload `sqrt()` to accept and return `Complex` as well as `double`, the overload on `double` which should use the standard C `sqrt()` will not match the function in the C library.

Before Release 2.0, the solution to the problem was to exploit a weakness in C++'s scope rules (Sec. 4.3.3). Releases 2.0 and later provide a syntax to declare that certain symbols are to be submitted to the linker as though they were C symbols.

```
extern "C" double sqrt( double );

extern "C"
{
    double atof( const char* );
    int write( int, const char*, unsigned );
}
```

The second form can contain entire functions and even `#include` directives, making it useful in the initial stages of a conversion from C to C++. To properly support `#include` operations, the linkage directive may be nested.

The linkage directive does not create a new scope. Within it, all objects have external scope, all `extern` objects have program extent, and all `static` objects have file extent.

In theory, linkage to languages other than C could be supported. Because of the close relationship between C and C++, C linkage should be supported by all Release 2.0 and later implementations. ANSI/ISO C++ requires that every C++ implementation provide "C" and "C++" linkage.

Overloads whose first argument is an `enum` must be nonmembers, since an `enum` has no member functions.

4.2.3 Member function overloads

Member functions may be overloaded without special declaration. This is the rule that permits constructor overloading.

```
class   Act
{
  public:
        Act( double );

        void scene();
        int scene( char*, int = 0 );
        const Act& scene( const Act& );

        void exeunt( Act& );
          ... ...

  private:
        Act( unsigned long );
        void scene( double );
          ... ...
};
```

These overloads of `Act::scene()` are all legal.

```
void
Act::scene()
{
        ... ...
}

void
Act::scene( double d )
{
        ... ...
}
```

```
int
Act::scene( char* cp, int ip )    // Remember: we
{                                 // DON'T repeat the
        ... ...                   // default value!

}
const Act&
Act::scene( const Act& aa )
{
        ... ...
}
```

They also illustrate a hazard of overloading, and a surprise in the public/private mechanism. And they probably indicate a misuse of overloading.

What if we write

```
Act a;
a.scene( 2 );    //      Act::scene( int )  ???
```

There are two possible resolutions of this overload:

```
Act::scene( double( 2 ) );
```

and

```
Act::scene( Act( 2 ) );
```

The first involves only a built-in conversion, and so is preferred.

On the other hand, if we write

```
a.exeunt( 2 );  //     Act::exeunt( int )  ???
```

we have an unresolvable ambiguity:

```
a.exeunt( Act( double( 2 ) );
```

and

```
a.exeunt( Act( (unsigned long) 2 ) );
```

Both are two-step conversions involving one built-in conversion and one user-defined conversion. In both cases, the built-in conversions are true conversions and not just promotions. If the second involved a promotion to `long`, it would be preferred to the conversion to `const Act&`.

This expression, then, is illegal. (Remember that before Release 2.0, C++ may not make these nice distinctions.)

What if the call of `Act::exeunt()` is outside the class scope and the constructor `Act::Act( unsigned long )` is private?

Even though the constructor is private, it is visible to the function call and overloading resolution mechanism, and it will *cause an ambiguity.* It's neither usable nor accessible, but it is visible and it is checked for a match.

In other words, the public/private mechanism controls *access* and *use,* but *not visibility.* (Experience has shown that this is safer than the alternatives.)

There may be a worse problem with such code as

```
class   Act
{
  public:
        Act( double );

        void scene();
        int scene( char*, int = 0 );
        const Act& scene( const Act& );

        void exeunt( Act& );

  private:
        Act( unsigned long );
        void scene( double );
          ... ...
};
```

It seems very unlikely that these different overloads of `Act::scene()` do anything remotely alike. If they don't, overloading is probably misused. *Overloads of a given function should all "do about the same thing."*

All constructors for a given class initialize the class. All overloads of `::sqrt()` perform (or should perform) computations with similar *conceptual* mathematical effect.

If `Act::scene()` were a static member function, it might be different; after all, the different `sqrt()` functions take different arguments and return different types. But for a nonstatic member function, the different return types suggest strongly that the overloads do different things with different internal data.

"Functionoids" and overloading of the function call operator (Chap. 5, Sec. 5.1.1) provide plenty of temptation to violate this rule. There are a few good places to violate it, but not many.

Consider this variation on an example from Chap. 5 (Sec. 5.5.2):

```
class   Mem_pool
{
  public:
        Mem_pool( size_t ch_size )
          : chunk_size( ch_size )
        { … … };

        void* alloc( size_t n_bytes )
        { … … };
        void free( void* p, size_t n_bytes );
        { … … };
        … …

  private:
        /*
         *      Instead of 'r_alloc', we could overload 'alloc';
         *      likewise for 'r_free' and 'free'. If this code goes
         *      in a library, the different names are probably a
         *      better choice so that errors on the function signature
         *      do not confuse library users; if this code is going into
         *      a single program, the extra name might be more confusing.
         */
        void* r_alloc();
        void r_free( void* p );

        const size_t chunk_size;
        . . .
};
```

4.3 Implementation

When a C++ program is linked under the standard compile-then-link-edit model, the various overloads of a function must appear to the linker under separate names so that the linker can distinguish between them. These names are formed by encoding each function's signature and complete name in a character string and passing that string to the linker as the function's name.

4.3.1 Name encoding ('name mangling')

Transforming the function's name, signature, and related information into the encoded name string is called 'name encoding' or 'name mangling.' (Microsoft delicately calls it 'decorating the name,' and the name thus processed is called a 'decorated name.') The mangled name includes

- The function name written by the programmer
- The class (if any) within which the function is nested
- The class (if any) of which the function is a member
- The type of each argument expected by the function
- The return type of the function

Before Release 2.0, only member function names and function names explicitly declared overload were encoded; in Release 2.0 and later, all function names are encoded *unless* they are declared for C linkage (Sec. 4.2.2).

This means that tools which examine object or executable files and report function names (namelisters, debuggers, etc.) will report mangled names unless they are modified to understand the name encoding scheme on the machine at hand. Some implementations of C++ (e.g., AT&T's 'cfront') provide a 'filter' (`c++filt`) program to convert mangled names to demangled, fully qualified names with the complete type, membership, and signature information.

4.3.2 The name mangling algorithm

Name encoding is an implementation technique, not a language feature. There is no single approved version of name encoding; every C++ implementation is free to use any system, or none at all if the linker available is smart enough. Nevertheless, the 'ARM' (Ellis and Stroustrup, 1990) offers a version which gives an idea of the difficulties involved. That scheme is outlined here.

All mangled names contain a double underscore: '__' . A C++ symbol containing a double underscore may confuse the linker and tools that read mangled names. Double underscores should be avoided in symbol names in code meant to be portable (Chap. 1, Sec. 1.1.2).

The mangling algorithm adds an informative string to the end of the function name. The function name is separated from the informative string by a pair of underscores ('__'). Thus, a function named `funct()` is encoded

```
funct__<added information>
```

The informative string consists of class membership and signature. For our `int f()` we get

```
funct__Fv()
```

This reads as "`funct`, function, arguments: void." The `F` means 'function' and `v` is the signature, in this case `void`.

The basic types are encoded thus:

int	`i`
short	`s`
long	`l`
char	`c`
float	`f`
double	`d`
long double	`r`
ellipsis arg	`e`

A user-defined type is encoded by preceding its name by the length of the name. Thus `funct( Xyzzy )` is encoded

```
funct__F5Xyzzy()
```

Type modifiers are encoded by single letters:

signed	`S`
unsigned	`U`
const	`C`
volatile	`V`

They are prepended in alphabetical order to the type in question, so `funct( signed char, const Xyzzy )` is encoded as

```
funct__FScC5Xyzzy()
```

C++ builds types with pointer, reference, array, function, and pointer-to-member declarations. These are order-dependent (a pointer-to-const is not the same as a const pointer) and they are encoded in their order. Pointer and reference types are indicated by prepending `P` or `R`. `funct( int*, const Xyzzy& )` is encoded

```
funct__FPiRC5Xyzzy()
```

Arrays are indicated by `A` followed by the size of the array, so `funct( int (*)[ 3 ] )` (function of pointer-to-array-of-three-int) is encoded

```
funct__FPA3i()
```

Pointers-to-member are indicated by `M` followed by the encoded type name, so `funct( const char Xyzzy::* )` is encoded:

```
funct__FM5XyzzyCc()
```

With the right declarations, we *can* write this. In C++, operators as well as functions may be overloaded. Nearly every C++ operator can be overloaded on user-defined types. Operator overloads are written as functions with special names. C++ uses its expression and operator syntax as a synonym for calls of these specially named functions.

Most overloads can be written as either member or nonmember functions. If an operator overload is written as a nonmember, it must have at least one operand of a user-defined type. This rule prevents redefinition of (for instance) *int* + *int* or definition of *float** + *float*. These would create exactly the kind of chaos that led to operator overloading's longstanding ill repute.

Because overloaded operators are used in the same way as built-in operators, a bug in an overloaded operator can be hard to find. The overload is easily overlooked when the code is read. Likewise, overloaded operators may offer more hiding places for malicious code.

When operators such as | (bitwise OR) are overloaded on enums, the values that result may match no enumerator (identifier in the enumeration). This is permitted, but the programmer must stay within the bounds of the 'underlying' integral type, which may be signed or unsigned (Chap. 2, Sec. 2.3.5) and which is large enough to hold all the values represented by enumerators. The arithmetic must be done in an integral type (prior to ANSI/ISO C++:)

```
enum Muddel { … … };

Muddel
operator| ( Muddel lhs, Muddle rhs )
{
        return (Muddel) ( (unsigned long) lhs | (unsigned long) rhs );
}
```

4.4.2 Operators which may be overloaded

Most C++ operators can be overloaded. Those which cannot be overloaded are

`::` Name Qualifier (both binary and unary; this is an operation on name spaces, not on objects.)

`sizeof()`

`?:` Ternary Conditional operator

`throw` (Chapter 10)

`.`

`.*`

Prior to Release 2.0, add `->`, `->*`, and the comma operator to this list. (There are proposals to allow the overloading of operators `.` and `.*` . It appears unlikely that the ANSI/ISO committe will accept any of them.)

No additional operators may be defined. The precedence and associativity of operators may not be changed.

Certain operators have additional restrictions placed on how they may be overloaded. These restrictions help to ensure sane behavior. The rest of the operators obey a uniform set of rules and restrictions. Special rules apply to

`[]`	(subscripting)
`()`	(function call)
`new`	
`delete`	
`++`	(both pre- and postfix)
`--`	(both pre- and postfix)
`->`	
`->*`	
`&&`	
`||`	
all assignment operators (=, +=, -=, etc.)	
,	(comma operator)

Default arguments may not be used for operator overloads. (But default arguments may be used in an overload of the function call operator, because the overload's RHS operand is the *argument list.*)

A full list of C++'s operators, C++'s grammar for expressions, and a summary of the nonoverloaded and overloaded properties of each operator are found in App F.

4.4.3 Mechanics

An operator is overloaded by creating a function that implements the overload. The function's name is the keyword `operator` followed by the operator itself:

```
ostream& operator << ( ostream&, const Complex& );

// Binary + and -
Complex operator + ( const Complex&, const Complex& );
Complex operator - ( const Complex&, const Complex& );
// Unary -
Complex operator - ( const Complex& );
    ... ...
```

```
Complex
operator + ( const Complex&, const Complex& )
{
    ... ...
}
```

With the prototypes in scope, it becomes legal to write

```
Complex c1 = ... ...
Complex c2 = ... ...

Complex c3 = operator + ( c1, c2 );
```

Or, as we would prefer to write it:

```
Complex c4 = c1 + c2;           // operator + ( c1, c2 )
Complex c5 = c1 + c2 + c3 + c4; // operator + (
                                //    operator + (
                                //       operator + ( c1, c2 ),
                                //       c3 ),
                                //    c4 );
```

The precedences and associativities of C++'s operators may be found in App. F. An overloaded operator may be declared to return any type; remember that the return type plays no part in selecting the overload to use. (It may affect a different overloaded operator surrounding it in the expression.)

These are written as nonmember functions. Operators can also be written as nonstatic member functions:

```
Complex& Complex::operator += ( const Complex& );

c1.operator += ( c2 );
```

or, as we would prefer to write it:

```
c1 += c2;
```

In this example, a binary operator (assignment addition) is implemented by what appears to be a unary function. For member operators, the first operand becomes the object on behalf of which the operator function is called. Other arguments (if any) are passed as ordinary arguments to the member function.

Invoking an operation with the 'algebraic syntax' form specifies the operation whether it is a built-in, is provided by a member function, or is provided by a nonmember function. It is both the most maintainable and the most understandable form. The others are provided for completeness and for a few special cases surrounding special operators.

Some operators must be provided by member operator functions. See Chap. 5, Secs. 5.3, and 5.5.

What if both

```
Complex operator + ( const Complex&, const Complex& )
```

and

```
Complex Complex::operator+( const Complex& ) const
```

are defined? It is an error to represent a single overload by both a member and nonmember operator; C++ would not be able to choose between them. Notice that

```
Complex operator + ( const Complex&, const Complex& )
```

and

```
Complex Complex::operator+( const Complex& )
```

do not conflict because of their different signatures. One requires a first argument that is const, the other accepts a non-const first argument.

Inline operators are permitted:

```
class   Complex
{
  public:
        Complex( double r, double im )
          : re( r ), imag( im )
        { };
        ... ...
        double real() const { return re; };
        double imaginary() const { return imag; };
        ... ...
  private:
        double re;
        double imag;
};
            ... ...
inline Complex
operator + ( const Complex& lhs, const Complex& rhs )
{
        return Complex( lhs.real() + rhs.real(),
                lhs.imaginary() + rhs.imaginary() );
}
```

There's a lot going on in `operator+( const Complex&, const Complex& )`.

First, the arguments are passed by reference, so no new argument objects will be constructed. This matters in an operation that is likely to be written as often and freely as built-in arithmetic. If there are no side effects, the actual arguments may just be substituted in the inline expansion.

Second, the return statement uses a value builder explicitly, giving C++ a chance to optimize out all the temporaries. Returning a just-created object avoids memory-management bookkeeping. For small 'arithmetic' types, this is usually the most economical way.

Third, this operator requires only public member functions of the operands, so it can be written as a nonmember without friendship. The member functions it uses are access functions written to be inlined. For many types, the operator must be either a member or a friend; even in this case it might well be made a friend.

On most machines, this implementation of `Complex` can produce code just about as good as code for a built-in type. We are not always so fortunate, but we can often come close for simple types. For types which may be heavily used in a program's 'inner loop' computations, it's worth some work.

Notice the importance of reference arguments, quite apart from efficiency concerns. They allow the any operator's operands, lvalue or rvalue, to be written naming the operand objects themselves instead of pointer to them. The C++ requirement that all operator overloads involve a class object and the maintenance requirement that all operator-containing expressions be written the same way regardless of whether their operands are built-in types or class types are both satisfied by reference arguments.

4.4.4 Nonmember interfaces

Consider the nonmember addition on `Complex`:

```
Complex operator + ( const Complex&, const Complex& )
```

If we also have a constructor `Complex::Complex( double )`, we can write

```
Complex c1;
Complex c2 = … …;
… …
c2 = 5 + c1;     // operator+( 5, c1 )
```

which can match `operator + ( const Complex&, const Complex& )` by

1. trivial conversion of the RHS
2. built-in conversion of the LHS to double

3. user-defined conversion of the LHS from double to Complex via the constructor

No such match is possible if the operator is a member, since `5` is not a class object, and since we would not want to modify `int` to accommodate `Complex` even if it were. (In 'pure' OOPLs, there may be special mechanisms to deal with numeric 'objects.')

When the operation should support arithmetic 'mixed modes,' where the same conversion behavior is needed on both the LHS and RHS, or where any conversion is needed on the LHS, use a nonmember operator function. This function may be a friend of the class involved, or it may be an interface that calls member functions of the class to do the job. Using member functions to perform the actual operation (distinct from the conversions leading up to it) allows the 'polymorphic' capabilities described in Chaps. 6 and 7 to be used, but if conversions are needed, polymorphism often isn't.

Various tricks can be performed with nonmember functions and argument matching. Some are respectable:

```
class   String
{
  private:
        int compare( const String& s2 ) const
                { return ::strcmp( value, s2.value ) ; };

        int compare( const char* s ) const
                { return ::strcmp( value, s ) ; };
        ... ...

        char* value;     // The text of the string
        int length;      // The actual length of the string
        ... ...

  public:
        int operator > ( const String& s2 ) const
                { return compare( s2 ) > 0; };

        int operator >= ( const String& s2 ) const
                { return compare( s2 ) >= 0; };
        ... ...

        int operator > ( const char* s ) const
                { return compare( s ) > 0; };

        int operator >= ( const char* s ) const
                { return compare( s ) >= 0; };
        ... ...
```

```
        friend operator > ( const char* cp, const String& s )
                { return s < cp ; };

        friend operator >= ( const char* cp, const String& s )
                { return s <= cp ; };
        ... ...
};
```

This is a quick and safe way of getting the comparisons written correctly, and a compiler that can inline `strcmp()` (and there are some) can generate for these operations code whose space and speed efficiencies rival those of a built-in type. The code is more cluttered than we might like and keeping inlines around consumes compiler resources, so a balance must be struck between compilation cost and performance, between a fast implementation of a safe-to-use type (contributing to reuse through widespread use) and maintainability (contributing to reuse through mutation). As personal computers skyrocket through the 64-Mbyte main memory barrier, and microprocessor speed bounds into the 100's of MIPS, these economics change.

For unary operators other than ++ and --, the operation can usually be written as either a nonmember function or as a member const function. The nonmember usually is simpler for arithmetic types:

```
Complex
operator - ( const Complex& c )
{
        return Complex( -.real(), -c.imaginary() );
}

Complex
operator ~ ( const Complex& c )
{
        return Complex( c.real(), -c.imaginary() );
}
```

For “status” operators, members are generally better:

```
class   Go_No_go
{
  public:
        operator const void*() const
                        { return  status ?  this  : 0 ; };
        int operator ! () const { return ! status ; };
        ... ...
};
```

4.4.5 Maintenance value

Operator overloading allows the same expressions to be written whether the values belong to built-in or user-defined types. This benefits program maintenance and growth.

Let's say that we need, one day, to replace a `long int` datum in a program with an arbitrary length int, or with a fixed-point type.

The datum will probably be a member of some class; changing the class header will change the type of the member in every instance of the class. There may be a few instances of the the conceptual type in the member functions; they will be easy to find, especially if we deliberately omit some operators at first, causing compile-time errors on the unexpected "mixed-mode" operations.

If the Problem/Subject-domain type is used extensively throughout the program and in more than one class, it should have been typedef'd when the program was first written. If it was not, diagnostics from C++'s type system can help hunt down all uses of the datum. Then we can replace the original type with either the class name or with a typedef for the Problem/Subject-domain type in terms of the type that represents it. If distances everywhere in the program must be kept as a number of parsecs with *N* fractional bits of precision, there should be a class for the particular precision and a typedef for distance.

What we need not do—*anywhere*—is change the expressions which perform computations with the expressions. The expressions which worked for `long int` will continue to work for the new type, so long as we provide the full set of arithmetic overloads. If there is a problem with a computation somewhere producing a trash value, we can, as a last resort, insert into every instance of an arithmetic or assignment operator a probe that will print what is happening—all without changing one line of code outside our type.

All of this flexibility comes from class types; the program with class structure and discipline is incomparable to the program without them.

One problem with extended arithmetic types should be noted. Let's say we have defined an `Int_48` (a 48-bit integer type). We may have a set of (truncating) conversions:

```
class   Int_48
{
  public:
        ... ...
        operator int() const { ... ... };
        operator short() const { ... ... };
        operator long() const { ... ... };
        ... ...
};
```

If we want to test an `Int_48` against zero, we might be tempted to write

```
Int_48 i48 = ... ... ;
... ...

if( i48 )
    ... ...
```

The `if()` will invoke `Int_48::operator int() const` which may truncate. Then, on a 32-bit twos-complement machine, a value of `1 << 38` would test as zero—clearly not what was wanted.

There are several solutions. One solution is to modify the conversions such that an out-of-range value is converted to the maximum or minimum value in the "to" type. This adds code to every such conversion and, if they are expanded inline, to every expansion of them. It also slows the program a bit. A second solution is not to use the expression of the previous example, writing instead

```
if( i48 != 0 )
    ... ...
```

This will invoke a (presumably) overloaded `operator!=()` that can perform the test correctly. This requires the programmer using the class type to do something special because it is a class type.

The most sweeping solution is to modify C++ to use a different conversion for the `if()` -test (and the `int` or `void*` conversion if the new one isn't available); this has been seriously proposed, but the ANSI/ISO committee does not seem disposed to act on it.

4.4.6 Applying common sense and consistency

We expect the built-in operators to provide certain relationships. For instance:

```
A > B    ==  B <= A
A == B   !=  B != A
A + B    ==  B + A

*&A      ===  A
A[ B ]   ===  *( A + B )

A = A + B has the same effect as A += B
```

Overloaded operators do not provide these relationships automatically. Where they make sense for the type at hand, your types should support them. Appropriate design and coding practices will reduce the danger of inconsistencies.

Where only one of the operations really makes sense, support just the one. Perhaps the B in A[B] is a const char* which is used as a key in a database lookup of some sort. A[B] is usually much clearer than *(A + B) for const char* B.

When the type defies the "expected C conventions," it is the type which must have the final say. Matrix multiplication will not be commutative and should not be made commutative.

4.4.7 Overloading << for output

Sometimes the intended use of a type or responsibility for its authorship preclude the member operator.

```
cout << Complex( u, v ) ;
```

The operator can't be a member of Complex because Complex is not on the LHS of the operator. It can't be a member of ostream because the programmer of Complex doesn't 'own' ostream; besides, ostream is meant to be 'extended' in this way without modifying it with knowledge of everything that is to be output.

The solution is to use a nonmember function to call a member function.

```
inline ostream&
operator<<( ostream& o, const Complex& c )
{
        return c.put( o );
}
```

where

```
ostream& Complex::put( ostream& ) const;
```

(Remember the consts! Remember also that the operator must return the reference to the ostream.)

If the stream insertion operator is a friend of Complex, then Complex::put() may be private.

By making the operator inline, we save a little time and space. More than that, if the operator is never used, it never forces the stream I/O system to be loaded (Chap. 3, Sec. 3.6.8).

This operator's circumlocution provides the expected user (client programmer) syntax and semantics. And using the member of Complex means that we can use polymorphism (Chaps. 6 and 7) if we need it. For Complex we probably won't.

4.4.8 Overloads that *should* be written

In Chap. 2, Sec. 2.1.4 we saw that overloads make constructors useful and safe. C++'s conversion rules imply that some overloads should be written for safety when a function (member or nonmember) or operator is overloaded.

Consider:

```
class   Fixed_rational
{
        ... ...
        Fixed_rational( double );
        ... ...
};

class   Arb_Rational
{
        Arb_rational( const Fixed_rational );
};
        ... ...

Fixed_rational fr( 3.14159 );     // OK
Arb_rational ar( fr );            // OK
Arb_rational arfr( 3.14159 );     // OK, one user-def conversion

void im_general( const Arb_rational& );

im_general( 3.14159 );  // No good!  Two conversions are needed.
```

One of the conversion steps should be replaced by an overload. Here it would appear that `Arb_Rational` should have a constructor converting from `double`. If this is to be a fully general arithmetic package, there probably should be constructors from `float`, `int`, `short`, and `long` as well, for both classes.

4.4.9 Name mangling of overloaded operators

Overloaded operators and special functions (constructors, destructors, `new`, and `delete`) must be mapped into names that can be handled by external systems like linkers. This can be done by giving them special names beginning with '__'. The AT&T compilers use these:

```
->      __rf
->*     __rm
!       __nt
~       __co
++      __pp
```

Section 4.2.1 In older versions of C++, nonmember functions to be overloaded had to be declared with the `overload` keyword. In newer versions this requirement and this keyword have been removed.

Section 4.2.2 Nonmember functions written in C may be overloaded; just one overload for each such function may be in C, and it must be specially declared with the `extern "C" . . .` syntax (foreign language linkage).

Section 4.2.3 Member functions may be overloaded without special declaration. Access control (by public and private) is considered *after* the best overload is selected.

Section 4.3.1 To allow overloaded functions to be separately compiled, then linked by conventional linkers, C++ encodes (or "mangles," or "decorates") the name of all functions except those declared to be compatible with C (with the `extern "C" . . .` syntax).

Section 4.3.3 In releases that are too old to support the `extern "C" . . .` syntax, only overloaded function names will be mangled, and only the second and subsequent names. The first name will not be encoded, and will be compatible with C.

Section 4.3.4 Name encoding increases the type safety of linkage and can allow a compiler to use calling sequences that are more efficient but that rely on closer mutual understanding between the calling and called functions. Some linkers, however, apply Pascal rules (case insensitivity) and require the compiler to use a special mangling scheme or risk erroneous code.

Section 4.4 C++ allows its operator symbols to be overloaded.

Section 4.4.1 Operator overloading has both notational and maintenance benefits; it allows a new user-defined type to be used just like a built-in type. C++ has sufficient safeguards to keep operator overloading reasonably safe.

Section 4.4.2 Most of C++'s operators can be overloaded; a list is provided.

Section 4.4.3, 4.4.4 An operator is overloaded by a function whose name indicates the operator and whose arguments are arranged according to certain rules. Most operators may be overloaded using either member or nonmember functions; there are properties peculiar to each.

Section 4.4.5 A built-in type identified by a typedef can be replaced throughout the program by a class type of the same name if all operators used by the old type are properly overloaded in the new type. This allows the source code *using* a type to be preserved in spite of changes to the type itself. (There are a very few things that may not work right for arithmetic types.)

Section 4.4.6 The programmer who provides overloaded operators is responsible for ensuring that they have the 'expected' consistent operation (commutivity when appropriate, == means the opposite of !=, etc.)

Section 4.4.7 Circumstances may force the use of the member or nonmember overload, or require a nonmember overload to invoke a member function (e.g., to get the semantics of *virtual functions*—see Chap. 6, Sec. 6.4).

Section 4.4.8 Certain overloads may improve the safety or maintainability of a program. Generally, these control conversions or reduce the need for conversions. (See also Chap. 2, Sec. 2.1.4 on constructors.)

Section 4.4.9 Current C++ compilers encode the operator functions as functions whose names involve special sequences of underscores and mnemonics. A list is provided.

Section 4.5 Special rules govern the overloading of assignment. If overloaded assignment does not obey its intended semantics, it can jeopardize the encapsulation of any type, not just the type to which it is applied. The rules for assignment prevent errors from destroying the safety of uninvolved types.

Sections 4.5.1, 4.5.2, 4.5.3 C++ can create default assignment operators, which will be correct for many types. The rules are 'memberwise,' recursive, and similar to those for copy constructors (Chap. 2, Sec. 2.1.7). C++'s default assignment operators will not be correct when the existence of an object implies relationships among the object and its members, nor can C++ create an assignment operator when one or more members cannot be assigned. Special rules apply to unions.

Section 4.5.4 The String class example in this section illustrates a wide range of overloads.

Section 4.6 A type should be given those overloaded operators that contribute to its intended semantics and its intended uses. Some characteristics of type semantics and uses can be delineated.

```
void
Array_Int_Int::fail() const
{
        ::abort();
}
```

This provides a checked array of `int` indexed by `int`. In a real-world program, this class would be provided by a template (Chap. 8) which would allow the same program logic to be used for arrays of many different types, and `fail()` would 'throw an exception' (Chap. 9) to allow client code to regain control after the failure.

ANSI/ISO C++ will probably include a dynamic array template called `dyn_array()`, which may use `operator[]()`.

5.1.4 Using classes to compose operations (surrogate objects)

The subscripting operator may be overloaded with any type for its second argument. This includes `const char*`, `double`, or `Database_query`. Programming some of these requires cleverness.

Consider a 'string map,' an array which holds strings and is indexed by strings. Most of the values which a subscript can take on map to null or empty strings and are not represented in the map's internal data structures (i.e., its *object representation*). We say that the array or map is 'sparse.' (Sparse arrays are heavily used in certain types of numerical problems.) Nevertheless, when such a subscript is provided, a value must be returned from the call or (on assignment) entered in the map's data structures.

When an access to null or empty array element requires an rvalue, it is enough to return (a reference to) an empty or null string. Likewise when a `const` lvalue is returned.

When the access requires a nonconstant lvalue this won't work. An assignment or non-`const` lvalue reference of any kind creates an entry in the data structures.

```
#include <iostream.h>

        Array_String_String str_map;
            ... ...
        String hello = "Hello" ;
        str_map[ hello ] = "world" ;
            ... ...
        cout << hello << "" << str_map[ hello ] << ".\n" ;
```

It can be made to work, and everyone should understand how. Whether the results are worth the complexity depends on the application.

The technique is to have `Array_String_String[ String ]` return not a reference to a `String`, but an object with 'magic' properties. This 'surrogate' object can be freely converted to a const (rvalue) `String`, and supports assignment by informing the `Array_String_String` to create the internal data structures to represent a nonnull array element.

```
class   Array_String_String
{
  private:
        class   Surr
        {
                friend class Array_String_String;
          public:
                operator const String&() const
                {  return *st; };

                operator const char*() const
                {  return (const char*) *st; };

                const String& operator = ( const String& s )
                {  return st = as.assign( st, s ); };

                const String& operator = ( const char* cp )
                {  return st = as.assign( st, cp ); };

          private:
                Surr( Array_String_String& a_as,
                                const String a_index,
                                const String* a_st )
                  : as( a_as ), index( a_index ), st( a_st )
                { };
                ~Surr();

                Array_String_String as&;
                const String index;
                const String* st;
        };
        friend class Surr;

        /*
         *      Perform an assignment to an array 'element'.
         *      For the use of Surr::operator=() .
         */
        const String* assign( const String* to,
                                        const String& from );
        const String* assign( const String* to,
                                        const char* from );
```

```
  public:
        Array_String_String();
        ~Array_String_String();

        Surr operator[] ( const String& index );
        const Surr operator[] ( const String& index ) const;

  private:
        ...implementation of the Array_String_String...
};
   ... ...
Array_String_String::Surr
Array_String_String::Array_String_String::operator[]
                                        ( const String& index )
{
        ... ...
        return Surr( *this, index, ...string we looked up... );
}
```

A couple of notes on mechanics: First, within member function for the `operator[]`, `Surr` is in scope, so we don't need to qualify it. Second, in a 'real program,' a function like this would be constructed using templates (Chap. 8), bringing the length of the class names under control.

As of December, 1992, code with surrogate objects may not be legal C++. The ANSI/ISO C++ committee is studying the lifetime of temporary objects (including such surrogate objects). The issues are not simple, but surrogate objects will probably be permitted under the final rules. (See Chap. 3, Sec. 3.3.6.) 'Real compilers' through C++ Release 3.0 seem to handle surrogate objects properly.

Tracing the calls through the assignment and lookup:

```
str_map[ hello ] = "world" ;
```

becomes

```
str_map[ hello ].operator=( "world" );
```

which in turn becomes

```
( str_map.operator[]( hello ) ).
        Array_String_String::Surr::operator=( "world" );
```

where the parenthesized expression on the LHS evaluates to the `Array_String_String::Surr` returned by `Array_String_String::operator[]()`. It contains a reference back to the `Array_String_String` that created it and a pointer to the `String` that is 'returned.' In this call, that will be a single empty String instance maintained by Array_String_String.

The technique has limitations. First, an 'array' expression cannot be used everywhere a String can be used because one of the available conversions has been used to get the String from the surrogate object. In some cases, an explicit conversion will be needed. Second, since (in general) no ordinary conversions will be performed on the object on behalf of which a member function is called, we could not write something like

```
#include <iostream.h>

        Array_String_String str_map;
            ... ...
        String hello = "Hello" ;
        str_map[ hello ] = "world" ;
            ... ...
        cout << hello << "" << str_map[ hello ].substring( 2 )
                                                          << ".\n" ;
```

Instead, the last statement must be written

```
cout << hello << " "
        << String( str_map[ hello ] ).substring( 2 )
                                                  << ".\n" ;
```

Of course, if String::Surr has a substring() function of its own, this is legal. Whether it means the same things depends on how it is written. (A class's users would probably expect the two functions to have the same effect.)

Because inheritance (Chap. 6) introduces 'conversions' on the object on whose behalf the member function is called, and because multiple inheritance (Chap. 7) allows types with different properties to share their lines of inheritance, clever solutions are possible. They do require the String class to be designed for them.

Another possibility involves the overloading of operators ->() and ->*(), (Sec. 5.3.1).

There's further difficulty to be managed. As we have written it, a const Array_String_String is useless because it cannot produce an Array_String_String::Surr. It's not enough to declare an overload of operator[]() for const objects and have it return a const Surr because even the const Surr will have a reference to non-const Array_String_String. We need a second version of the Surr to provide for the Array_String_String. This Surr_const will need the conversion to `const String`, but not the assignment operator. (A single type can be tricked into serving as surrogate of both `const` and non-`const`, but the problems must be addressed either way.)

5.2 Operators for Wheels

We can overload `operator()()` in the Wheels problem. Both the 'add a wheel' and 'return string/advance' operations are candidates for `operator()()` overloads. We'll show both, although using the same operator (or function) overload for both is poor practice. (Do both perform 'the same' operation with different types? In this example, no.)

Recall from Chap. 3, Sec. 3.7 that we want to make the individual `Wheel` a private class. Recall also that we made the 'step' operation a recursive inline which 'recursed' down a list of `Wheel`s. Here we make it a static member function that loops to walk from one to another. Some compilers will reject an inline with a loop, so here we'll make it out-of-line. On the assumption that this code *might* dominate the execution time of program, we'll use an inline to check the first `Wheel`, calling the out-of-line function as needed.

The previous `Wheel` examples used a return of 'true' to indicate the end of the sequence. This is un-C-like; we should use 'false' to indicate the end of the sequence, allowing a loop to run `while(` *advance* `)`.

```
class   Wheel
{
        friend class Wheel_set;
  private:

        Wheel( const char**, Wheel* next_w = 0 );

        // Note the recursive call to the destructor ...

        ~Wheel() { delete sides; delete next_wheel };

        /*
         *      We advance the wheels by advancing this wheel;
         *      if it has rolled over, we look for another; if
         *      there is none, or if IT, when advanced, says
         *      that we have wrapped around, then we have
         *      wrapped around.
         */
        int advance()
        {       return advance_me()
                    || advance_following( next_wheel );
};
```

```
        static int advance_following( Wheel* );

        int copy_rev( char* );

        int advance_me()
        {       if( *++next ) { return 1; }
                else { next = sides; return 0; }
        };

        int copyout( char* );
        const char** sides;
        const char** next;
        Wheel* next_wheel;
};

class   Wheel_set
{
  public:
        Wheel_set() : wheels( 0 ) {};
        ~Wheel_set() { delete wheels; };

        /*
         *      Add a wheel, linking it into the list.
         */
        void operator() ( const char** sides )
        {  wheels = new Wheel( sides, wheel );  };

        /*
         *      Advance the wheels and return true if the
         *      operation succeeded.  The first part of
         *      the test ensures that wheels have been added.
         */
        int operator()() { return wheels
                                && wheels->advance() ; };
        int copy( char* );

  private:
        Wheel* wheels;          // Store a pointer into a
                                // linked list.
};
int
Wheel::advance_following( Wheel* w )
{
        for( ; w ; w = w->next_wheel )
        {
                if( *++next )
                        return 1;
```

```
                next = side;
        }

        return 0;
}

int
Wheel::copy_rev( char* to )
{
        int st = next_wheel ? next_wheel->copy_rev( to ) : 0;

        st += copyout( &to[ st ] );

        to[ st ] = '\0';

        return st;
}

int
Wheel::copyout( char* to )
{
        for( const char* s = *side ; *s ; s++, to++ )
                *to = *s;

        return s - side;
}

/*
 *      The Wheel constructor sets up the "next Wheel"
 *      pointer to help create the linked list.  This makes
 *      the Wheel and the Wheel_set very close partners indeed.
 */
Wheel::Wheel( const char** strings, Wheel* next_w )
  : next_wheel( next_w )
{
        if( sides )
                delete sides;

        const char** s = strings;
        while( *s++ )  // Loop past the null ...
                { }

        sides = new char* [ s - strings ];

        for( s = strings, next = sides ; next++ = s++ ; )
                { }

        next = sides;
}
```

5.3 Special Operators II: Miscellaneous Special Operators

Various other operators have special properties when overloaded.

5.3.1 Operators `->()` and `->*()`

In C++ Release 2.0 and later, the member selection operators `operator->()` and `operator->*()` may be overloaded as member functions. These operators select members by name or pointer from a class's name space. Overloading them allows an object of one class to pretend that is a pointer to another class. (It also helps C++ simulate *delegation;* see Chap. 7, Sec. 7.9). With the proper overloads on these operators in `Gate`, the following are legal. (The pointer-to-member operator `->*` is described in Chap. 2, Sec. 2.7.1.)

```
Gate gate;
Gate* gp = &gate;

/*
 *  With pointers to objects
 */
gp->member_of_gate();      // Ordinary

gate->member_of_gee();     // Gate pretends to be a Gee*, and
                           // somehow a call is made ...

/*
 *  And using pointers to members
 */
void (Gate::*gate_mp)() =          // Assuming that
         Gate::member_of_gate;     // member_of_gate() returns
                                   // void ...
void (Gee::*gee_mp)() =            // Assuming also that
         Gate::member_of_gee;      // member_of_gee() returns
                                   // void ...

(gp->*ga_mp)();          // Ordinary

(gate->*ge_mp)();        // gate pretends to be a Gee*, and
                         // somehow a call is made ...
```

The calls of `Gee::member_of_gee()` written on behalf of a `Gate` must result in calls to `member_of_gee()` on behalf of some object of type `Gee`. What object, and how?

The overloaded member selection operators return a pointer or reference to an object of a *different* class type (here, `Gee`). Then the members (data and function) of that class may be used as though they were addressed by a pointer to that class. The appropriate member operator will be called to provide the pointer or member needed. (As usual, 'class' includes structs and unions.)

```
class   Gee
{
    ... ...
};
        ... ...
class   Gate
{
  public:
        Gee* operator->() { return &gates_s_gee; };

        Gee* operator->*() { return &gates_s_gee; };
        ... ...
  private:
        ... ...
        Gee gate_s_gee;
        ... ...
};
    ... ...

        gate.member_of_gate();  // Ordinary

        gp->member_of_gate();   // Ordinary
        gate->member_of_gee();  // gate.operator->()->member_of_gee()

        (gp->*ga_mp)();          // Ordinary
        (gate->*ge_mp)();        // ( (gate.operator->*() )->*ge_mp)()
```

The ANSI/ISO C++ standards committee has had several incompatible proposals to allow overloading `operator.()` and `operator.*()` as member functions. It now seems highly unlikely that any will be adopted by the committee.

`Gate` ought to have const versions of the operators so that a call on behalf of a `const Gate` (whose member `gate_s_gee` is also `const`) can be used to access `const` members of `Gee`.

```
class   Gate
{
  public:
        Gee* operator->() { return &gates_s_gee; };
        const Gee* operator->() const { return &gates_s_gee; };

        Gee* operator->*() { return &gates_s_gee; };
        const Gee* operator->*() const { return &gates_s_gee; };

        ...
  private:
        ...
};
```

We've written these operator functions inline; this usually makes sense, but they are legal C++ whether written inline or out-of-line.

These overloads must always return a valid, nonnull pointer. Ensuring this may require keeping a spare object around (as a static member, perhaps?) so that there will always be an object to use for the return pointer or reference. If this is impossible, or if the lack of an object to use indicates a serious error, it may be best to throw an exception (Chap. 9) instead, aborting some part of the operation.

These operators may be overloaded once in any class (or struct or union) type.

Another way to look at overloading the member selection operators is that they add the members of the 'converted-to' class to the set of names which may appear on the RHS of the selection operators. This 'combining of name spaces' is a useful illusion, not the reality. Using the previous example,

```
void
Gate::member_of_Gate()
{
        member_of_gee();            // Illegal, Gee's members
                                    // are NOT members of Gate

        (*this)->member_of_gee();   // Ok, Gee's members can be
                                    // SELECTED from a Gee using
                                    // the operator overloads.
}
```

Besides simulating delegation, overloads of the member selection operators can simulate 'access-oriented' programming. In access-oriented programming, accessing an object causes an action to occur or a value to be propagated. (Spreadsheet programs are strongly access-oriented: updating one cell results in updates to other cells.) If access orientation and object orientation are mixed carelessly, the program's operation may become hopelessly subtle and badly tangled. Used carefully, access orientation has good uses usually in a particular problem-based or algorithm-based level of abstraction.

5.3.2 `operator++()` and `operator--()`

Operators ++ and -- may be overloaded as member or nonmember operators. (C++ Release 2.0 permitted only nonmember overloads as well.) Each actually represents two operators (prefix and postfix) and the distinction between the two differs depending upon the release.

In C++ Release 3.0 and later, the prefix and postfix versions of `operator++()` and `operator--()` are handled differently. The prefix versions are unary operator overloads. The postfix operators are binary operator overloads whose RHS is of type `int` and is not written when using operator notation.

```
class   Fixed_in_ANSI
{
  public:
        const Fix& operator++();        // Prefix
        Fix operator++( int );          // Postfix
        const Fix& operator--();        // Prefix
        Fix operator--( int );          // Postfix
        ... ...
};

        Fixed_in_ANSI poppycox;

        flamer( const Fixed_in_ANSI& );
            ... ...

        flamer( ++poppycox );   //      { poppycox.operator++();
                                //        flamer( poppycox ); }

        flamer( poppycox++ );   //      { flamer( poppycox );
                                //        poppycox.operator++( 0 ); }

        flamer( --poppycox );   //      { poppycox.operator--();
                                //        flamer( poppycox ); }

        flamer( poppycox-- );   //      { flamer( poppycox );
                                //        poppycox.operator--( 0 ); }
```

As usual, it's legal to call the operator overloads using function call sequence:

```
poppycox.operator--();          // Prefix
poppycox.operator++();          // Prefix

const int ala_carte = 45;
poppycox.operator++( ala_carte );          // Postfix
```

Most postfix overloads will ignore the integer parameter but they don't have to; they can use it for whatever purpose they like.

In C++ through Release 2.1, only one overload was permitted for each operator (++, --) for each class. This overload was used for both the pre- and postfix operators, applied pre- or post- as written:

```
class   Fix
{
  public:
        const Fix operator++();
        unsigned short operator--();
```

```
    ... ...
};
   ... ...

        void gargantugripe( const Fix& );
        void gargantugripe( unsigned short, const char* =
                                                "FLAME ON!" );

        ... ...
        Fix black_sox = ...
        gargantugripe( ++black_sox );    // Calls the increment
                                         // operator, then calls the
                                         // first overload.
        gargantugripe( black_sox++ );    // Calls the first overload,
                                         // then calls the
                                         // increment operator.
        gargantugripe( --black_sox );    // Calls the decrement
                                         // operator, then calls the
                                         // second overload.
```

5.3.3 `operator , ()` (Comma operator)

In C++ Release 2.0 and later releases, the comma operator may be overloaded. The default comma operator accepts operands of any type on the LHS and RHS. It evaluates the operand on the LHS, including all side effects, discards the LHS value, evaluates the operand on the RHS, and returns the value of the RHS with the type of the RHS.

The comma operator may be overloaded as a nonstatic member or as a nonmember so long as one of its operands is a class (or struct or union) or enum type (or a trivial conversion from one). The overloaded comma operator does not ensure that the LHS is evaluated first, nor does it guarantee that all side effects of the LHS are completed before the RHS is evaluated.

The comma operator is left-associative. The C++ expression grammar looks something like this:

```
expression:
        assignment-expression
        expression "," assignment-expression
```

This overload is supported because there is no good reason to prohibit it. It can be used to create exotic expressions:

```
( assign , x , ( plus , a , b ) );
```

If `assign` and `plus` have appropriate types, this code can be both legal and useful. (The technique can be used to build queries for database systems, for instance.)

It's probably futile to argue that writing LISP code is an inappropriate use of C++. Some programmers would never dream of doing such a thing; others perhaps have long dreamt of it.

5.3.4 `operator &&`, `operator ||`, `operator &` (unary), and `operator *` (unary)

`operator && ()` and `operator || ()` may be overloaded as nonstatic members or as nonmembers, so long as one of the arguments is a class (or struct, or union) or enum type, or a trivial conversion of such a type.

The built-in definitions of these operators have strict short-circuit operation: they evaluate left-to-right and only as far as necessary. User-defined overloads of these operators do not have this property.

The unary `&` (address-of) and `*` operators may be overloaded as members or as nonmembers whose argument is a class (or struct or union) type (or a trivial conversion from such a type).

Overloading unary `operator&()` hides the built-in 'address-of' operator. Member functions can still see the address of the object on behalf of which they are called; it is simply `this`. Overloading unary `operator*()` doesn't hide anything, since there is no default 'points-to' operator.

Overloading the 'address-of' and 'points-to' operators is probably necessary for any 'smart pointer' type.

5.3.5 More on member conversion operators: ambiguities

A user-defined conversion may be specified by either a constructor or a member operator conversion (Chap. 3, Secs. 3.3, 3.5). If both are specified for a given conversion, the conversion is ambiguous and cannot be invoked implicitly.

Thus, if we have

```
class A;
class B;

class   A
{
  public:
        A();
        A( const B& );
        ... ...
};
class   B
{
  public:
        B();
```

```
        ...
        operator A() const;
        ... ...
    };
    ... ...

        A an_a;
        B a_b;
```

this statement's RHS expression is ambiguous:

```
an_a = a_b;      // Ambiguous
```

We can explicitly request the operator conversion:

```
an_a = a_b.operator A();        // OK.
```

An explicit cast will also be given the operator conversion:

```
an_a = (A) a_b;          // OK.  Will use  B::operator A()
```

A functional-form cast (value builder expression) remains ambiguous:

```
an_a = A( a_b );         // Ambiguous.
```

The only way to invoke the constructor is to write an explicit initialization:

```
A nuther_a( a_b );      // Ok, uses  A::A( const B& )
```

Explicitly naming the constructor is illegal.

```
an_a = A::A( a_b );     // Error: for class A, A::A() may not be
                        //        invoked by that syntax.
```

It is best to avoid this ambiguity, even at the cost of writing an extra parameter for the constructor, or making the constructor accept a pointer-to-const instead of the reference-to-const.

5.4 Wheels: Dressing Them to the 0x09's

This is our last set of variations on the Wheels example, begun in Chap. 1, Sec. 1.3 and last seen in Sec. 5.2. Using the tools we now have, we can give the Wheels system many different external semantics. For instance, we might overload the comma operator to add a `Wheel`:

We've made an objects-and-mechanisms mountain out of an algorithmic molehill (albeit a troublesome molehill). For some purposes, all the changes would be worthwhile; for others, just the first few. But for almost every problem, those first few steps would be profitable. The algorithm is at first clearer after being fit into an explicit mechanism than before; in making the interface prettier we muddled it again, bit by bit, as we added code that shifted our attention and effort from the algorithm to the interface. Whether this was a good bargain depends on issues discussed in Sec. 5.6.6.

5.5 Special Operators III: Overloading `new` and `delete`

C++ provides free store management with the `new` and `delete` operators (Chap. 3, Sec. 3.1). C++ allows these operators to be redefined and overloaded. These overloads can replace the default versions of `new` and `delete` for objects and for arrays, and can provide additional overloads for `new`. The operators can also be redefined for use with objects of a particular class type. Redefinition of `new` and `delete` was introduced in C++ Release 1.2; per-class redefinition was introduced in C++ Release 2.0.

Replacement versions of `new` and `delete` will be used just as the built-in versions are, both for calls from user code *and for calls from the built-in library,* so redefining these operators must be done with care.

5.5.1 Global `new` and `delete`

The global `new` and `delete` operators are provided by operator functions:

```
void* ::operator new( size_t nbytes ) ;            // new
void ::operator delete( void*, size_t nbytes ) ; // delete
void ::operator delete( void* ) ;         // alternate form of
                                          // delete

void* ::operator new[]( size_t nbytes ) ;          // new for
                                                    // arrays
void ::operator delete[]( void*, size_t nbytes ) ;  // delete for
                                                      // arrays
void ::operator delete[]( void* ) ;       // alternate form of
                                           // delete for arrays
```

(`size_t` is a typedef found in `<stddef>`.* Prior to C++ Release 2.0, the proper type for these parameters is `long`.)

* Prior to ANSI/ISO C++, this is `<stddef.h>`.

(The :: indicating that the operator function is global is superfluous if these declarations are written at the top level of the program, and some versions of C++ may parse it incorrectly.)

Notice that `operator delete()` and `operator delete[]()` may take two forms, either with or without the second (length) argument. C++ will accept each operator either with or without the length argument; it will not accept both forms of one operator.

These 'global' new and delete operators will be used for:

- all invocations of new and delete for all individual objects of nonclass types
- all invocations of new and delete for individual objects of classes which do not have a class-by-class version available (Sec. 5.5.4, Chap. 6, Sec. 6.4.7 for interactions with inheritance)
- all invocations of `new` and `delete` for all arrays *prior to the introduction of ANSI/ISO C++*
- all invocations of `new[]` and `delete[]` for arrays of nonclass types (in ANSI/ISO C++)
- all invocations of `new[]` and `delete[]` for arrays of classes which do not have a class-by-class version available (in ANSI/ISO C++) (see Sec. 5.5.5 and Chap. 6, Sec. 6.4.7)

("Class type" includes structs and unions in this list.)

5.5.2 Array `new[]` and `delete[]`

(This section is based on a proposal which the ANSI/ISO C++ committee seems certain to approve.)

ANSI/ISO C++ has two more operators, `operator new[]` and `operator delete[]`.

```
void* ::operator new[]( size_t ) ;
void ::operator delete[]( void*, size_t ) ;
void ::operator delete[]( void* ) ;      // alternate form of
                                          // delete
```

(The square brackets and the keywords 'new' and 'delete' are each separate tokens; white space between them will not affect the program.)

5.5.3 `operator new()` and the `new` operator

Recall that C++ converts the `void*` returned by the `operator new()` to the actual type needed for the call of the `new` operator. There is a nice distinction to be made here. The code which invokes the allocation operator invokes 'the `new` operator'; in response, C++ invokes `operator new()`, converts the return type, and calls a constructor if necessary. Likewise, code which calls the deallocation operator invokes 'the `delete` operator'; in response, C++ invokes the destructor (if appropriate), converts the type of the pointer, and invokes `operator delete()`.

In some uses, especially around Object-Oriented Programming, this distinction is critical (Chap. 6, Sec. 6.4.6).

Notice the type proprieties of this structure: the free store operators deal only with memory described by `void*`. It is the call of constructor and destructor that converts 'heap space' into an object, and vice versa.

C++ is free to implement the behavior by embedding the call to the operator function inside the code for the constructor or destructor and calling or not calling the free store operator according to the value of 'hidden' arguments. Postmortem stack traces can show the free store operator called from within the constructor or destructor; this does not necessarily indicate a bug in the compiler.

At this writing, there is a proposal before the ANSI/ISO committee that would allow a C++ to preallocate fixed memory for a `new` invocation if there is a corresponding `delete` that must take place. The rationale is that workspace needed by such things as matrix operators would otherwise be allocated and deallocated repeatedly in loops, slowing numerical code and interfering with vectorization. There seems to be no reason why this proposal should not pass; it is an extension of the 'as if' principle ("it must work *as if* it were computed this way") but there is no guarantee.

5.5.4 Free store exhaustion

A user-defined `operator new()` should participate in whatever mechanism is used to deal with free store exhaustion. The proper handling of memory exhaustion is as follows:

- Try to find more memory, if possible. If more memory is available, seize it and return an appropriate chunk.
- If the `new_handler` pointer-to-function is not null, call the function. It may return, it may terminate the program, or it may throw an `xalloc` exception which `operator new()` and `operator new[] ()` almost certainly *should not catch.*
- If the `new_handler` returns, check if memory has become available. If so, return it; otherwise, examine `new_handler` again.

To summarize the operation of `new_handler` (from 3.1.3)*:

- There is an external variable declared

```
void (*new_handler) ();
```

- Although `new_handler` is publicly writable, there is a function to set it, returning the old value as it does so:

```
typedef void (*PF_v)(); // Assume this typedef . . .
extern PF_v set_new_handler( PF_v );
```

- The default value of `new_handler` is 0 (pointer null) before ANSI/ISO C++, and a function that will throw an `xalloc` exception in ANSI/ISO C++. If the value is nonnull when memory exhaustion occurs, free store management should call the function at which it points.

What if `operatornew()` returns null, and there is a constructor? Will there be a call to `( (X*) 0)->X::X( . . . )`? The answer is "No."

Allocation through the new operator has two parts. First, `operator new()` is called to get the memory. Then, *if the memory was actually found* (that is, if `operator new()` returns a nonnull pointer), the appropriate constructor (if any) is called to actually build the object. *If the return value from the* `new` *operator is null, no constructor was called.*

5.5.5 Class-by-class `new` and `delete`

(Class-by-class `new` and `delete` were introduced in C++ Release 2.0.)

`operator new()`, `operator new[]()`, `operator delete()`, and `operator delete[]()` may be defined as members of a class, struct, or union. These operators are static members of the class: they can access the class's scope, but have no class scope themselves.

5.5.6 Writing class-by-class new and delete

For a class `X`, `X::operator new()` will be used for any `new` operator invocation on a single object of that class type. Likewise, `x::operator delete()` will be used for any `delete` operator invocation for a single object of that class. If the class has no such operator defined, and if it does not inherit an operator from a base class (Chap. 6, Sec. 6.4.7), the corresponding global operator will be used.

An array of a class type will be handled by either by the class's `operator new[] ()` if the class has one, otherwise by the global `operator new[] ()`, and by the class's `operator delete[]()` if the class has one,

* Please see Chap. 3, Sec. 3.1.3 for issues not discussed here.

otherwise by the global `operator delete[]()`. (Prior to ANSI/ISO C++, there are no 'array-new' and 'array-delete' operators, and array allocation is handled by the global `new` and `delete` operators.)

The `new` and `delete` operators may not assume that the size of the memory chunk to be allocated or freed is the size of an object of their class. It might not be, because under inheritance a `new` or `delete` operator may be used for classes other than the exact class of which it is a member (Chap. 6, Sec. 6.4.7).

5.5.7 Designing class-by-class `new` and `delete`

Here's a plausible implementation of `new` for a class. It uses a pool-based allocator, and is patterned after one the author used for the namespace management classes of an interpreter for a research programming language:

```
class  Expr_node
{
  public:
        /*
         *      Although these operators are static members, we
         *      do not write 'static'.  C++ makes new and delete
         *      static automatically.
         */
        void* operator new( size_t n_bytes )
        {  return pool.alloc( n_bytes ) ;  } ;

        void* operator new[] ( size_t n_bytes )
        {  return pool.alloc( n_bytes ) ;  } ;

        void operator delete( void* p, size_t n_bytes )
        {  pool.free( p, n_bytes ) ;  } ;

        void operator delete[] ( void* p, size_t n_bytes )
        {  pool.free( p, n_bytes ) ;  } ;

  private:
        static Mem_pool pool;

        ... ...
};
    ... ...
        /*
         *      This declaration/definition is put in a source file
         *      somewhere, not in the header file ...
         */
        Mem_pool Expr_node::pool( sizeof ( Expr_node ) ) ;
```

Here we assume that `Mem_pool` actually implements the allocation and deallocation behind `Expr_node`'s `new` and `delete`. `Mem_pool` might hold freed chunks of space in a freelist ('pool') instead of returning them to the free store manager. If many objects of a fixed size will be created and deleted in cycles, this can save considerable time.

The `Mem_pool` for the `Expr_node` is initialized with the size of the pool to be maintained; for requests to allocate or release chunks of memory of other sizes, it turns the request over to the system's general-purpose new (allocating the memory as an array of `char*`). Presumably, several `Mem_pool`s of the same size will share the same pool, so that if the system alternately replaces all the `Expr_node`s with `Reverse_expr_node`s of the same size, and then changes them all back, chunks of space freed from one use can be put to the other as soon as they are available.

Behavior such as this that implements the behavior of a class can often be incorporated into a virtual-base class (Chap. 7, Secs. 7.2, 7.8.3).

5.5.8 Overloading `new` and `delete`

It is also possible to overload the `new` operator. The overload is based on additional arguments to the operator, and there is a special syntax, called placement syntax to provide them when the `new` or `new[]` operator is invoked:

```
int* special = new ( arg1, arg2, arg3 ) int;

int* a_special = new ( arg1, arg2, arg3 ) int [ length ] ;
```

If the types of `arg1`, `arg2`, and `arg3` are `A_type1`, `A_type2`, and `A_type3`, this call needs an `operator new` or `operator new[]` with one of these prototypes:

```
void* operator new( size_t, A_type1, A_type2, A_type3 ) ;

void* operator new[] ( size_t, A_type1, A_type2, A_type3 ) ;
```

Thus a call of

```
Grumble grump* = new ( 5, DONT_WANNA, cout )
                                Grumble( "And I won't!" ) ;
```

would invoke

```
void* operator new( size_t, int, Grumble::reason, ostream& ) ;
```

The "And I won't" is passed to `Grumble::Grumble( const char* )`.

The syntax is called 'placement syntax' because the standard C++ header <new.h>* provides one overload of global `operator new()` and global `operator new[]()`:

```
void* operator new( size_t, void* there ) { return there; } ;
void* operator new[]( size_t, void* there ) { return there; } ;
```

These operators simply return the address provided. They are used to build an object or an array in a known place:

```
long buf[ long_enough ] ;

new ( buf ) Buffer( ... ... ) ;
```

This creates a `Buffer` object in the space defined by `buf`. This operator is actually used by the stream I/O system and should be not be redefined.

Similar overloads are permitted for the class-by-class `new` and `new[]` operators.

There is a serious limitation on overloaded `new` and `delete`. It is easiest to see if we consider allocation from *arenas*. An arena is a pool or 'heap' used by a free store manager. A program might use different arenas for memory that will be used and released quickly, and another for memory that will be allocated and kept around for a while. Or it might select an arena according to rules that reduce randomness of memory reference, reducing paging.

It is easy to provide an arena argument to new:

```
Xform_3to2d* xform = new ( temp_arena ) Xform_3_to_2d;
```

But how do we indicate to what arena the memory is to be returned? `delete` cannot be overloaded, and it is *not* safe for `Xform_3to_2d::delete()` to assume that it knows the memory layout of the space it is given (Chap. 7, Sec. 7.4). Where the choice of arena is managed by inheritance (Chap. 6), the problem can be solved (Sec. 6.4.7). Otherwise, the deallocation of the object must be managed by something other than `delete`, typically a static member function. Separating deallocation from `delete` is a serious maintainability risk.

5.5.9 Invoking a destructor in place

Placement syntax and `operator new( void* )` allow us to invoke a constructor for memory that we provide, bypassing any actual free store

---

* Or `<new>`, if the proposal of Chap. 1, Sec. 1.8.2 should be accepted.

manipulation. C++ allows a destructor to be explicitly invoked on memory as well:

```
char buffer[ BIG_ENOUGH_FOR_TO_BE ];

To_be* const want_to_be = new ( (void*) buffer ) To_be ;

... ...

want_to_be->To_be::~To_be();    // Destroys the To_be in buffer
```

What if we have

```
typedef Complex V_s_type;

V_s_type* vs_p = new ( (void*) buffer )
                                   vs_group [ vs_group_size ] ;
```

So far, so good. We've created an array of `Complex` under the typedef `V_s_type`. The `[ vs_group_size ]` will cause the constructor (if any) for `V_s_type` to be called for each object 'created.' When it comes time to destroy the array, we must write this:

```
for( int i = vs_group_size - 1 ; i >= 0; i++ )
        ( &vs_p[ i ] )->V_s_type::~V_s_type() ;
```

Again, so far, so good. We are simply invoking the destructors, quite properly, for `V_s_type`. We carefully destroy the objects in the opposite order of their creation. For `Complex` it doesn't matter, but for other types it might. What if the objects in the 'array' represent a linked data structure (say, the nodes in a tree)? We want to take it apart in the order opposite that in which it was built.

In Chap. 2, Sec. 2.1.11 we stated that a typedef name may be used to invoke a constructor. A typedef name may also be used to invoke the destructor, as we have done here. But that raises another question: What if we later change the typedef for `V_s_type` to a type that does not, or cannot, have a destructor?

```
typedef double V_s_type;
  ... ...

for( int i = vs_group_size - 1 ; i >= 0; i++ )
        ( &vs_p [ i ] )->V_s_type::~V_s_type() ;
```

The call controlled by the for loop is tantamount to

```
( &vs_p [ i ] )->double::~double() ;
```

Can we make a call to `~double()` ? `double` is a built-in type and cannot have a destructor. The answer is 'Yes.'

C++ allows the explicit call of a destructor for any type, whether it has a destructor or not. If it does not, the call has no effect and results in no actual code being generated.

Without this, code which explicitly calls a destructor or which *should* explicitly call a destructor would depend upon the details of the type. The change from 'has a destructor' to 'has no destructor' would be caught by the compiler, but the change from 'has no destructor' to 'has a destructor' would not be because there's no indication that there should be a destructor call there.

5.5.10 Using `new` for nontrivial types

Recall that in some contexts (e.g., member operator conversions) we must have a simple type name; if the type is not simple, we need to write a typedef.

The type argument to `new` must be a 'restricted-type-name,' or else it must be parenthesized. If it is parenthesized, any type name at all is allowed. A 'restricted-type-name' is a set of tokens representing a type name (`int`, `long int`, `unsigned short`, etc.), possibly followed by some number of 'ptr-operator's (`*` or `&` or `class-name ::`).

```
/*
 *      ten_p is a pointer to an array of ten pointers-to-
 *      function-of-no-args-returning-int
 */
int ( *(*ten_p) [ 10 ] )() = new ( int ( * [10])() ) ;
```

A typedef would easily be better than this!

5.5.11 Class-by-class allocation before Release 2.0

Class-by-class allocation is possible before C++ Release 2.0.

The technique is incompatible with Release 2.0 and beyond. It may be supported as an anachronism for a few releases. It is ugly and will not work with some of the improved OOP capabilities of Release 2.0 (especially multiple inheritance, Chap. 7).

Prior to Release 2.0, a constructor may, in carefully limited circumstances, assign to its object's this pointer.

This requires that

- All constructors must have their own copy of the allocation code.
- All manipulation of the this pointer must be done *before* any members are accessed (thus the constructor may not use the initializer-list).

- The this pointer must be tested for zero/nonzero value. If the value is nonzero, allocation has already been done or the object has nondynamic extent.
- On *all* paths, the this pointer must receive an assignment. Where the this pointer is to be left unchanged, the assignment this = this; must be written.

The last of these requirements ensures that certain code which the compiler may have to insert can be inserted correctly for all paths.

- The destructor must zero the this pointer of any object which was actually allocated by user code, and must do so after all operations on members.

This questionable usage is supported (so long as it is supported) only to allow pre-C++ Release 2.0 code to compile. It should be changed as soon as possible, and should *never* be used in new code.

5.5.12 Garbage collection: the Boehm-Weiser garbage collector

Not all programming languages support explicit deallocation of free store (or 'dynamic memory'). Instead, they periodically recover, or 'garbage collect,' memory which has been lost. (It is lost if there are no pointer references to it, either from nondynamic memory or from dynamic memory which is not lost.) Garbage collection is not, in general, a good choice in C++. With garbage collection, there is no clean end to an object's lifetime; it just sort of fades into the background and gets swept up later. But there are some places where garbage collection makes sense. In particular, the links and multilinks used by some data structures could be 'dropped on the floor' without ever calling a destructor, and cleaned up later.

Conventional wisdom holds that garbage collection requires the cooperation of the compiler and language run-time. After all, only they know where to look for pointers that might reference the memory in question. But Hans J. Boehm of Rice University has shown that C and C++ can have garbage collection and even type-by-type garbage collection. (See Boehm and Weiser, 1988.)

The Boehm-Weiser garbage collector is extremely conservative; it remembers what memory has been parcelled out of its heap and scans all of memory for possible pointers to that memory before declaring a chunk of memory garbage to be collected. This means that some garbage memory may be left uncollected.

The Boehm-Weiser garbage collector is available to the public in source form from a number of archives, including by *ftp* across the

Internet, by *uucp* from the for-profit *uunet* system, and from various Internet mail servers. It contains some compiler and machine dependencies.

Garbage collection is most needed under circumstances described in Sec. 5.6.6.3.

5.6 Changing Viewpoints on the Meaning of a 'Class Type'

(The reader is warned that this section describes the author's thinking—and his prejudices. They complement, rather than describe, 'conventional wisdom.')

Here we detour again into 'philosophy of programming.' We pick up where we left off, looking at the roles played by types in a program. We frame some of the observations of Chap. 2, Sec. 2.8 and Chap. 3, Sec. 3.10 within a larger approach.

Object-Oriented methodologies for large systems call for a top-level 'partition' of a program or system. Some provide policies which shape the partition; some provide multiple policies.

The approach presented here develops such a partition organically from knowledge of what the various types represent. It provides opportunities for reuse that grow with the organization's specialization in one or another type of program. It enhances cohesion, reduces coupling, and relates the 'top-level modules' directly to the both the program's type structure and to the types of knowledge the program embodies.

This approach is suitable for large programs (10,000 to probably 1 million lines of C++, and perhaps more) and can probably be extended hierarchically for at least another factor of 10. It will become harder to apply and enforce as programs pass the million-line mark, and may need help from either the programming language (it is not specific to C++) or the development environment.

5.6.1 The class as the smallest semantic unit

The AVL tree example (Chap. 2, Sec. 2.8.3) showed how a program's meaning should be represented in the meaning and behavior of its classes. These types represent 'Objects' and not just data structures by which Objects are implemented. If these 'semantic loci' are poorly chosen, the program will be needlessly complex.

Such classes are the smallest program units embodying problem-domain behavior or semantics. Enumerations, consts, and the like help to represent the semantics of other types, but embody no problem-domain semantics of their own.

To understand a program, we must understand not only the inner workings of the types but also the roles they play in the program. These roles are determined both by the type's behavior in isolation and by why it was introduced into the program: Does it directly provide a feature or fulfill a specification? Does it model a part of the problem domain? Does it fill a supporting role?

The Architecture of a system is the collection of information which specifies, for each component of the system, (1) what tasks the component performs, (2) what resources the component has with which to perform them, and (3) what the component contributes to the system thereby.

A type's intended role defines its *External Semantics*—its meaning to the world around it. A system's Architecture is also the collection of external semantics of its semantic loci and semantic systems.

The service manual for an electronic device typically describes the roles of its various circuits and devices under the heading "Theory of Operation." Such a description would benefit software systems as well. But uncontrolled complexity can make it difficult to formulate a cogent Theory of Operation for a software system.

5.6.2 Organizing classes

Classes use other types either as explicit resources (e.g., the input and output streams) or as part of their basic vocabulary (e.g., complex numbers, string types).

Since only classes (and structs used as Objects) are capable of activity, only they can 'use' other types. Only they can be said to have a 'vocabulary,' which is the set of types they name, and the things they name by them. Here 'type' does not just mean 'int,' but 'distance in nautical miles stored as an int'—and if we have designed and programmed correctly, we will have a C++ type just for that.

Just as we group functions around data to construct classes, we can group classes around common vocabulary. A class associated with one vocabulary (e.g., a network representing an electronic circuit) may use a class with the same basic vocabulary (e.g., one that 'transforms' the circuit by replacing one subnetwork with another that behaves identically) or a class which has a very different basic vocabulary (e.g., a linear algebra systems-solver).

The two circuit analysis classes share a basic *mission:* to represent the circuit. The linear algebra systems-solver's mission is to provide a mathematical description of a system given mathematical descriptions of the system's parts. It neither knows nor cares that the parts belong to a circuit; they might as well be girders in a truss. It solves a problem in circuit theory because the circuit analysis classes cast their problem in its vocabulary (linear algebra) and give the problem to it.

These *changes of abstraction* delineate the basic architecture of the solution. To represent the solution properly in the program, we should represent these abstraction boundaries explicitly.

5.6.3 Semantic systems: domains

The term 'Domain Analysis' is used to mean either of two kinds of analysis. The more common meaning is an analysis of subject areas commonly encountered in a programming organization. This analysis can be reused from one program to another, often in the form of 'subject matter' libraries and header files. The second meaning is a study of the various 'domains' that appear in a program and how those domains interact. We are interested in the second meaning, using domains as a model for program architecture. This will lead back to the first meaning.

A *Semantic Domain* (or just *Domain*) is the set of concepts needed to understand and describe something, or the representation of those concepts in a program. Such a Domain is a part of a problem or program constituting a 'universe' of its own. The 'problem' it represents exists independent of programs that use it.

A Domain has a lexicon or vocabulary. Within a program, a Domain also has a 'mission.' Types that share a common mission will share their vocabulary as well, so types can be grouped into Domains by shared mission as well as by shared vocabulary. By organizing a program around Domains, we localize the concepts and the types needed to understand any Domain in the program.

One of the 'missions' that a circuit analysis package must perform to fulfill its own mission is solving the linear equations that describe the circuit. It can use a general-purpose linear equation solver, or it can use one 'tuned' for its needs. But even if the linear equation solver is specially written for the program, it will be clearer if written as a general solver for linear systems, uncomplicated by circuit theory.

The linear-systems solver represents a separate domain of circuit analysis. It has its own mission and its own vocabulary (matrices, determinants, reduction and elimination, etc.) that may overlap another domain's but that is nonetheless distinct. Should another domain invoke it, it will apply its own vocabulary and mission to the types the other domain presents to it, independent of what they are and of what they represent. (This is another form of the 'change of abstraction' described at the end of Sec. 5.6.2 and of the 'separation of concerns' mentioned in Chap. 1, Sec. 1.8.1.6.)

A Semantic Domain's types represent and share a common vocabulary; together, they are solely responsible for some sub-mission within the program. The vocabulary may include types provided by other domains (e.g., a Matrix type in a circuit analysis program, used by the network analysis domain, but provided by an arithmetic domain).

If the class is a semantic locus or semantic center of the program, the Semantic Domain is a *complete semantic system* which embodies the entire meaning and behavior of a well-defined and separable module.

Because a Semantic Domain has a self-contained mission and vocabulary, it can be reused as a unit. A Graphical User Interface may be represented by a top-level domain, and can be used by many programs. If the GUI uses a process-management system, that process manager should be programmed as a self-contained domain that can serve other GUI's and other non-GUI domains.

Returning to the older meaning of Domain Analysis, the analysis of various problem domains independent of any specific program: if the various problem and solution domains can be analyzed and solutions designed for them independent of any particular program but usable by any program, the Semantic Domain model becomes a powerful and valuable tool for reuse. It is a better-defined form of the 'application libraries' long used for special purposes. (Linear systems solving and circuit analysis are among the oldest such libraries.)

It does not appear that present-day CASE tools are equipped to actively manage reusable and interacting domains.

The integrity of a program's Semantic Domain structure is essential to the clarity of the program. Clarity is the absence of obstacles to understanding. If we interleave Semantic Domains, the issues central to a given Domain become obstacles to the understanding of other Domains. Thus, even a small-to-medium-sized program (500 to 50,000 lines) may be helped by a properly defined domain organization.

5.6.4 Clients, servers, and bridges

Domains interact with each other. Their interaction is mediated by functions and types which one domain provides for the use of the other. These 'access ports' are sometimes called *bridges*. The Domain which provides the service is the the *server* Domain; the Domain which uses it is the *client* domain. The bridge is provided by the server for access by the client.

Each Domain reexpresses its semantics in terms which its server Domains can accept. (For instance, the circuit analysis package converts the circuit network into a matrix representing a system of linear equations.) A client may have many servers and a server many clients. The circuit analysis program may convert the network of electronic components it is given into an AC model of circuit elements and a DC model of circuit elements. Each of those models may convert the network into a (different) set of linear equations, using the same linear equations solver for each.

A program's Domains and bridges can be represented as a graph whose nodes are Domains and whose edges are bridges. The client-server relationship is one-way; the edges are *directed*. It may be multiply connected, so it is not a tree. And because the problem's semantics are progressively reexpressed until they can be solved by the binary logic circuits of the computer, the graph must be *acyclic*. Putting that together, we get a *Directed Acyclic Graph* or *DAG*. (See Fig. 5.1.)

One measure of a program's quality is how decoupled it is—or how coupled it isn't. A program's 'modules' should be coupled loosely to a small number of other modules. Coupling by invocation without dependence on external variables is the loosest possible, and the class and Domain organizations limit the number of functions which can be seen and can be called. Within a class, a member function may call any other member function. It may call any function in its Domain. And it may call the bridge functions (or use the bridge types) of other Domains. The ANSI/ISO C++ Namespace Management facility may become a valuable tool for controlling access to the inside of other Domains.

A good Domain structure offers the possibility that the number of types and functions visible at any point in the code will expand more slowly than the size of the program. To expect it to expand only logarithmically is probably too optimistic. But as more and more programs

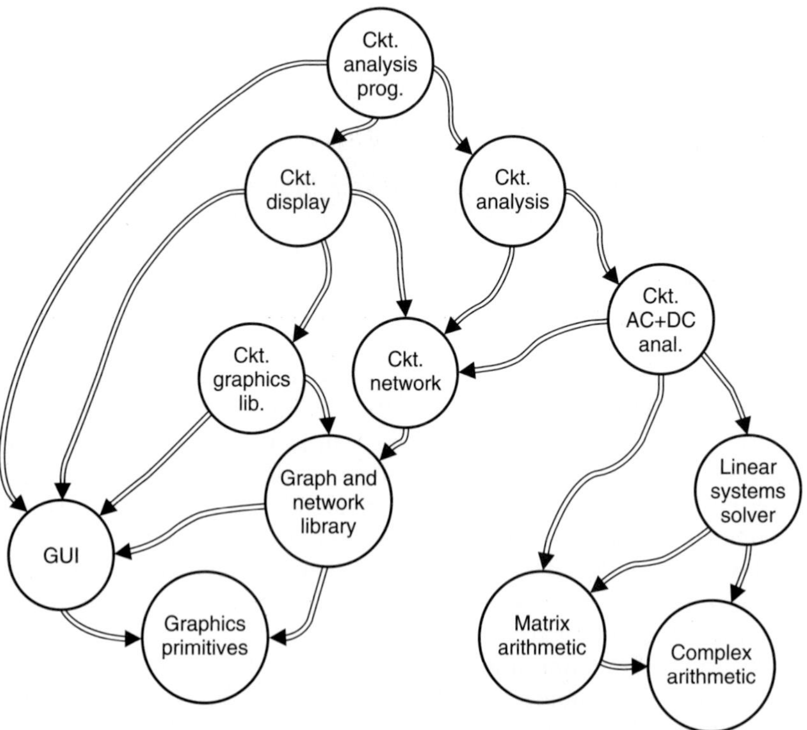

Figure 5.1 Domain diagram for hypothetical circuit analysis program.

pass the million-line mark and 10-million-line programs become common, linear expansion of the set of names visible at any given part of the program would be disastrous.

5.6.5 Domain origins

The DAG of a program's domains is not infinite; it has (usually) one top-level domain whose clients are users at terminals, or pilots in an aircraft cockpit, or whomever. It also has one or more domains that represent a program's ultimate resources: the computer executing instructions, the operating system, a file system manager or database manager or process manager.

Every domain in a program derives from some combination of four 'elements.' They are

- the services the program provides (Application)
- programming technologies (arrays, loops, searches, lists, procedure calls, etc.) (Programming)
- the technologies (circuit analysis, library science) from which the solution (with or without the program) is built (Subject)
- the external, ultimate resources on which the program draws (Environment)

We can visualize these as 'Elementary Domains,' fixed points in a 'Domain spacE.' We find or create Domains at these 'APSE' points as the first part of our analysis; indeed, we may go out and buy a DBMS or graphics 'assist' hardware to make the set more palatable, and we may research related subjects to find more desirable ways of performing this or that mission. (Is there any value in applying clipping speedup algorithms in a GUI? Does Operations Research have anything to say about this problem?) (See Fig. 5.2.)

'Subject Matter Experts' are custodians of knowledge vital to the solution of problems in their areas of expertise. The better the match between the subjects as they understand them and the Domain boundaries, the more effective they can be in verifying and validating the design and programming within their Domains, and the more certain you can be that their expertise has been translated properly into the program.

Careful study can reveal separable 'subject' or 'programming' Domains that can be reused in other programs. These may have a very high payoff, *both in reuse and in the ability to develop Subject Matter Experts for them.*

5.6.6.1 Offices of a type. Within a Domain, there are four basic parts a type may play; for want of a better word, the author calls these *Offices*. The Offices which a type (or object, or function, or macro) may fill are these:

- *Vocabulary.* A type may provide a term in the basic lexicon or vocabulary with which the Domain describes its abstractions. A Vocabulary type is either a built-in type of the programming language (or system) or a Service type provided by another Domain.
- *Model.* A type may provide some part of the abstraction which the Domain implements using its vocabulary. Such a type is a Model type. Model types may be Service types provided by other Domains. (This is more likely when generic types are available—see Chap. 8 on C++ templates.)
- *Service.* A type may provide the services which are the Domain's raison d'être. These Service types are the 'bridge' by which this Domain's clients make requests of this Domain. (Notice that a Vocabulary type which appears in the interface of a Service type remains a Vocabulary type.)
- *Instrumentation.* A type may allow the workings of the Domain to be studied, either for debugging or for some form of performance or cost measurement. Such a type is *not* seen by the Domain's ordinary clients and is *not* a part of the type's basic model or vocabulary, hence it has an Office of its own.

The care paid to a type, making it 'bulletproof,' making it agree with interface standards, making it general so that it can be easily reused, etc., will usually vary with the Office of the type. This can be condemned as sloppiness or praised as effective use of the engineering staff-hours available. In general, the Service types of a Domain merit the most attention, and the Instrumentation types, the least.

5.6.6.2 Nature of a type. A type's *Nature* determines the form of the type and what is expected of it. This classification would be incomplete, save for the inclusion of the category 'Other,' but it covers most of the field. It is a two-level classification scheme. These are the top-level categories:

- *Entity.* An Entity is anything which exists more or less of itself, and which can be called a 'thing' rather than a property or dimension.
- *Relationship.* A Relationship is something that exists by virtue of other things, or that describes in some way the relationship between other things.

- *Temporality.* A Temporality is something whose reason for existence is its behavior in the fourth dimension, time.
- *Information.* Information covers any type which describes a property or a quantity rather than a 'thing.'
- *Other.* An object that falls into none of the other categories can be put here.
- *Combinations.* A type or object which seems to have some of the characteristics of two or more of these categories is put with the characteristic that predominates. If none predominates, then choose Temporality over Relationship, Relationship over Entity, Entity over Information. It's normal for a Combination object to move from category to category as the analysis and design evolve.

Within each of the top-level categories there are three subcategories. If you need to add 'Other' or some other subcategory for your application area, do so.

Within Entity:

- *Thing.* A thing is a physical entity, with a real existence, and known by its real name. (Persons may be considered Things here.)
- *Specification.* A specification is a collection of information that describes how another object is to be built, how a process is to proceed, etc.
- *Role.* A role is a name by which another type may be known. For instance, a Person may also be an Employee; an Automobile may be a Fuel_consumer or a Conveyance.

Within Relationship:

- *Association.* An association is a relationship between two or a few particular, distinguished object instances, often of different types.
- *Agglomeration.* An agglomeration is a relationship between zero, one, or many object instances that are not distinguished from each other.

The difference between an association and an agglomeration is essentially the difference between a C `struct` and an array: in the `struct`, different things are brought together and each is named; in the array, things of the same type are brought together and known by their place in the collection.

- *Organization.* An organization is a collection of things wherein the thing's place in the collection holds information about the thing. This applies equally well to people in a corporation and to strings in a hash table.

Within Temporality:

- *Event.* An event is something that has a known beginning, and a known ending, and possibly some time between them. Other objects bring it about, and other things react to it. It has no time-structure other than its beginning and end.
- *Transaction.* A Transaction describes one or more interactions between objects that take place according to certain rules and that involve some common state information. Often a transaction requires each object to make a request of the other, and other operations may intervene between the operations that constitute the transaction. A Transaction is subordinate to the objects that make requests of it.
- *Process.* A Process is a sequence of operations that are driven from one store of state information (and therefore one object). The process makes requests of other objects, and they may occasionally make requests of it. A process dominates the objects with which it interacts, excepting perhaps the object that created it.

Within Information:

- *Quantity.* Quantity is any measurement of 'how much,' 'how many,' 'how long,' 'how far,' or 'how strong'; indeed almost any property that can be described with the word 'how' followed by an adjective.
- *Quality.* Quality is a property that is not a Quantity, and not a Selection. 'What color,' 'What shape,' 'What type'; any phrase that contains 'what' followed by the name of a property is a candidate Quality.

Many Qualities can be converted to Quantity: 'What size' (how big, how heavy), 'what color,' (how much red, green, blue, how much cyan, magenta, yellow, black).

- *Selection.* Selection is a choice ('one of') from a small set of alternatives. 'Which' is a good indicator of a Selection: 'Which route,' 'which fork,' 'which brand of cake mix.'

5.6.6.3 Identity/value semantics of a type. The distinction between Identity and Value semantics is well known to the designers of programming languages (under different names), but less well known among programmers, analysts, and such. Since it profoundly affects how Objects are built, how they can be used, and just what features of the problem they can represent, it deserves wider understanding.

The difference between Value and Identity semantics is illustrated by the difference between a C++ `int` and a record in a linked list. For the `int`, all that matters is the pattern of bits stored; one instance of an `int` is as good as another. Not so with the record in the linked list; if you transfer the bit-pattern 'value' elsewhere and rewrite the record, you have invalidated the list (what the list represents) and probably corrupted the list (destroyed the infrastructure of the representation) as well. Once an object is part of any kind of linked structure, its identity is part of its representation of the 'problem.'

Note that a type can have external Value semantics and internal Identity semantics; a `String` is the perfect example. It's even possible for a type to have internal Value semantics but external Identity semantics; an Object in an array means one thing by what it contains and something else by where it *is*. The contents can be rewritten almost arbitrarily without invalidating the information of its position (i.e., with just what index this Object is associated). And some data storage mechanisms combine both value and identity information. The hashed and linked string trees used by the LZW variant of the Lempel-Ziv compression algorithm are a frightening masterpiece of economy. (For a brief overview of the LZW technique, see App. B.4.)

An Object with Identity semantics—internal or external—uses its solution-domain relationships with the environment or other Objects as part of the representation of its problem-domain value. Identity semantics allow self-referential and recursive data structures, at a cost in complexity, time to set up, time to read data, and time to update the data structure.

Some application areas make heavy use of such data-storage techniques. And some of these expect the individual Object to be implemented by Value semantics so as to minimize execution cost. The internal data structure of the LISP programming language, for example, does not track allocation and deallocation; when it uses an object-in-memory it expects to use value semantics, rewriting pointers without checking if they are the last live pointers to the data to which they refer. Instead, a LISP system 'garbage-collects' from time to time, searching for unreferenced data. A variety of optimizations can make this a reasonably efficient way to conduct business.

Data structures which present Identify semantics to their users, but which are implemented using Value Semantics rules, may require Garbage Collection.

In C++, Object Identity is frequently used to represent problem-domain relationships between Objects (Chap. 3, Sec. 3.1.5), and Object lifetime is also available to store problem-domain information. This makes C++ generally inhospitable to Garbage Collection (GC). Nevertheless, some GC techniques work in C, and they can probably be made to work in C++ for those algorithms and problem domains to which GC-based data structures are well-suited. (See Sec. 5.5.12 for more information.)

5.7 Summary

Certain C++ operators are 'special'; they have special properties, either in general or when overloaded.

Section 5.1.1 The function call operator can be overloaded for a class type, with an object of the type taking the place of the function, and an arbitrary argument list corresponding to the signature of the operator overload function.

Section 5.1.2 There are some good uses for objects that look like functions, or for 'functions' that are really objects. One kind, the "functionoid," can be used to represent a transaction that must be performed a piece at a time. Another depends on deliberate confusion between function call on a function, function call on an object, and construction of an object by value builder.

Sections 5.1.3, 5.1.4 The subscripting operator can be overloaded. An overload can provide 'smart' arrays, subscript-checked arrays, maps (arrays subscripted by values other than integers), etc. Making these work often requires some sophistication and some "helper" types.

Section 5.3.1 The pointer-to-structure member selection operators (arrow and arrow-star) can be overloaded. Such an overload has very specific semantics, which have the effect of allowing a conversion on the LHS of these operators, one conversion available for each overload in a class, struct, or union. If one of these operators receives an overload in a class, the others should probably receive corresponding overloads.

Section 5.3.2 The increment and decrement operators may be overloaded for class types. The prefix operators are overloaded as unary operators; the postfix operators are overloaded as binary operators whose RHS is of type int and will usually be ignored. When C++ calls them, the argument for the RHS will be zero.

Section 5.3.3 The comma operator may be overloaded. Such overloads can provide various syntactic niceties; they can also be used to write "LISP with semicolons."

Section 5.3.4 The logical AND and OR operators may be overloaded; the overloads do not have any short-circuit property. The address-of and indirection (star) operators may also be overloaded. When address-of is overloaded, it hides the built-in address-of. Member functions still get their object's address as the this pointer.

Section 5.3.5 Conversion-by-member and conversion-by-constructor, taken together for a given pair of classes, may be ambiguous. In some cases, the ambiguity can be resolved in the direction of conversion-by-member; it cannot be resolved in the direction of conversion-by-constructor.

Section 5.4.2 Various transformations of the "Wheels" problem and examples show how the semantic center or "locus" of a system can be changed, and how the external and internal structure of the programmed solution change with it.

Section 5.5 The dynamic memory allocation operators `new` and `delete` can be replaced or overloaded, either for class types or as global operators, for individual object or (in ANSI/ISO C++) for arrays.

Section 5.5.1 Replacing `new` and `delete` is done by defining these operator functions:

```
void* ::operator new( size_t nbytes ) ;          // new
void ::operator delete( void*, size_t nbytes ) ; // delete
void ::operator delete( void* ) ;               // alternate form
                                                // of delete

void* ::operator new[] ( size_t nbytes ) ;       // new for
                                                 // arrays
void ::operator delete[] ( void*, size_t nbytes ) ; // delete for
                                                    // arrays
void ::operator delete[] ( void* ) ;      // alternate form of
                                          // delete for arrays
```

Section 5.5.2 The array forms, `operator new[] ()` and `operator delete[] ()`, are introduced by ANSI/ISO C++. In earlier versions of C++, the global new and delete operators are used for all array allocations and deallocations.

Section 5.5.3 The allocation process is divided into the new operator, which knows the type of the object or array, the constructor, if any, which initializes it, and `operator new()`, which deals with the memory as `void*`. A similar distinction is made for deallocation. There is an important interaction with virtual member functions (Chap. 6, Sec. 6.4.6).

Section 5.5.4 Any redefinition or overload of the various `new` operators should handle free store exhaustion consistent with the built-in handling of free store exhaustion.

Section 5.5.6 `new`, `new[]`, `delete`, and `delete[]` may be defined as member operator functions. These are implicitly static (Chap. 2, Sec. 2.6.2) and will be used to allocate objects or arrays of the class, and of derived types (Chap. 6, Sec. 6.4.7) (whose size may differ from the size of objects of this class).

Section 5.5.8 `new` and `new[]` may be overloaded as well as redefined, both for the global operators and for class member operators. These overloads use *placement syntax,* and one overload is provided by the standard library to allow an object or array to be built in a preallocated place.

Section 5.5.9 To correspond with placement syntax, it is possible to invoke a destructor 'in place,' without deallocating the memory occupied by an object.

Section 5.5.11 Special techniques must be used to provide class-by-class allocation before C++ Release 2.0. These are unspeakable kludges, and should be expunged as soon as possible.

Section 5.5.12 C++ does not provide Garbage Collection, and its model of computation is not conducive to any kind of Garbage Collection. Nevertheless, it has been done and at least one working version is available in (machine-dependent) source code.

Section 5.6.1 A class is the smallest recognizable unit of meaning in a large system.

Section 5.6.2 Classes should be organized around abstractions that are found in the problem and its solution. *Vocabulary* or (lexicon) and *Mission* are the characteristics around which the problem will organize 'naturally.'

Sections 5.6.3, 5.6.4 The *Semantic Domain* is the expression of a common Vocabulary and Mission. Semantic Domains in a well-organized program form client-server relationships in a DAG.

Section 5.6.5 The extremes of the Domain DAG are set by four 'fixed points': the problem to be solved, programming technology, solution technology, and the resources available in the programming environment.

Section 5.6.6 A program's types may be introduced (or discovered) during different stages of the Analysis-Architecture-Design process. The type will reflect the stage at which it is introduced.

Section 5.6.6.1 A type can fill four different 'offices' within a Semantic Domain: Vocabulary, Model, Service, and Instrumentation.

Section 5.6.6.2 A type can represent different 'Natures,' and the type's Nature determines in large measure what the type will look like and how it must behave. The five common Natures are Entities (things, people, specifications, roles), Relationships (association, agglomeration, organization), Temporalities (events, transactions, processes), Information (quantity, quality, selection), and combinations of these. A very few types will fall outside this grouping.

Section 5.6.6.3 A type's representation can be based on the Object's Rvalue, or upon the Object's Identity (lvalue). An object can have one representation semantic externally and the other internally.

Chapter

6

Inheritance

Overview

We can now examine Object-Oriented programming ('OOP') in C++. Sections 6.1 through 6.5 address C++'s basic tools for OOP. In Sec. 6.6 we examine some of the practical requirements of OOP in C++. Those requirements vary considerably with who is using it.

There are three major communities using Object-Oriented technologies. They are the 'prototyping' community, the 'simulation' community, and the 'engineered software' community.

The prototyping community performs very directed research: "How does this user interface work? How do we fine-tune it? Can this algorithm be tweaked to make it do a new job?" Their software is short-lived and used by few people, though exhibited to many. Prototypers must convert an idea into working software quickly. Their product is not software but algorithms, data structures, and conclusions: in other words, technology.

The engineered software community develops production code. Their product is delivered to meet a commitment. It must be maintained over years or decades. It must be easy to verify and validate. It must be as cheap as possible to build *and maintain.* Engineers-in-software must express a problem in a way that is malleable and plastic, that can absorb forced change without crazing and shattering.

The simulation community performs research. Unlike the prototyping community, they research a subject that is not the program, nor its programming technologies, nor its interfaces. For prototypers, the tool itself is under study; for simulators, the object of study is elsewhere. The needs of simulators lie somewhere between those of prototypers and engineers-in-software. They need malleability less than engineers-in-software and fast programming somewhat less than prototypers.

This text is slanted towards the needs of engineers-in-software. C++ seems to be slanted in this direction as well, though less severely. Those with different needs should consider the advice herein on its own merit for their own situations.

6.1 Introduction: Polymorphism and OOP

Polymorphism is the ability of different types of objects to support the same operation. Operator overloading is one kind of polymorphism: both `int` and `complex` can support the + operator. This polymorphism is completely static and arranged entirely at compile time.

Object-Oriented Programming uses run-time polymorphism. Objects of class `X1` can substitute for objects of class `X`, allowing `X::fun()` to be called on behalf of an `X1`, or even on behalf of an `X1` that we *think* is an `X`. *The function actually called is not* `X::fun()` *but* `X1::fun()`.

6.2 Derived Classes

Some Object-Oriented programming languages allow *any* 'member function'* to be called on behalf of any object. If the object has no function of that name, a run-time error results. Such languages also allow any object to be referenced through a generic object pointer, so a request can be sent to an object whose actual type is completely unknown; the object interprets the request and either acts on it or bails out. This is suitable when the programmer is the chief user of the program, or when the program is itself an experiment.

When software is mission-critical, or when it is used by a customer, this is rarely acceptable. C++ verifies at compile time that no object will be called for an operation that it does not possess. (See Sec. 6.4.3 for the one place where this cannot be verified.) As usual, the type system can be overridden. Even then, it can still help to provide type safety.

Types that will be used for Object-Oriented polymorphism must be properly declared. First one class (the *base class*) is declared, then another class is 'derived' from it. A *Derived class* object can substitute for an object of its base class. The derived class, by default, has all of the properties of the base class. We say that the derived class *inherits* the properties of the base class. (Multiple base classes are allowed; this is *Multiple Inheritance* or *MI*. See Chap. 7.)

---

* In such languages, 'member functions' are typically called *methods* and their invocation is called a *message* to the object.

Derived and base classes retain C++'s support for data abstraction (public and private). Base classes can provide extra support for their derived classes. All of the usual C++ class properties apply to derived and base classes; only properties explicitly declared polymorphic (*virtual*) take on new behavior.

Some terminology: in some Object-Oriented Programming Languages and literature, base classes are called 'supertypes' and derived classes 'subtypes.' These terms come from Data Modeling, some methods of which recognize inheritance. In C++ this is confusing: an object of the derived ('sub') type incorporates an object of the base ('super') type. When describing C++, C++ terminology is clearer.

6.2.1 Deriving classes

A base class is written just as any other class, except that it may have special provisions to support its derived classes (Secs. 6.2.3.2, 6.4):

```
/*
 *      We'll use this as a base class . . .
 */
class   Babble
{
  public:
        int base_func() const { return bab; };
        ... ...

  private:
        int bab;
};
```

Any class, including a derived class, may be used as a base class.

A derived class is declared with a *base class list:* a colon and a comma-separated list of existing classes. (Classes with multiple bases are covered in depth in Chap. 7.) Each class name is qualified by one of `public`, `private`, or `protected` (Sec. 6.2.3.2):

```
/*
 *      . . . and derive this class from the one above.
 */
class   Diddle
  : public Babble      // Babble  is a  base class  of  Diddle
{
  public:
        int derived_func() const { return did; };
        ... ...
```

```
  private:
        int did;
};
        ... ...

        Babble b;
        Diddle d;

        cout << b.base_func();        // Of course:  base_func()
                                      //   is a member of  Babble .
        cout << d.derived_func();     // Likewise:  derived_func()
                                      //   is a member of Diddle .
        cout << d.base_func();        // Yes, Ok!   Diddle *inherits*
                                      //   Babble::base_func()
                                      //   and  Babble::bab .
```

Consider the third "<<" expression. It is legal to call a member function of `Babble` on behalf of a `Diddle` because a `Diddle` *is* a `Babble`—a `Babble` with something extra.

> *A derived class object* is *an object of its base classes*—
> with any extras the derived class adds.

C++ builds a `Diddle` by constructing a `Babble`, then adding the extra parts needed for a `Diddle`. Within every derived class object (`Diddle`) lies a base class object (`Babble`).

Friendship is not inherited. If `Babble` is a friend of `Scuttlebutt`, `Diddle` gains no privileges thereby. Nor, if `Scuttlebutt` is a friend of `Babble`, does `Scuttlebutt` gain any privileges with respect to `Diddle`.

6.2.2 Direct and indirect derivation

Any class or struct, even a derived class, can act as a base class. (Unions, however, may not.) And a class may have many derived classes. A derived class is derived *directly* from its own bases (base classes), and *indirectly* from any direct or indirect bases of its own bases.

```
/*
 *      Flumdiddle is derived from Diddle, which
 *      is derived from Babble . . .
 */
class   Flumdiddle
  : public Diddle
```

```
{
public:
    int flum_func() const { return flummery; };
    ... ...

private:
    int flummery;
};

    Babble b;
    Diddle did;
    Flumdiddle deedee;

    cout << b.base_func();          // Babble has  base_func() . . .

    cout << did.derived_func();     // Diddle has  derived_func()
    cout << did.base_func();        //   AND  base_func() ...

    cout << deedee.flum_func();     // But Flumdiddle has
                                    //    flum_func() and
    cout << deedee.derived_func();  // derived_func() and
    cout << deedee.base_func();     //    base_func() .
```

Within each `Flumdiddle` there is a `Diddle`, and within that `Diddle` there is a `Babble`—so *somewhere* within the most deeply derived `Flumflimmeryflumdiddledeedee` there sits a `Babble`.

Some Object-Oriented approaches encourage 'deep inheritance': capabilities accrete bit by bit through repeated derivation (Incremental Programming). Others encourage 'wide inheritance': no deriving from derived classes is allowed. Still others hold that the 'correct' use of inheritance is an architectural issue, and depends on (1) the program (or library, or system), (2) the architectural structure the inheritance represents, and (3) what the classes themselves represent.

The author agrees with the last group. Some uses of inheritance do work better than others in engineered software; there *are* right and wrong uses of inheritance, both as a programming construct and as a tool for modeling a system. But these distinctions follow from what sort of things the inheritance is to model.

6.2.3 Access control

A derived class's base classes are either `public`, `private`, or `protected`. This establishes the access control applied to the derivation.

The access control keyword may be omitted. It defaults to `private`. Omitting the keyword is considered bad practice, and in some versions, generates a warning. In C++ Release 3.0 and ANSI/ISO C++, it may be omitted only if the `virtual` keyword is present. (This a different use of `virtual` than the one examined in Sec. 6.4. See Chap. 7, Sec. 7.2.)

6.2.3.1 Public and private derivation. The previous examples use the keyword `public` to provide *public inheritance.* Under public inheritance, the inherited nature of the derived class is accessable everywhere the class is. Only the private parts of derived and base classes are completely inaccessible to the world at large.

In a class derived with *private* inheritance, the inherited nature of the class is inaccessible outside the derived class's own scope. The world at large has no access to the base part of the class; only members and friends of the derived class can use the derived class as the base class. (Access control for a private base class can be relaxed member-by-member; see Sec. 6.2.3.3 and 6.2.3.4.)

In neither case does the private part of the base class become any more visible.

Even under private inheritance, the derived class itself knows itself as the base class, and can pass itself by pointer or reference to anything else as a base class object.

```
class   Hush
  : private Babble          // Hush knows itself as a Babble
{
  public:
        /*
         *      The  gossip()  functions give access to  Hush
         *      as the Babble it is.
         */
        Babble* gossip() { return this; };
        const Babble* gossip() const { return this; };

        int true_straight_dope() const;
};

/*
 *      As a member of Hush, we're in on the
 *      secret: Hush is really a Babble (!)
 */
int
Hush::true_straight_dope() const
```

```
    {
        return base_func();    // Babble::base_fun()!
    }
        ... ...

        Hush secret;

        secret.base_func();    // ILLEGAL!  We don't know out
                               //   here that Hush has a
                               //   base_func() :  that's
                               //   private . . .
        /*
         *     . . . but only so long as Hush keeps
         *     quiet about it . . .
         */
        Babble* blather = secret.gossip();

        blather->base_func();   // . . . and by the time we
                                //   get here, there's
                                //   nothing to connect what
                                //   blather is pointing at
                                //   with the Hush secret--
                                //   even though they are
                                //   "really the same."
```

`blather` is a pointer-to-`Babble` and in the absence of coercions (casts) to violate the type system, whatever the object at which it points, that object is a `Babble`. Yet in this case we know that the object that `blather` 'actually' points at is a `Hush`.

We say that `Hush` is `secret`'s *exact* type, and that `Babble` is its *apparent* type *when it is accessed through* `blather`.

The exact type is the type of the *complete object.* The base class objects within the complete object are *incomplete objects.* (These definitions are not limited to base class objects that are privately derived.)

6.2.3.2 Protected. We've assumed that a base class such as `Babble` is ignorant of the classes derived from it. This ignorance is good; if `Babble` were coded with knowledge specific to some derived classes, this coupling would interfere with other attempts to derive from it.

How does a base class provide services for a derived class without harmful coupling? The base class must embody a minimal set of assumptions about the derived classes and their needs. They, in turn, should provide services of a sort compatible with the base class. (What 'compatible' means depends on what we are using derivation to achieve. See Sec. 6.6.4.)

```
class   Random_number_gen
{
  public:
        long sequence() const { return seq; };
        long inc_seq() { return ++seq; };
        ... ...
  private:
        long seq;
        ... ...
};
```

Here the position in the random number sequence is common to all generators derived from this class; it is a service provided by the base class. The actual mechanisms for generating the random number sequence will be provided by the derived class, allowing generators with many different properties.

Code which knows it has a `Random_number_gen` but doesn't know its exact type can still request the position-in-sequence of the generator. This capability is public because it should be usable by all 'clients' of the generator.

Here the ability to increment the position-in-sequence is public. This allows the derived classes to increment it as needed—but also allows the 'outside world' to tinker with the sequence abstraction.

This isn't right; a base class designed as a base class ought to present a special, cooperative interface to its derived classes. For this, C++ has a third kind of access, *protected:*

```
class   Random_number_gen
{
  public:
        long sequence() const { return seq; };
        ... ...
  protected:
        long inc_seq() { return ++seq; };
        ... ...
  private:
        long seq;
        ... ...
};
```

`Random_number_gen::inc_seq()` can be used by a directly derived class, and by an indirectly derived class whose inheritance from `Random_number_generator` is public—*or* protected.

In C++ Release 3.0 and ANSI/ISO C++, a base class can be protected. This makes sense if our derived classes should have access to our base class. For a random number generator, it might make sense.

Data abstraction implies data should not be public; public services and operations should be provided through member functions. Should protected access be strictly data-abstracted or should there be protected data?

"It depends." Data shared between base and derived types can reflect a 'universal' of the problem entities that the classes represent. It can sometimes be justified by a need for efficiency. In either case, shared data must be carefully engineered.

Constructors can be `protected`; these can be invoked only by an immediate derived class, not to declare or `new`-allocate objects of the class. Destructors can be protected, likewise `new`, `delete`, conversion operators, static members, nested types, and just about anything else in a class.

There's a subtlety in the access granted to protected members. If `prot` is a protected member of `Base`, and if `Derived` is derived from `Base`, protected access to `prot` means that `Derived` has access to the protected part of `Base` *as a base class of* `Derived` *only.*

```
#include <string.h>

class   Base
{
        ... ...
  protected:
        ... ...
        const char* prot_memb;
};

class   Some_other_base_child
  : public Base
{
        ... ...
};

class   Derived
  : public Base
{
  public:
        int prot_cmp( const Base* bp ) const
        {  return strcmp(
                prot_memb,      // OK: this->
                                //  Derived::Base::prot_memb
                bp->prot_memb   // Not Allowed:
                                //  bp->Base::prot_memb
                                //  and *bp's type is not
                );              //  Derived.
        };
```

```
        int prot_cmp( const Some_other_base_child* op ) const
        { return strcmp (
                prot_memb,      // OK: this->
                                //  Derived::Base::prot_memb
                op->prot_memb   // Not Allowed:
                );              //  op->Some_other_base_child::
                                //  Base::prot_memb and *op's
                                //  type is not Derived.
        };

        int prot_cmp( const Derived* dp ) const
        { return strcmp(
                prot_memb,       // OK: this->
                                 //  Derived::Base::prot
                dp->prot_memb    // OK: dp->
                                 //  Derived::Base::prot and
                );               //  *op's type IS Derived.
        };
};
```

6.2.3.3 Access declarations. Protected is more restrictive than public, and private more than protected. Sometimes it makes sense to relax the inheritance access control for a particular member. The derived class may do this with an *access declaration:*

```
class   Semi_hush
  : private Babble
{
  public:
        Babble::base_func;       // Make Babble::base_func()
        ... ...                  // public in Semi_hush
};
```

An access declaration in a class restores access that the class's declaration denies; it cannot relax the base class's own access control.

The access declaration does not specify any type information apart from the base class. An access declaration for an overloaded member function affects all the overloads of that member.

An access declaration cannot be used when the same member name occurs in both the base and derived classes. This is an important case (Secs. 6.3, 6.4). Access declarations are little-used; this may be one reason. They may also be a 'wart' of little use in a good design.

6.2.3.4 `using` definitions and access control. The version of Namespace Management (Chap. 1, Sec. 1.9) most likely to be adopted defines the inheritance of scopes in terms of the `using` of namespaces. In this model, a `using` definition can 'promote' a base class member (static or nonstatic) into the derived class, changing access control as well:

```
class   My_Derived
  : protected My_Base
{
  public:
        ... ...
        using My_Base::prot_memb;       // Now My_Base::prot_memb
                                        //  has an alias of the
                                        //  same name in the
                                        //  public part of
                                        //  My_Derived .
};
```

If the proposal passes in this form, Namespace Management's `using` definition will be the preferred form for changing access form to a base class member.

6.2.4 Derivation, creation and destruction

A derived class object contains an instance of its base class, and of any base classes of the base class, etc. Creating or destroying a derived class object requires creating or deleting those base class objects. (For MI, this is even more interesting; see Chap. 7, Sec. 7.3).

6.2.4.1 Explicit constructors for derived classes. A derived class constructor provided by the programmer can provide arguments to the base class constructors, thereby controlling the construction of the base class. (Constructors can be provided by C++; see Chap. 2, Secs. 2.1.7, 2.1.8, and Sec. 6.2.4.2.)

```
class   Babble
{
  public:
        Babble();
        Babble( const char* );
        ... ...
  protected:
        Babble( int, const char* = 0 );
        ... ...
};

class   Diddle
  : public Babble
{
  public:
        Diddle( const char* = "" );
        ... ...
```

```
        Ullage* const alp = &al;

        short_N( alp->tonnes );  // No Good!  This  tonnes
                                 // means  Ullage::tonnes ,
                                 // which is a  long .

        long_N( alp->tonnes );   // Ok--Ullage::tonnes is long
}
```

We can still name the base class member by qualifying it explicitly:

```
short_N( alp->Burthen::tonnes ); // Ok--Burthen::tonnes
                                 // is a short.
```

For pointers-to-class (or-to-struct), it is the *apparent type* (indicated by the pointer) that matters for data members, *not the actual type.* C++ may not know the actual type at the point of the object's use:

```
Burthen* dray( int some, const char* arg )
{
        ... ...
        if( ... ... )
                return new Ullage( some, args );
        else
                return new Burthen( some, args );
}
... ...

Burthen* burgeon = dray( 16, "tons" );  // Is *burgeon actually
                                        // a Burthen or an
                                        // Ullage?

short_N( burgeon->tonnes );     // Uses Burthen::tonnes.
```

References work the same way. (Several compilers from different vendors failed to recognize that references are 'actually' pointers and mishandled this case; this problem occurred in compilers corresponding to C++ Release 2.0 and C++ Release 2.1.)

6.3.2 Ordinary (nonvirtual) member functions, overloading and inheritance

Overriding ordinary member functions (and operators) is slightly more complicated than overriding member data; functions may be overloaded. A member function in a derived class overrides *all* overloads of that name in the base class, whether or not it matches any of their signatures.

```
class   Car
{
  public:
        void fuel( float gas );
        … …
};

class   Electric_car
  : public Car
{
  public:
        void fuel( float kilojoules );  // Hides Car::fuel()
        … …
};

class   Turbine_engine_tank
  : public Car
{
  public:
        void fuel( float gas, float diesel,      // Also hides
                float jp2, float lpg );          //  Car::fuel()
        … …
};
        … …

        Turbine_engine_tank grin_g( "Grinnin' Gus" );

        grin_g.fuel( 350.0 );          // No good!
        grin_g.Car::fuel( 350.0 );     // That's more like it.

        Car& anonymous_car = grin_g;

        anonymous_car.fuel( 80.0 );    // Ok, a car can
                                       //   take gasoline.
        anonymous_car.fuel( 0.0, 0.0, 610., 0.0 );  //No good! A
                                       //   'car' (that we don't
                                       //   know is a special
                                       //   kind of car) can't
                                       //   take on fuel like a
                                       //   turbine-engine'd tank.
```

There are good reasons for the overriding of all overloads, but they are subtle and the behavior surprises many newcomers to C++.

6.3.3 Inheritance and conversions

In Chap. 4, Sec. 4.1 we saw how C++ inserts implicit conversions, and mentioned that the built-in conversions include conversions for inheritance.

There are three cases: from `Derived*` to `Base*`, from `Derived&` to `Base&`, and from `Derived` to `Base`.

The type system can disallow conversions (Chap. 3, Sec. 3.4); here we will assume that the conversions of interest are legal in the type system. We will also assume that all base classes are accessible; if they are not, the conversions will be illegal (Sec. 6.2.3).

These examples all use direct *base classes. Indirect base classes obey the same rules.* C++ selects the shortest conversion sequence that covers the distance between derived and base type.

6.3.3.1 Pointer conversions. When a derived class object is used as an object of a base class, conversions may occur.

```
class   Pastry
{
        ... ...
}:

class   Napoleon
  : public Pastry
{
        ... ...
};
        ... ...

        void diner( Pastry* );

        Napoleon napol;

        diner( &napol );        //      (Pastry*) Napoleon
```

A pointer to a derived class (`Napoleon`) can be converted to a pointer to one of its base classes (`Pastry`). Here the compiler inserts a conversion:

```
diner( (Pastry*) &nap );
```

When `diner()` is called, its argument is initialized by a `Pastry*` that points to the `Pastry` object within `Napoleon napol`. (`diner()` knows `napol` by an apparent type.)

6.3.3.2 Reference and reference-object conversions. References have derived-to-base conversions corresponding to those of pointers:

```
class   Pastry
{
        ... ...
}:
```

```
class   Napoleon
  : public Pastry
{
        ... ...
};
      ... ...

        void desserter( Pastry& );

        Napoleon napol;

        desserter( napol );
```

The conversion inserted in the call to `desserter()` is

```
(Pastry&) napol
```

This conversion yields a reference to the `Pastry` object within the `Napoleon napol`.

The conversion is allowed even though `napol` is an object, not a reference. What matters is that it can *initialize* the reference (Chap. 1, Sec. 1.2.4).

As before, this conversion allows the function to know the object by an apparent type instead of its exact type.

Conversion-to-reference, like other conversions, may be written explicitly to disambiguate when needed (e.g., to disambiguate possible overload matches) (but see Chap. 3, Sec. 3.4.2 and Sec. 6.3.3.4 on the different semantics of conversions).

6.3.3.3 Object conversions and 'slicing.' Consider our `Pastry` and `Napoleon` classes from the previous section:

```
Napoleon napol( ... ... );

Pastry& slicer = napol;

slicer = Pastry( ... ... );
```

When we initialize the reference with a derived class, the reference only 'refers to' part of the derived class object. If we assign to that 'slice' we may alter the base class in a way inconsistant with the expectations of the derived class. In particular, if the base class stores some pointer the derived class needs, this will break the relationships between the two.

```
Pastry presliced( napol );
```

Here the copy constructor for Pastry initializes a Pastry from something that is a Pastry and yet is more than a Pastry.

This behavior is called *slicing,* and when it is unexpected or undesirable, it is called the *slicing problem.* It is particularly insidious when it happens to function parameters:

```
void sweeteater( Pastry& );
void omnivore( Pastry );

Napoleon napol;

sweeteater( napol );      // The called function MAY
                          //   slice the parameter
                          //   and damage our variable.
omnivore( napol );        // The function call DOES
                          //   slice the parameter, but
                          //   does not damage our variable.
```

Slicing is rarely desirable. Long consideration failed to find any way to avoid it that did not do worse damage to C++. Slicing can happen with pointers as easily as with references, but it is more insidious with references.

Slicing occurs when the reference is used to create an object, or when the object is the target of a memberwise assignment by other than it's exact type. When planning these operations on objects that may be polymorphic, make sure that the class has made provision for them; if it has not, the operations are probably invalid and unsafe.

6.3.3.4 Checked conversions. In Chap. 3, Sec. 3.4.2, we saw that there are three different semantics and (ANSI x3j16/ISO WG21 willing) three different syntaxes. The third case, the *dynamic* conversion, we have deferred until now.

Given two pointers or references to class types, we know the apparent types of the objects at which they point, but not their exact types:

```
Ct1* p1 = … …;  // Ct1 or a type derived therefrom.
Ct2* p2 = … …;  // Ct2 or a type derived therefrom.
```

Run-time type identification allows us to ask 'is the object identified by p1, which object we know is of Ct1, also an object derived from Ct2?'

Under single inheritance, this can be determined statically: either Ct1 is derived from Ct2, or Ct2 is derived from Ct1, or neither is derived from the other. Under multiple inheritance, this doesn't hold:

```
class  Ct3
  : public Ct1, public Ct2
{
        ... ...
};
      ... ...

         Ct1* p10 = new Ct3( ... ... );
```

p10 points to an object that is both a Ct1 and a Ct2. This pointer could be returned by a function and assigned to p1. *The declarations of* p1 *and* p2 *do not have to have either* Ct3 *or* p10 *in scope!* (Chapter 7, Sec. 7.7) (Multiple Inheritance has many interesting ramifications; Chap. 7 describes some of the commonly encountered ones.)

Conversions of this type are sometimes called 'downcasting' because inheritance diagrams usually place the derived classes below their base classes in a top-rooted tree or graph.

Enquiring at run time of the type of an object is usually bad practice; the virtual functions in the next section make it almost pointless. There are a few cases where it can be acceptable, especially when you want to know if a pointer you have been given is 'really one of your own' given back.

The syntax for dynamic conversion is still tentative as of June 1993. Here is the probable final form:

```
Ct2* p2 = dynamic_cast< Ct2* >( p1 );
```

The conversion returns a valid pointer to a p2, or a null pointer if there is no inheritance conversion available.

If references are used instead of pointers, and the conversion is found to be impossible, an exception (name unchosen as of this writing) is thrown (Chap. 9).

The types to which dynamic conversion applies are exactly those with virtual functions, as described in Sec. 6.4.

6.3.4 Covariant return types

Covariance between types involved in an operation means that as one operand varies from base class to derived class, the other operand also changes from base to derived.

In an Object-Oriented Programming Language like C++, it means that if a class's member functions have arguments of the class's type, a derived class (of that class) will have arguments of the derived class. *In general, covariance is* not *typesafe and cannot be implemented without run-time checks.* (But parameterized types can be typesafe; see Chap. 8.)

While covariant parameters are inherently type-unsafe, covariant return types can be defined and implemented safely. The rules governing covariance are these:

- When a member function in a derived class overrides one in the base class, the derived function's parameters must have the same types as the base class functions.
- The return type of the derived class function must be either the same as the base class function's return type *or* derived from the base class's return type (e.g., `Base` and `Derived`, `Base*` and `Derived*`).

This feature has been accepted for ANSI/ISO C++. It is not present in any version of C++ available as of spring 1993.

6.4 Virtualization

A derived class object can be passed by address or reference to a function that expects an object of one of its base classes. With ordinary member functions, the object looks and acts like the base class object. The members visible are those of the incomplete base class object, and the object's exact type does not contribute to its behavior.

Object-Oriented Programming calls for an object to act according to its exact type, even when accessed by code that knows it by an apparent type. C++ *virtual member functions* provide this behavior.

6.4.1 Virtual functions and polymorphic behavior

A class's protected members give it an interface for its derived classes. Virtual member functions give the derived class an interface accessible to anything that knows the object by its base class type. Since one of any number of derived classes may be accessed through one type's interface, it is called *polymorphic*. This kind of polymorphism distinguishes Object-Oriented programming from programming with Objects.

Virtual member functions are inherited from a base class:

```
#include <iostream.h>

class   A_day
{
  public:
        virtual ostream& have( ostream& ) const;
};
ostream&
A_day::have( ostream& o ) const
{
        return o << "Have a day.";
}
```

```
A_day ad;

  ad.have( cout ) << "\n";          // Prints
                                    //      Have a day.(\n)
```

A_day::have() is declared *virtual.* By itself this does not change the behavior of A_day. (It does enable checked casts and RTTI for the class; see Sec. 6.3.3.4 and Chap. 7, Sec. 7.10.)

The effect of an inherited virtual function is seen when a derived class overrides the virtual member function:

```
class A_nice_day
  : public A_day
{
  public:
        ostream& have( ostream& ) const;
};
```

A_nice_day::have() overrides A_day::have(). *Because the base class function is virtual, all derived class functions which override it* and *match its signature will also be virtual.*

```
ostream&
A_nice_day::have( ostream& o ) const
{
        return o << "Have a NICE day." ;
}
      ... ...

        A_day a_d;
        A_nice_day a_n_d;

        a_d.have( cout ) << "\n";       //     Have a day.(\n)
        a_n_d.have( cout ) << "\n";     //     Have a NICE
                                        //     day.(\n)
```

No surprise here. But let's wrap it in a function that hides the exact type:

```
ostream&
operator<<( ostream& o, const A_day& a )
{
        return a.have( o );
}
```

This operator knows its second argument only by the base class A_day. Were have() an ordinary member function, this operator would always print Have a day\n.

But this is a virtual member function, and *a virtual member function is called according to the exact type,* not the apparent type:

```
cout << a_d << "\n";     // Operator << calls
                         //   a_d.have() which is
                         //   A_day::have(), which
                         //   prints
                         //      Have a day.

cout << a_n_d << "\n";   // Operator << calls
                         //   a_n_d.have() which is
                         //   *virtual*, meaning that
                         //   the operator's 'a.have()'
                         //   calls A_nice_day::have()
                         //   for A_nice_day objects,
                         //   printing
                         //      Have a NICE day.
```

A call to a virtual member function is managed by the object itself, identifies the correct version of the member function, and calls that function. A virtual member function associates with the complete object, and with the exact type.

If the derived class does not override a virtual function, it inherits that function from its base class, just as for an ordinary member function. (See Sec. 6.4.2 for an exception in certain versions of C++.)

```
class   A_dull_day
  : public A_day
{ };

        cout << A_dull_day() << "\n";   // Uses A_day::have()
                                        //   and prints
                                        //      Have a day.(\n)
```

(For name clashes that can occur with multiple base classes, see Chap. 7, Sec. 7.1.2.)

When a derived class overrides a virtual function, the override also becomes virtual. The derived class may include the `virtual` keyword, but it does not have to.

The base class version of a virtual function knows that it is a member of the base class, and has access to the base class members. The derived class version of that function knows that it is a member of the derived class, and has access to its own members, and to the public and protected parts of the base class.

```
class   A_variable_day
  : public A_dull_day
{
  public:
        A_variable_day( const char* c = 0 )
          : day_type( c )
        { };

        /*
         *      Here we include the redundant 'virtual' .
         */
        virtual ostream& have( ostream& o ) const;

  private:
        const char* const day_type;
};

ostream&
A_variable_day::have( ostream& o ) const
{
        return o << "Have a " <<
                ( c ? c : "--BLANK--" ) << " day." ;
}
      ... ...

        A_variable_day a_v_d( "Humpty-Dumpty" );

        cout << a_v_d
                << "\n";    // Prints
                            //   Have a Humpty-Dumpty day.(\n)
```

Neither the insertion operator nor `A_day` know about the derived class's member `c`. It belongs to `A_variable_day`, and it is used when by `A_variable_day` is invoked for `a_v_d`.

Operator member functions may be virtual (on the LHS operand, if they are binary); likewise operator conversions.

Sometimes the virtual behavior must be overruled. The common case is that of a derived class function needing to use it's corresponding function in the base class. To overrule the virtual function mechanism, qualify the class explicitly:

```
class   A_double_day
  : public A_day
{
  public:
        ... ...
```

```
        ostream& have( ostream& o ) const;

        ... ...
  private:
        A_variable_day another;
};

ostream&
A_double_day::have( ostream& o )
{
        A_day::have( o );       // Calls the base class function
                                //   for our base class object.
        another.have( o );      // Calls the base class function
                                //   for our member.
}
```

Here's some plausible output from this example:

```
Have a day.
Have another a day.
```

The base class must provide a virtual interface that makes sense for its derived classes. They must provide the same 'operation' as the base class, but in a different flavor. What constitutes a different operation and what constitutes a different flavor depends on the types involved, and in particular upon what they represent. The program designer and programmer *must* without fail have a clear, simple, complete definition of what this is, and they must communicate it to those who work on the program, and they must write the classes around that definition.

6.4.2 Pointer-to-member and overriding

When a virtual member function is invoked through a pointer-to-member (Chap. 2, Sec. 2.7.1), it is not possible to overrule the virtual function call mechanism:

```
ostream&
A_double_day::anyfun( ostream& o,
                ostream* (A_double_day::*fun) ( ostream& ) )
{
      (this->A_day::*fun) ( o );  //Illegal!  Not only
                                  //    is there no syntax
                                  //    to allow this, the
                                  //    compiler doesn't
                                  //    have the information
                                  //    to support it.
       ... ...
       (another.*fun) ( o );      // Ok.
}
```

6.4.3 Pure virtual functions and abstract classes

A class's virtual member functions define the services common to it and its derived classes. Sometimes the base class is meant to define the services, but not to actually provide them. Such a base class shouldn't be created as a complete object and it shouldn't be asked at run time to provide those services.

Beginning in C++ Release 2.0, a class may declare that it may not be used to declare a complete object by making one or more of its virtual member functions *pure*. A class with pure virtual functions is called an *abstract* class:

```
class   A_pure_day
  : public A_day
{
  public:
        virtual ostream& have( ostream& ) const = 0;
};
```

The `= 0` defines `A_pure_day::have()` as pure. The program need not provide an implementation for a pure function, and often will not. In that case, C++ will create a version of the function that will cause a run-time error if called. (Officially, the behavior is 'undefined'; an ANSI/ISO C++ implementation will probably throw an exception in this case.) (In Release 2.0, the program *may not* provide an implementation of a pure virtual function.)

Because an `A_pure_day` may only be created as a base class, and not as a complete object, it can be called only by explicit qualification (`A_pure_day::have(` *ostream* `)`) (Sec. 6.4.1) or by mistake from a constructor (Sec. 6.4.5). This makes sense for virtual functions whose base class version is 'incomplete,' but which provides facilities that derived classes will need.

In C++ Release 2.0, any class inheriting a pure virtual member function must either override it or redeclare it as pure. In later versions this isn't required; the pure virtual member function can simply be inherited.

An abstract class may have no complete objects, but there may be pointers and references to the class and they may point at derived class objects:

```
A_pure_day pure_daily_func( A_pure_day );        // Illegal!
A_pure_day* p2_pure_daily_func( A_pure_day& );  // Legal.
```

6.4.4 Virtual and inline

A virtual function may be declared `inline`. Where the compiler is sure of the exact type of the object, it is free to make the calls inline. Generally this occurs only when the object is locally declared, and is accessed itself, not through any pointer or reference.

6.4.5 Constructors and destructors

When a derived class object is constructed, it is built 'from the base upwards,' with the 'innermost' (least derived) base class the first thing built. (This is more complicated under multiple inheritance; see Chap. 7, Sec. 7.3). While a base class is being built, the object *is* an object of the base class, and nothing more. Then, once construction of the derived part begins, the object becomes a derived class object.

If a virtual function call is made directly or indirectly from the base class constructor, it will activate the virtual function *appropriate to its type at the moment.* If the functions have side effects, this can be seen easily:

```
/*
 *      Assume that these constructors are declared in their
 *      respective classes:
 */

A_day::A_day( ostream& o )
{
        have( o << "Building ''" ) << "''\n";
}

A_nice_day::A_nice_day( ostream& o )
  :A_day( o )
{
        have( o << "Building ''" ) << "''\n";
}

A_nice_day a_n_d( cout );
```

In this example, while `A_day` is being built, the exact type of `a_n_d` is `A_day`. Once `A_day` is completed, the exact type is adjusted to `A_nice_day`. Then the output produced by the declaration is

```
Building ''Have a day.''
Building ''Have a NICE day.''
```

Destructors operate in reverse. If these destructors are declared in the class header and defined thus:

```
A_day::~A_day()
{
        have( cout << "Razing ''" ) << "''\n";
}
```

```
A_nice_day::~A_nice_day()
{
        have( cout << "Razing ''" ) << "''\n";
}
```

the output upon destruction of a_n_d is

```
Razing ''Have a NICE day.''
Razing ''Have a day.''
```

This property can lead to accidental calls of pure virtual functions that are not defined:

```
class   An_abstract_day
{
  public:
        An_abstract_day( ostream& );
        ostream& have( ostream& ) const = 0;
};

class   A_tangible_day
  : public An_abstract_day
{
  public:
        A_tangible_day( ostream& );
        ostream& have( ostream& ) const;
};

ostream&
operator<<( ostream& o, const An_abstract_day& a )
{
        return a.have( o );
}

An_abstract_day( ostream& o )
{
        o << *this;
}

A_tangible_day( ostream& o )
  : An_abstract_day( o )
{
        o << *this;
}
    ... ...
```

```
A_tangible_day a_t_d( cout );   // Whuppps !!
                        //   This calls
                        // A_tangible_day::A_tangible_day()
                        //  Which calls
                        // An_abstract_day::An_abstract_day()
                        //  to build the base part of the
                        //  class and the base class function,
                        //  Which calls
                        // ostream& operator<<( ostream&, string )
                        //  which calls the pure virtual function
                        // An_abstract_day::have ( ostream& )
```

This is illegal. The result of such a call is presently undefined. A specific implementation may ignore the call, or translate it into a run-time error, or even into an exception which is thrown (Chap. 9) and which may be caught. The ANSI/ISO C++ committee may leave it undefined, or it might specify an exception to be thrown.

6.4.6 Virtual destructors

When we destroy an object, we must destroy it by its exact type.

```
    void one_use( A_day*, ostream& );

    one_use( new A_variable_day( "bodacious" ) );
  ... ...

void
one_use( A_day* no_deposit_no_return, ostream& o )
{
        o << no_deposit_no_return << "\n" ;

        delete no_deposit_no_return;    // Do we use
                        //   A_variable_day::~A_variable_day()
                        //   or A_day::~A_day()  ???
}
```

If we destroy only the apparent type, we will not execute the correct destructor, and we may also corrupt the free store system. To correct this, we make the destructor for `A_day` virtual. (Its derived classes inherit the virtual destructor, and their destructors are also virtual.)

In general, *any class that has any virtual functions should have a virtual destructor.* Virtual functions indicate that polymorphic behavior will be used, and code which exercises polymorphic behavior may lose track of the exact types of objects that it must destroy.

```
class   A_day
{
  public:
          … …
          virtual "A_day();
          … …
};
```

Why not simply declare all destructors (and all functions) virtual?

Virtual function calls have a small overhead. It's cheaper than almost any alternative you could program, but it is not zero. Further, any class which has any virtual functions must have some extra data hidden inside it (Sec. 6.5), making the object bigger. If the object is small and simple (e.g., `class Complex`), the price may be excessive. Also, a non-derived struct with no virtual members can have the same memory layout as a matching C struct, allowing C++ to share data structures with C code. If there are virtual functions, C++ cannot do this.

6.4.7 `new` and `delete` as (static) member functions

Class-by-class `new`, `new[]`, `delete`, and `delete[]` are implemented by static operator member functions (Chap. 5, Sec. 5.5.4). They are inherited just like any other members. If a base class `new`, `new[]`, `delete`, or `delete[]` operator is called for a derived class, it will be passed the appropriate size parameter(s) for the derived class.

In general, an object allocated by `X::operator new()` should be deleted by `X::operator delete()`, and not by `Y::operator delete()`. But if `X` is derived from `Y`, an `X` object may be known as a `Y` when it is deleted:

```
class   Y
{
          … …
};

class   X
  : public Y
{
          … …
};
     … …

          Y* wye_pea = new X( … … );

          … …

          delete wye_pea;
```

Selecting the correct `delete` is as important to polymorphism as selecting the correct destructor. The circumstances that call for virtual behavior for `operator delete` are exactly those that call for a virtual destructor.

C++ distinguishes between `operator delete` and the `delete` operator. In the last example we invoke the `delete` operator. In response, C++ calls a version of `operator delete()`, either the global operator or a static member operator. The invocation of `operator delete()` is tied into the call of the class's destructor. *If the destructor is virtual, then the call of* `operator delete()` *will behave as though it too is virtual,* and the appropriate free store operator will be called.

6.4.8 Pointer arithmetic and pointer-to-base

An object identified by a pointer has the apparent type of the pointer, but may have a different exact type. With inheritance, this is not only possible, but likely. With a pointer used for polymorphism, we know neither the exact type nor the precise size of the object.

C and C++ permit pointer arithmetic, assuming that the type of a pointer describes the pointer's length. Pointers may be moved around in arrays by adding and subtracting integers which are scaled by the pointers' lengths.

These two models contradict each other. Pointer arithmetic is safe only if (1) the pointer remains inside a homogeneous array, *and* (2) the pointer's exact type is the type of the array element. Polymorphic behavior is useful only if a pointer's apparent and exact types may differ.

Neither model can be discarded. C++ needs both polymorphism and pointer arithmetic. *It is up to the programmer to know whether the pointer at hand can be used for pointer arithmetic or not.*

6.4.9 Polymorphism and copy semantics

Destructors can be virtual; constructors cannot be. If virtual constructors were supported, they could provide a way around the slicing problem (Sec. 6.3.3.3). What we must do instead is this:

```
class   Copy_it_right
{
  public:
        Copy_it_right( const Copy_it_right& );
        virtual Copy_it_right* copy() const
        {       return new Copy_it_right( *this );     };
        ... ...
};
```

```
class   Copy_it_left
  : public Copy_it_right
  {
   public:
          Copy_it_left( const Copy_it_left& );
          virtual Copy_it_right* copy() const
          {        return new Copy_it_left( *this );        };
          … …
  };

class   Copy_it_up
  : public Copy_it_right
  {
   public:
          Copy_it_up( const Copy_it_up& );
          virtual Copy_it_right* copy() const
          {        return new Copy_it_up( *this ); };
          … …
  };
```

This has a serious problem: the derived class *must* define the `Copy_it_right`. The burden of the interface falls on every derived class. This cries out for some kind of "metaclass" facility. C++ templates (Chap. 8) do *not* answer this need. There have been proposals for facilities that would, by giving classes some of the properties of templates. To date, none of these has been shown to be simple to use, simple to learn, properly orthogonal to the rest of C++, and simple enough to be implemented somehow.

Assignment operators are created implicitly or explicitly for each class, not inherited. A class can invoke a base class's assignment explicitly:

```
this->my_base::operator=( that_other_object );
```

A larger issue lurks behind both initialization and assignment. What constitutes correct copying of the "object"? If it has a tree beneath it, do we copy the entire tree, or do we simply create an extra reference to the tree? These are called 'deep copy' and 'shallow copy,' respectively. The answer must be "it depends." It depends on what the object represents in the program's model and design; it depends also on how the representation is designed and implemented. Whether copy even makes sense depends intimately upon what relationships the object has with entities within and without the program. See also Chap. 3, Sec. 3.1.5.

Some programming languages or environments favor one copy semantic or the another. A language or environment with Garbage Col-

Section 6.6 C++ lends itself to certain uses and certain styles of use. It is well suited to design and programming approaches that stress planning and understanding. It requires some discipline to avoid confusing the problem and the solution. It can express both, and in a typical program, it will express both. Different aspects of problem and solution do tend to appear in different, recognizable ways. And while C++ supports techniques that support reuse, it cannot automatically guarantee reusability.

Section 6.7 *Double dispatching* and *multimethods* are programming language capabilities that extend virtualization across multiple classes. C++ does not support them; they can be simulated (kludged) in simple cases.

Chapter

7

Multiple Inheritance

Overview

This chapter generalizes the Single Inheritance in Chap. 6 into Multiple Inheritance (inheritance from more than one base class). Chapter 6 explains how one class is *derived* from another and how the derived class *inherits* members from its base class. This chapter assumes that the details of this feature are established and do not need explanation.

Many of the examples in this chapter will seem artificial or strained. This has two causes: first, that Multiple Inheritance (MI) is usually used with much larger problems and examples and second, that the good and bad uses of MI are still not entirely understood. (But see Sec. 7.11 for some criteria by which to judge.)

Multiple Inheritance was introduced with Release 2.0 of C++. Some of the features described here are not yet part of C++, but are under very serious consideration by the ANSI/ISO committee, and are presented in anticipation of their adoption.

7.1 What Multiple Inheritance Means

A derived class inherits the interface and members of its base classes. When there are several base classes, the new class inherits the interfaces and members of all of them *and gains the ability to coordinate their behavior* so that one object behaves both as a single, unified object and as a set of separate, cooperating objects.

7.1.1 Multiple base classes

Multiple Inheritance combines the inherited public and protected interfaces of two or more base classes:

```
class   Param_canvas
  : public Display_canvas;
{
        … …
        virtual Data set_field( const char* fieldname,
                                const Data& val );
        … …
};
class   Gauge_display
  : public Gauge, public Param_canvas, public Window
{
        … …
        Data load( Data );              // Overrides virtual
                                        //   Gauge::load( Data );

        Window& load( const Display_canvas& dc )  // Overrides the
        {  return Window::load( dc ); };          //   member of Window
                                                  //   that it calls.

        … …
        int set_image( Param_image );     // Overrides virtual
                                          //   Param_canvas::
                                          //    set_image( Param_image );
        … …
        int frame( Extent );              // Overrides virtual
                                          //   frame( Extent ) in BOTH
                                          //    Window  and  Param_canvas
        … …
};
```

These classes might operate an industrial plant control system's 'glass console,' whose instruments are images on a screen—or a simulator whose glass console can model any one of many plants.

The member functions override virtual functions in the various base classes, and coordinate them so that the three base class objects work together:

```
/*
 *      To update the display gauge with a value uploaded
 *      from a sensor, load the gauge, set the parameter
 *      into the image canvas, load the window from the
 *      image canvas, and then update the window.
 */
Data
Gauge_display::load( Data d )
{
        Gauge::load( d );          // First bring the gauge up to date,
        set_field( "Field.1", d );   Param_canvas::set_field(
                                         const char* fieldname,
                                         Data )
```

```
        Window::load( *this );
        display();                                  Window::display()

        return Gauge::value();
}

/*
 *      When readjusting the window, we have to repaint the
 *      whole gauge image.  If the gauge cannot be reframed
 *      in the new size, display the hash pattern.
 */

int
Gauge_display::frame( Extent e )
{
        int ok = Param_canvas::frame( e );

        Window::frame( e );

        Window::load( ok ? *this : hash_canvas );

        display();                  Window::display()

        return ok;
}

/*
 *      When loading a new gauge face, we have to set the fields
 *      and load the face into the window.  Again, if it cannot
 *      be loaded for some reason we use the hash pattern.
 */
int
Gauge_display::set_image( Param_image pi )
{
        if( ! Param_canvas::set_image( pi ) );
                Window::load( hash_canvas );
        else
        {
                set_field( "Field.1",             Param_canvas::
                        Gauge::value() );               set_field( const
                                                        char* fieldname,
                                                        Data)

                Window::load( *this );
        }
        display();                  Window::display()
}
```

Each of these member functions of `Gauge_display` routes its 'request' to the corresponding base class, then directs the other base classes to accomodate the change.

This is the unique capability of Multiple Inheritance. It can be simulated under single inheritance only by programming relationships between classes and engineering close cooperation between them.

The `public` access specifiers are written explicitly for the three base classes. Omitting them is a common error:

```
class   Gauge_display
  : public Gauge, Param_canvas, Window
{
          ... ...
};
```

C++ will read it thus:

```
class   Gauge_display
  : public Gauge, private Param_canvas, private Window
{
          ... ...
};
```

Each base class needs its own access specifier. A missing specifier is taken to be private. Some releases issue a warning when this happens, but ANSI/ISO C++ explicitly allows the missing access specifier in certain cases (if the `virtual` keyword is present—Sec. 7.2), so the compiler cannot always call it an error. It is safest to treat the missing specifier as an error anyway.

7.1.2 Namespace collisions

With multiple base classes, the same name may be inherited from more than one base class. This includes member names, type names *and* base class names. In the previous example, `load()` is inherited from both `Window` and `Gauge`. The two inherited functions have different parameters, and so they cannot be mistaken for each other—but they cannot be used either, unless they are qualified.

`frame()` is also inherited from both `Window` and `Param_canvas`, but both inherited members have the same parameters. One version of `frame()` overrides them both.

We are fortunate in this case (or we have planned carefully); the functionality of both the base class `frame()` functions and of the derived class `frame()` function are the same. This isn't always the case, and it causes major complications:

```
class   Printing_press
  : public Equipment
{
        ... ...
        int print();            // Returns total # of pages.
        ... ...
};

class   Equipment_controller
{
        ... ...
        int print();            // Dump the configuration to
                                //   the diagnosic port; return
                                //   zero if the port does not
                                //   respond.
        ... ...
};

class   Automated_press
  : public Printing_press, public Equipment_controller
{
        ... ...
};

        Automated_press printerator( ... ... );

        printerator.print();    // Error--Ambiguous

        Printing_press& press = printerator;
        press.print();          // Legal: Printing_press::
                                //   print() (Roll the presses!)

        Equipment_controller& automator = printerator;
        automator.print();      // Legal: Equipment_controller::
                                //   print() (Tell us what
                                //   you're doing.)
```

Additional things happen when the derived class overrides such member functions. See Sec. 7.6.

7.1.3 Conversion ambiguities

Conversions of *Multiple_Derived** to *Base_n** and from *Multiple_Derived&* to *Base_n&* work as they do under single inheritance (Chap. 6, Sec. 6.3.3), except that Multiple Inheritance creates an additional opportunity for ambiguity:

```
class   Wind
  : public Aeolus, public Notus, public Eurus, public Zephyr
{
        ... ...
};

        Aeolus& sow( Aeolus* );
        Eurus& sow( Eurus* );
        Notus& sow( Notus* );
        Zephyr& sow( Zephyr* );
                ... ...

        Wind fourwinds;

        sow( &fourwinds );      // Ambiguous!

        sow( (Aeolus*) &fourwinds );    // Ok-- North
        sow( (Eurus*) &fourwinds );     // Ok-- East
        sow( (Notus*) &fourwinds );     // Ok-- South
        sow( (Zephyr*) &fourwinds );    // Ok-- West
```

C++ cannot determine, without the cast—or some equivalent syntax—which conversion-to-base class is intended. All four have equal precedence.

Casts such as these are dangerous; they will convert even if there is no legal conversion within the type system. Worse, if this code is correct in version *N*, a change to the type structure in version $N + 1$ could render it invalid—without causing any compiler warnings.

Such coercions are liable to lead, sooner or later, to addressing errors. The ANSI/ISO C++ committee is examining alternatives, including three new and distinct conversion forms (Chap. 3, Sec. 3.4.2). The casts in the `Winds` example correspond to the `static_cast< >()` of Sec. 3.4.2: convert only if there is a known safe conversion within the type system.

Where possible, such ambiguities should be avoided and not merely resolved. Where it is not possible, `static_cast< >()` will be the correct solution.

7.1.4 Dynamic conversions, RTTI, and exceptions

In Chap. 6, Sec. 6.3.3.4 we saw that MI removes one of Single Inheritance's guarantees: Under SI, if one type has two base types, one of those base types is derived from the other, directly or indirectly, and the more derived will 'know' about the less derived, and permit pointer and reference conversions from itself back to the less derived.

Under MI, this does not hold. In the example of Sec. 7.1.2, we saw how both `Printing_press` and `Equipment_controller` could be base classes of `Automated_press` without either of the base classes 'knowing' of the other. (See Fig. 7.1.)

Then if an `Automated_Press` is known by a pointer or reference to either one of its base classes, that pointer points to an object with a base class unknown to it:

```
Automated_press printerator( … … );

Printing_press* press_p = &printerator;
            //  press_p  points to a  Printing_press  and
            //    knows it.  press_p  also points to an
            //    Equipment_controller  and does NOT know it.

Equipment_controller& automator = printerator;
            //  automator  names an  Equipment_controller
            //    and knows it.  automator  also names a
            //    Printing_press  and does NOT know it.
```

In C and C++, any pointer-to-object can be cast to any type. We might try one of these:

```
Equipment_controller* ec_from_pp =
                        (Equipment_controller*) press_p;
Printing_press& pp_from_ec =
                        (Printing_press&) automator;
```

These won't work properly because neither type has the inheritance information needed to 'adjust' the pointers (either explicit or internal to the reference) to point to the correct base class object within the Automated_press. It is for this case that the *dynamic_cast* is proposed. (This is one of the three described in Chap. 3, Sec. 3.4.2.)

```
Equipment_controller* ec_from_pp =
        dynamic_cast< Equipment_controller* >( press_p );
                        //  Attempt a run-time conversion
                        //    of  press_p  from
                        //    Printing_Press*  to
                        //    Equipment_controller*

/*
 *      The conversion will return the null pointer if the
 *      object at which press_p points isn't also an
 *      Equipment_controller
```

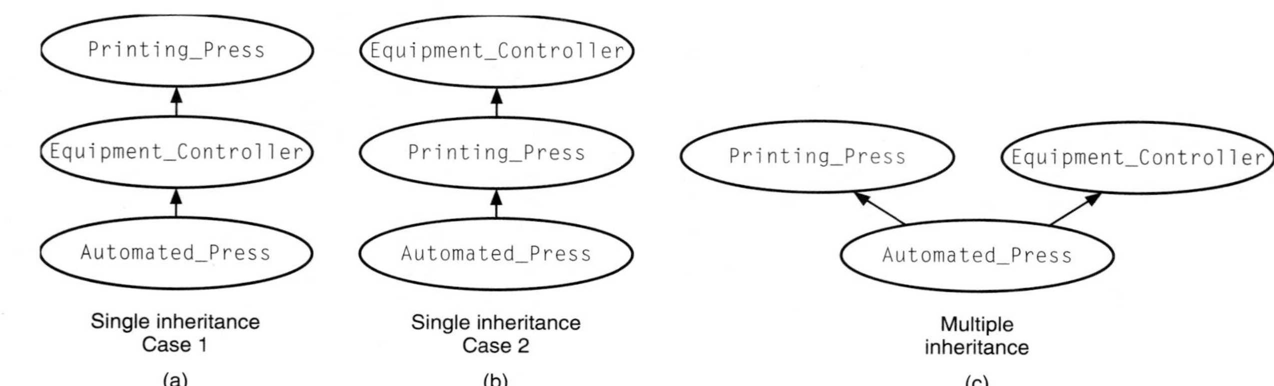

Figure 7.1 (Arrows from derived class to base class symbolize the derived class's use of base class facilities.)

```
*/
if( ! ec_from_pp )
{
        ... ...
}

Printing_press& pp_from_ec =
                dynamic_cast< Printing_press& >( automator );
                        //  Attempt a run-time conversion
                        //    of  automator  from
                        //    Equipment_controller&
                        //    to  Printing_press&

/*
 *      If the object named by  automator  is not also a
 *      Printing_press , the conversion will fail by throwing
 *      an exception.  Unless we do something special here,
 *      this part of the thread of execution will be
 *      abandoned on that failure.
 */
```

(As of this writing, this is still a proposal before the ANSI/ISO committee, albeit one with a stellar chance of acceptance. The need for it is recognized by several influential members of that committee. Consult your reference manual for the final word.)

`dynamic_cast` is allowed only if there is at least one virtual function in the object. It will only allow conversions involving public base classes (i.e., it will not violate the access declarations). It's implemented using the 'Run-Time Type Identification' (*RTTI*) system described in Sec. 7.10.2.

When a dynamic conversion involving pointers fails, a null pointer is returned. When a dynamic conversion involving references fails, an exception (whose name is not yet determined) is thrown. This means that the execution of this code is abandoned. It resumes with the smallest enclosing scope that is willing to catch and handle the exception. That smallest scope may be in the function that called this function, or in the function that called that function, or anywhere in the 'stack' of function activations that led to this point. If nothing is willing to handle the exception, the program will terminate. The throwing, catching, and handling of exceptions is described in Chap. 9.

The behavior of a dynamic conversion is undefined if the pointer is not null and does not point to an object of the type to which it is declared to point, or if the object named by the reference is not a valid object of the correct type. Put differently, the pointer or reference value given to a dynamic cast must be a valid value for that pointer or reference type.

7.2 Ordinary and Virtual MI

Multiple Inheritance creates design decisions not possible under Single Inheritance:

```
class   A
{  ... ... };

class   M
  : public A
{  ... ... };

class   N
  : public A
{  ... ... };

class   Y
  : public M, public N
{  ... ... };


    ... ...

        Y wye_indeed( ... ... );

        A* ap = &wye_indeed;     // Ambiguous!

        A* am = static_cast< M* >( &wye_indeed );
                                  // Get access to the  A  part of
                                  //    the  M  part of  wye_indeed .
        //  (M*) &wye_indeed   -- Use this expression until the
        //                        static_cast< >() becomes available.

        A* an = static_cast< N* >( &wye_indeed );
                                  // Get access to the  A  part of
                                  //   the  N  part of  wye_indeed .

        // (N*) &wye_indeed;   -- Use this expression until the
        //                        static_cast< >() becomes available.
```

First we have an ambiguity; the initialization of ap is illegal because there are two different incomplete instances of A buried in the derivation of Y. We correct the ambiguity by introducing intermediate, explicit conversions—static casts if they are available, otherwise C pointer casts.

Then we have a question: Is this what we really want? If A, M, N, and Y are Account, Checking_account, Savings_account, and Customer_account, then it makes all the sense in the world. (See Fig. 7.2.)

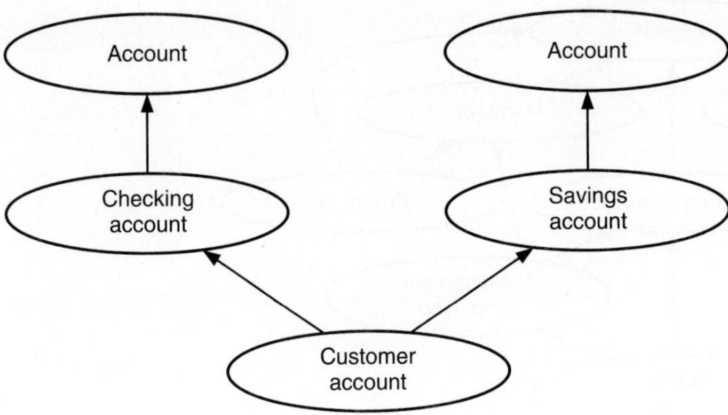

Figure 7.2

7.2.1 Base classes for the complete object

But if instead `A`, `M`, `N`, and `Y` are `Person`, `Manager`, `Engineer`, and `Senior_Engineer` (who is both `Engineer` and `Manager`), it's all wrong; what we need is shown in Fig. 7.3.

To make things more interesting, we may wish to include `Consulting Engineer` and the `Proprietor`. These folks are not employees; if we have carelessly put employee information in with `Person`, we have to move it out, as shown in Fig. 7.4.

The diagram of Fig. 7.4 contains the dangerous assumption that all employees are persons. Come the day that computers become sentient—or at least smart enough to work for pay—this assumption will depend on whether they are considered persons. (That day seems far enough off, but the assumption should always be stated.)

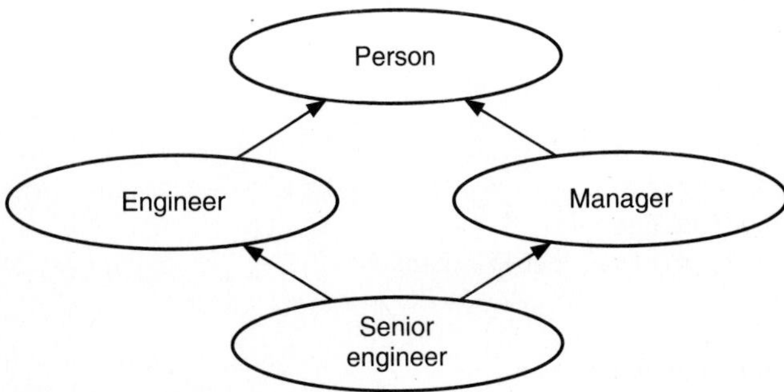

Figure 7.3

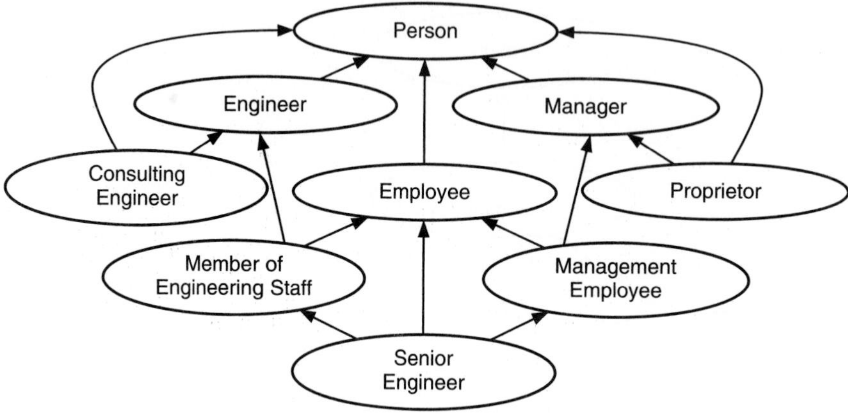

Figure 7.4

For this application, we don't want a `Person` to be constructed once in everything that represents a person; just one `Person` object per complete object is all we need and want.

C++ can do this. Recall that a virtual function belongs to the exact type and the complete object, not to the apparent type and an incomplete object. By analogy, a *virtually inherited base class* (or *virtual base class*) belongs to the complete object:

```
class   Person
{  ... ...  };

class   Engineer
  : virtual public Person
{  ... ...  };

class   Manager
  : virtual public Person
{  ... ...  };

class   Employee
  : virtual public Person
{  ... ...  };

class   Consulting_Engineer
  : public Engineer, virtual public Person
{  ... ...  };

class   Member_Engineering_Staff
  : public Engineer, virtual public Employee
{  ... ...  };
```

```
class   Management_Employee
  : public Engineer, virtual public Employee
{  … …  };

class   Senior_Engineer
  : public Member_Engineering_Staff, public Management_Employee,
    virtual public Employee
{  … …  };
```

For Single Inheritance, the inheritance graph is linear. For ordinary Multiple Inheritance, a type's inheritance graph is a tree with the edges pointing away from the most-derived 'root' and towards the base class(es). With Virtual Inheritance added, the inheritance graph can rejoin. It is no longer a tree but a 'directed acyclic graph' or *DAG*. In some programming languages, all types belong to a single, connected inheritance graph. In C++, there may be many separate subgraphs, each with a few types, or just one, or many. (The built-in types are never part of these graphs.)

7.2.2 Rules for virtual inheritance

In the bank account example near the beginning of Sec. 7.2, there were two base classes to `Customer_account`, each of which had `Account` for a base class. This code, then, is ambiguous:

```
Account*
extract_account( Customer_account* ca )
{
        return ca;    // Ambiguous: There is no way to tell whether
                      //    this means
                      // Customer_account::Checking_account::Account
                      //    or
                      // Customer_account::Savings_account::Account
}
```

(By the way, this is a poor design for a bank's overall accounts, although it might be useful for an ATM or even a statement generator, things whose view of the system is limited.)

Here's the corresponding code for our 'Engineers and Managers' example:

```
Person*
extract_person( Member_Engineering_Staff* mes )
{
        return mes;  // Unambiguous; because  Person  is
                     //   inherited virtually,
                     // Member_Engineering_Staff::Engineer::
```

```
                        //  Person is the same object as Member_
                        //  Engineering_Staff::Employee::Person
}
```

Although the conversion from a derived class to a virtual base class is always defined and unambiguous, the reverse conversion, from virtual base to derived class, requires run-time information. If the `dynamic_cast< >()` operator (or its equivalent) is available in the version of C++ at hand, and if the type in question has run-time type information available (see Secs. 7.1.4 and 7.4.2), the `dynamic_cast` operator may be used to perform the conversion from a virtual base class to a derived class. If the conversion is illegal, it may fail at run time, as described in Sec. 7.1.4.

Because inheritance graphs are drawn with arcs pointing toward the base class, a conversion from base to derived is often called *downcasting*. (This usage is generic to Object Orientation, not peculiar to C++.)

A class may be inherited both virtually and nonvirtually:

```
class   Basic
{  ... ...  };

class   Virtually_Basic
  : public virtual Basic
{  ... ...  };

class   Mixup1
  : public Basic, public Virtually_Basic
{  ... ...  };

class   Mixup2
  : public Basic, virtual public Virtually_Basic
{  ... ...  };

class   Scramble
  : public Basic, virtual public Virtually_Basic,
    public Mixup1, public Mixup2
{  ... ...  };
```

A diagram is the simplest way to make sense of this tangle. See Fig. 7.5. Such a maze of inheritance over and over on the same types may reflect a poor design—but see Sec. 7.11.

7.3 Multiple Inheritance, Constructors and Destructors

When an object is created or destroyed, its base class subobjects must be created or destroyed with it. For nonvirtual Multiple Inheritance,

```
class   Three_C
  : public C1, public C2
{
  public:
        int sum() const
        { return sum_thing

};
```

As with single inheritance (C
help to resolve ambiguity betw
classes:

```
class   D1
{
  public:
        int f() const;
};

class   D2
{
  public:
        int f( int ) const;
};

class   Two_D
  : public D1, public D2
{
        ... ...
};

int
f( const Two_D& td )
{
        td.f( 77 );      // A
        return td.f();   //
                         //
                         //
}

int
g( const Two_T& td )
{
        if( ! td.D2::f( 0 ) )
                return 0;
```

7.4 Memo

7.4.1 Memo

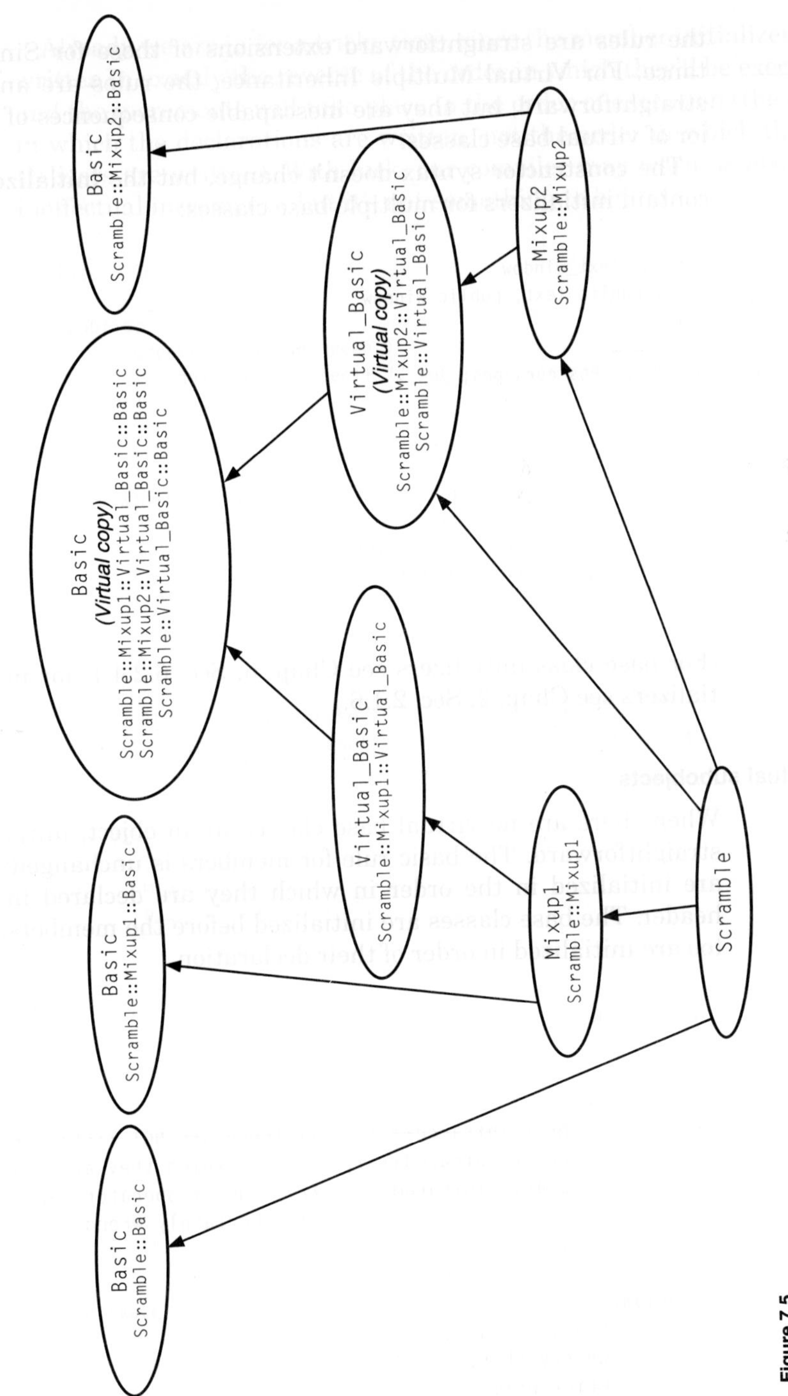

Figure 7.5

```
        else
                return td.D2::f( td.D1::f() );
}
```

7.7 Virtualization and Multiple Inheritance

Virtualization and multiple inheritance together can provide some surprises—which, on examination, should be no surprise at all.

Consider a class which combines management of a process with displayability:

```
class   Operation_buffet
{
  public:
        virtual int suspend();
        virtual int resume();
        ... ...
        virtual ostream& display( ostream& ) const;
        ... ...
};

int      Operation_buffet::suspend()     { return 1; };
int      Operation_buffet::resume()      { return 1; };
ostream& Operation_buffet::display( ostream& os ) const
                                         { return os; };
   ... ...

class   Proc
  : virtual public Operation_buffet
{
  public:
        ... ...
        virtual int suspend() ;
        virtual int resume() ;
        ... ...
};

class   Displayable
  : virtual public Operation_buffet
{
  public:
        ... ...
        ostream& display( ostream& );
        ... ...
};
```

```
class   Display_proc
  : public Proc, public Displayable
{
        … …
};
```

The inheritance diagram (see Fig. 7.13) is almost identical to that of Fig. 7.3.

For a first cut, let's assume that we haven't yet overridden any virtual functions in `Display_proc`.

Now watch carefully:

```
Display_proc disppr( … … );

Display_proc* dspr_p = *disppr;

disppr->suspend();                  // Calls Proc::suspend()
disppr->display( cout ) << endl; // Calls
                                   //   Displayable::display()
Displayable* dyp = dspr_p;        // dyp  points at
                                   //   the  Displayable
                                   //   part of  disppr .
Proc* prp = dspr_p;               // and  prp  points at the
                                   //   Proc  part of  disppr .
                           //  Neither  Proc  nor  Displayable
                           //    inherits from the other ... BUT
dyp->suspend();            //  A call through a  Displayable*
                           //    invokes a member of  Proc ,
                           //    which member doesn't know
                           //    anything about  Proc ...
```

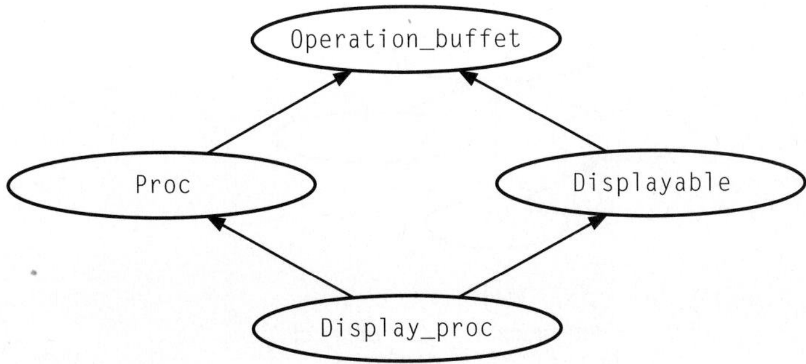

Figure 7.13

```
prp->display( cout ) << endl;    // and . . . a call through
                                 //   a Proc* invokes a member
                                 //   of Displayable , which
                                 //   know as little about Proc
                                 //   as Proc knows about it.
```

There is not a little magic here! But, upon reflection, we see that it must be this way—indeed, virtual base classes were designed to (among other things) provide just this behavior.

Notice that once we override `suspend()`, `resume()`, and `display()` in `Display_proc`, the virtual functions invoked will know about both legs of the inheritance graph—and about both the `Displayable` and `Proc` natures of `Display_proc`.

7.7.1 Dominance

Dominance is the key principal in resolving conflicts between virtual functions that occur when inheriting from several base classes. One instance dominates the other if the first instance overrides the second, directly or indirectly, in the inheritance hierarchy. Unless there is a single dominant instance of a virtual function, there is no way to choose an instance of that function for the complete object. Each virtual function overload must have a single dominant instance or the derived class declaration is in error. (See Fig. 7.14.)

In Fig. 7.14*a*, `B::f()` dominates `A::f()`. `B` is derived from `A`. But there is no dominance relationship between `A::h()` and `D::h()`.

In Fig. 7.14*b*, `B::f()()` dominates `A::f()` because `B` is derived from `A`. `B::h()` also dominates `A::h()` but the fact is valueless because neither does it dominate `D::h()`, nor does `D::h()` dominate `B::h()` (although it does dominate `A::h()`). Without a single dominant instance of the member function, the class declaration is invalid.

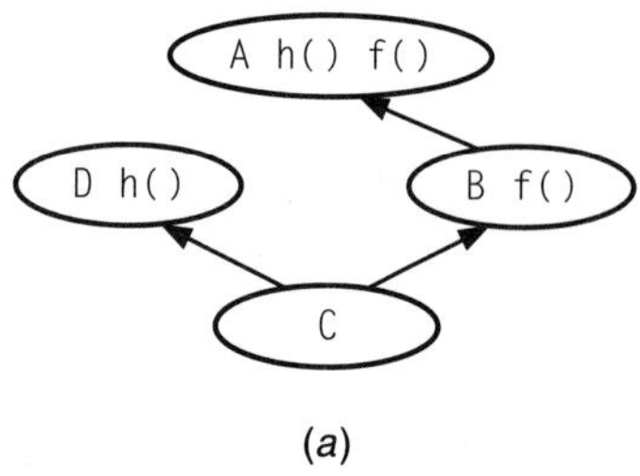

(*a*)
`B::f()` dominates `A::f()`, but neither of `B::h()` nor `D::h()` dominates the other.

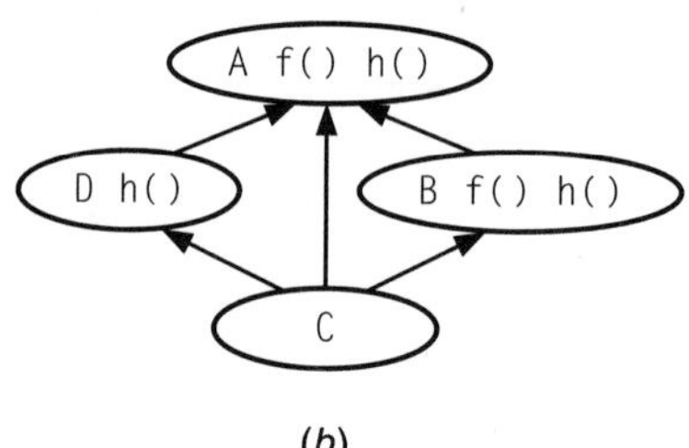

(*b*)
`B::f()` dominates `A::f()`. Either of `B::h()` or `D::h()` dominates `A::h()`, but neither dominates the other.

Figure 7.14

7.7.2 Using the many faces of an object

There are proper uses and there are improper uses of Multiple Inheritance. Just as misuse of pointers leads to Pointer Stew, of the preprocessor to Preprocessor Pudding, and of the class-and-object structure to Type Chutney, so misuse of Multiple Inheritance can curdle into MI Mulligatawny. MI Mulligatawny usually begins as a plausible-looking design and turns into something opaque, incongruous, and indigestible, along the lines of chipped beef with marshmallow fudge and alfalfa sprouts.

Multiple Inheritance is usually not appropriate unless you are bringing together things from several different domains. We use 'domain' here in a broader sense than the Semantic Domain of Chap. 5, Sec. 5.6.3. A domain may be a semantic domain. It may be a larger unit, such as the 'model' of a simulation, as opposed to the scenario of the simulation, as opposed to the tracing or instrumenting of the simulation. It may be a component of a program that models the problem directly, as opposed to a component that implements an algorithm or models some other abstract solution. Or the domain distinction may be the difference between a user's view of the system and a view of the underlying implementation, between the human interface of an ATM machine and the networked transaction system which serves the ATM.

So long as there is a clear distinction rooted in some architectural feature of the problem, the solution, the platforms, or any combination of these, it is probably safe to bind classes from different sides of the distinction together as base classes to another class.

Probably the safest use of multiple inheritance occurs when Semantic Domains offer their services by means of inheritance rather than object creation or function calls. Then a type which needs to use the services of two or more must inherit from several of them.

On virtual inheritance: it is the author's opinion that virtual inheritance is more suited to implementing facilities that support types than it is to modeling problems in the real world. The `Pool` example of Sec. 7.8.3 is such a facility.

One use of Multiple Inheritance deserves mention. It is almost the inverse of a Semantic Domain providing services by Inheritance.

In some programming environments, when an external event occurs, the environment will invoke a prearranged function with a previously stored pointer (typically stored and passed as `void*`).

```
/*
 *      Register a function and an object for alert on an event.
 */
void set_callback( EVENT, void (*) ( void* ), void* );
```

This limited interface can be packaged safely for general-purpose use:

```
/*
 *      Manage and dispatch callbacks.
 *      The actual callback object should be derived from
 *      Dispatch and any other appropriate classes.
 *
 *      When a callback occurs, the environment will call our
 *      static call_alert, which will in turn call the virtual
 *      callback() . This should be overridden to take the action
 *      necessary on the callback.  Since we will have converted
 *      the environment's void*  back into a  Dispatch* , we'll be
 *      typesafe and home free.
 */
class   Dispatch
{
  public:
        ~Dispatch();
        void set_callback( EVENT );
        void clr_callback();

        static void call_alert( void* );        // To be used by the
                                                // environment to
                                                // call us back; it
                                                // doesn't really
                                                // have to be public.
  protected:
        Dispatch()
          : event( E_Idle )
        { };
        virtual void callback() = 0;      // What will _really_
                                          //    happen on callback.

  private:
        Dispatch( const Dispatch& d );  // Disallow copying of the
                                        // callback.

        EVENT event;
};
void
Dispatch::call_alert( void* cb )
{
        if( cb )
                ( (Dispatch*) cb )->callback();
}

void
Dispatch::set_callback( EVENT e )
{
        event = e;
```

```
        ::set_callback( e, &call_alert, (void*) this );
}

void
Dispatch::clr_callback()
{
        ::set_callback( event, 0, 0 );
        event = E_Idle;
}
```

Any class can safely inherit from `Dispatch` and use it to negotiate the callback. An existing class can be 'augmented' for dispatching by deriving a new class from both it and `Dispatch`.

(In `Dispatch::set_callback()`, recall from Chap. 2, Sec. 2.7.1 that taking the address of a static member function yields an ordinary pointer-to-function.)

7.8 Virtual MI and Operations on Incomplete Objects

The 'memberwise' operations (default constructor, compiler-generated copy constructor, and assignment) map naturally onto ordinary multiple inheritance: the various subobjects are initialized or assigned in the order specified in Sec. 7.3. All the rules of Chap. 2, Sec. 2.1.7 and Chap. 6, Sec. 6.2.4.2 apply, and the caveats of Sec. 2.1.8 are even more important with multiple base classes and additional possibilities for relationships and dependencies.

Virtual inheritance, however, creates serious difficulties. The constructors are managed properly by C++, and so is default assignment. But a programmer-written assignment operator faces the same difficulties that inherited member functions face.

7.8.1 Orchestrating base class cooperation

We will consider nonvirtual base classes first.

For assignment operators and constructors provided by C++, the recursive 'memberwise' rules apply. Often, a member function or operator must be applied in a memberwise fashion. C++ has no way to declare that a compiler is to apply memberwise rules for any new functions or operators. Diagnostic operations like "print" or "dump" often fall into this category; so do transformations on graphical objects:

```
class   Gr_Object
{
  public:
        ... ...
        virtual Gr_Obj& transform( const Transform& );
        ... ...
```

```
  private:
        Point loc;
        Point extent;
};

class   Linked_Gr_Object
  : public Gr_Object
{
        virtual Linked_Gr_Object& transform( const Transform& );
        ... ...
  private:
        Gr_Object* next;
        ... ...
};

Gr_Object&
Gr_Object::transform( const Transform& tr )
{
        loc = tr.position( loc );       // Position, rotation,
                                        // and scaling.
        extent = tr.displacement( loc, extent ); // Rotation and
                                                 // scaling.

        return *this;
}

/*
 *      The use of a derived type instead of the original type as
 *      the return value type of a virtual function is an
 *      anticipated ANSI/ISO feature--see Sec. 6.3.4 on Covariant
 *      Return Types. Until then, don't try this at /home.
 */

Linked_Gr_Object&
Linked_Gr_Object::transform( const Transform& tr )
{
        Gr_Object::transform( tr );     // Apply the transform to
                                        //   our base class ...

        if( next )
                next->transform( tr );  // . . . and then to
                                        //   our dependent.

        return *this;
}
```

Managing this cooperation in the absence of virtual bases isn't tricky, just tedious.

7.8.2 Managing the virtual base interactions

In this section, we will demonstrate the problem faced by user-defined assignment operators. The same techniques apply to other member functions and operators as well.

All of the basic problems facing assignment still exist. In particular, multiple inheritance provides more opportunities for accidentally 'slicing' objects on assignment or copy (Chap. 6, Sec. 6.3.3.3).

The peculiar problem of a virtual base class is that the virtual base class belongs to the complete object, but there is no way for a given class to determine if it represents a complete object or not. If we could, we might write something like this:

```
const Mult_derived&
Mult_derived::operator=( const Mult_derived& md )
{
        if( this == &md )
                return *this;

        if( i_am_complete() )
        {
                vBase_1::operator=( md );  // Use Mult_derived::vBase_1
                vBase_2::operator=( md );  // Use Mult_derived::vBase_2
        }

        nvBase_1::operator=( md );
        nvBase_2::operator=( md );
        nvBase_3::operator=( md );

        mem1 = md.m1;

        mem2 = md.m2;
        mem2->ref++;

        return *this;
}
```

Lacking some kind of `i_am_complete()`, we must kludge a solution. The kludge is to write two 'assignments' for every class. One is the `operator=()`; the other is named something like `assign()`.

```
class Mult_derived
  : public virtual vBase_1, public virtual vBase_2,
    public nvBase_1, public nvBase_2
{
  public:
        /*
         *      The assignment operator is called from the
```

```
         *      outside world; it assumes that we are a
         *      complete object.
         */
        const Mult_derived operator=( const Mult_derived& );
        ... ...
    protected:
        ... ...
        /*
         *      assign() is called from derived classes (and
         *      from the assignment operator); it assumes
         *      that it is dealing with an incomplete object
         *      (so it is not responsible for the virtual
         *      bases).
         */
        void assign( const Mult_derived& );
        ... ...
};

const Mult_derived&
Mult_derived::operator=( const Mult_derived& md )
{
        if( this == &md )
                return *this;

        /*
         *      Do the virtual bases ...
         */
        vBase_1::assign( md );  // Use Mult_derived::vBase_1
        vBase_2::assign( md );  // Use Mult_derived::vBase_2

        /*
         *      ... and then do the incomplete object stuff.
         */
        assign( md );

        return *this;
}

/*
 *      Since we are only to be called for an incomplete
 *      object, we worry neither about the virtuals nor about
 *      assignment to ourselves; that is the province of
 *      operator=() .
 */
void
Mult_derived::assign( const Mult_derived& md )
{
```

```
        nvBase_1::assign( md );     // Use md::nvBase_1
        nvBase_2::assign( md );     // Use md::nvBase_2
        nvBase_3::assign( md );     // Use md::nvBase_3

        mem1 = md.m1;

        mem2 = md.m2;
        mem2->ref++;
}
```

Refer to Fig. 7.15.

This solution requires that all virtual bases be declared in the most derived class, or else that the assignment operator know about those that are not, and explicitly invoke `assign()` for those base classes. This is potentially vulnerable to changes deep in the inheritance graph, so changes to an inheritance graph involving virtual inheritance should be made with the greatest care.

Such brittleness in the structure of a program is asking for trouble. The situation may be less damaging than it seems. If a virtual base class is being used to manage some aspect of an object's representation (e.g., providing storage allocation, central resource tracking, etc.), assignment for that class may make no sense. In that case, `assign()` for that class can be defined as an empty (null) function.

If `assign()` is a null function, and especially if it is inline, there is no harm in invoking it repeatedly. If so, it doesn't matter how many times it does or does not get invoked out of the inheritance hierarchy; derived classes can simply ignore it. (But this behavior should be carefully described in the class's design documents, and echoed in the class's comments!)

7.8.3 The memory pool: an example of programming with virtual inheritance

One way to speed up the allocation of memory is to create pools of memory chunks of the sizes most often needed. In a program which rapidly allocates and deallocates large numbers of linked records, allocating from and returning to such a pool can be dozens of times faster than allocating from a general-purpose 'heap.'

To use it, we must make the appropriate classes allocate and deallocate from it. Since this is a facility to be 'built into' a type instead of being 'contained' or 'called' by it, inheritance is an appropriate way for the facility to provide its services. And, since an object can be allocated or deallocated only as a complete object, the properties of this mechanism belong to the complete object and the inheritance should be virtual.

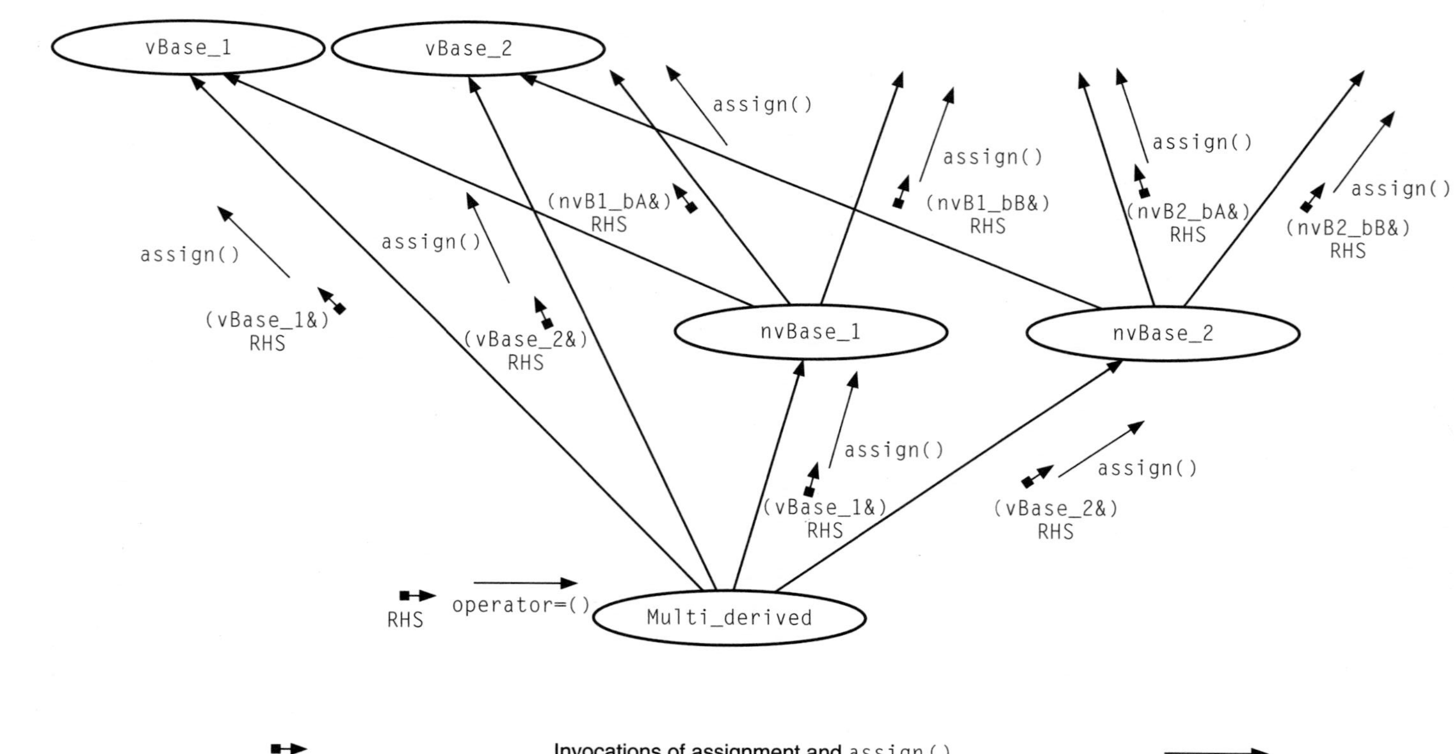
vBase_1
vBase_2
assign()
assign()
assign()
assign()
assign()
assign()
(nvB1_bA&)
RHS
(nvB1_bB&)
RHS
(nvB2_bA&)
RHS
(nvB2_bB&)
RHS
assign()
(vBase_1&)
RHS
assign()
(vBase_2&)
RHS
nvBase_1
nvBase_2
assign()
(vBase_1&)
RHS
assign()
(vBase_2&)
RHS
RHS
operator=()
Multi_derived
Parameter
Invocations of assignment and assign()
Function

Figure 7.15

This type provides a service that supports representations and algorithms, but that does not model the problem directly. It lies completely within the sphere of the 'P-for-programming' origin of the APSE model (Chap. 5, Sec. 5.6.5).

```
class   Pool_service
{
  public:
        … …

        class   Pool
        {
                … …
        };

        /*
         *      A Pool_mgr must be given a pool to work with,
         *      and the pool must be created and tracked
         *      somewhere--which must lie within or beneath
         *      of_size() .
         *
         *      If the Pool constructor is passed a size of
         *      zero, alloc() will set the size of the pool from
         *      the size of the first memory block requested.
         */
        static Pool& of_size( size_t );

        Pool_service( size_t sz );

        /*
         *      The guts of Pool_service: get a block from the
         *      pool, return it to the pool, find out what size
         *      block the pool deals in.
         */
        int my_size() const { return … … };
        void* alloc();
        void free( void* );
  private:
        … …
};
```

From the pool manager we can derive a 'new-and-delete' class:

```
class   New_and_Delete
  : protected Pool_service
{
  public:
        /*
```

```
         *       For scalars only . . .
         */
        void* operator new( size_t nbytes )
        {       return nbytes == my_size() ?
                    alloc() : (void*) new char[ nbytes ];
        };

        void operator delete( void* there, size_t nbytes )
        {       nbytes == my_size() ?
                    free( there ) : delete (char*) there;
        };

    protected:
        New_and_Delete( size_t sz = 0 )
          : Pool_service( sz )
        { };

        virtual ~New_and_Delete() {};

        /*
         *       Assignment should have no effect; if we
         *       get called by a memberwise assignment, we
         *       don't really want to do anything.
         */
        const New_and_Delete& operator=(
                                const New_and_Delete& )
        { return *this; };
};
```

New_and_delete provides a service to classes that derive from it. The client classes naturally call its operator new() or operator delete() with the correct parameters. What they can't do automatically is determine the size of the object and initialize the New_and_delete base with it.

Templates (Chap. 8) can manage the initialization: if derivation from New_and_delete is managed through a template, the template can provide New_and_delete's initializers. Getting other base class initializers through a template requires some 'protocol' between the base classes, the derived classes, and the template (Chap. 8, Sec. 8.3.4). A better solution, not supported by C++, would be to somehow combine the template and the base class, so that the base class could include a declaration of code to be expanded by the derived class in order to satisfy the interface provided by the base class.

Pool_service could be changed to always determine which pool to use at first allocation. But that is unreliable; something might find a way to call New_and_delete::operator new() the first time with the wrong size. So New_and_delete's constructor can take an optional size.

A derived class can always provide the constructor parameters for a virtual base class, even if it does not directly derive from that base class. Without violating or changing the program's inheritance structure, the 'correct' initializer can be added as an 'efficiency tweak' later if it is desired.

7.9 Delegation and How to Simulate It

Some OO programming languages support a capability called variously *Delegation* or *instance-based inheritance* or *per-object inheritance.*

In C++, inheritance is type-based (per-class). If you derive `FooBar` from `Foo` and `Bar`, then any `FooBar` you create will have as its base class objects a subobject that is precisely a `Foo` and a subobject that is precisely a `Bar`.

Under per-object inheritance, a given `FooBar` object would be guaranteed to have two subobjects, a `Foo` *or an object of a type derived from* `Foo` and a `Bar` *or an object of a type derived from* `Bar`.

Under per-object inheritance, the rules for dominance become much more slippery. On the other hand, there may be some things for which per-object inheritance makes sense. Look back at the example at the beginning of Sec. 7.2.1, Fig. 7.4. The diagram "contains the dangerous assumption that all employees are persons." If we ever have 'semipersons' as employees (whether robots, programs, or—civilization forbid—slaves), we will have two choices. We can either duplicate much of the inheritance hierarchy, creating in effect a cross-product of the job type and the personhood, or we can let `Person` represent either a person or a semiperson.

We would, in effect, allow the `Person` subobject to determine, instance by instance, which kind of 'person' it represented. In C++, we would program this by simulating *Delegation.* Delegation is one way of implementing per-object inheritance.

The implementation is simple to program but trickier to design. There is a separate inheritance hierarchy for `Person`. Besides the 'real' derived types, there is a 'fake' derived type called (in Fig. 7.16) `Delegated_Person`. This class contains a pointer or reference to a `Person` and it is that instance of `Person` whose type is the derived type representing the actual person or semiperson.

The various virtual member functions of `Delegated_Person` do nothing but call the corresponding function in the object identified by their pointer, and pass back any return value. In other words, the `Person` nature of `Delegated_Person` is *delegated* to the actual object representing the person.

Simulating delgation in this way requires that we avoid any interaction between the job inheritance hierarchy and the person hierarchy

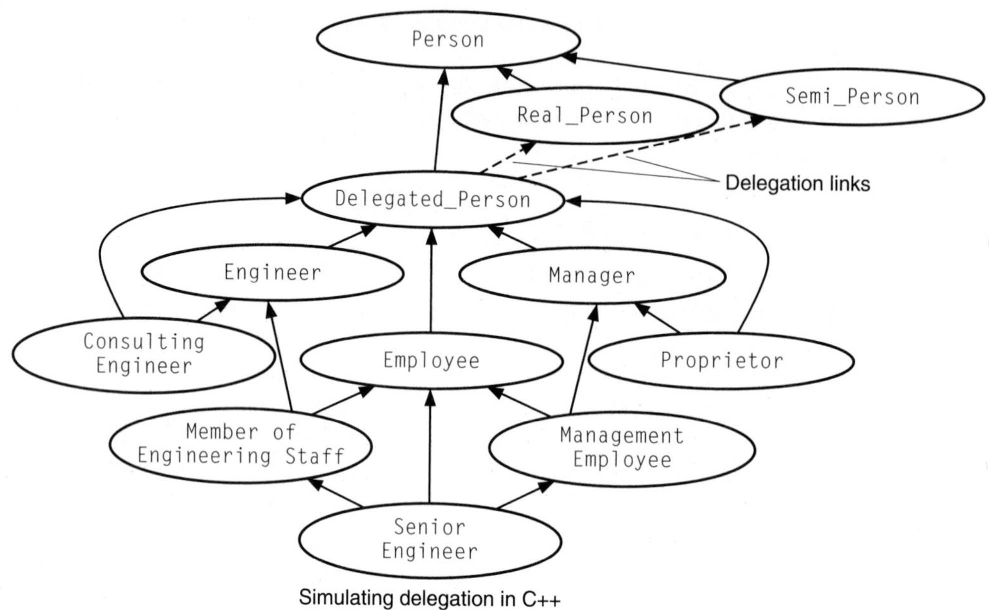

Simulating delegation in C++

Figure 7.16

that would change the dominance rules on the basis of which derived class of `Person` we were using. This means that all derived classes of `Person` must define the same virtual and nonvirtual function signatures. It also means that there are no true 'derived class member functions' to represent the individual combinations of derived-class-of-`Person` and derived-class-of-`Delegated_Person`.

7.10 Functions to Access the Type Structure

Prior to ANSI/ISO C++, C++ provides no way to access or query a program's type structure. This was by design; experience with SIMULA led Bjarne Stroustrup to expect such features to be misused (e.g., by using a `switch()` on types instead of virtual functions). By 1991 it was clear that this strict position was unacceptable; there were many things users wanted to do that they probably should be allowed to do.

7.10.1 Dynamic casting, and how to simulate it

The first such capability is *downcasting,* described in Sec. 7.2.2 as a conversion from a base class to the derived class of which it is a part. In Sec. 7.4.3 we saw that it will probably be added to C++ as a *dynamic cast,* which will use type information, including that in the virtual function tables, to determine if such a conversion is legal and sensible, and to make it if possible.

Until that is available, there is a way to simulate it. It is neither very extensible nor very maintainable, but it can work in certain families of problems.

The solution is this: the base class must know of every intended derived class, and provide a virtual function to convert its `this` pointer *if appropriate*. In the base class, it will not be appropriate, and the base class should provide a version of each that returns a null pointer. (In practice, two versions may be needed, one `const` returning a pointer-to-`const` and one non-`const`.) Each directly derived class overrides one function (or one `const`/non-`const` pair)—the function that returns a pointer to its own type. That function is modified to return `this`:

```
class   For_space;
class   For_speed;
class   For_compromise;

class   Does_it
{
  public:
        ... ...
        virtual For_space* xFor_space()
        { return 0; };

        virtual const For_space* xFor_space() const
        { return 0; };

        virtual For_speed* xFor_speed()
        { return 0; };

        virtual const For_speed* xFor_speed() const
        { return 0; };

        virtual For_compromise* xFor_compromise()
        { return 0; };

        virtual const For_compromise* xFor_compromise() const
        { return 0; };
        ... ...
};

class   For_space
  : public Does_it
{
  public:
        ... ...
```

```
            virtual For_space* xFor_space()
            { return this; };
            virtual const For_space* xFor_space() const
            { return this; };
            ... ...
};

class   For_speed
  : public Does_it
{
  public:
            ... ...
            virtual For_speed* xFor_speed()
            { return this; };
            virtual const For_speed* xFor_speed() const
            { return this; };
            ... ...
};

class   For_compromise
  : public Does_it
{
  public:
            ... ...
            virtual For_compromise* xFor_compromise()
            { return this; };
            virtual const For_compromise* xFor_compromise() const
            { return this; };
            ... ...
};
```

It's not pretty, it's unmaintainable, and it has much potential for trouble, especially if it is used several times in close quarters, but it can be made to work.

7.10.2 Run-time type identification (RTTI)

Run-time type identification or RTTI is, at this writing, a proposal before the ANSI/ISO C++ committee. It has two parts, a basic part which is well understood and which will probably be accepted, with some changes in the syntax, and an 'extended' part which some vendors want very badly, if only an efficient, reliable, and portable way can be found to implement it.

Basic RTTI has four parts:

- a 'pseudotype' that represents types
- a way to create a value of that pseudotype for any type

- a way to create a value of that pseudotype for any object's type
- a way to compare two values of the pseudotype to determine if the types represented by the values are the same

This would allow such code as this:

```
void
Base_class::outgrabe( Base_class& other )
{
        if( Typeof< Base_class > == typeof( other ) )
        {
                ... simple case ...
        }
        else
        {
                /*
                 *      The RHS is a derived class and it
                 *      should know best; use the 'reverse'
                 *      function in the derived class.
                 */
                other.ebargtuo( *this );
        }
}
```

This may seem vaguely familiar; it is a small part of a technique to simulate double-dispatching in C++ (Chap. 6, Sec. 6.7).

The syntax finally accepted into C++ will probably not be this syntax.

7.10.3 Extended run-time type identification (XRTTI)

Vendors of databases, of libraries that provide persistent objects (objects that survive from one execution of a program to another), and of run-time debugging systems have often requested a way to interrogate the type structure of an object at run time. They want to know not only about its base classes but about its member data and functions (including static members) so that they can copy an arbitrary object out to a file system (*freeze* it) and later read it back in (*thaw* or *reconstitute* it), or otherwise interpret it during execution.

Many members of the ANSI/ISO C++ committee represent such vendors; several are working together to prepare a report and perhaps a proposal to present to the Working Group on Language Extensions and, it is hoped, to the committee in general. They have a difficult task and it is not certain that an economical solution exists. If such a facility is adopted into C++, whether by language syntax or by standard libraries, it will probably be of interest primarily to the vendors as described in the previous paragraph.

7.11 Design Issues: The Roles of Classes (*continued*)

A typical example of Multiple Inheritance will fall into one of two patterns. The first is an 'implementation' structure, the second a 'taxonomic' structure. The first is typified by a Graphical User Interface (GUI), the second by a database organized by subtype.

A quick review of Chap. 5, Secs. 5.6.5 and 5.6.6.1 follows.

A program can be viewed as a collection of *Semantic Domains,* interacting in client-server relationships. Each Semantic Domain has a vocabulary, a mission, and a model. The client-server relationship is a DAG with one ultimate client [the Application (A)] and three ultimate servers [Programming technology (P), Subject technology/expertise/knowledge (S), and the execution Environment (E).]. This is called the 'APSE' model.

Within a Semantic Domain, a type can hold one or more of four offices: it can provide the Domain's Services to other domains; it can help to implement the Domain's Model; it can provide part of the Domain's basic Vocabulary; or it can serve to Instrument the Domain. A Domain's Model and Vocabulary types are likely the Service types of some other Domain.

Thus Semantic Domain boundaries are the natural Architectural boundaries of the problem and the solution resources and the Offices guide the design to separate out distinct things which must be done within each Domain.

We can make an additional observation now: there are just six ways for a Domain to provide its services. It can provide them through global functions (and data); this is typical of the FORTRAN 'subroutine package.' It can provide them through class functions (static member functions). It can provide them by providing objects whose member functions can be invoked (stream I/O's `cin`, `cout`, and `cerr`). It can provide types to instantiate (most classes do this). It can provide types from which to inherit and derive other types (some C++ types do this; the `Pool` type of Sec. 7.8.3 is one example). And, finally, it can provide services through *genericity.*

Genericity is the subject of the Chap. 8; in brief, it is a macrolike facility which allows an entire class or function to have parameters which are types; from one generic class or function, many classes or functions can be created, each operating over a different set of parameter types.

Types in different Offices and Services of Domains in different parts of the APSE DAG will tend to use different means of providing services. Domains near the P origin of the DAG will provide algorithms and data structures; genericity is especially suited to providing these as services (`T max( T, T)`). Domains that insulate the rest of the system from the E origin will commonly use functions, class objects, and classes (`cout, cin`). Domains near the S origin will more often use classes and inheritance, at least in an OO programming environment.

An 'implementation' Inheritance structure, as typified by a GUI, usually risks becoming a disorganized tangle of interfaces, derivation, and 'glue' functions and derivation, so that the system becomes monolithic (and megalithic) in spite of itself.

This happens because the GUI is a soil too fertile to plant inheritance and let it grow wild. First of all, such systems are rarely organized into semantic domains, and the nature of the services provided to a given system component isn't made clear. A class may inherit one base class to provide access to the visual system (servicing the Application), another to gain memory and object management services (providing Programming-heavy services), and a third to manage text in a window (providing a Subject-specific Vocabulary).

Without some discipline in creating and viewing the type hierarchy, there is little to prevent the DAG from turning into a snake pit.

Discipline is needed in creating the type graph; the system should first be organized around Semantic Domains (Architecture) and the Services and the ways that they are to be provided must be clearly enumerated.

Discipline is also needed in viewing such a type graph; an inheritance relationship (or any other service relationship) should be carried to the first Domain boundary and just far enough across it to understand how the service is accessed. Types in different Offices within a Domain should be viewed separately first, then together. And the contribution of each base class should be understood in terms of the problem at hand (Analysis contribution), the APSE components it furnishes (Architecture contribution), and the Offices it fills (Design contribution).

If the types are created, used, and viewed under these disciplines, it will be much harder for a mona- megalithic system to accrete.

The second 'typical' example for Multiple Inheritance is the taxonomy, wherein the Universe of Animals or Workers or Political Views is divided into types, and types into subtypes, and so forth. Multiple inheritance is invoked for the species that is both Fish and Fowl, the Engineer who is also a Manager, the Conservative who votes with Organized Labor on tax bills.

These examples can lead into a trap. The definitive textbooks on Entity-Relationship modeling use inheritance just as we have here, as a subtyping mechanism. But the inheritance provided by C++ (and some other OOPLs) is primarily an inheritance on *Behavior;* you derive not to subdivide a universe of things but to extend a behavior pattern to another class of things, modifying it to suit the needs of that new class of things. (This may have the effect of subtyping, but the motives differ.) Inheritance should always be viewed as a way of granting the derived class the right to use the interface of the base class.

7.12 Summary

Chapter 7 describes C++'s facilities for *Multiple Inheritance,* the inheriting of the facilities of several unrelated base classes. Multiple Inheritance was introduce in C++ Release 2.0. (The following all apply to structs as well as to classes.)

Section 7.1 A derived class inherits the interface and members of its base classes. There may be several base classes, in which case the base class inherits from them all.

Section 7.1.1 When a class inherits from multiple base classes, it effectively combines their interfaces and their sets of members into one interface and one member set of its own.

Section 7.1.2 When the interfaces and member sets of two or more classes are combined, names may clash. In this case, they can be disambiguated by qualifying the member name with the class name and the `::` . Overloading resolution is *not* used to disambiguate.

Section 7.1.3 It is possible to convert a pointer or reference to a derived class so that it may point at a base class; the opposite cannot be done safely in all circumstances.

Section 7.1.4 To remedy the deficiencies of Sec. 7.1.3, there is a proposal to store additional type information and to make it available in some safe, general-purpose way. The proposal stands a very good chance of passage in the ANSI/ISO C++ committee after some changes are made. The feature—or part of a feature—that will support this is called *dynamic conversion.* In some circumstances, it can lead to the throwing of an exception (Chap. 9). (See also Chap. 3, Sec. 3.4.2).

Section 7.2 When multiple classes are inherited, several may all inherit from the same 'deep' base class. Should there be one copy of the object, or several?

Section 7.2.1 When a single base class object is stored for multiple derivations, the derivation from that base class is said to be *virtual.* Virtual base classes belong to the complete object, not to any incomplete object within it.

This means that the inheritance diagram, instead of being a tree, will be a directed acyclic graph (DAG).

Section 7.2.2 The cases of Sec. 7.2.1 create—and resolve—various possibilities for ambiguity. In particular, a virtual base class reference is never ambiguous; however many times the virtual base class appears, there is only one instance of it.

Section 7.3 The 'memberwise' rules of object creation are modified under Multiple Inheritance. Base classes are all done first, and virtual bases first among bases. Determining what must be initialized first is a nontrivial matter. Virtual base classes are initialized only once, by the most-derived class.

When a base class is inherited virtually, the most-derived class provides the initializers. If they are not specified, then default constructors are used. An initalizer may be provided for an indirect virtual base class.

Section 7.4 An object with multiple or virtual base classes must have a more complicated memory layout than an object with no base classes or only single base classes.

Section 7.4.1 The crucial steps in the increase in complexity of the object's memory layout are (*a*) the C struct, (*b*) ordinary member functions, (*c*) single inheritance (*d*) virtual member functions, (*e*) ordinary multiple inheritance, (*f*) virtual inheritance.

Section 7.4.2 An object with a complicated memory layout may have pointers of different types pointing to the various base classes within it. In some cases, C++ provides standard, static conversions from certain such pointers to others, thus changing our view of the object.

Section 7.4.3 The proposal to support dynamic conversion between types would permit all conversions of the sort previously described.

Section 7.5 The access permissions, *public, private,* and *protected* still apply in the case of multiple inheritance. A few extra rules are needed to deal with MI and virtual MI.

Section 7.6 Multiple inheritance provides extra opportunities for name conflicts, which are not resolved by overloading. In some cases, however, one name *overrides* another, hiding the other from virtual or nonvirtual function calls.

Section 7.7 The interaction of overriding and virtualization under Multiple Inheritance has some additional rules and some additional cases of behavior.

Section 7.7.1 For each virtual function that appears in more than one branch of the inheritance DAG, there must be one instance that overrides (*dominates*) all others or the function will be unusable.

Section 7.7.2 There are proper and improper uses of Multiple and Virtual Inheritance; improper uses can make the program much more complicated.

Section 7.8 Under virtual inheritance, the virtual base class belongs to the complete object, but not to any of the subobjects within—not even to the most derived object. When operations like assignment must be propagated down into the base class components of a class, this property adds some complications.

Section 7.9 A facility called *Delegation* may be simulated in C++. Under delegation, inheritance is effectively object by object instead of type by type.

Section 7.10 C++, as of Release 3.0, does not provide any functions which can yield or act on type information at run time.

Section 7.10.1 The proposed facility called *dynamic conversion* (Sec. 7.1.4) would allow the legality of conversions to be analyzed at run time. Until it becomes available, there is at least one work-around.

Section 7.10.2 Another proposed facility, Run-Time Type Identification (RTTI), would allow a program to enquire of the types of its objects and adjust its behavior appropriately.

Section 7.10.3 An extension of the proposal in Sec. 7.10.2, extended RTTI (XRTTI) would contain enough information, in a standard format, to store an object to disk ("freeze it") and later restore it to life ("thaw it").

Section 7.11 Architectural and Design considerations, combined with some basic knowledge about a class type and its intended use, can control the complexity of a program, both as it is built and as it is viewed. Key concepts include the Semantic Domain, the APSE model, and the Offices a type may hold in the Semantic Domain.

Chapter

8

Templates

Templates (also called *parameterized types*) provide C++ with a capability called *genericity*. Genericity promises to be a powerful and valuable programming tool. As of mid-1993, neither templates themselves nor any implementation of templates is mature.

The ANSI/ISO C++ committee is engaged in heated discussions on the nuances of template behavior. This debate should provide C++ with mature, reliable, portable templates. Among the issues before the committee are these:

- How the specialization of a template receives type information from the scopes of the template's declaration and from the definitions of the parameter types must be completely defined and given some controls.
- How function templates interact with overloading must be clarified.
- Some trivial conversions may be allowed to the matching of template functions.
- Should templates themselves be allowed as parameters to templates?
- Should there be templates for typedefs or namespaces?
- What syntactic and semantic checks may be made at template declaration and definition and what must be deferred until specialization?
- How should template declarations and definitions be arrayed in header and source files?
- Template parameter lists make for long type names. It appears that they can be omitted in many places. Should C++ allow this?
- Should overloading or default parameters be allowed for template parameters?

This list may fairly be taken as a list of current (Release 3.0 and 3.0.1) deficiencies.

Overview

Templates are C++'s implementation of *genericity,* providing *generic classes* (class template) and *generic functions* (function templates). Class templates are also called *parameterized classes.*

Templates allow a kind of reuse which C++ inheritance does not permit. (In some other languages, notably Smalltalk, inheritance can provide what C++ templates provide.)

8.1 The Limitations of Inheritance

Inheritance allows a derived class to add its operations to those of a base class, or to substitute its own operations for some of the operations provided by the base class. The derived class differs from the base class by those operations. Inheritance, as C++ defines it, cannot allow a derived class to substitute a *type* for a type in the base class. If the base class has a member whose type is `char*`, the derived class cannot replace it with a member whose type is `String`. Nor can the derived class change the size of a member array, since the array's type includes its size.

8.1.1 Composing types

Suppose we create an AVL tree (Chap. 2, Sec. 2.8.3) of `char*`. We may also wish to have an AVL tree of `String` or of `Date`, or of `Personnel_record`: we want to *compose* the AVL tree and some other type into a new type. Most data structures (distinct from C `structs`) do just this: they impose some organization on instances of a particular type, in which the organization of instances and their addresses stores information about relationships between those instances.

8.1.2 You can't derive from an `int`

With derived types, composition can sometimes be faked using inheritance. If `Fixed_String`, `Variable_String`, `Persistent_String`, and `LZW_Substring` are all derived from `String`, then an AVL tree for `String` may be able to substitute for an AVL tree on any of `String`'s derived types. This often requires that something, somewhere, convert a `String*` back to a pointer to the derived type.

Such 'downcasting' isn't safe in the general case, nor are the techniques which use it fully general. If, instead of `String`, we have `char*`, it can't be used; you can't derive from `char*`.

8.1.3 Heterogeneous and homogeneous collections

Types such as our hypothetical AVL tree type are sometimes called 'collections.' A collection of objects of the same type, or of the same apparent type (Chap. 6, Sec. 6.3.1) is called a *homogeneous* collection; a collection of objects of different types is called a *heterogeneous* collection.

A programming language whose typing is managed wholly at run time and in which a reference or pointer or variable can name or point to or hold any type at all can support fully heterogeneous collections. A language like C++ with static typing can, in the end, support only homogeneous collections. All the objects in a single collection must *appear* to be objects of a common base type, whether or not their exact types are the same.

In practice, this is rarely a problem. We gather objects in a collection so that they may be treated in a common way; this means they have some common property or common nature, and it is that common nature (i.e., a common base class) by which they are known to the collection. If we want to take paragraphs out of a list, it doesn't matter whether they are justified paragraphs or footnote paragraphs; if we want to take taxpayers out of a list, it doesn't matter whether they are individuals or corporations so long as they are all derived from the taxpayer type by which they are known to the list.

8.2 Parameterized Types (Templates)

C++ provides composition of types by 'parameterized types' or *templates*. A template is a description of a type (or a function) that is not complete; it requires one or more parameters (types or constant values) to be provided before the type (or function) is fully defined. (We will discuss type templates first; most of what we say about types will apply to function templates as well.)

When a template is used to name a type, the missing parameters are provided. The result is a ready-to-use type. Creating the type from the template is called *specializing* the template. It is also sometimes called *instantiating* the template.

8.2.1 Introduction and syntax

A template for a dynamic array of an arbitrary type could be declared like this:

```
/*
 *      A template definition. Note that the parameters
 *      go after the "template," in the definition,
 *      _not_ after the class name.
 *
```

```
 *      And yes, the parameter list is delimited by
 *      angle brackets (aka brokets, aka greater-than
 *      and less-than signs).
 */
template < class T >     //   "class" indicates that  T is
class Var_array_T        //   a type parameter (user-defined
{                        //   _or_ built-in).
  public:
        Var_array_T( int init_size = 0 );
        Var_array_T( const Var_array_T< T >& ); //Both  T  and
        virtual ~Var_array_T ();          //   Var_array_T< T >
                                          //   are valid type
                                          //   names within the
                                          //   class template's
                                          //   scope.
        /*
         *      Reference, store a value,
         *      get the current array length.
         */
        const T& operator[]( int ) const;
        const T& set( int, const T& );
        int sz() const;

  private:
        T** array;      // The actual storage is managed
dynamically         ... ...
};
... ...

/*
 *      Now some specializations, both direct (vary_int)
 *      and by typedef (vary_str).
 *
 *      The parameter list follows the type name.
 */
Var_array_T< int > vary_int;

typedef Var_array_T< char* > Var_ch_s;

Var_ch_s vary_str( 65 );
```

(Most of the template names in the examples of this chapter will end in _T. This is the author's convention, neither a requirement nor universal.)

Please note how, in the declaration of the copy constructor, the template parameter is *not* part of the class-name-as-constructor name, but it *is* part of the class name when the name is used to declare the parameter to the constructor:

```
... ...
Var_array_T( const Var_array_T< T >& ) ;
... ...
```

If a template has multiple parameters, they are separated by commas:

```
template< class From, class To >
class Map_T
{ ... ... };
```

The parameter list attaches to the class name in most places; only where the name is used to declare or define a constructor or destructor is the template parameter list omitted. (This is awkward and will probably be relaxed in ANSI/ISO C++.)

There is no overloading on template names, nor are there default arguments to templates.

A *template class* is a class created by *specializing* a template; a template that gives rise to a class when it is specialized is a *class template:*

```
template< class T >       // Var_array_T is a _class template_
class   Var_array_T
{  ... ...  };

Var_array_T< int > indices;      // indices is an object of
                                 //   a _template class_.

typedef Var_array_T< Var_array_T< String > > Ragged_strs;
Ragged_strs clauses_and_provisions;  // clauses_and_provisions
                                     //   is also an
                                     //   instance (object)
                                     //   of a
                                     //   template class,
                                     //   Ragged_strs,
                                     //   which is a
                                     //   specialization
                                     //   of the class
                                     //   template
                                     //   Var_array_T .
```

Templates may be written only at the 'top level' (external or file scope) or at the top level of a namespace.

Because template specializations produce long names, they lend themselves to typedefs. Random typedefs, like randomly created 'scratch' variables, will obscure rather than clarify. The typedefs written as shorthand for template instantiations should be 'good' typedefs on their own; they should make sense in the program and participate in the exposition of the program's type structure.

As usual, anyplace where `class` may appear, `struct` may also appear. Although `union` may not introduce a type in the parameter list, the template type itself may be a union:

```
template < class T1 >
union U_T
{
        int i;
        T1* tp;
        T1** tpp;
        T1 T1::* tmp;
};
```

Member functions that are not defined in the class header are defined as templates, using the template argument lists:

```
template< class T >
inline int
Var_array_T< class T >::sz() const
{
        return n_elem;
}

template< class T >
const T&
Var_array_T< class T >::operator[] ( int i ) const
{ ... ... }
```

8.2.2 Parameters: types and values

There are two kinds of template parameters: types and constant values. The `Var_array_T` example uses one type parameter:

```
template < class T >
class Var_array_T
{
        ... ...
};
```

The parameter declaration `class T` makes `T` a parameter name and a type name within the scope of `Var_array_T`. Outside the class template's scope, it has no effect.

The keyword `class` really means 'type' in this context; any type at all can be used to supply the parameter in the template instantiation:

```
typedef Var_array_T< int > Vary_int;

typedef Var_array_T< String > Vary_str;
```

Constants can be used as parameters as well. They must be 'constant at link-time,' that is, they must be arithmetic or character constants, or enumerators, or the names of external or static functions, variables, or arrays.

We can declare a template for an array type whose size is 'compiled in,' but which provides checking for overflow and underflow:

```
template< int max_el, class T >
class   Fixed_array_T
{
        ... ...
        const T& operator[]( int ) const;
        const T& set( int, const T& ) ;
  private:
        T array[ max_el ] ;
};
... ...

template< int max_el, class T >
const T& Fixed_array_T< int max_el, class T >::operator[]
( int index ) const
{
         if(index < 0
         || index > max_el )
        {
                ...error handling code...
        }

        return array[ index ];
}
```

The template parameter list is a troublesome lexical and syntactic construct.* The list is delimited by tokens that are also used as operators (the angle brackets). This means that any template parameter which involves a relational expression *must* be parenthesized:

---

* C++ declarations in general have deep lexical and semantic difficulties; determining whether a sentence is an expression statement or a declaration can require both deep lookahead and tentative guesses which are only discarded when they become syntactically *or* semantically untenable.

```
Converter_T< T_1, T_2, ( sizeof( T_1 ) > sizeof( T_2 ) ) >
                                        T_one_to_two;
```

The third template argument is the expression

```
( sizeof( T_1 ) > sizeof( T_2 ) ).
```

Expressions involving templates are also affected:

```
if( ( Randomizer_T< double >( 0.0, 1.1 ) ) () > 0.66667 )
        ... ...
```

Template `Randomizer_T` with `operator()()`, when used in this value builder, gives an almost unreadable expression.

Finally, those who are not in the habit of writing white space around operators and delimiter tokens will probably get caught by templates:

```
typedef Linked_list<Fixed_array_T<Personnel_record,sort_sz>>
                                                   Sort_list;
```

The two angle brackets, `>>`, at the end of the first line will be tokenized as the right shift operator. White space should always be used between tokens in template parameter lists.

8.2.3 Creating classes and types

When templates are specialized, two specializations yield the same type if

- They are specializations of the same template, and
- They have identical arguments

"Identical" means that type parameters resolve to the same type (after all typedefs are applied) and all value parameters evaluate to the same value. "Same value" must be taken exactly:

```
template< class Out_stream, const char* key >
class   Encrypter_T
{
  public:
        Encrypter_T( Out_stream& ) ;
        ... ...
};

Encrypter_T< ostream, "hither and thither" > hither( cout );
Encrypter_T< ostream, "hither and thither" > thither( cout );

const char* all_over_the_place = "here and there" ;
```

```
Encrypter_T< ostream, all_over_the_place > here( cout );
Encrypter_T< ostream, all_over_the_place > there( cout );
```

In this example, here and there have the same type, since their type and value parameters are identical.* Whether hither and thither have the same type is implementation-dependent: a compiler is permitted to fold the two identical character literals into a single string, but is in no way required to do so. Nor is it required to document whether it does so, so that this example is implementation-dependent but not implementation-defined.

This is probably a misuse of templates: the parameter key should almost certainly be a parameter of the object, not of the type:

```
template < class Out_stream >
class   Encrypter_T
{
  public:
        Encrypter_T( Out_stream&, const char* key ) ;
        ... ...
};

Encrypter_T< ostream > hither( cout, "hither and thither" );
Encrypter_T< ostream > thither( cout, "hither and thither" );

const char* all_over_the_place = "here and there" ;

Encrypter_T< ostream > here( cout, all_over_the_place );
Encrypter_T< ostream > there( cout, all_over_the_place );
```

Now hither, thither, here, and there all have the same type.

The program text in a template assumes much. It may use types, functions, and objects declared externally. It may call functions and operators which depend on its type parameters. It may use members, nested types, and static members of its parameter types—and of their nested types. This has two ramifications.

First, only tentative syntactic and semantic checks may be applied to the template's declaration and definitions. The final check must be deferred until the template is specialized. This means that it is usually

---

* That is, they have the same type so long as the template specializations are in the same source unit. Because consts have internal linkage by default, if the templates occur in different source units, or if they are included by different source units, they will refer to different template specializations.

This is exactly the sort of subtlety that may escape the authors of an individual compiler; one benefit of the standardization effort is that various compiler writers have a chance to compare their interpretations of the standard-in-progress.

easiest, safest, and fastest to develop a template by developing a non-template version first and then parameterizing it.

Second, it means that C++ must gather information about types and objects to the point of the template's specialization. In effect, the template specialization takes place in a synthetic scope that is not quite the same as any other in the program. (As of mid-1993, how this scope is gathered is not yet standardized.)

Recall from Chap. 5, Sec. 5.5.9 that a destructor may be explicitly called for a type that lacks a destructor, and even for a built-in type.

```
char buffer[ BIG_ENOUGH_FOR_TO_BE ];

To_be* const want_to_be =                        // Placement Syntax;
                new ( (void*) buffer ) To_be;    // See Sec. 5.5.5
        ... ...

want_to_be->To_be::~To_be();     // Destroys the To_be in buffer
```

This applies likewise to template parameters:

```
template < class T >
class Thingamabob_T
{
        ... ...
        void j_random_function()
        {
                T* tee = ... ... ;
                ... ...
                tee->T::~T();    // Explicit destructor call for T.
        }
        ... ...
};

Thingamabob_T< int > thingie;
... ...
thingie.j_random_function();     // Results in a "call" of
                                 // int::~int() .
```

The "call of `~int ()`" is quietly turned into nothing when `Thingamabob_T` is specialized for `int`.

8.2.4 Creating functions

Member functions of class templates become function templates:

```
template< int max_el, class T >
class   Fixed_array_T
{
```

```
        ... ...
        const T& operator[] ( int ) const;
        const T& set ( int, const T& );
    private:
        T array[ max_el ];
};
... ...

template< int max_el, class T >
const T& Fixed_array_T( int max_el, class T ):: set(
                                int index, const T& new_val )
{
        if( index < 0
         || index > max_el )
        {
                ...error handling code...
        }

        array[ index ] = new_val;
        return array[ index ];
}
```

Once defined, member functions of template classes may be called as though they were ordinary member functions:

```
const int max_pos = 30;
    ... ...
Fixed_array_T< max_pos, int > intie;
Fixed_array_T< 4, Environment > environs;
... ...
/*
 *      These all call
 *      Fixed_array_T< 4, Environment >::set():
 */
environs.set( 0, Environment( "Internal" ) );
environs.set( 1, Environment( "External" ) );
environs.set( 2, Environment( "Alternate" ) );
environs.set( 3, Environment( "Library" ) );

for( int i = 0 ; i < max_pos ; i++ )
{
        /*
         *      This calls
         *      Fixed_array_T< 30, int >::set()
         */
        intie.set( i, max_pos - i );
}
```

For member functions of a class template, overloading works as it otherwise would. Static member functions can be used normally once the template class has been created by specializing the template.

Two member function templates belonging to the same class template may use different names for their identical template parameters. This is probably very poor practice, and may provide a hiding place for malicious code. In the author's opinion, it should not be done.

Nonmember function templates have extra restrictions because a nonmember function lacks two things. There is no object or pointer to reveal the instance of the template that is to be used (so it must be deduced from the parameter types) and there is no class declaration to actually specialize the function. It must be specialized either explicitly or implicitly. Finally, *nonmember function templates may not have any value parameters.* (This can be circumvented with a static member function, as described in Sec. 8.2.6.)

8.2.5 Template class static members

A static member of a class template becomes a template for a static member:

```
template< class Tee, class Ewe >
class   Recurser_T
{
        ... ...
        static Tee zero;
        static int depth;
        ... ...
};
```

Recurser_T's instances have two static members for which initialization must be provided (Chap. 2, Sec. 2.6.2). A template's static member data can be initialized either explicitly or implicitly.

An explicit initialization for a static data member of a template class can be made into a template of the initialization class:

```
template< class Tee, class Ewe >
    int Recurser_T< Tee, Ewe >::depth = -1;
```

Such an initialization template can be overridden for individual instances created from the class template (Sec. 8.2.7).

An implicit initialization isn't written. Instead, it is supplied automatically by C++ for static member data for which no initialization is found; such static members receive default initialization (so, in the example, any type used as the first parameter to `Recurser_T` must have default initialization, either provided by C++ or written as a default constructor).

Each specialized template class of `Recurser_T` will have its own instance of `zero` and `depth`. If this isn't desired, the class template should derive from a class or struct that provides the shared static data:

```
struct  Shared_proc_count
{
  protected:
          int n_proc;
};

template< class Process, Message_router m >
class   Proc
  : protected Shared_proc_count
{ ... ... };

int Shared_proc_count::n_proc = 0; // Not a template!
```

8.2.6 Overload and conversion interactions

A nonmember function may be specialized explicitly:

```
template < class T >
inline const T&                      // The "inline" must come
max( const T& t1, const T& t2 ) //   after the template header.
{
        return t1 >= t2 ? t1 : t2;
}
  ... ...

int max( int, int );      // Explicitly introduces
                          //   max( int, int )  as a
                          //   function which can receive
                          //   the ordinary overload
                          //   resolution.
```

When a function template specialization (*template function*) is declared explicitly, the template function behaves like an ordinary function in how overloads are matched and how conversions are applied implicitly to parameters.

A nonmember function template may also be specialized implicitly:

```
        ... ...
        double d1 = 4.4 ;
        ... ...
```

```
double d2 = max( d1, 0.0 );      // Calls
                    // max< double >( double, double )
```

A different overload matching process is applied to template functions that have not been explicitly specialized:

- First, the overload resolution searches for an exact match, permitting trivial conversions. This search includes all functions including explicitly specialized template functions.
- Then it searches for a match among function templates for one that can provide a 'super-exact' match if specialized. No conversions are allowed. (This may be relaxed to allow certain trivial conversions, but no others. `T -> T&` and `T& -> T` are the likely candidates.)
- Then it searches for matches involving conversions, as described in Chap. 4, Sec. 4.1.4.

```
... ...
double d1 = 4.4 ;
double& d_ref = d1;
... ...

double d3 = max( d1, 1e15F );    // Does not match the
                                 //   unspecialized max< >() ;
                            //   one parameter is a double, the
                            //   other a float.

double d2 = max( d_ref, 0.0 );   // Will match the
                                 //unspecialized max< >()
                            //   if ANSI/ISO allows the trivial
                            //   conversion from T to T&

double d4 = max( d1, d_ref );    // Will match the
                                 //   unspecialized max< >()
                            //   if ANSI/ISO allows the trivial
                            //   conversion from T& to T.
```

There has been discussion about permitting the template instance to be specified explicitly:

```
... ...
double d1 = 4.4 ;
double& d_ref = d1;
... ...

double d2 = max< double >( d_ref, 0.0 );
```

This syntax matches the new conversion syntax. Template arguments may also be used in value builders (Chap. 3, Sec. 3.3). It is possible to 'fake' the foregoing syntax by making the function a static member of a class template:

```
template< class T >
class   Min_max_T
{
  public:
        static T& max( T& t1, T& t2 )
        {   return t1 >= t2 ? t1 : t2;  }

        static T& min ( T& t1, T& t2 )
        {   return t1 <= t2 ? t1 : t2;  }
};
         ... ...

        double d2 = Min_max_T< double >::max( d_ref, 0.0 );
```

8.2.7 Overriding a template's specialization

For any template, including a member function template, C++ can specialize that template for a given set of parameter types and values. Ordinarily, it will specialize the template as it needs the specialization.

Instead of allowing C++ to provide the specialization, we can define the specialized function ourselves:

```
/*
 *      This 'sign' is 1 if the argument is zero or positive.
 */
template< class T >
int sign( const T& t )
{
        return t >= 0;
}

/*
 *      For unsigned types, the sign is always 1.
 */
int
sign< unsigned char >( const unsigned char& )
{
        return 1;
}

int
```

```
sign< unsigned short >( const unsigned short& )
{
        return 1;
}

int
sign< unsigned int >( const unsigned int& )
{
        return 1;
}
    ... ...

/*
 *      For a matrix, the sign is 1 if the matrix
 *        is positive semidefinite ...
 */
int
sign< const Matrix >( const Matrix& m )
{
        return m.positive_semi_def();
}
    ... ...
```

Classes too can be ‘manually specialized’:

```
template< class T >
class   Formatter_T
{
  public:
        Formatter_T( T& );
        ~Formatter_T();
                ... ...
};
    ... ...

/*
 *      Character strings are special; we must
 *        allow the ignore-case option, but we can
 *        do a lot of the conversions directly ...
 */
class   Formatter_T< const char* >
{
  public:
        Formatter_T( const char*, int ignore_case = 0 );
            ... ...
};
```

And likewise for the member functions of templates that the compiler specializes:

```
/*
 *      There's no need to actually _do_ anything for  Invis .
 */
ostream&
Formatter_T< Invis >( ostream& os, const Invis& )
{
        return os;
}
```

There's a distinction to be observed here: If the *declarations* of the templates' specializations provided by the programmer appear in the header file or in the program file before the code that uses them, the overload resolution changes. If the declarations do not appear there, the overload resolution is unchanged, but so long as the *definitions* of the template specializations appear somewhere in one or another of the source code units compiled, those specializations will be chosen over any that the compiler might provide.

8.3 Combining (Multiple) Inheritance and Templates

Templates and Inheritance together are more powerful than either alone. Let's say we have a sorted dynamic data structure template like an AVL tree. We can layer inheritance and templates around it.

The example that follows is both large and incomplete; this is almost inevitable, since these facilities are used for organizing large parts of systems. But even though the definition of each component is fairly large, the use of that component takes only a very little code.

The "lvalue access" functions and operators return a surrogate object. (Surrogate objects are described in Chap. 5, Sec. 5.1.4.)

```
/*
 *      Map_bases_T provides two nested classes for use as base
 *      classes.  One is a dynamic array; it stores a collection
 *      of arbitrary objects by an index, which must be a signed
 *      integral type.  The other maps a value of some type into
 *      an integer using an unspecified data structure.  If the
 *      integer is positive, it corresponds to a lookup key for
 *      the first base class (or one of its derived classes); if
 *      it is negative, it indicates that the value was not found.
 *      If the value is to be inserted, the negative integer may
 *      be used to indicate where the insertion is to take place.
 */
template < class From, class To, class Index >
class   Map_bases_T
{
```

```
public:
    /*
     *      The indexed collection.
     */
    class   I_coll
    {
      protected:
            I_coll () {};

      public:
            virtual ~I_coll () {};

      protected:
            const To& get( Index ) const = 0;
            const To& set( Index, const To& ) = 0;
            Index create( const To& ) = 0;
            void remove( Index ) = 0;

            /*
             *      This requires some little explanation.
             *      null_value() returns a reference to the
             *      value, if any, which is to be returned
             *      on a lookup of a non-existant index.
             *      If no value is to be returned in that
             *      situation, null_value() should throw an
             *      appropriate exception (see Chapter 9).
             *
             *      The null value corresponds to a null
             *      string in a string=>string map, or
             *      to a zero in a sparse array.
             */
            virtual const To& null_value() = 0;
            /*
             *      is_null(), on the other hand, just
             *      determines if the to_value is equal
             *      to the null value (if there is any
             *      null value).  (But if is_null () can
             *      return true, null_value() should not
             *      throw an exception.)
             */
            virtual int is_null( const To& ) = 0;
    };

    /*
     *      The map from From to Index.
     */
    class   I_map
    {
      protected:
            I_map() {};
      public:
            virtual ~I_map() {};

      protected:
            Index find( const From& ) const = 0;
            void store( const From&, Index at, Index value ) = 0;
            void unstore( Index at ) = 0;
```

```
        };
};

/*
 *      An arbitrary map using an arbitrary lookup method and an
 *      arbitrary storage method.  The parameters  I_coll  and
 *      I_map  must be derived from appropriate instantiation of
 *      Map_bases_T< >::I_coll  and  Map_bases_T< >::I_map ,
 *      respectively.  They are each expected to provide a nested
 *      class or typedef called  Init  by which they are to be
 *      initialized.
 *
 *      For a nicer interface, derive from this and provide a
 *      constructor which takes its arguments in a more appropriate
 *      form and presents them to the Init constructor/value
 *      builder as needed.
 */
template< class From, class To, class I_map, class I_coll, class Index >
class   Arb_map_T
  : public I_coll, public I_map
{
  protected:
        typedef I_coll::Init Ic_init;
        typedef I_map::Init Im_init;
        typedef Arb_map_T< From, To, I_map, I_coll, Index > A_map;

        /*
         *      Here we use a "magic" helper class; it is
         *      returned by our operator[] and it can be
         *      converted into a const From& or assigned to
         *      in order to store into the A_map.
         *
         *      There's a special version called R_val for use
         *      with const A_map's; it lacks the assignment.
         */
        class L_val
        {
          public:
                L_val ( A_map& a_am, const From& a_fr )
                  : am( a_am ), fr( a_fr )
                { };
                ~L_val() {};

                operator const To&() const
                {  return am.lookup( fr ); };

                const To& operator=( const To& tu ) const
                { return am.assign( fr, to ); };

          private:
                A_map& am;
                From& fr;
        };
        friend class L_val;

        class   R_val
        {
```

```
            public:
                  L_val ( const A_map& a_am, const From& a_fr )
                    : am( a_am ), fr( a_fr )
                  { };
                  ~L_val () {};

                  operator const To&() const
                  {  return am.lookup( fr ); };

            private:
                  const A_map& am;
                  From& fr;
          };
          friend class R_val;

  public:
          Arb_map_T( const Ic_init& ici, const Im_init& imi );
          virtual ~Arb_map_T();

          L_val operator[] ( const From& f )
          { return L_val ( *this, f ); };

          R_val operator[] ( const From& f ) const
          { return R_val ( *this, f ); };

  protected:
          const To& lookup( const From& ) const;
          const To& assign( const From&, const To& );
};

template< class From, class To, class I_map, class I_coll, class Index >
Arb_map_T< From, To, I_map, I_coll, Index >
                ::Arb_map_T( const Ic_init& ici, const Im_init& imi )
  : I_coll( ici ), I_map( imi )
{ }

template< class From, class To, class I_map, class I_coll, class Index >
Arb_map_T< From, To, I_map, I_coll, Index >::~Arb_map_T()
{}

template < class From, class To, class I_map, class I_coll, class Index >
const To&
Arb_map_T< From, To, I_map, I_coll, Index >
                              ::lookup( const From& fr ) const
{
        /*
         *      find()  comes from our  I_map  heritage;  get()
         *      and  null_value()  come from our  I_coll  heritage.
         */
        Index ix = find( fr );

        return ix >= 0 ? get( ix ) : null_value();
}

template< class From, class To, class I_map, class I_coll, class Index >
const To&
```

```
Arb_map_T< From, To, I_map, I_coll, Index >
        ::assign( const From& fr, const To& to )
{
        Index ix = find( fr );

        /*
         *      If there's a null case, we have to handle it
         *      differently; normally we act to create a record
         *      if it's not there; here we remove it if it is
         *      there.
         */
        if( is_null( to ) )
        {
                if( ix >= 0 )
                {
                        /*
                         *      Remove the item from the
                         *      I_coll and take it out of
                         *      the I_map.
                         */
                        remove( ix );
                        unstore( ix );
                }

                return to;
        }

        /*
         *      Otherwise, if the From value already has a
         *      record, we just re-assign the to-side.
         */
        if( ix >= 0 )
                return set( ix, fr );

        /*
         *      Otherwise, create a map entry and a record.
         */
        Index jx = create( to );
        store( fr, ix, jx );
        return get( jx );
}
```

At least one compiler for C++ Release 3.0 will not allow a base class of a template class to depend on a template parameter, or one severely restricts the dependencies possible. It also has trouble with some typedefs in class and local scope. This example can't be compiled under that compiler, and is too incomplete to test properly, but it does represent legal C++ types and templates. The nested types and typedefs are pervasive; with them the code is quite hard to read; without them it would be nearly impossible to read.

This of course is just one example of how inheritance and templates can be used together. There are some things which C++ could do, but doesn't. For example, it would be nice to be able to specify directly that the `I_coll` and `I_map` parameters are derived from the appropriate classes within the appropriate instance of `Map_bases_T`.

8.3.1 Roles of classes, roles of templates

Just as we can classify the 'roles' and 'offices' held by types (Chap. 3, Sec. 3.10.4; Chap. 5, Sec. 5.6.6; Chap. 6, Sec. 6.6.4), so we would like to classify the roles or offices of templates. Since templates provide genericity over functions or classes, the role or office filled by a template may be precisely that filled by the function or class were it not parameterized. A type which would provide a Domain's services were it not parameterized still provides that Domain's services.

But templates also permit one Domain to provide services to another. Recall that the Vocabulary types of one Domain are generally Service types of another Domain (Chap. 5, Sec. 5.6.6). One Domain can provide templates (function or class) that provide algorithms and data structures; these can serve a client Domain not only as Vocabulary types but also as Model types. Template functions permit an algorithm to be specified generically for use by arbitrary types.

It seems likely that template classes and functions will appear as Service types, first of the Programming Domain and Domains that incorporate a strong Programming component, providing generic data structures and algorithms. Generic Service types will become model types in other domains. (See Chap. 5, Sec. 5.6.5 for a description of the Elementary Domains in the APSE model.)

8.3.2 Collections, iterators, generators, etc.

Template classes lend themselves to data structures and to 'stateful' operations on those classes.*

Today, template classes are most often used to provide Generic data structures are an obvious use of template classes. Many of these are collections of some sort. Recall from Sec. 8.1.3 that we are usually interested in collections that can be treated as though they are homogeneous, whether they be homo- or heterogeneous.

In implementing an operation over the elements of a set or collection, we may need to store information about where in the set we are. There are two OO ways of doing this: generators and iterators.

A *generator* is an object which can be invoked to return a value from a sequence of values; each invocation yields a 'subsequent' value until

---

* *Stateful* is the popular OO antonym of 'stateless.' A more conventional construction would be 'stated' (by analogy with 'nameless' and 'named'), but that would probably be confusing.

the sequence is exhausted, at which time the generator might fail, or might restart the sequence, or might obtain a new sequence. If the collection of objects or values is internal to the generator, it can be stored in any convenient way and the state of the sequence can also be stored as convenient. (See Chap. 3, Sec. 3.8.)

Generators based on data structures are good candidates for parameterization as classes; likewise, templates that implement data structures can be helpful in implementing generators.

If the generator's data structure is separated from its control or sequencing abstraction, it is no longer a generator, but an *iterator.* An iterator is an object that maintains state information about a sequence of objects or values stored in a collection that can be separated from the state of the sequence. While the iterator is not part of the collection, nor the collection of the iterator, the iterator needs intimate knowledge of how the collection is represented (e.g., by what data structures).

Iterators can be simple or complicated. Here's a very simple example:

```
template< class A_type >
class   Flex_array_T
{
  public:
        ... ...
        const A_type& operator[]( int ) const;
        ... ...
        int n_elem() const
        { return n_elements; };
        ... ...
};

/*
 *      Iterator base for arbitrary Flex_array
 */
class   F_array_it_b
{
  public:
        F_array_it_b( int a_max ) : n( 0 ), n_el( a_max ) {};
        ~F_array_it_b() {};

        int operator()() { return n >= n_el ? -1 ; n++; };
  private:
        int n;
        const int n_el;
};

/*
 *      Interator for arbitrary Flex_array_T
```

```
 */
template< class A_type >
class   F_array_it
    : private F_array_b
{
  public:
        F_array_it( Flex_array< A_type >& ada)
          : F_array_it_b( ada.n_elem() ), da( ada )
        { };

        ~F_array_it() { };

        const A_type* operator()()
        { int i = Flex_array_b::operator()();
          return i ? &ada[ i ] : 0;
        };

  private:
        Flex_array< A_type >& da;
};
```

`F_array_it< A_type >` steps through the elements of a `Flex_array< A_type >` one at a time, starting with the zeroeth, returning a new value each time its `operator()()` is invoked. This simple generator does not support a reset-to-beginning operation, nor a start-with-new-collection operation. More complicated iterators can serve linked lists, trees, etc.

An interator has one problem that a generator does not have: since the collection through which it iterates is visible to the outside, it is vulnerable to changes in that collection between invocations of itself. This problem can be ignored (in which case the iterator should carry a notice to that effect) or the collection and the iterator can cooperate to manage the interaction.

If the interaction is to be managed, the collection must maintain a relationship by which it can notify the iterator, either while the change is occurring or when the iterator accesses it. And if it supports multiple iterators, more data structures ('collections of objects') will be needed to manage those iterators and the relationships with them. If the collection is to support only one iterator, it may suffice to put the iterator's state information into the collection object itself. In this case, the collection is really a 'collection-with-iterator' and is just one step from a generator (that step being to hide the collection from outside tinkering after it has been initialized).

Template classes can also be used to manage the lifetime of some object:

```
template< class Owned >
class   Owner_T
{
        Owner_T( const Owned::init& o_i )
           : o( new Owned( o_i ) )
        { };

        ~Owner()
        { delete o; };

        operator Owned*() const { return o; };

  private:
        Owned* o;
};
```

By itself, this isn't very interesting; we could just as well have made the Owned object a member of Owned_T. If we add a constructor to accept a function that will create such an object, however, it becomes more interesting:

```
template< class Owned, class Generator, class Gen_param >
class   Virt_owner_T
  : public Owner_T < Owned >
{
        Virt_owner_T( const Owned::init& o_i )
           : o( new Owned( o_i ) )
        { };

Virt_owner_T( const Generator& (*gen_fun) ( const Generator::init& ),
                                                 const Generor::init& ini )
           : o( (*gen_fun )( ini ) )
        { };

        Virt_owner_T()
        { delete o; };

        operator Owned*() const { return o; };

  private:
        Owned* o;
}
```

Now Virt_owner_T can hold not only a pointer to an Owned, but to an object of any type derived from Owned. The example can be expanded almost without limit with the constructor accepting generator objects, generator objects with member functions, etc. Of course, deriving a type from the appropriate specialization of Virt_owner_T will allow these to be added on later.

know what it means for that matrix to be singular. Perhaps it is an internal error; perhaps it is a linear system that is badly designed. Perhaps, in the situation at hand, it is even good news.

Matrix packages tend to have thorough error recovery and reporting, but they can only report the error to the level that invoked them. If that level cannot assign meaning to the failure, the failure must be deferred again to the next level above that, and so forth.

To program this in the conventional way, every part of the system must be festooned with tests that guard against unforeseen conditions in every function called. This distracts from the problem being solved, especially because *these 'exceptional' cases are what happens when the fundamental problem statement no longer applies.* A better way is needed.

C++ helps by supporting exception handling. A failure can be routed back dynamically to the last code prepared to handle it, abandoning work in progress. The improvement isn't free: in a world that includes exceptions, functions that allocate resources must either allocate them through class objects whose destructors will release them, or themselves catch the exception, release the resources, and then re-initiate the exception. In C++, both are possible, and are already good practice.

Exception handling in C++ is designed to deal with events that occur as a result of program execution; it is not, in general, suitable for dealing with asynchronous events such as signals.

9.1.2 Approach

Exception handling in C++ exploits C++'s system of objects with types. An exception is represented by an object of some type. A function which detects an exceptional condition creates an object to represent the exception; the type of object represents the type of the exception. The object may contain whatever information will help in reporting or recovering from the exception. The function 'throws' the exception, which travels upwards through the current function, the current function's caller, the caller's caller, and so forth, looking for the last function invoked that is willing to 'catch' this exception. As it progresses, it 'unwinds' the stack of function invocation records, terminating the function invocation and destroying local objects by calling their destructors.

```
Some_type
Low_level_drudge::slavey( ...args... )
{
        ...And a GHASTLY error occurs...
                Throw an exception.
}
```

```
some_high_level_and_mighty_function()
{
        ...

        Low_level_drudge laborer;

        Try
                laborer.slavey( ... );
        and catch a GHASTLY exception if one occurs
       and if one is caught, then
             Do Something Useful.
}
```

Each function that is searched and found unwilling to catch the exception is terminated. The active local variables of the function are destroyed, their destructors being called as necessary.

An exception may be represented by a class or struct type, by a basic type, by an enum or a pointer or a reference.

In C++, a derived class object may stand in for an object of any of its base types. When a derived class or struct exception searches backwards for an active function invocation to catch it, all publicly visible base classes of the exception's type are used in the search; the exception object can be caught by any of the types by which it is publicly known.

For example, a failure to find an intermediate work file that should exist may be represented by a `Temp_file_error`, which might be derived from both a `File_error` and a `Program_logic_error`; the latter might in turn be derived from an `Internal_error`. If a `Temp_file_error` is thrown, it can be caught by any active handler prepared to catch one of `Temp_file_error`, `File_error`, `Program_logic_error`, or `Internal_error`.

Servicing an exception may involve considerable run-time overhead. This is acceptable; exceptions are assumed to occur infrequently and it is more important (within limits) to deal with them succinctly and correctly than to deal with them rapidly.

9.2 Programming Exceptions in C++

9.2.1 `try` and `catch`

To catch an exception thrown within code, that code must be enclosed in a *try-block.* The *try-block* is followed by *handlers,* which might also be called *catch-clauses:*

```
/*
 *      Main calculator loop.
 */
```

```
for( ; ; )
{
        Formula f();

        try
        {
          cin >> f ;
        }
        catch( Formula::Syntax_err se)
          {
                /*
                 *      There is an inserter overload
                 *        for Syntax_err; Syntax_err
                 *        contains pointers to the
                 *        error message and to the text
                 *        that caused the error ...
                 *        and then we'll try again.
                 */
                cerr << se ;
                continue;
          }
        catch( Formula::Except e )
          {
                /*
                 *      If it's not a syntax problem,
                 *        we might as well bug out.
                 */
                cerr << e << "Exiting." << endl ;
                break;
          }
        ...
}
```

This code assumes a number of things. First, it assumes that something, somewhere in the evaluation of `cin >> f`, may throw an exception with the type `Formula::Syntax_err` (that is, of a type named `Syntax_err` within the `Formula` class). If not, the handler for `Formula::Syntax_err` will never be activated.

9.2.2 `throw`

What about the code that throws an exception such as `Formula::Syntax_err`? Let's get a better picture of our `Formula` class:

```
class   Formula
{
        /*
```

```
         *      Input a Formula.
         */
        friend istream& operator>>( istream& is, Formula& f )
        { f.parse( is ); return is; };

  private:
        /*
         *      A token read in:
         */
        enum Tok_type { t_identifier, t_left_parens, t_right_parens,
                                                         … … };

        class   Token
        {
          public:
                Token( …whatever… );
                ~Token();

                operator Tok_type() const
                                { … …; };

            … …
        };

        /*
         *      Tokenizer for input.  Reads a whole line, returns it
         *      token by token.  Stores the line in its original form
         *      to help error reporting or recovery.
         */
        class   Tokenizer
        {
          public:
                tokenizer( istream& );
                ~tokenizer();
                Token operator()();
            … …
        };
  public:

        /*
         *      Except provides a common interface for Formula
         *      exceptions.
         */
        class   Except
        {
          public:
                friend ostream& operator<<( ostream& os, const Except&
ex )
                { return ex.put( os ); };
                Except();
                virtual ~Except();

          protected:
                virtual ostream& put ( ostream& ) const = 0;
                    … …
        };
```

```
        class   Syntax_err
          : public Except
        {
          public:
                Syntax_err( tokenizer );
                ~Syntax_err();

          protected:
                ostream& put( ostream& ) const;
                    ... ...
        };

        class   Allocation_err
          : public Except, public ::Allocation_err
        { ... ... };

        class   Internal_err
          : public Except
        { ... ... };

        Formula( Memory_base& );
        ~Formula();
          ... ...

  private:
        void parse( istream& is );

        void parse_assign( Token& lhs, Tokenizer& );
        void parse_expr( Tokenizer& );

        void count_error();
        int num_errs() const;
            ... ...
};
    ... ...
```

Now we can examine how `Formula::parse()` might recognize exceptional cases and throw exceptions:

```
void
Formula::parse( istream& is )
{
        Tokenizer tok_stream( is );

        Token t = tok_stream();

        switch( t.type() )
        {
        // identifier = ...
        //            ^
        case t_identifier:
```

```
                parse_assign( t, tok_stream );
                break;

        // ( expression ...
        //   ^
        case t_left_parens:
                parse_expr( tok_stream );

                t = tok_stream();

                /*
                 *  If we don't have a matching ')'
                 *  we have an error, period.
                 */
                if( t.type() != t_rght_parens )
                        throw Syntax_err( tok_stream );

                break;

        ... ...

        default:
                /*
                 *      Neither assignment nor a
                 *      parenthesized expression ???
                 */
                throw Syntax_err( tok_stream ); // Throw an
                                                // exception
        }
}
```

There are two `throw` expressions, each corresponding to a particular unexpected circumstance. The keyword `throw` is a unary operator. It returns `void` and takes an expression of any type, built-in or user-defined. Its priority is just slightly higher than that of assignment. (The *throw* operation is represented as an expression rather than as a statement to allow the future possibility of a way to resume operations after an exception instead of simply terminating the current operation.)

9.2.3 Matching and inheritance

Here are the handlers (`catch` clauses) which cover the attempt to read a `Formula`:

```
try
{
        ... ...
```

```
        ... ...
}
catch( Formula::Syntax_err se )
  {
        cerr << se ;
        count_error();
        continue;
  }
catch( Formula::Except e )
  {
        cerr << e << "Exiting." << endl ;
        break;
  }
```

The two `throw` expressions both create `Syntax_err` objects (using the `Syntax_err` constructor as a *value builder*—see Sec. 3.3). C++ then searches backward from the `throw` for the nearest enclosing `try` that has a `catch` of a matching type.

Both of these two `catch` clauses (handlers) can catch the `Syntax_err`, since `Syntax_err` is derived from `Formula::Except`. The *first applicable match is used,* so the first `catch` is taken, and the *continue* is executed.

To catch any exception at all, the ellipsis can be used:

```
catch( ... )
  {
        cerr << "Unknown failure.  Exiting." << endl ;
        ... ...
  }
```

There's not much that can be done with an exception whose type is unknown; see Sec. 9.2.7.

9.2.4 Inheritance and slicing

What if an `Internal_err` is thrown instead?

Since `Formula::Internal_err` is derived from `Formula::Except`, the second `catch` clause can be used:

```
catch( Formula::Except e )
  {
        cerr << e << "Exiting." << endl ;
        break;
  }
```

Unfortunately, this isn't quite right. The parameter to the `catch` is initialized the same way a function argument is initialized. In this case, that means that the original `Formula::Internal_err` is used to initialize a local `Formula::Except`. The functions which implement `operator<<( ostream&, Formula::Except& )` will operate 'polymorphically' and print according to the actual type of their parameter, but the handler as written cuts them off by forcing that parameter's actual type to the base class. This is precisely the 'slicing' problem of Sec. 6.3.3.3. The same solution applies: the handler must accept its parameter by reference:

```
catch( Formula::Except& e )
  {
        cerr << e << "Exiting." << endl ;
        break;
  }
```

The same reasoning can be applied to the first handler:

```
catch( Formula::Syntax_err& se )
  {
        cerr << se ;
        count_error();
        continue;
  }
```

9.2.5 Pointers as exceptions

The slicing problem can also be avoided by throwing and catching an exception as a pointer to the object that represents the exceptional condition. Unfortunately, this requires that the thrower and catcher agree on how the memory is to be allocated and released. Free store management during exception handling is unreliable; if an exception occurs during the throwing of an exception, `terminate()` (Sec. 9.4, below) is invoked.

One solution is for classes which expect to throw an exception to allocate the space for it in a static member, and to throw a pointer or reference to it. If necessary, a large-enough array can be preallocated and the exception object built in it and destroyed using placement syntax and destruction-in-place (Secs. 5.5.8 and 5.5.9).

9.2.6 Implementation-defined limits

Careful study of the design of this feature reveals a problem: the execution model of exception handling in C++ demands that a temporary be created somewhere *in the calling frame of the function with the handler,* but only the function with the `throw` knows exactly how large the object is. Because exceptions may be thrown in response to failures in free store management, free store cannot be used to provide a variable-length memory. Many implementations will use a static area or preallocated area of some fixed size. This will set an implementation-defined maximum size for the exception object.

Throwing a pointer, reference, or enum, or a small object with a pointer or reference in it, and storing the actual information in a static class member (Sec. 9.2.5) can deal with this, if the space for the static member can be spared.

9.2.7 Rethrowing an exception

An exception handler might know or discover that it cannot deal completely with an exception, and that the exception should be handed off to the next enclosing try-block with a handler for the exception (whether in this function or another):

```
int
Golliwog::read( ...args... )
{
        try
        {
                ...

                return whatever ;
        }
          /*
           *    Catch anything at all ...
           */
        catch( ... )
          {
                /*
                 *        ... Protest ...
                 */
                cerr << "Hey!  I was READING!" << endl ;

                /*
                 *      And rethrow the current exception.
                 */
                throw;
          }

                /*
                 *      No return statement here: we never
                 *      actually get here!
                 */
}
```

Rethrowing works just as well with an exception caught by type as with an exception caught by the ellipsis.

9.3 Exception Specifications

Locality, the stronger coupling of things near to each other and the weaker coupling of things more remote, is essential to controlling the complexity of a program. C++ exceptions are necessarily nonlocal. Uncontrolled, they complicate a program beyond recovery.

C++ provides a means of control. It is possible to declare that a function will throw or pass only certain exceptions. Other exceptions will be caught and turned into invocations of `unexpected()` (described in the next section). If the program is organized around semantic domains (Sec. 5.6.3), the domains can be made into 'exception-tight compartments,' which stop the flow of all exceptions except those which the domain is specifically meant to generate or propagate. This approach is applicable to other large-scale modularity techniques as well.

The actual unit of control is the function. All functions, whether member or nonmember, may have *exception specifications* (or *throw-specifications*):

```
/*
 *      biff_pow() may throw or pass along Bam, Wham, Socko
 *      or any exception derived from one of them.
 */
Oomph&
biff_pow() throw( Bam, Wham, Socko )
{ … … }

/*
 *      Moonshine::mountain_dew() may throw or pass along
 *      Revenoower* or any pointer exception to a type
 *      derived from Revenooer.
 */
Demijohn
Moonshine::mountain_dew( Sugar&, Water&, Fire& ) const
        throw( Revenooer* )
{ … … }
/*
 *      Innocuous is not expected to throw or pass along any
 *      exception at all.
 */
void
innocuous() throw()
{  … …  }

/*
 *      Without an exception specification, a function may
 *      throw or pass along any exception.
 */
```

```
void
abandoned( int, void* )
{ ... ... }
```

The exception specification is *not* part of the function's type; a pointer to the function does not carry the exception specification with it. Neither does a pointer-to-member-function.

As of this writing, there is little practical experience with designing exception specifications in C++.

Exception specifications do *not* guarantee that no disallowed exception will be thrown; they guarantee that any such exception is handed over to `unexpected()`, which may choose to throw any exception, or none.

9.4 `terminate()` and `unexpected()`

Throwing or attempting to throw an exception can lead to further exceptional circumstances. These can be divided into two broad cases: those where an exception specification is violated and those where another exception is attempted. In addition, failing to catch an exception requires some action.

Violating an exception specification causes the function `unexpected()` to be invoked; attempting to throw one exception before another has reached its handler causes the function `terminate()` to be invoked. Failing to catch an exception will also cause `terminate()` to be called.

Because throwing an exception while exceptions are being handled will cause `*terminate()` to be called, destructors must be careful not to cause exceptions, or to catch those that get thrown before they can terminate a destructor used in unwinding the stack and trigger the call to `*terminate()`.

These functions operate in a manner similar to the `new_handler` discussed in Sec. 3.1.3. Each stores a pointer to a function whose signature is

```
void HANDLER();
```

Functions are provided to set the handlers:

```
typedef void (*HANDLER_P) ();

HANDLER_P set_unexpected( HANDLER_P* );
HANDLER_P set_terminate( HANDLER_P* );
```

When unexpected() or terminate() is called, it calls the handler function pointed to by its handler pointer. There are special restrictions on these functions. In particular:

The terminate handler function *must not return.*

If the unexpected handler returns, the function in which the unexpected exception is recognized will simply return. This is not usually a good idea, as something is almost surely not finished, closed out, or cleaned up. More often, the unexpected handler should throw another exception. There is no restriction placed on the exception thrown; it may even rethrow the exception that caused it to be called.

Unlike new_handler, the unexpected and terminate handler function pointers should not be null. A program begins with default values for them: the default value for the unexpected handler is terminate(); the default value for the terminate handler is abort(), which arranges for the program to be terminated and an error reported to the environment. On some systems, abort() may result in a copy of the program's image being stored for later debugging (a "core dump").

9.5 Managing Resources and Relationships in a World of Exceptions

Many resources must be allocated and deallocated as functions or objects come into existence and are destroyed. This is a special case of the programming of relationships: the resource and the object or the activity represented by the function have a one-to-one relationship that must be maintained. There are some subtleties.

Consider a class with one constructor and destructor:

```
class   Come_and_go
{
  public:
        Come_and_go();
        ~Come_and_go();
        ...
  private:
        A a;
        B b;
        C c;
        char* buf;
};
```

(We are neglecting the possible need for a copy constructor to simplify the example.)

Let's examine how the constructor and destructor might work.

```
Come_and_go::Come_and_go()
  : a(), b(), c()
{
        // Before we enter this block,  a ,  b, and
        // c  are created.

        buf = new char[ NBUF ];

        // Stuff is done here.
        dangerous();
}

~Come_and_go::Come_and_go()
{
        delete [] buf;

        // After we leave the destructor's body block,  c,
        // b , and  a  are destroyed.
}
```

What happens if an exception occurs somewhere in the constructor for Come_and_go? The stack-unwinding in the destructor will begin at a corresponding place. If the exception occurs in building one of the members a, b, or c, the destructor will resume in the corresponding part of that member when the time comes to unwind the stack. *But what happens if the exception occurs in the function* dangerous()*?*

If the exception occurs in the constructor body, the destructor will resume *after the destructor body.* In other words, the delete [] buf; will never be executed! This is clearly a grave error.

The solution—which must be adopted pervasively throughout any C++ program which will deal consistently with exceptions—is to embed the management of the character array represented by buf in a member object that will perform the allocation and deallocation:

```
template< class T, int n >
class   Fixed_array
{
  public:
        Fixed_array() : t( 0 ) { t = new T[ n ]; };
        ~Fixed_array() { delete [] t;

        operator T*() { return t; };
        operator const T*() { return t; } const;
```

```
private:
        T* t;
};

class Come_and_go
{
  public:
        Come_and_go();
        ~Come_and_go();
        ... ...
  private:
        A a;
        B b;
        C c;
        Fixed_array< char, NBUF > buf;
};
```

Now, no matter what exceptions occur in the body of `Come_and_go::Come_and_go()`, when the destructor for `Come_and_go` is executed, the memory allocated to `Come_and_go::buf` will be released.

9.6 Summary and Reference

Exception handling allows a program to deal with unexpected circumstances—or at least to address them.

Section 9.1.1 Unexpected events usually violate some assumption underlying the program's abstractions, and thus the *model* of the program. Guarding every part of the program with tests to defend against this distracts from the problem at hand—without properly addressing the problem. The failure must percolate upward through the active functions until it is found to deal with it. This expensive operation is acceptable for rare events.

Section 9.1.2 C++ exceptions are represented by objects with their type and value. The handler is chosen on the basis of the object's type; the value is used for whatever information the exception's originator and handler care to exchange. Functions that are offered the exception to handle and that cannot handle it are terminated and their member data destroyed.

An exception can be handled according to either its exact type or any of its publicly visible apparent types.

Section 9.2.1 Exceptions are caught by a `try`-*block* surrounding the statement in which they occur; they are handed to the appropriate catch-*clause* (or *handler*), if the function has one. Otherwise the function is terminated and the exception offered to the next function. To catch any exception at all, the ellipsis can be used.

Section 9.2.2 Exceptions are thrown by throw-*expressions* which construct an object of the appropriate type and set the exception-handling mechanism in motion.

Sections 9.2.4, 9.2.5, 9.2.6 Exceptions are subject to the slicing problem of Sec. 6.3.3.3. Using dynamic allocation to avoid the slicing problem is unreliable because exceptions can occur when memory allocation fails. Preallocating space can defend against the problem, and also against the limited amount of space that a C++ program might set aside to build a temporary exception exception object.

Section 9.2.7 An exception handler can rethrow an expression it has caught if it cannot deal with it completely.

Section 9.3 Exceptions violate locality. If a program is to handle exceptions in a comprehensive fashion, there must be a way to limit the scope which an exception may affect. C++ allows a function to declare that it may propagate certain exceptions; if any other exception would be propagated, it is turned into a call to *unexpected().

A function organized into domains may use them as boundaries across which only declared exceptions may pass.

Section 9.4 Exceptions that are not handled are turned into calls to *unexpected() (if they violate exception specifications) or *terminate() (if they are not called at all).

Section 9.5 To manage resources properly when exception handling is available, all resources must be tied firmly to some scope, so that exiting the scope will cause them to be freed.

Chapter

10

Stream I/O

Overview

C++ relies on the stream I/O system for portable and extensible input and output. *Extensible* means that the I/O system can be extended to serve user-defined types as well as built-in types, *and* can be extended to use different sorts of 'input character sources' and 'output character sinks.' (For instance, stream I/O could be extended to encrypt and decrypt blocks of characters as they are moved in and out of the program.)

The stream I/O system is simple to use, somewhat harder to extend to deal with new types, and fairly complicated to extend to new input and output sources and sinks. It also has some esoteric capabilities.

The stream I/O library has changed with every release of C++, and will likely change again. Until the ANSI/ISO standard is approved and published, there will be differences between the versions provided by different compiler vendors. The classes described here belong to the C++ Release 3.0 I/O stream library, except where noted. In particular, the I/O manipulators are described first in terms of a simple and plausible ANSI/ISO interface, and then in terms of the current, obscure interface.

(A late note: the ANSI/ISO committee has adopted a manipulator interface similar to the one presented here.)

Previous chapters have described the C++ language itself; this chapter describes a set of types, functions, and templates that are written mostly in C++.

10.1 Overall Structure

Recall that the basic use of stream I/O is with the overloaded << (insert) and >> (extract) operators:

```
int ntrials;

for(;;)
{
        cout << "Number of trials: " ;

        cin >> ntrials ;

        if( ntrials > 0 )
                break;
        cout << "Number of trials must be > 0.  " ;
}
```

These input and output operations involve

1. Recognizing a type for conversion.
2. Converting between a value of that type and the character representation of that value.
3. Moving those characters in or out of the program.

The first step is accomplished by overloading the insert and extract operators. The second step is accomplished by those operators, whose LHS operands are objects of types derived from an 'I/O stream' class.

The third step is accomplished by an object that accepts the characters from the operators (output) or provides them to the operators (input), while buffering them as necessary. This is an object of class `streambuf`. In practice, the actual object is of a class derived from `streambuf`; the `streambuf` part manages the buffer and the derived class part moves the characters in or out of the program.

10.1.1 Classes and relationships in stream I/O

Figure 10.1 is a *class-relationship diagram* of the stream I/O system. The class-relationship diagram is a variation of the *entity-relationship diagram* long used in data modeling and information modeling.

The boxes indicate classes with objects. The heavy lines indicate inheritance relationships, with the base class above the crossbar (in general, on the side of the bar that has just one stem). The lighter lines indicate other relationships, with information about the relationships indicated on the lines. The heavy dotted lines (crossbar and stem, like an inheritance relationship) indicate that a relationship is constrained by inheritance: when the `ios` is really an `fstreambase`, then the `streambuf` to which it is related is actually a `filebuf`.

The numbers at the end of relationship lines indicate the *cardinality* of the relationship: For every `ios` there are zero or one `streambufs`. For

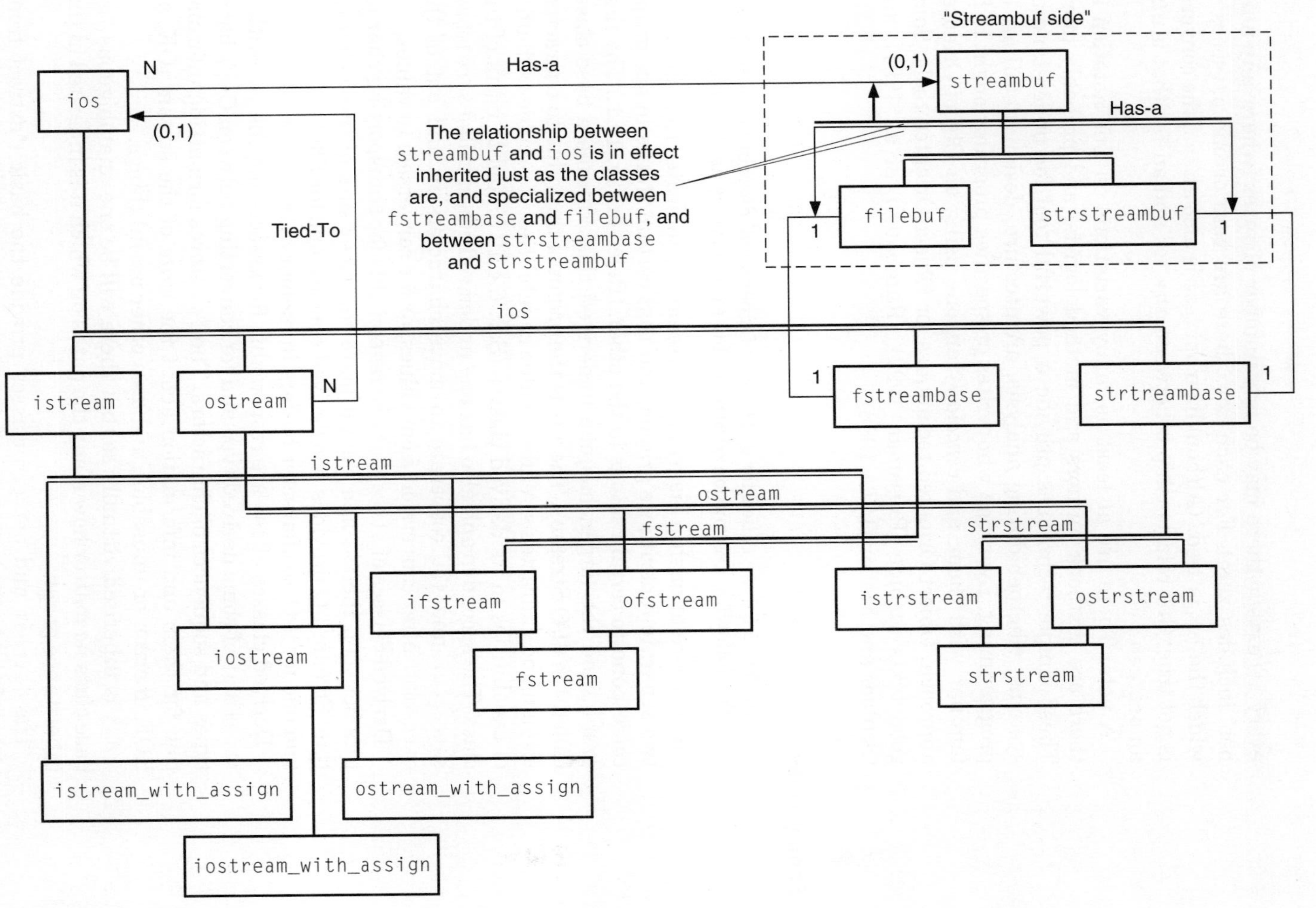
"Streambuf side"
Has-a
N
ios
(0,1)
streambuf
Has-a
The relationship between streambuf and ios is in effect inherited just as the classes are, and specialized between fstreambase and filebuf, and between strstreambase and strstreambuf
Tied-To
filebuf
strstreambuf
1
1
ios
istream
ostream
N
1
fstreambase
strtreambase
1
istream
ostream
fstream
strstream
ifstream
ofstream
istrstream
ostrstream
iostream
fstream
strstream
istream_with_assign
ostream_with_assign
iostream_with_assign

Figure 10.1

every `streambuf` there may be any number of `ios`es (where 'any number' includes zero). For each `ios`, there are zero or one `ostreams` to which the `ios` is 'tied.' (Although an `ostream` is also an `ios`, the converse is not true; this relationship is between *any* `ios` and an `ios` that is *also* an `ostream`.)

A note: There are at least as many variations on this notation as there are textbook authors and methodologists, and probably more. These simple techniques provide a powerful tool for understanding systems, whether during analysis, architecture, design, detailing, or programming. Everyone who writes or specifies programs ought to be familiar with them, and *especially* anyone using an Object-Oriented approach, Object-Oriented techniques, or Object-Oriented tools. Some good texts include (Pressman 1992), (Rumbaugh, et al. 1991), and (Schlaer and Mellor/DATA 1988).

10.2 Family Trees

In Sec. 5.6.1 we called for a 'Theory of Operation' description of software. The following description of Stream I/O may serve as an illustration.

The class-relationship diagram for stream I/O indicates that there are two separate inheritance graphs, and that certain things in one graph correspond to certain things in the other. (Refer to Fig. 10.1.) The first graph, and the larger, has one underived class (ultimate base class) called `ios` ('I/O Stream'). The `ios` is the origin of the value-to-character-stream and character-stream-to-value capabilities. It provides a 'buffet' of capabilities to its derived classes (Sec. 6.4.10.3) and to users of the class. The second graph also has one underived class, called `streambuf`. `streambuf` and `ios` cooperate to move characters in and out of the `streambuf` after conversion from values, or for conversion to values.

Derived classes of `streambuf` are responsible for transporting characters between the `ios` and the ultimate source or sink of those characters. Stream I/O provides two derived classes, one for file I/O (`filebuf`) and one for 'I/O' to character buffers in memory (`strstreambuf`).

Derived classes of `ios` are responsible for associating the `ios` with a `streambuf` of some derived type and for converting between C++'s basic types and sequences of characters. The `ios` stores formatting information for them and information about the *state* of the stream (OK, at EOF, in error, or unusable), and does other useful things.

`ios` is inherited virtually so that there will be one unambiguous `ios` base class no matter how many the paths on which it is inherited in the inheritance graph.

The `istream` and `ostream` classes provide the basic ("extract from stream") and output ("insert in stream") operations. `iostream` inherits from both, and has the capabilities of both. These three act as base classes for istream_withassign, ostream_withassign, and iostream_withassign, which in turn add the assignment operator to the capabilities of their base classes. Assignment causes the LHS stream to use the same streambuf as the RHS stream. (This capability is used at program start-up. It is not legal to assign to an ios or to most of the types derived from it.)

Two additional base classes are derived directly (and virtually) from ios. fstreambase and strstreambase ensure that their ios is initialized with a filebuf or a strstreambuf, respectively. This initialization may include connecting the streambuf with a file outside the program or establishing the connection between a strstreambuf and the memory it is to use. They also ensure that the streambuf is properly flushed and deallocated when the stream is destroyed, ensuring the integrity of the relationship between stream and streambuf. From each of these 'intermediate bases' are derived stream classes for input (ifstream, istrstream), output (ofstream, ostrstream), and both input and output (fstream, strstream).

10.3 Principal Constructors and Setup Functions

Since the constructors and setup functions adapt their objects to the task at hand (setting up relationships, etc.), understanding their calling sequences (and the basic province of each class) reveals how each class is meant to be used.

Of the constructors for the various classes, probably the most widely used use are those for the file streams and the string streams.

The file streams have a particular problem: opening a file can fail. Once exceptions become available, constructors will be able to 'report' errors by throwing an exception. Until then, it's important to check the stream state (Sec. 10.4) before trying to use a file stream whose construction attempted to 'open' a file.

A number of parameters are shown as ints in the implementation here. In an ANSI/ISO implementation, the parameters which give the length of any array will probably be size_t.

10.3.1 ios

Public constructor and destructor:

```
ios( streambuf* );
~ios();
```

Protected constructor:

```
ios();  // Doesn't actually initialize; used
        //   by some derived classes.
```

Protected setup function:

```
void init( streambuf* );     // Used to complete
                             //   the initialization.
```

Private constructors:

```
ios( ios& );        // In fact, it's not defined;
                    //   this prevents an accidental
                    //   pass-by-value parameter.
```

The `ios` does not take any responsibility for managing its `streambuf`.

```
sync_with_stdio:
        static void sync_with_stdio();
```

By default, the buffering of the stream I/O system and C-style standard I/O interfere with each other. After a call to `ios::sync_with_stdio()`, all stream I/O and standard I/O will interleave without interference. This imposes a performance penalty when the two are synchronized.

There is no way to undo `sync_with_stdio()`.

10.3.2 Basic streams

(Several 'obsolete' members are omitted here.)

10.3.2.1 `istream` public constructor and destructor:

```
istream( streambuf* );
virtual ~istream();
```

Protected constructor:

```
istream();        // Like ios::ios();
```

The `istream` does not take any responsibility for managing its `streambuf`.

10.3.2.2 `ostream` public constructor and destructor:

```
ostream( streambuf* );
virtual ~ostream();
```

Protected constructor:

```
ostream();          // Like ios::ios();
```

The `ostream` does not take any responsibility for managing its `streambuf`.

10.3.2.3 `iostream` public constructor and destructor:

```
iostream( streambuf* );
virtual ~iostream();
```

Protected constructor:

```
iostream();         // Like ios::ios();
```

The `iostream` does not take any responsibility for managing its `streambuf`.

10.3.3 `_withassign` streams

The `_withassign` streams act as aliases for another stream; assignment simply makes the LHS stream use the streambuf of the RHS stream.

Public constructors and destructors:

```
istream_withassign()
virtual ~istream_withassign()

ostream_withassign()
virtual ~ostream_withassign()

iostream_withassign()
virtual ~iostream_withassign()
```

Public assignment operators:

```
istream_withassign&
    istream_withassign::operator=( istream& );

istream_withassign&
    istream_withassign::operator=( streambuf* );
```

```
ostream_withassign&
    ostream_withassign::operator=( ostream& );

ostream_withassign&
    ostream_withassign::operator=( streambuf* );

iostream_withassign&
    iostream_withassign::operator=( iostream& );
iostream_withassign&
    iostream_withassign::operator=( streambuf* );
```

Because the `_withassign` streams assume that something else is managing the streambuf, they do not attempt to manage it.

10.3.4 File streams

The file streams are specialized to files. They are derived from `fstreambase` and they use an `fstreambuf`.

10.3.4.1 `fstreambase`. The `fstreambase` manages its own `streambuf`, which is a `filebuf`. The `filebuf` is created and destroyed along with the `fstreambase`. The various file management operations are passed through to the `fstreambuf`.

Public constructors:

```
public:
fstreambase();  // Used to create an fstreambase
                //   to be used a little later.

fstreambase( const char* name,            // Creates the
        int mode,                         //   fstreambase
                                          //   and connects
                                          //   it to a file.
        int prot=filebuf::openprot );     // See  open()
                                          //   below.
fstreambase( int fd );          // This is a UNIX version.
                                //   It passes the 'file
                        //   descriptor' of an already
                        //   open file to the fstreambuf
                        //   for use by the fstreambuf.
fstreambase( int fd, char* p, int l );  // Like the
                                        //   constructor
                        //   above, but it also provides
                        //   the fstreambuf with memory
                        //   for its buffer.  See the
                        //   matching fstreambuf constructor.
~fstreambase();
```

Public setup functions:

The success or failure of `open()` in the various file stream classes in C++ Release 3.0 is reflected not in a return value but in the setting of a state variable in the `ios`. (See Sec. 10.4.) In ANSI/ISO C++, an exception will probably be thrown (Chap. 9).

```
void open( const char* name,          // This is a UNIX or
        ios::open_mode mode,          //  POSIX interface.
        int prot = filebuf::openprot ); // The first
                                      //   argument is
                //   the filename, the second is a mask
                //   of bits given by the enumerators
                //   in ios::open_mode (for input,
                //   output, append, do not replace
                //   existing file, etc.)
                //
                //   In C++ Release 3.0 the second
                //   argument must be an int; in ANSI/ISO
                //   C++, it must be an ios::open_mode.
                //
                //   The third parameter sets the access
                //   permissions on the file if the
                //   file is new. This is specific to
                //   UNIX/POSIX.
void attach( int fd );          // See the constructors
                                //   above that take a 'file
                                //   descriptor' parameter.
void close();                   // Close the file.  Uses
                                //   fstreambuf::close(), which
                                //   flushes the file first.
```

10.3.4.2 Derived `fstreams`. Classes derived from `fstreambase` are meant to be instantiated to gain access to the file system in the environment in which the program is executing. Most of the functions are derived from `fstreambase` and most of the constructors correspond directly to those in `streambase` (Sec. 10.3.4.1), so no further explanation is provided here.

`ifstream` public constructors and destructors:

```
ifstream();
ifstream( const char* name,
        ios::open_mode mode = ios::in,
        int prot = filebuf::openprot );
ifstream( int fd );
ifstream( int fd, char* p, int l );
~ifstream();
```

`ifstream` **open function:**

```
void open( const char* name,
        ios::open_mode = ios::in,
        int prot=filebuf::openprot );
```

`ofstream` **public constructors and destructors:**

```
ofstream();
ofstream( const char* name,
        ios::open_mode = ios::out,
        int prot = filebuf::openprot );
ofstream( int fd );
ofstream( int fd, char* p, int l );
~ofstream();
```

`ofstream` **open function:**

```
void open( const char* name,
        ios::open_mode = ios::out,
        int prot = filebuf::openprot );
```

`fstream` **public constructors and destructors:**

```
fstream();
fstream( const char* name,
        ios::open_mode,
        int prot = filebuf::openprot );
fstream( int fd );
fstream( int fd, char* p, int l );
~fstream();
```

`fstream` **open function:**

```
void open( const char* name,
        int mode,
        int prot = filebuf::openprot );
```

10.3.4.3 `strstreambase`. The `strstreams` ('string streams') manage their own streambuf which is actually a `strstreambuf`. `strstreambufs` are associated with a region of memory, either allocated by themselves or by the user, into which or from which the stream will move characters. If they have not allocated the memory, they will not free it; if they have allocated the memory, their user may ask for it. If the user does not ask for the memory, the `strstreambuf` will free it.

Memory allocated by the `strstreambase` is managed dynamically by the `strstreambase`: if the characters inserted overflow the memory the `strstreambase` allocated, it will allocate a larger area and copy the characters to it. This is convenient if the final size is known, even approximately, it may be less costly for the class's client to provide an appropriately sized memory area.

strstreambase has no public constructors or initialization functions. The protected interface is of interest only to those who need to provide yet another kind of strstream.

Protected strstreambase constructors and destructors:

```
strstreambase( char* charbuf,    // Create a strstreambase,
        int len,                 //   using memory provided
        char* put_ptr );         //   outside the
                //   strstreambase.  The first argument
                //   identifies the memory.  The second
                //   argument is the length of the memory.
                //   If zero, it is assumed that there is
                //   a null-terminated string beginning at
                //   the beginning of the memory, and the
                //   strstreambuf's 'get' pointer (see
                //   Sec. 10.10) is set to the start of the
                //   buffer area.
                //   The third argument, if not null, is
                //   assumed to point into the character
                //   buffer.  It identifies the start of
                //   the 'put' area (see Sec. 10.10).
strstreambase();
~strstreambase() ;
```

10.3.4.4 Derived strstreams

istrstream public constructors and destructors:

```
istrstream( char* str ); // Create an input stream with
                         //   the buffer named by 'str'
                         //   (preloaded with characters).
                         //  The buffer is assumed to be
                         //   null-terminated.
istrstream( char* str, int size );      // As above,
                                        //   except that
                         //   the buffer's size is fixed
                         //   by the second argument.
istrstream( const char* str );          // As in the
                                        //   first case,
                         //   but for a const buffer.
istrstream( const char* str, int size ); // As in the
                                         //   second case,
                         //    but for a const buffer.
~istrstream() ;
```

`ostrstream` **public constructors and destructors:**

```
ostrstream( char* str,          // Create an ostrstream
            int size,           //   (output strstream) with
            ios::open_mode = ios::out);//  a fixed size
                                //   buffer of length  size
                                //   beginning at  str .
ostrstream();                   // Create an ostrstream
                                //   with a dynamically
                                //   managed buffer.  The
                                //   strstreambuf will
                                //   allocate and reallocate
                                //   memory as necessary.
~ostrstream();
```

`strstream` **public constructors and destructors:**

```
strstream();            // Create a strstream for both
                        //   insertion and extraction
                        //   (a circular strstream).
                        //   the strstream's buffer will
                        //   be automatically allocated
                        //   and reallocated as necessary.
strstream( char* str,           // Create a strstream for
        int size,               //   both insertion and
        ios::open_mode mode );  //   extraction using
                                //   a fixed buffer
                        //   of length  size  at the
                        //   location identified by  str .
~strstream();
```

10.3.5 `streambuf`

The interface between `ios` and `streambuf` is intricate. It is described in detail in Sec. 10.10. We need some terms here. The *reserve area* is another name for the buffer. The *get area* and *put area* are disjoint regions of the reserve area identified by the *get pointer* and *put pointer.*

`streambuf` **constructors and destructors:** (These are public in C++ Release 3.0 but may be made protected in ANSI/ISO C++.)

```
streambuf();            // Create a streambuf which will
                        //   allocate its own reserve area.
streambuf( char* res, int len );// Create a streambuf
                        //   with an externally provided
                        //   reserve area of length  len
                        //   starting at  res .

virtual ~streambuf();
```

10.3.6 Derived streambufs

filebuf **public constructors and destructors:**

```
filebuf();                  // Create a filebuf unassociated
                            //    with any file.
filebuf( int fd );          // Create a filebuf associated with
                            //    with the file already open on
                            //    file descriptor  fd .  This
                            //    is a UNIX/POSIX interface.
filebuf( int fd,            // Like above, but use a buffer
                            //    (reserve area) of length
        char* ptr,          //    length beginning at ptr.
        int len );

filebuf* open( const char *name,// Create a filebuf
        ios::open_mode mode,    //   associated with the
                                //   file named by the
                                //   first parameter.
        int prot = openprot );  // Open the file with the
                                //   mode (read, write,
                //   append, etc.) given by the second
                //   parameter.  The third parameter
                //   sets the access permissions on the
                //   file if the file is new.  This is
                //   UNIX/POSIX-specific.
~filebuf();
```

filebuf **public setup functions:**

```
filebuf* attach( int fd );      // Associate the filebuf
                                //   with the file
                //   identified by the file descriptor
                //   fd . This is UNIX/POSIX-specific.
virtual streambuf* setbuf( char* ptr,   // Assign the
                int len );              //   (not-yet-
                                        //   active)
                //   filebuf the reserve area of  length
                //   len  beginning at ptr .
```

strstreambuf **public constructors and destructors:**

```
strstreambuf();             // Create a strstreambuf with
                            //   automatic management of
                            //   the string memory.
strstreambuf( int len ); // Create a strstreambuf with
                            //   automatic management of
                //   the string memory, starting with
```

```
                //    enough memory for  len  chars.
strstreambuf(                        // Create a strstreambuf
    void* (*allocator) ( size_t ),        //   with
    void (*deallocator) ( void* ) );      //   automatic
                                          //   management
                //   of the string memory, using the
                //   argument functions to allocate and
                //   deallocate memory. If the allocator
                //   function pointer is null, global
                //   operator new is used; if the
                //   deallocator function pointer is null,
                //   global operator delete is used.
strstreambuf( char* r,  // Create a strstreambuf using
        int size, //   reserve area (buffer) of
        char* pstart = 0 ); //   length  size .  If
                //   size is zero, assume that the
                //   reserve area is a get area containing
                //   a null-terminated string.  If the
                //   pstart argument is non-null, assume
                //   the pointer identifies the beginning
                //   of a put area.
strstreambuf( signed char* r,            // Like the previous
        int size,                        //   constructor,
        unsigned char* pstart = 0 );     //   but using an
                        // array of signed chars instead
                        // of 'natural' chars.

strstreambuf( unsigned char* r,          // Like the previous
        int size,                        //   constructor,
        unsigned char* pstart = 0 );     //   but using
                                         //   an array of
                //   unsigned chars instead of
                //   'natural' chars.

~strstreambuf();
```

`strstreambuf` **public setup functions:**

```
virtual streambuf* setbuf ( char* ptr,   // Convert the
        int len );       //   (unused) strstreambuf to use
                         //   a fixed (buffer) reserve
                         //   area of length len at the
                         //   location identified by  ptr .
```

10.3.7 Program startup

Program startup poses special challenges for classes which depend upon external initialization (which stream I/O does, for the predefined streams cin, cout, and cerr) and which are also of such general use that other external or static constructors are likely to want to use them. Stream I/O accomplishes this by a truly awful kludge of very general use. (If a language enhancement that improves this at acceptable cost can be found, ANSI/ISO C++ will probably incorporate that enhancement and ANSI/ISO stream I/O will use it.)

The kludge is this: *the constructors written for those predefined external streams do nothing at all!* Instead, initialization is handled by a friend class called Iostream_init. The iostream.h header, uncharacteristically, declares a static instance of that class, which must be initialized before anything in any header file that follows it will be initialized:

```
#include <iostream.h>     // As its last step,
                          //   iostream.h initializes a
                          //   static instance of
                          //   Iostream_init.
#include <kinky.h>        // Now kinky.h can
                          //   use any of the predefined
                          //   I/O streams…
```

When an instance of Iostream_init is created, it checks its own static variable to see if it is the first instance created. If so, *it* performs the initialization of the predefined external I/O streams. On destruction, a similar protocol is followed.

10.4 ios State

Every ios has associated with it a *state,* which is set by various operations and which may be interrogated in various ways.

Also important to the usability of the stream is the stream's buffering strategy. Related to stream buffering is the concept of a *tied* stream, which helps to coordinate interactive input and output.

10.4.1 The I/O state and its values

The state is represented by an enum:

```
class   ios
{
            … …
        enum io_state { goodbit = … …,
                        eofbit = … …,
                        failbit = … …,
                        badbit = … … … } ;
            … …
};
```

The enumerator names describe the way the state information is stored. One state indicator can hide another (e.g., `failbit` can hide `eofbit`). This means that there are four externally visible states: good, eof, fail, and bad. *good* means that the stream is ready to perform I/O. *eof* means that the stream has reached end-of-file. *fail* means that some operation (typically formatted input) has failed, and that another operation might succeed after the stream is reset. *bad* means that there has been an I/O failure of some sort and recovery is nontrivial, either because there is an external I/O error (e.g., a network failure) or because characters have been lost.

10.4.2 Reading the stream state

The stream state can be read in a number of ways. First, the `ios` has an implicit conversion defined to `void*`. This means that we can write

```
if( cin )
        ... ...
```

The conversion returns a nonnull value if the stream state is *good,* null otherwise. (Typically, the value is just the value of the conversion operator's *this* pointer—see Sec. 3.3.4.)

The insert and extract operators return a reference to the stream so that

```
if( cin >> boffin )
        ... ...
```

also invokes `ios::operator void*()`, but *after* the operation has taken place. If the operation has succeeded, the test succeeds; if the operation has failed, the test fails. There are two subtleties to notice.

First, if the stream state was not *good* to begin with, no operation is attempted. Second, if the operation is attempted and fails, *the RHS variable is not changed.* We'll see in Sec. 10.8 that this is a great convenience in writing extractors for class types, but also a great responsibility. These properties also make code like

```
cin >> biffin >> boffin >> buffin ;
```

both safe and sensible in many situations.

Besides `operator void()`, `ios` has `operator!()`. This returns nonzero if `operator void*()` would return null, zero otherwise.

The member function `rdstate()` returns the actual state variable value. The `int` member functions `good()`, `eof()`, `fail()`, and `bad()` return `int` one or zero as the `ios` is or is not in that state.

10.4.3 Setting and resetting the stream state

When a stream is created, it is by default in the *good* state. If it is not attached to a file or string or other source or sink of characters (through its `streambuf`), an attempt to perform I/O will change its state. An attempt at input will result in setting the state to *fall.* It will also set the `eofbit`. An attempt to write to the stream will set the stream state to *bad.*

(These are not yet standardized and may differ somewhat from implementation to implementation. The results presented in this section were achieved with the AT&T Release 3.0 'cfront' translator. The ANSI/ISO standard will provide definitive values.)

To set the stream state, the member function `clear()` may be used:

```
class   ios
{
        ... ...
        void clear( newstate = goodbit ) ;
        ... ...
```

The default argument to `clear()` sets the state to *good.* The other `ios::io_state` enumerators may be used as well. This is important when writing extractors and inserters for user-defined types.

10.4.4 Stream buffering and tied streams

To achieve any kind of efficiency on bulk file input and output, the stream must be buffered so that it communicates with the environment (OS, file system, etc.) in a way that is convenient for the environment. To operate properly with interactive input and output, buffering must be defeated at certain times and certain places.

Stream I/O provides two ways of defeating this. First, there is 'unit buffering,' which buffers a single built-in insertion operator. This facility is not well-enough standardized to present here. Second, there is 'tying' of an input stream to an output stream. Any attempt to read on the input stream causes the output stream to be flushed. For example, `cin` may be tied to `cout`. A read on `cin` will first flush any waiting characters from `cout`.

Tying is accomplished by `ios::tie()`:

```
class   ios
{
  public:
        ... ...
        ostream* tie( ostream* ) ;
        ... ...
```

```
};
... ...
ifstream caller_in( ...args... ) ;
ofstream caller_out( ...args... ) ;

caller_in.tie( &caller_out ) ;

... ...
caller_out << "Enter Account Code: " ;
caller_in >> acct_code ;
... ...
```

`tie()` returns the previous value of the class's tied-to variable, allowing tied streams to be saved and restored as need.

More control over the `streambuf` is possible using the `streambuf`'s public functions (see Sec. 10.10). To get the identity of the `streambuf` used by a stream, use `ios::rdbuf()`:

```
class   ios
{
  public:
        ... ...
        ostream* rdbuf() ;
        ... ...
```

10.4.6 `flush` and `endl`

It is also possible to explicitly flush an ostream's buffer. Stream I/O provides two special objects (*not* classes!) to do this.

One of these objects is called `flush`:

```
buffered_stream << a << ' ( ' ;

buffered_stream << b << ', ' << c << ', ' << d << ', ' ;
buffered_stream << e << ', ' << f << ', ' << g << ', ' ;

buffered_stream << h << ' );' << flush ;
```

Inserting `flush` into the stream produces no output; instead it causes the buffer(s) in `buffered_stream` to be flushed.

`endl` is similar, except that `endl` *does* produce output. It inserts a new line into the output stream, then flushes the stream:

```
cout << "Time into phase 1: " << my_time_object << endl ;
```

Objects which are used like `flush` and `endl` are called *manipulators* and are presented in Sec. 10.9.

10.5 Formatted I/O

The I/O operations provided by stream I/O can be divided into *formatted* and *unformatted* operations.

Formatted operations are performed using the (heavily overloaded) insertion and extraction operators. They obey certain format specification variables (field widths, input radix, etc.) in the `ios`, and there are some functions in the input and output streams to assist user-defined extractors and inserters.

Unformatted I/O deals with moving characters without conversions, but in some cases monitoring the character stream to read a record delimited by a sentinel (typically new line). Unformatted I/O is presented in Sec. 10.7.

The formatted inserters and extractors can in turn be divided into 'normal' inserters and extractors (for `int`, `char`, `double`, etc.) and those which perform 'special' operations (for the I/O manipulators and other special things).

10.5.1 Normal inserters

The inserters (and extractors) for built-in types are members of `ostream`.

```
class  ostream
{
  public:
    ... ...
        /*
         *      The  const char*  inserter handles such things
         *      as  cout << "Hello, World."
         */
        ostream& operator<<( char ) ;
        ostream& operator<<( signed char ) ;
        ostream& operator<<( unsigned char ) ;

        ostream& operator<<( const char* ) ;

        ostream& operator<<( int ) ;
        ostream& operator<<( short ) ;
        ostream& operator<<( long ) ;

        ostream& operator<<( unsigned int ) ;
        ostream& operator<<( unsigned short ) ;
        ostream& operator<<( unsigned long ) ;

        ostream& operator<<( double ) ;
        ostream& operator<<( float ) ;
```

```
        /*
         *      The void* and const void* inserters print a
         *      pointer in a machine-dependent (but usually
         *      hexadecimal) format.  (This is unlike the
         *      const char*  inserter, which prints what the
         *      pointer points at.)
         *
         *      Since just about every pointer can be
         *      converted to a  void* , every pointer save
         *      pointer-to-char can be converted to characters
         *      directly by this inserter.  (Pointer-to-char
         *      requires an explicit conversion to  void*  to
         *      avoid using the overload for  char* -- or
         *      const char* .)
         */
        ostream& operator<<( void* ) ;
        ostream& operator<<( const void* ) ;
    ... ...
```

We may presume that inserters for `long double` and for `wchar_t*` will also be provided in ANSI/ISO C++.

10.5.2 Normal extractors

The extractors (and inserters) for built-in types are members of `ostream`.

```
class ostream
{
  public:
    ... ...
        /*
         *      These three are DANGEROUS!  They don't
         *      control how many characters will be read
         *      unless format control is used, so array
         *      overflow is quite possible.
         */
        istream& operator>>( char* ) ;
        istream& operator>>( unsigned char* ) ;
        istream& operator>>( signed char* ) ;

        istream& operator>>( char& )
        istream& operator>>( unsigned char& )
        istream& operator>>( signed char& )

        istream& operator>>( int& ) ;
        istream& operator>>( short& ) ;
        istream& operator>>( long& ) ;
```

```
        istream& operator>>( unsigned int& ) ;
        istream& operator>>( unsigned short& ) ;
        istream& operator>>( unsigned long& ) ;

        istream& operator>>( float& ) ;
        istream& operator>>( double& ) ;
    ... ...
```

We may presume that extractors for `long double` and for `wchar_t*` will also be provided in ANSI/ISO C++.

10.5.3 Special inserters

Special inserters do special things.

```
class   ostream
{
  public:
    ... ...
        ostream& operator<<( ostream& (*f)( ostream& ) )
                                { return (*f)( *this ) ; } ;
        ostream& operator<<( ios& (*f)(ios&) ) ;
                                { return (*f)( *this ) ; } ;
        ostream& operator<<( streambuf*) ;
    ... ...
```

The first two inserters are used by manipulators. For example, `endl` could be defined like this:

```
ostream&
endl( ostream& o )
{
        o << '\n';
        o.flush() ;

        return o;
}
```

The inserter for this function type (actually pointer-to-function type) takes the function and applies it to the stream itself! This is the basic modus operandi of manipulators.

The third inserter shown in this group is used to transfer characters from one `streambuf` to another. All the available characters are transferred.

10.5.4 Special extractors

Special extractors do special things.

```
class   istream
{
  public:
     ... ...
        istream& operator>>( istream& (*f)( istream& ) )
                                   { return (*f)( *this ) ; } ;
        istream& operator>>( ios& (*f)( ios& ) ) ;
                                   { return (*f)( *this ) ; } ;
        istream& operator>>( streambuf* ) ;
     ... ...
```

The first two extractors support manipulators. There is a manipulator called `ws`, which might be defined (in part) like this:

```
istream&
ws( istream& is )
{
        /*
         *      Eat leading whitespace characters
         */
        ... ...
        return is;
}
```

Then an extraction of the form

```
cin >> ws
```

is turned into a call like this:

```
ws( cin )
```

The third extractor shown in this group is used to transfer characters from one `streambuf` to another. One extraction transfers as many characters as the RHS buffer can absorb.

10.6 Format Control (`ios` Format Settings)

The `ios` has a number of formatting controls. It also has provision for adding more at run time for use with inserters and extractors written for user-defined types.

The built-in controls come in two flavors: those that are flags and those that are variables. The flags are given by an enum in the `ios` and set and reset by member functions and manipulators. So are the variables, but the variables have one function and (sometimes) one manipulator each. The flags are handled in a less regular way. Every `ios` has a set of these flags and variables.

These facilities are described as they occur in AT&T's C++ Release 3.0 (except for changes which are necessary for overloading, and type system proposals already accepted by x3j16/WG21). They may be completely rethought for ANSI/ISO C++.

10.6.1 Formatting flags

The `ios` defines these formatting flags:

Skip whitespace. `ios::skipws` set.
Skip leading whitespace on input when converting a numeric type.

Padding location. One of `ios::left`, `ios::right`, or `ios::internal` selected from `ios::adjustfield`.
When fill characters must be added on output, where are they added? To the left, to the right, or between the sign indicator (if any) and the rest of the characters.

Conversion base. `ios::dec`, `ios::oct`, or `ios::hex` selected from `ios::basefield`.
On output, which base should be used for conversion? On input, which base should be assumed in the absence of an indicator (leading 0 or 0x)?

Indicate base. `ios::showbase` set.
On output, generate the leading 0 (for octal) or 0x (for hexadecimal).

Show decimal point. `ios::showpoint` set.
On output, indicate the decimal point and trailing zeros, even if they are not significant.

Indicators in uppercase. `ios::uppercase` set.
On uppercase, make the 0x into 0X (hexadecimal indicator prefix) and the e into E (when indicating the exponent in scientific notation).

Use plus sign. `ios::showpos` set.
On output, use a leading plus sign for non-negative values on numeric conversions.

Use scientific notation always. `ios::scientific` set out of `ios::floatfield`.
On output, convert all floating point numbers into scientific notation (default is to select scientific or fixed-point according to the value).

Use fixed point notation always. `ios::fixed` set out of `ios::floatfield`.
On output, convert all floating point numbers into fixed-point notation (default is to select scientific or fixed-point according to the value).

Note that the formatting of numbers depends upon `locale.h` (App. A, Sec. I3). In particular, the 'decimal point' in some national locales will be a comma rather than a period.

10.6.2 Accessing the format flags

Format flags that stand on their own ("`ios::skipws` set") are accessed slightly differently from those that belong to a field ("`ios::scientific` set out of `ios::floatfield`").

All the flags can be read at once and set at once with the `ios::flags` function:

```
class   ios
{
  public:
    ... ...
        format_flags flags() const;
        format_flags flags( format_flags f );
    ... ...
```

Warning: The `format_flags` *type doesn't really exist!* In Release 3.0, the type is `long`. In ANSI/ISO C++, there will have to be a named enum for this type in accordance with the new rules for enum types in arithmetic expressions.

The 'set' overload of `flags()` is used when saving and restoring the flags as a unit. The return from that overload is the *previous* value of the flags. Thus, save-and-change can be done in one operation.

To set and clear flags that are not part of a field, use

```
class   ios
{
  public:
        ... ...
        format_flags setb( format_flags flags_to_set ) ;
        format_flags unsetb( format_flags flags_to_clear ) ;
        ... ...
```

These also return the previous value of the form at flag variable.

For flags that are part of a field, use

```
class   ios
{
  public:
        format_flags setf( format_flags flags_to_set,
                                  format_flags field_to_use ) ;
        ... ...
```

`ios::setf()` first clears all the flag bits in the field, then sets the bits associated with the flags to be set.

Some of these capabilities are also available in manipulators.

10.6.3 Format control variables

Besides the flags, every *ios* has a set of form at control variables (data members). These are *field width, precision,* and *fill character.* They are accessed and managed with these functions:

```
class   ios
{
  public:
        int width() const;
        int width( int new_width ) ;

        int precision() const;
        int precision( int new_precision ) ;

        char fill_char() const;
        char fill_char( int new_fill_char ) ;
        ... ...
```

In all cases the 'set' overloads return the previous value. Taking them in reverse order:

The fill character is used on output whenever a field width is greater than the number of characters available to place in it. The extra characters have the value of the fill character. The default fill character is a blank.

The precision is used on output when converting a floating point number. It is the minimum of the total number of significant digits (on either side of the decimal point). The default value for the precision is six. The precision is *not* the same in fixed precision as the number of digits after the decimal point. 1234e-8, printed with a precision of 3 in fixed-point, will print as 0.0000000123. Three digits of precision are supplied.

The field width is used on output as the minimum total field width for the conversion, including all signs, decimal indicators, and so forth. It is used *on input* for character strings (`char*`, `signed char*`, `unsigned char*`, and `wchar_t`). Exactly how it will be applied to `wchar_t`, which may on some systems translate variable numbers of printable characters to one `wchar_t`, is not clear. The field width is unusual in that it resets to its default value of 0 after every insertion or extraction. If an inserter or extractor for a class needs to save the value to use a second time, it must preserve the value itself.

These three formatting variables may also be set by manipulators (see Sec. 10.9). This facility is especially convenient for the field width, which clears after each extraction or insertion:

```
cout << setw( 8 ) << account.name() << ": " <<
        setw( 10 ) << account.num() << " " <<
        setw( 6 ) << account.type() << " " <<
                account.standing() << endl ;
```

10.6.4 Extending the formatting flags and variables

User-defined types may demand additional formatting flags and variables. Each instance of an `ios` must have its own instance of the extra data, but all instances of the `ios` in that program must have the same 'schema' for those data. The `ios` accomplishes this with a mixture of static members (to manage the schemas) and ordinary members.

Accordingly, if a class needs to allocate some of these 'extended' flags or variables, it is up to the class to remember which belong to it, and to use them accordingly. The class will probably need static data to manage the flags or variables.

Extended formatting flags and variables are allocated and accessed by means of member functions in the `ios`.

```
class   ios
{
  public:
        ... ...
        long bitalloc() ;

        int xalloc() ;
        long& iword( int ) ;
        void*& pword( int ) ;
        ... ...
```

`ios::bitalloc()` returns a `long` with a single bit set. This bit belongs to the `flags` variable and is set and gotten with those various 'flags' functions. Each call to `bitalloc()` returns a different bit, so that `bitalloc()` should be called once for each flag that must be added to the `ios` *type*. These flags are a very finite resource. (This interface will almost certainly have to change in ANSI/ISO C++, but the direction of change is not now obvious.)

`ios::xalloc()` ('eXtension ALLOCate') returns an index into an array of `long`s which every `ios` possesses. (This array is also a finite resource, and should be husbanded in the same way as the `bitalloc()` flags.)

The `ios::iword()` and `ios::pword()` functions return references or pointers to the `long` 'word' indicated by the index returned from `ios::xalloc()`. (These interfaces may also change in ANSI/ISO C++. The need for change is smaller in this than in the flag allocation.)

10.7 Unformatted I/O

Unformatted I/O is used when characters must be moved without any formatting control, but (possibly) with respect for single-character record sentinels (e.g., newlines).

Unformatted I/O also supports a seek-and-tell mechanism. An input stream has a 'get' pointer buried within it; an output stream has a 'put' pointer, and a stream for both input and output has both.

10.7.1 Input

An `istream` has these 'get' member functions:

```
class  istream
{
  public:
        ... ...
        int get() ;                          //Like  getchar()  or
                                             //  getc(), it returns
                                             //  EOF on attempt to
                                             //  read past end-of-
                                             //  file.

        istream& get( char& ) ;              //These three extract a
        istream& get( signed char& ) ;       //  char (unless at EOF)
        istream& get( unsigned char& ) ;     //  and storeit in their
                                             //  argument. They can
                                             //  be embedded in a
                           // sequence of extractors, viz.:
                           // ( cin >> a ) .get( b ) .get( c ) >> d ;

        istream& get( char*,                 //These three read a
                      int lim,               //  sequence of up to
                      char delim = '\n' );//  lim - 1  chars,
        istream& get( signed char*,          //  stopping if the
                         int lim,            // 'delimiter' character
                         char delim = '\n' );//is encountered. EOF
        istream& get) unsigned char*,        //  is set if it is
                int lim,            //  encountered; FAIL is set if
                char delim = '\n' );//EOF is hit before any chars
                         //  are read.  The array stored will be
                         //  null-terminated, (even if it is
                         //  empty) ; the delimiter char will NOT
                         //  be read.

  istream& getline( char*,          //These three are like the
                int lim,            //  previous three ( get(,,) ),
                char delim = '\n' );//except that the delimiter
  istream& getline( signed char*  //  char WILL be stored if it
```

```
                    int lim,        //  was hit while reading the
                    char delim = '\n' );//maximum number of chars.
istream& getline( unsigned char*//  If the delimiter char is
                    int lim,        //  next-to-be-read, it will
                    char delim = '\n' );//remain on the stream.

istream& get( streambuf&,       //Move chars into the
                    char delim = '\n' );//streambuf until the
                                    //  streambuf can take no
                                    //  more (in which case FAIL
                                    //  is set) or until  delim
                                    //  is encountered on the
                                    //  input stream.  (It's
                                    //  left there.)
```

The 'get' functions treat character streams in a C-like fashion: there are individual characters and there are lines terminated with newlines.

An `istream` also has an `ignore` function:

```
class   istream
{
  public:
        ... ...
        istream& ignore( int lim,        //Like getline( char*,
                char delim ) ;           //   lim, delim ) , but
                                         //   throws away the
                                         //  chars.  The delim
                                         //  char is consumed.
```

An `istream` has these 'read' member functions:

```
class   istream
{
  public:
        ... ...
        istream& read( char*,   //Extracts  count  characters and
                int count );    //    places them in the array
        istream& read( signed char*,//identified by the first
                int count );    //    argument.  On end-of-file
        istream& read( unsigned char*,//they set FAIL, and the
                int count );    //    number of characters
                                //    transferred is available
                                //    from  gcount() .

                int gcount();   // Returns the number of
                                //   characters successfully
                                //   transferred by the last
                                //   unformatted input.
                ... ...
```

It is likely, but in no way certain, that the `int` parameters in these function declarations may become `size_t` in the ANSI/ISO version of C++.

10.7.2 Output

An `ostream` has a 'put' function:

```
class   ostream
{
  public:
        ... ...
        ostream& put( char ) ;    // Inserts the paramter into
                                  //   the ostream .   Sets
                                  //   the  FAIL state if for
                                  //   some reason it can't be
                                  //   done.
```

An `ostream` has these 'write' functions:

```
class   ostream
{
  public:
        ... ...
        ostream& write( const char*,                //Insert into the
                        int count                   //   ostream
        ostream& write( const signed char*,         //   count
                        int count                   //   characters.
        ostream& write( const unsigned char*,       //   Null
                        int count                   //   characters
                                                    //   may be
                                                    //   included in
                                                    //   the array
                                                    //   transferred.
```

An `ostream` has a `flush()` function which forces the `streambuf` to send any characters currently buffered out to their ultimate sink (if any), 'completing' the I/O.

10.7.2 Pointer movement

On streams where it makes sense, the 'read pointer' or 'write pointer' for the stream may be retrieved, stored, and set to a previously retrieved value. It makes sense to do so on streams whose streambufs are associated with character sources or character sinks which support such operations (e.g., disk files but not interactive terminals or communication links). The functions that do this are sometimes called 'pointer movement' or 'positioning' functions.

These functions use and return variables of type `streampos` (stream position) and `streamoff` (stream offset). The *stream position* is a 'magic cookie' describing the location of the `streambuf`'s get or put pointer in the character stream. On some systems it may be implemented in such a way that arithmetic can be performed on it. This is not true on all systems and cannot be relied upon.

The *stream offset,* on the other hand, is an ordinary integral type (e.g., `long` or `size_t`). It describes character-count offset in the character stream.

A stream that provides both input and output (e.g., an `fstream` or a `strstream`) has both a get pointer and a put pointer. (Functions to operate on the get pointer end in 'g'; functions to operate on the put pointer end in 'p'.) The behavior of these pointers is determined by the `streambuf`, to which they really belong. For some `streambuf`s, the two pointers are 'locked together.' `fstream`s behave this way. For others, the two pointers identify different ends of one queue. `strstream`s behave like such a queue.

Some of the pointer movement functions use a 'seek direction.' This is an enum in `ios`:

```
class   ios
{
  public:
        ... ...
        enum seek_dir    { beg=0, cur=1, end=2 } ;
        ... ...
```

The three enumerators of `ios::seek_dir` mean

- The offset provided is taken relative to the beginning of the character stream (absolute position in a file) (`ios::beg`).
- The offset provided is taken relative to the current position of the pointer in the character stream (relative position in a file) (`ios::cur`).
- The offset provided is taken relative to the end of the character stream (or end-of-file) (`ios::end`).

For input streams, the pointer positioning functions are these:

```
class   istream
{
  public:
        ... ...
        streampos tellg();              // Return a  streampos  for
                                        //   the current get pointer.
        istream& seekg( streampos );    // Move the get pointer to the
```

```
                                        //   position indicated by the
                                        //   streampos  parameter.
        istream& seekg( streamoff,      // Move the stream pointer to
                ios::seek_dir );        //   the position indicated by
                                        //   the  streamoff , the seek
                                   //   direction and (for seek direction
                                   //   ios::cur) the current position.

        ... ...
class   ostream
{
  public:
        ... ...
        streampos tellp() ;             // Return a  streampos  for
                                        //   the current put pointer.
        ostream& seekp ( streampos ) ;  // Move the put pointer to the
                                        //   position indicated by
                                        //   the streampos parameter.
        ostream& seekp( streamoff,      // Move the stream pointer to
                ios::seek_dir ) ;       //   the position indicated
                                        //   by the  streamoff , the
                                   //   seek direction and (for seek
                                   //   direction ios::cur) the current
                                   //   position.
        ... ...
```

Note that on some systems, and for some files, these operations may be unduly expensive, especially if the file is stored in some sort of compressed format by the file system.

10.8 Inserters and Extractors for User-Defined Types

The insertion and extraction operators can be overloaded on user-defined types. Extractors will be tricky because they parse input. Inserters are bipolar in their difficulty. It's easy to write a naive inserter, but to cooperate fully with the stream interface is a little more complicated.

The basic rules for overloading the << and >> operators are the same as for overloading any other ordinary operators (Sec. 4.4).

10.8.1 Naive inserters

A simple inserter is easy to write. For a `Point` template, it might look like this:

```
#include <iostream.h>

template< class Base_t >
class   Point
{
```

```
    ... ...
        friend ostream& operator<<( ostream& o,
                                    const Point< Base_t > ap )
        {       return o << "( " << ap.x()
                        << ", "
                        << ap.y() << " )" ;
        } ;

        friend istream& operator>>( istream&, Point< Base_t > ap ) ;

        Base_t x() const { return x_val; };
        Base_t y () const { return y_val; };

    ... ...
    private:
        Base_t x_val;
        Base_t y_val;
} ;
```

This is quick and easy. It doesn't manage the field width properly, nor does it do anything special to cooperate with the internals of the I/O system. (To be fair, it doesn't have to.)

10.8.2 First-class inserters

The things which make an inserter more sophisticated fall into two categories: using, propagating, and adjusting formatting parameters; and building formatted I/O around unformatted I/O.

10.8.2.1 Inserters and formatting parameters. Three kinds of formatting parameters affect inserters: field width, other built-in parameters, and extended formatting parameters. The first two are discussed here. The third is too dependent upon the actual types involved and their meaning.

Consider the inserter for `Point`, above. Let's say we write

```
Point p = ... ...

cout << width( 12 ) << p << endl;
```

The width parameter is good for only one formatted operation. But the inserter for `Point` is made up of other inserters:

```
return o << " ( " << ap.x()
         << ", "
         << ap.y() << " ) " ;
```

The naive inserter will apply the field width to the insertion of the left parenthesis. This is probably not what we want.

Since all we have is a width, not a breakdown of expected widths, we have to do some guessing. Here's one way to approach it:

```
ostream& friend operator<<( ostream& o, const Point< Base_t >& ap )
{
	int t_wid = o.width();

	int w1;
	int w2;

	if( t_wid <= 4 )
		w1 = w2 = 0;
	else
	{
		w1 = ( t_wid - 3 ) / 2;
		w2 = t_wid - 3 - w1;
	}

	return o << width( 0 ) '(' << width( w1 ) << ap.x()
			<< ',' << width( w2 ) << ap.y()
			<< ')' ;
}
```

We also have to take into account the 'nonvolatile' field width issues: precision, padding direction, etc. The version above will cause padding to be provided for both numeric fields, placing it *within* the outer parentheses even if the `ios::adjustfield` bits are not set to `ios::internal`.

To do this really well requires heroic measures:

```
/*
 *	We'll need all three of these:
 * #include <iostream.h>
 * #include <strstream.h>
 * #include <iomanip.h>
 */

/*
 *	Some little help doing the output.  There's a matter
 *	of the interface between formatted and unformatted
 *	I/O.  It would be handy if the I/O system provided
 *	this class.  The members of ostream used here are
 *	described in the text.
 */
class	Bracket_format
```

```
{
  public:
        Bracket_format( ostream& o )
          : ost( o ), ok( ost.opfx() ) {} ;

        ~Bracket_format() { if( ok ) ost.osfx() ; }

        operator int() const { return ok; } ;

  private:
                ostream& ost;
                int ok;
};

template< class Base_t >
ostream&
operator<<( ostream& o, const Point< Base_t >& ap )
{
        /*
         *      We'll separately convert the X and Y parts of
         *      the point into x_part and y_part.
         *
         *      We could spare some memory allocation effort
         *      in an implementation for a built-in numeric type,
         *      but we can't risk it in the general template.
         *      Who knows what our Base_t might be?  (But how
         *      much recursive strstreaming will we do?)
         */
        strstream x_part;
        strstream y_part;

        const int tot_wid = o.width() ;

        if( ( o.flags() & ios::adjustfield ) != ios::internal )
        {
                x_part << ap.x() ;
                y_part << ap.y() ;
        }
        else
        {
                int w_x;
                int w_y;

                if( tot_wid <= 4 )
                        w_x = w_y = 0;
                else
                {
                        w_x = ( tot_wid - 3 ) / 2;
                        w_y = tot_wid - 3 - w_x;
                }
```

```
        x_part.setf( ios::internal, ios::adjustfield ) ;
        x_part << setw( w_x ) << ap.x();

        y_part.setf( ios::internal, ios::adjustfield ) ;
        y_part << setw( w_x ) << ap.y() ;
}

/*
 *      See Sec. 10.10 on the streambuf ...
 */
const int tot_in_field = x_part.rdbuf()->in_avail()
                    + y_part.rdbuf()->in_avail() ;

int to_pad = tot_wid - tot_in_field - 3;
if( to_pad < 0 )
        to_pad = 0;

/*
 *      We need to play the ipfx()/opfx() games
 *      because we may begin or end our operations
 *      with unformatted output, which we need to
 *      include under the opfx()/osfx() umbrella.
 */
Bracket_format bf( o ) ;
/*
 *      If the opfx() fails, we are done.
 */
if( ! bf )
{
        if( o )
                o.clear( ios::failbit );

        return o;
}

const char padchar = o.fill() ;
/*
 *      It's a shame this isn't provided by the
 *      ostream ...
 */
if( ( o.flags() & ios::adjustfield ) == ios::right )
{
        for( int i = 0 ; i < to_pad ; i++ )
                o.put( padchar );
}

o.width( 0 ) ;
o.put( '(' ) << x_part.rdbuf() ;
o.put( ',' ) << y_part.rdbuf() ;
o.put( ')' ) ;
```

```
        if( ( o.flags() & ios::adjustfield ) == ios::left )
        {
                for( int i = 0 ; i < to_pad ; i++ )
                        o.put( padchar ) ;
        }

        return o;
}
```

This mass of code actually works. On the author's computer (UNIX System V Release 4 on an Intel 80486) it compiles to almost 1900 bytes. In the absence of better assistance from the I/O library, writing such functions may not be worth the cost except for heavily used classes. (It took the author about two hours to get this operator right, including test driver.)

This inserter uses `ostream::opfx()` and `osfx()` (via the `Bracket_format class`). These and their counterparts in the `istream` are the subject of the next section.

10.8.2.2 Beginning and ending formatted I/O. When a formatted output or input operation (an insertion or an extraction) takes place, certain 'prefix' and 'suffix' actions must take place. For the predefined inserters and extractors, these are taken care of. For inserters and extractors that begin and end with *other* inserters and extractors, it's a nonissue—the prefix and suffix operations are performed by the inner inserters and extractors. Thus, the naive inserter of Sec. 10.8.1 does not need to perform any prefix or suffix operations. But the inserter of Sec. 10.8.2.1 can perform unformatted output either before or after all the formatted operations, and needs to perform the prefix and suffix operations. (The `Bracket_format` class allows an arbitrary return to cause the suffix operation to be invoked without cluttering the function.)

The prefix and suffix functions are

- `istream::ipfx()`, the input prefix function. It returns an `int` to be interpreted as *true* or *false*. If *false,* the input operation can't be performed and must be abandoned.
- `istream::isfx()`, the input suffix function. It returns `void`.
- `ostream::opfx()`, the output prefix function. It returns an int to be interpreted as *true* or *false*. If *false,* the output operation can't be performed and must be abandoned.
- `ostream::osfx()`, the output suffix function. It returns `void`.

In various versions of the library, some of these are absent; other are null. The absent functions will make portable code difficult; the null functions should be invoked even though they have no effect in that particular implementation of C++. Among the responsibilities of the prefix functions are assuring that tied streams are flushed (for input) and that unit buffers are flushed (for output).

10.8.3 Extractors

Because extractors have to parse input, their job is always hard. The ability of a stream to record its state makes the job a little easier. On the other hand, facilities for error recovery are very limited, and in many cases the stream state must be set to `ios::bad` because characters are consumed and cannot be returned.

We'll examine two extractors here. They are similar, but the second will have a complication missing in the first. The first extractor will be a dual of the inserters above:

```
template< class Base_t >
istream&
operator>>( istream& is, Point< Base_t >& p )
{
        Base_t x;
        Base_t y;

        char c = 0;
        /*
         *      Check the first character; if it's not an '(', we
         *      can put it back and declare failure rather than
         *      bad.  We try the putback even after skipping
         *      leading whitespace here because if we've skipped
         *      any, we did it by the authority of skipws .
         */
        if( ! ( is >> c )
         || c != '(' )
        {
                is.putback( c ) ;
                is.clear( ios::failbit ) ;

                return is;
        }

        /*
         *      Skipws might not be set, but we still want
         *      to accept imbedded whitespace.
         */
        if( ! ( is >> ws >> x >> ws >> c )
```

```
        || c != ','
        || ! ( is >> ws >> y >> ws >> c )
        || c != ')' )
                is.clear( ios::badbit ) ;
      else
      if( is )
                p = Point< Base_t >( x, y ) ;

        return is;
}
```

Notice that this code respects internal settings for dealing with octal and hext constants, etc. It has to; all it does is defer the actual input conversions to other extractors.

Notice the call to `is.putback()`. It can push one character back onto the istream. More than one character of pushback may work, but it is not guaranteed. Also, the character pushed back must be the one just taken off.

The extractor for `Point` does not have to make any decisions about what is meant to be read. The limited amount of pushback and the inability to recover characters read by another extractor make the job difficult. Nevertheless, it can sometimes be managed. This extractor reads not a `Point` but a `Rectangle`. Two formats are supported:

```
( Point , Point )
```

or:

```
( X1 , X2 , Y1 , Y2 )
```

The `Rectangle` stores its location and extent by two points, but two of `Rectangle`'s constructors correspond to the two input formats and they take care of arranging the values and storing them internally.

```
template< class Base_t >
class   Rectangle
{
  public:
        typedef Point< Base_t > Point_t;

        Rectangle() {} ;
        Rectangle( Point_t, Point_t ) ;
        Rectangle( Base_t x1, Base_t x2, Base_t y1, Base_t y2 ) ;
        ~Rectangle() {} ;

        Point_t lower() const { return low; } ;
        Point_t upper() const { return high; } ;

        friend ostream& operator<<( ostream& o,
                                    const Rectangle< Base_t >& r ) ;
```

```
        friend istream& operator>>( istream&, Rectangle< Base_t >& ) ;

  private:
        Point_t low;
        Point_t high;

        /*
         *      This manipulator is present to make input a
         *      little cleaner.
         */
        static istream& eatcomma( istream& ) ;

        … …
} ;

/*
 *      This static member function provides an input
 *      manipulator.  See Sec. 10.5--4 and Sec. 10.9.  The expression
 *      ( istream >> Rectangle< sometype >::eatcomma )
 *      will throw away whitespace, a comma, and more
 *      whitespace.  If the comma isn't found, the
 *      istream is set to fail .
 */
template< class Base_t >
istream&
Rectangle< Base_t >::eatcomma( istream& is )
{
        … …
}

    … …

template< class Base_t >
istream&
operator>>( istream& is, Rectangle< Base_t >& r )
{
        char c = 0;

        /*
         *      Check the first character; if it's not an '(', we
         *      can put it back and declare failure rather than
         *      bad.  We try the putback even after skipping
         *      leading whitespace here because if we've skipped
         *      any, we did it by the authority of  skipws .
         */
        if( ! ( is >> c )
         || c != '(' )
        {
                is.putback( c ) ;
                is.clear( ios::failbit ) ;

                return is;
        }
```

```
/*
 *      Remember, skipws might not be set, but we
 *      still want to accept imbedded whitespace!
 */

/*
 *      Now, are we collecting two Points or four
 *      Base_t 's ?  This assumes, right or wrong, that
 *      the Base_t does not begin with a '(' .
 */
c = ' ';
if( ! ( is >> ws >> c ) )
        return is;

is.putback( c ) ;
/*
 *      Another open paren means
 *      ( Point< Base_t >, Point< Base_t > ) .
 *      The open paren belongs to the first Point,
 *      so we have to put it back.
 */
if( c == '(' )
{
        Point< Base_t > p1;
        Point< Base_t > p2;

        if( !( is >> p1 >>
                        Rectangle< Base_t >::eatcomma >>
                        p2 >> ws >> c ) )
                return is;

        if( c != ')' )
        {
                is.clear( ios::badbit );
                return is;
        }

        r = Rectangle< Base_t >( p1, p2 ) ;

        return is;
}

/*
 *      Otherwise we have four  Base_t , seperated by commas.
 */
Base_t x1;
Base_t x2;
Base_t y1;
Base_t y2;

c = ' ';
if( ! ( is >> ws >> x1 >> Rectangle< Base_t >::eatcomma
```

```
                        >> x2 >> Rectangle< Base_t >::eatcomma
                        >> y1 >> Rectangle< Base_t >::eatcomma
                        >> y2 >> ws >> c ) )
                return is;

        if( c != ')' )
        {
                is.clear( ios::badbit ) ;
                return is;
        }

        r = Rectangle<Base_t>( x1, x2, y1, y2 ) ;

        return is;
}
```

Instead of reading a character and pushing it back on the stream with `istream::putback()`, we can use `istream::peek()`:

```
/*
 *      Now, are we collecting two Points or four
 *      Base_t 's ?  This assumes, right or wrong, that
 *      the Base_t does not begin with a '(' .
 */
if( ! ( is >> ws ) )
        return is;

c = is.peek() ;
if( ! is )
        return is;

/*
 *      Another open paren means
 *      ( Point< Base_t >, Point< Base_t > ) .
 *      The open paren belongs to the first Point,
 *      so we have to put it back.
 */
if( c == '(' )
{
        ... ...
```

10.9 Manipulators

A *manipulator* is an object (or expression) that is written on the right-hand side of a stream I/O inserter or extractor, and that does something besides cause input or output of that object (or the value of that expression).

Predefined manipulators are found in the header `<iomanip.h>`.

10.9.1 Fixed manipulators

Recall (from Sec. 10.5.3 and Sec. 10.5.4) that the input and output streams have special extractors and inserters:

```
class   ostream
{
  public:
     ... ...
        ostream& operator<<( ostream& (*f)( ostream& ) )
                                    { return (*f)( *this ) ; } ;
        ostream& operator<<( ios& (*f)(ios&) ) ;
                                    { return (*f)( *this ) ; } ;
     ... ...
} ;

class   istream
{
  public:
     ... ...
        istream& operator>>) istream& (*f)( istream& ) )
                                    { return (*f)( *this ) ; } ;
        istream& operator>>( ios& (*f)( ios& ) ) ;
                                    { return (*f)( *this ) ; } ;
     ... ...
} ;
```

Any function that matches any of these signatures can be used as an inserter. Here's a stripped-down version of `eatcomma()`:

```
istream&
eatcomma ( istream& is )
{
        char c = '';

        is >> ws >> c;

        if( ! is )
                return is;

        if( c != ',' )
        {
                is.clear( ios::failbit ) ;
                is.putback( c ) ;
```

```
            return is;
        }

        return is >> ws;
    }
```

The first of istream's special inserters can be used with eatcomma(), allowing expressions such as this:

```
cin >> eatcomma;
```

The inserter, when evaluated, executes

```
eatcomma( cin ) ;       // istream& eatcomma( istream& )
```

Exactly the same mechanism evaluates the insertion 'into' ws within eatcomma(); ws is declared as

```
istream& ws( istream& ) ;
```

The I/O system provides these 'function' manipulators:

`ws` 'White space.' Extracting ws from an istream consumes leading whitespace.

`flush` 'Flush.' Inserting flush into an ostream forces all characters in the stream's buffer to be sent out to their ultimate destination.

`endl` 'End line.' Inserting endl into an output stream issues a newline and flushes the streambuf.

`ends` 'End stream.' Inserting ends into an output stream writes a null character (in ASCII, NUL) into the stream as a string terminator.

`dec` 'Decimal.' Inserting dec into an output stream or extracting it from an input stream sets the ios::basefield bits in the ios formatting flags to ios::dec.

`hex` 'Hexadecimal.' Inserting hex into an output stream or extracting it from an input stream sets the ios::basefield bits in the ios formatting flags to ios::hex.

`oct` 'Octal.' Inserting oct into an output stream or extracting it from an input stream sets the ios::basefield *bits in the* ios formatting flags to ios::oct.

The example of eatcomma() shows that any function with an appropriate signature may be used as a manipulator.

10.9.2 Manipulator objects

This function can serve as a manipulator; it sets the field width to nine:

```
ios&
width9( ios& io )
{
        io.setw( 9 ) ;
        return io;
}
```

This is not very flexible; what if we need to set various field widths? Template functions won't work; the parameters of a function template must be types, not values. And template classes are overkill; ordinary classes can do the job:

```
class   set_width
{
  public:
        set_width( int a ) : parm( a ) {} ;
        ~set_width() ;

        friend ios& operator>>( ios& io, const set_width sw )
        { io.setw( sw.parm ) ; return io; } ;

        friend ios& operator<<( ios& io, const set_width sw )
        { io.width( sw.parm ) ; return io; } ;

  private:
        const int parm;
};

        ... ...

        cout << set_width( 9 ) << i << endl;
```

The constructor for `set_width` is used as a value builder (Sec. 3.3) to create the object on the fly. This technique is not limited to one argument, nor to integer arguments. All that is needed is that the inserter or extractor (or both) are defined for the object.

We can just as well create a general 'function-closure' and use it for whatever purpose we have in mind:

```
class   manip_closure
{
  public:
        manip_closure( ios& (*af)( ios&, int ), int ai )
          : fun( af ), parm( ai ) { };
        ~manip_closure() {};

        friend ios& operator>>( ios& is, const manip_closure& ai )
        {       return ai.fun( is, ai.parm );    };
```

```
        friend ios& operator<<( ios& os, const manip_closure& ai )
        {       return ai.fun( os, ai.parm );   };

  private:
        ios& (*const fun) ( ios&, int ) const;
        const int parm;
};

ios&
set_width( ios& io, int w )
{
        io.width( w );
        return io;
};

... ...

        cout << manip_closure( set_width, 7 ) << i << endl;
```

Any function that returns one of these 'closure' objects can act as an integer manipulator:

```
class   apply_int
{
  public:
        apply_int( ios& (*af)( ios& ) ) : fun( af ) {};
        ~apply_int();

        manip_closure operator() ( int parm )
        {       return manip_closure( fun, parm ); };

  private:
        ios& (*const fun) ( ios&, int ) const;
};

extern ios& setwidth_fun( ios&, int );
apply_int setw( setwidth_fun );

        ... ...

          cout << setw( 9 ) << i << endl;
```

`setw()` returns a 'closure' which is actually inserted; the closure applies the function and the parameter list (in this case, one `int`) to the `ios`.

Now we can create a whole family of manipulator-objects-as-functions-returning-objects without proliferating either types or overloads of the insertion and extraction operators:

```
extern ios& setwidth_fun( ios&, int );
extern ios& setbase_fun( ios&, int );
extern ios& setprecision_fun( ios&, int );
extern ios& setfillchar_fun( ios&, int );

apply_int setw( setwidth_fun );
apply_int setbase( setwidth_fun );
apply_int setprecision( setwidth_fun );
apply_int setfill( setwidth_fun );
```

This is, in fact, close to how the stream I/O manipulators are built.

10.9.3 Manipulator templates

For ANSI/ISO C++, class templates are provided in the standard library; these are used to create manipulators. In previous versions of C++, the manipulators are provided using macros which are described in Sec. 10.9.4.*

There are four degrees of freedom involved in manipulators. There is the actual function to be used, the type of argument and number of arguments to that function, and the type of stream (`ios`, `istream`, `ostream`, or `iostream`) to which it may be applied.

The actual function is stored as a datum in the 'apply' and 'closure' objects; the number of arguments must be expressed as explicit source code, and the type of parameter and the type of stream to which the functions may be applied can be expressed as templates. The type of stream to which it is applied could be expressed by template, but it affects whether the class must have an inserter or an extractor or both, so their are four different templates for the four different possibilities.

The templates look something like this:

```
/*
 *      For the  ios :
 *
 *      First, the manipulator 'closure' object:
 */
template< class M_type >
class   smanip
{
  public:
        smanip( ios& (*af) ( ios&, M_type ), M_type ap )
         : fun( af ), parm( ap ) { };
        ~smanip() {};
```

* This section originally described the manipulator templates as 'speculative'; the new ANSI/ISO proposed version became available right before the publication deadline for this book. The text has been revised to reflect the changes, but readers are advised to consult their reference manuals to verify the details of these templates.

```
        friend ios& operator>>( ios& s,
                                const smanip< M_type >& ap )
        {       return ap.fun( s, ap.parm ); };

        friend ios& operator<<( ios& s,
                                const smanip< M_type >& ap )
        {       return ap.fun( s, ap.parm );    };

  private:
        ios& (*const fun)( ios&, M_type ) const;
        const M_type parm;
};

/*
 *      Now the 'applier' class, with the  operator()() :
 */
template< class M_type >
class   sapp
{
  public:
        sapp( ios& (*af)( ios&, M_type ) ) : fun( af ) {};
        ~sapp() {};
        smanip< M_type > operator()( M_type parm )
        {       return smanip< M_type >( fun, parm ); };

  private:
        ios& (*const fun)( ios&, M_type ) const;
};

template < class M_type >
        istream& operator >>( istream&, const smanip< M_type >& );
template < class M_type >
        ostream& operator <<( ostream&, const smanip< M_type >& );

/*
 *      For the istream :
 *
 *      First, the manipulator 'closure' object:
 */
template< class M_type >
class   imanip
{
  public:
        imanip( istream& (*af) ( istream&, M_type ), M_type ap )
        : fun( af ), parm( ap ) { };
        ~imanip() {};

        friend istream& operator>>( istream& s,
                                const imanip< M_type >& ap )
        {       return ap.fun( s, ap.parm );    };
```

```
  private:
        istream& (*const fun) ( istream&, M_type ) const;
        const M_type parm;
};

/*
 *      Now the 'applier' class, with the  operator()() :
 */
template< class M_type >

class   iapp
{
  public:
        iapp( istream& (*af)( istream&, M_type ) ) : fun( af ) {};
        ~iapp() {};

        imanip< M_type > operator()( M_type parm )
        {       return imanip< M_type >( fun, parm ); };

  private:
        istream& (*const fun)( istream&, M_type ) const;
};

/*
 *      For the ostream :
 *
 *      First, the manipulator 'closure' object:
 */
template< class M_type >
class   omanip
{
  public:
        omanip( ostream& (*af)( ostream&, M_type ), M_type ap )
         :fun( af ), parm( ap ) { };
        ~omanip() {};

        friend ostream& operator<<( ostream& s,
                                const omanip< M_type >& ap )
        {       return ap.fun( s, ap.parm );    };

  private:
        ostream& (*const fun)( ostream&, M_type ) const;
        const M_type parm;
};

/*
 *      Now the 'applier' class, with the  operator()() :
 */
template< class M_type >
```

```
class   oapp
{
  public:
        oapp( ostream& (*af) ( ostream&, M_type ) ) : fun( af ) {};
        ~oapp() {};

        omanip< M_type > operator()( M_type parm )
        {       return omanip< M_type >( fun, parm ); };

  private:
        ostream& (*const fun)( ostream&, M_type ) const;
};
```

10.9.4 Faked manipulator templates

Releases of C++ before the introduction of templates do not provide template manipulators. Neither does AT&T's C++ Release 3.0. These releases fake manipulators using the preprocessor.

The macro IOMANIPdeclare(T) will declare for a type T (e.g., for int) eight types, corresponding to the eight templates in Sec. 10.9.3. They are

SMANIP*T* (e.g., SMANIPint), corresponds to smanip< T >.

SAPP*T* (e.g., SAPPint), corresponds to sapp< T >.

IMANIP*T* (e.g., IMANIPint)
IAPP*T* (e.g., IAPPint)
correspond to imanip< T > and iapp< T >.

OMANIP*T* (e.g., OMANIPint)
OAPP*T* (e.g., OAPPint)
correspond to omanip< T > and oapp< T >.

Note that the IOMANIPdeclare() macro actually writes class declarations, and so must appear just once in each compilation for each type for which the manipulator classes are to be created.

After IOMANIPdeclare() is invoked for some type, the various *XX*MANIP and *XX*APP macros become valid type names:

```
ios& murgetroyd( ios&, float );

OMANIP(float) heavensII( murgetroyd );
```

Because this is accomplished with preprocessor magic, the type name must be a simple identifier. These will not work:

```
SMANIPdeclare( unsigned char ); // No good!  Will try to
                                // compile names such as
                                // 'SMANIP_unsigned char' and
SMANIPdeclare( ios::io_state ); // 'SMANIP_ios::iostate'
```

To make them work, the types must be given typedef names:

```
typedef unsigned char UnChar;
SMANIPdeclare( UnChar );

typedef ios::iostate IosState;
SMANIPdeclare( IosState );
```

Errors of this sort in preprocessor macros often produce very misleading diagnostics from the compiler.

10.10 The `streambuf` Interfaces

There are two interfaces to the `streambuf`. The 'public' interface serves the I/O stream classes and other things as needed to manipulate a stream directly. The 'protected' interface serves classed derived from `streambuf`. These classes must operate the `streambuf`'s abstractions, and must also respond to the needs of those abstractions.

The division of labor between the base and derived parts of a `streambuf` is exactly the 'Dainty Embrace' of Sec. 6.4.9.1. The `streambuf` is used by everything for input and output and it is built for speed at the expense of convenience. Base and derived classes must cooperate across a closely coupled interface.

10.10.1 Public interface—nonvirtual

(This should be read in conjunction with Sec. 10.10.3.)

Recall that a `streambuf`'s basic model centers on the *reserve area,* the memory buffer in which it can store characters. Part of this area may be set aside as a *put area,* at the end of which characters may be inserted. A different part may be set apart as a *get area,* from which characters may be taken.

Here are the basic public interface functions for the `streambuf` (excluding constructors and setup functions; see Sec. 10.3), starting with the 'get' functions. Note that `int` is the return type for functions intended to return characters; this allows `EOF` as a return value.

These functions manage characters in the reserve area. Many of them are inline, helping the character management to run as fast as possible.

```
class   streambuf
{
  public:
```

```
... ...
int in_avail() const;   // How many characters are queued
                        //   incoming in the get area?
int sbumpc();           // Get the first character in the
                        //   get area, and advance the get
                        //   pointer.  Return EOF if no
                        //   characters are available.
int sgetc();            // Get the first character in the
                        //   get area.  Do NOT advance the
                        //   get pointer.  Return EOF if
                        //   no characters are available.
int sgetn( char*,       // Copy the next n_char characters
        int n_char );   //   out of the streambuf, or as
                        //   many as are available, if
                        //   there are less than n_char.
int snextc();           // Advance the get pointer
                        //   (discarding) the current
                        //   character) and return the new
                        //   'current character' (that is,
                        //   the next character).
int putback( int c );   // Push character c back under the
                        //   get pointer, and move the
                //   pointer back.  Only one character of
                //   pushback is guaranteed, and the
                //   character pushed back must be the
                //   last character read.

int out_waiting() const;        // How many characters are
                                //   queued outgoing in
                                //   the put area?
int sputc( int c );     // Put c at the end of the
                        //   characters in the put area
                        //   and advance the put pointer.
                        //   Returns EOF if an error
                        //   occurs.
int sputn( const char*, // Take n_char characters pointed
        int n_char );   //   at by the first argument and
                        //   put them at the end of
                //   characters in the put area (if
                //   possible).  Return the number of
                //   characters actually copied into the
                //   put area.

void stossc();          // Advance the get pointer by one
                        //   character if there are any
                        //   characters.

... ...
};
```

10.10.2 Protected interface—nonvirtual

The nonvirtual protected interface allows the derived class to manage the reserve area. The control is provided over and above the character management functions in the public interface.

```
        class   streambuf
{
        ... ...
   protected:
        ... ...
        char* base();           // Pointer to the reserve area.
        char* ebase();          // Pointer to the first character
                                //    AFTER the reserve area.

        int blen() const;       // Length of the reserve area.

        char* gptr();           // Get pointer.
        char* egptr();          // Pointer to the first character
                                //    AFTER the get area.
        void gbump( int nn );   // Adjust the get pointer by nn ,
                                //    which may be positive or
                                //    negative.  No range check
                                //    is applied.
        char* eback();          // Lowest (leftmost) possible
                                //    pointer value the get
                        //   pointer may assume.  Space from here
                        //   to gptr()  is available for putback.

        char* pptr();           // Put pointer.
        char* epptr();          // Pointer to the first character
                                //   AFTER the put area.
        char* pbase();          // Lowest (leftmost) possible
                                //   pointer value the put
                                //   pointer may assume.
        void pbump( int nn );   // Adjust the put pointer by  nn ,
                                //   which may be positive or
                        //   negative.  No range check is
                        //   applied.

        void setb( char* base_p,// Install a reserve area.
                char* ebase_p,  //   base_p will become base()
                                //   and ebase_p ebase().
                int auto_del = 0 );//If auto_del is non-zero, the
                                //   reserve area memory will be
                        //   deleted when setb() is called again
                        //   or when the streambuf is destroyed.
                        //   If base_p and ebase_p are both null,
                        //   there is no reserve area; if
                        //   ebase_p < base_p, the reserve area
                        //   has length zero ( blen() == 0 ).
```

```
        void setp( char* putp,  // Sets pptr() and pbase() to p
                char* eput );   //   and epptr() to ep.
        void setg( char* back,  // Sets eback() to back, gptr()
                char* getp,     //    to getp, and egptr() to
                char* eget );   //    eget.

         int unbuffered() const; // Return the 'unbuffered' flag
                                 //   for the streambuf.
        int unbuffered( int ub );//Set the unbuffered flag to ub .

        int allocate();         // Set up an automatic reserve
                                //    area. If there is a reserve
                        //    area, or if unbuffered()  is set,
                        //    this is a no-op that returns 0.  If
                        //    the space allocation fails, return
                        //    EOF, otherwise 1.  allocate() is
                        //    meant for the use of derived
                        //    classes, and is not called from any
                        //    non-virtual member function of
                        //    streambuf.

        void dbp(); // 'Debug print.'  Dumps information about
                        //   the streambuf on standard
                        //   out.  The information is meant to be
                        //   human-readable.
... ...
};
```

10.10.3 Public interface—virtual

Recall from Sec. 6.4.2 that a public virtual function represents part of a derived class interface to the base class's clients (rather than to the base class itself). It also represents a 'contract' to which the derived class must adhere.

Some of the public virtual members of `streambuf` are arguably part of the interface to `streambuf`; they are presented in the next section.

```
class   streambuf
{
  public:
        ... ...
        virtual streambuf* setbuf(      // This version of  setbuf()
                           char* p,     //    is given  p  as a
                           int len );   //    prospective reserve
                                        //    area (of length len ).
                      //   It may accept the reserve area and
                      //   return  this  or reject the area and
                      //   return 0.  The base class version will
                      //   accept the area if there is no reserve
                      //   area already set up.  (If called with
                      //   a null pointer or a  len  of zero, the
                      //   streambuf is to be unbuffered.)
```

```
        virtual streampos seekpos(      // See the description of the
                          seekpos,      //   seekp( . . . ) and
                          int mode );   //   seekg( . . . ) functions
        virtual streampos seekoff(      //   in the istream and
                          streamoff,    //   ostream (Sec. 10.7--2).
                          seekdir,      //   The base class version
                          int mode );   //    of seekpos()  calls
                                        //    seekoff() ; the base
                        //   class version of seekoff() does nothing
                        //   and returns EOF.

        virtual int sync();     // Force the streambuf and the
                                //   external character source or
                        //   sink into consistency.  Returns EOF on
                        //   error.  The base class version of
                        //   sync() returns 0 unless there are
                        //   characters left in the get area; then it
                        //   returns EOF.

... ...
};
```

10.10.4 Protected interface—virtual

Recall from Sec. 6.4.1 that a protected virtual function represents part of a derived class interface to the base class itself (rather than to the base class's clients). It also represents a 'contract' to which the derived class must adhere.

Some of these member functions are actually public, but are of use principally to `streambuf`.

The derived classes of `streambuf` must be able to produce or consume characters, moving them in and out of the reserve area upon request, and most of these functions are concerned with that activity.

```
class   streambuf
{
        ... ...
  protected:
        virtual int doallocate();//Called by allocate()  when
                                 //    that function actually
                        //   needs to allocate space.  The base
                        //   class version allocates a reserve
                        //   area using global  operator new() .

        virtual int underflow();// Called when characters are
                                //    needed and there are none in
                        //   the get area.  underflow()  must move
                        //   characters into the get area, and return
                        //   EOF.  If there is no reserve area,
                        //   underflow() must first allocate one with
                        //   allocate() (or possibly  doallocate()
                        //   directly).  The base class version
                        //   should not be called.
```

```
virtual int pbackfail(  // Called when an attempt to push
                int c );//    back character  c  has
                        //    failed for lack of pushback
                //   room before the get area.  Should
                //   perform the pushback if possible (by
                //   repositioning a file pointer, adjusting
                //   the get area, etc.) and return 1 if the
                //   pushback worked, EOF if it wasn't
                //   possible.  The base class version
                //   returns EOF and does nothing.

virtual int overflow(); // Called to move characters out of
                        //    the put area to their consumer.
                //   Must reset the put area to empty.  Must
                //   return EOF on failure, anything else
                //   on success.  The base class version
                //   should not be called.

    ... ...
};
```

10.10.5 Operation

The general operation of the streambuf, then, is this: efficient inline functions move characters in and out of the buffer (the put and get areas), and call underflow() and overflow() when characters need to be moved between the reserve area and the external source or sink of characters.

10.11 Summary and Reference

Stream I/O can be extended to deal with new types and new sources or sinks of characters.

Section 10.1. For basic input and output of typed objects, the >> and << operators are overloaded and called *extractor* and *inserter*. These can be overloaded for new user-defined types. They return their left-hand operand, and can be chained:

```
cout << "Hello," << ' ' << "World!" << endl;
```

These operators use an underlying *streambuf* abstraction to move the characters that represent the type values into and out of the program.

Section 10.2. There are predefined stream and streambuf types for input, output, and for both, for file I/O and for I/O to strings in memory. The fundamental types are the ios (basic stream management), istream (basic stream input), ostream (basic stream output), and streambuf (basic buffer for stream I/O).

Section 10.3. The constructors and setup functions presented here for the predefined stream and streambuf types reflect not only the basic stream and streambuf abstractions, but the particulars of the job and post the type occupies.

Section 10.4. Every stream has a *state* which describes whether the stream is functioning, and if not, why. The state information is limited to 'good,' 'eof,' 'failed,' and 'bad.' A failed stream is assumed to be completely recoverable; a bad stream is not. The state can be interrogated by member functions; alternatively it can be tested by conversion to `void*` (as in the test-part of an `if()` or `while()`) or by `operator!()`. 'Good' tests as true, anything else as false. The common idiom is

```
char c;
while( cin >> c )
{
        ... ...
}
```

Inserters and extractors for user-defined types must manage the stream state correctly so that the streams will continue to provide the expected behavior.

A variety of mechanisms control the buffering of streams, especially input stream. In particular, output streams may be *tied* to an input stream. When input is demanded, any character buffered for output will be written through.

Section 10.5. There are a variety of predefined inserters and extractors for the built-in types. There are also special inserters and extractors to support bulk transfer of characters to and from streambufs, and to support objects called *manipulators.* Manipulators affect the streams into which they are inserted or from which they are extracted. They do not necessarily result in characters being inserted or values being created.

Section 10.6. Streams have a variety of format settings to control such things as field width, output precision, justification, and conversion base. Inserters and extractors for user-defined types can and should use these consistently. There is also provision for additional formatting information for such inserters and extractors.

Formatting information can be set by member functions in the stream and by manipulator objects.

Section 10.7. Stream I/O also supports unformatted transfer of characters into and out of the program. The member functions which accomplish this can transfer records delimited by end-of-record characters (e.g., newlines).

The unformatted I/O support includes support for 'file positioning' on streams that support it.

Section 10.8. Inserters and extractors can be overloaded for user-defined types. For extraction (input), the various problems of parsing input and recognizing errors must be managed, the stream's formatting indicators must be observed, and the stream state set appropriately on failure. For insertion (output), simple functions can perform for many types. To cooperate fully with the stream I/O formatting system, more work must be done. For both input and output, if unformatted operations are used, special function calls may be needed to cooperate fully with the formatted I/O system.

Section 10.9. Inserting an object into a stream or extracting it from a stream ordinarily means converting between the object's value and a character-sequence representation of that value. *Manipulators* are objects which, when inserted into or extracted from a stream, cause the stream to do something else. Manipulators can be used to flush streams, to set formatting parameters, and for other purposes. Some manipulators are written as function calls returning the actual manipulator object; these allow manipulators to accept parameters.

Manipulators can be written by C++ users. The stream I/O library provides some assistance in this. The form of the assistance varies between releases that support templates fully and those that do not.

Section 10.10. The `streambuf` is responsible for moving characters between the stream I/O system and the ultimate producer or consumer of those characters. Types derived from the streambuf can perform I/O to files or to character arrays within the program.

The streambuf has public and protected interfaces for both the base and derived parts. These interfaces allow characters to be moved one at a time with reasonable efficiency with relatively simple programming. User-defined streambuf types must observe and fulfill these interfaces.

Appendix

A Summary of C

C++ is derived from the C programming language. In many ways, the two are incommensurate: C provides none of C++'s ability to define abstract data types or object (class) types. Nevertheless, C is a quite vital language on its own.

C was designed to be close enough to the machine that efficient code could be generated easily, but with flow control and data structure constructs sufficient to 'most' problems. In the 1970s C sparked a revolution: it became possible to move an entire operating system from a minicomputer to a small mainframe because the operating system was written mostly in C. At first, this was a happy byproduct: it had become easier to port the operating system than to port the many applications that ran on it. C's efficiency and expressiveness have made it possible for the UNIX operating system and its variants to run on countless machine architectures. The current success of Window System X also depends on an efficient, maintainable, universally available language whose environment dependencies can be isolated easily in a few hundred lines of header files within a system of hundreds of thousands of lines of code.

C is alternately criticized for being at too high a level and too low a level, for being too specific to optimize well on a given machine and for leaving too many decisions to the particular implementation. C is closer to the machine than anything higher-level, and more portable than anything lower-level. Its balance is nearly perfect, and it is surprisingly well thought out.

The version of C presented here is the dialect prescribed by the ANSI C standard, ANSI document number X3J11/88-001.

A.1 C Fundamentals

We assume here that you have programmed in some computer programming language, even if it is only the UNIX shell.

We will avoid introducing C features that become obsolete or deprecated in C++, except where absolutely necessary. One necessary area is input and output; C uses the 'standard I/O' system while C++ uses stream I/O.

We also assume that you are using C in a "hosted environment," that is, an environment with the usual support of an operating system, libraries, etc. If you are using C in a nonhosted environment (e.g., for writing a stand-alone program on a controller, or for actually writing an operating system yourself) the rules will be somewhat different. Consult the documentation for your environment and a good C text.

A.1.1 Getting started

A.1.1.1 The `Hello, World!` program. A C program consists of one or more 'source code files.' (What constitutes a file depends on the environment.) Here's a simple program to print 'Hello, World!' on the standard output:

```
#include <stdio.h>

/*
 *      A 'Hello, World!' program.
 */
int
main( void )
{
        printf( "Hello, World!\n" );
        return 0;
}
```

From the top we have:

- An *include directive,* which instructs the preprocessor to include the source stored in the system header file `stdio.h`.
- A comment, surrounded by /* and */. It is ignored by C, but should edify the human reader. (C's comments are just like PL/I's.)
- A definition for a function called `main()`, whose 'function body' contains two statements.
- The first statement, a function call to `printf()` followed by a semicolon. This function call generates the program's output.

- The second statement, a return statement that exits the function and returns a value of zero to the function's caller.

The program's effect is provided by the `printf()` function. The rest of the program is supporting skeleton. (This is not the simplest version of the program; it will still work if some things are omitted. We wouldn't omit them in a larger program, so we won't omit them here.)

A.1.1.2 Compiling the `Hello, World!` How we actually compile a C program depends on our computer, and also on the program. For a large program, we will probably compile it in separate, small pieces, then combine them into one executable. For a small program like our `Hello, World!`, we may compile the whole program at once. And in any case, we need to use some text editing tool or program to put a copy of the program in a file that can be compiled. On the UNIX Operating System, using the compiler provided with the operating system and assuming that the program has been placed in a file called `hello.c`, we can use

```
cc hello.c
```

which puts the executable in a file called `a.out`. Or we can use

```
cc hello.c -o hello
```

which puts the executable on a file called `hello`. (The native C compiler on UNIX recognizes a C program file by the '.c' on the end of its file name.)

Finally, on many versions of UNIX, we could just issue the command

```
make hello
```

If there is a `hello.c` that is younger than the `hello` executable, this will issue a C compiler command similar to the second one above.

A.1.1.3 `Hello, World!: main()` From the top, then:

The header file, `stdio.h`, contains a number of declarations, including those for `printf()`. It also contains macro definitions and other 'preprocessor things' (see App. C).

`main()` is the program's 'main function.' It's been years since serious programs had one 'main' calling subroutines one or two levels deep to do the work, but the idea persists: when a program is executed, `main()` is executed somehow from the operating system environment. (In a nonhosted environment, the C language startup will probably be different.)

main() is declared to take no arguments and return a value of type int, where int represents the 'most natural' signed integer type on the machine at hand.* That main() takes no arguments is indicated by the void between the parentheses; were there arguments, they would be declared there instead of the void. We'll say more on this later; for now, this is acceptable as both C and C++. Were we to omit the void we would be telling C that although main() takes no arguments, calls to it are not to be type-checked. (A C program may explicitly call main() recursively; a C++ program may not.) (And in C++, omitting the arguments would mean that no arguments are to be provided and would not prevent type-checking the arguments given in a function call.)

Notice the way we write the return type for main():

```
int
main( void )
{
        ...
```

There's no reason we couldn't have written this

```
int main( void )
{
```

or

```
int main( void ) {
```

or even

```
int main
( void
) {
```

C doesn't care much about line breaks; a line break generally means the same to C as a space or a tab. (Two exceptions: the preprocessor works in terms of lines, and spaces or tabs inside character or string constants are treated as part of the constant.) But there are conventional ways to use whitespace in programs, and consistent line and page layout makes it easier to read code quickly. The first two examples above are conventional, as is the original example; the last one is eccentric, at least.

* C's int is guaranteed to be least 16 bits wide.

The allowable declarations of `main()` depend upon the machine and the environment. In a 'hosted' environment (with a full compilation system, file system, command interpreter, etc.), these two declarations (at least) are permitted:

```
int main( void );
```

or

```
int main( int, char** );
```

We'll examine the second declaration in A.2.3.7.

In a nonhosted environment, everything about `main()` depends upon the environment.

C language functions are defined in pretty much the way `main()` is defined. They vary in their function name, their return type, their argument list, and the statements that make up their function bodies.

The name of a C variable, function, or other 'nameable thing' must be a character string composed of letters, digits, and underscores, and beginning with a letter or underscore. Any ANSI-conforming version of C will support at least 31 significant characters and any number of nonsignificant characters. (There are some places where fewer characters will be significant.) (Identifiers beginning with an underscore are reserved for use by the compiler or compiler-provided library. Identifiers beginning with certain character sequences are reserved for future use as 'external' identifiers—function names and other global names. See Sec. A.2.2.1.4.)

A.1.1.4 `Hello, World!` **: statements and the function body.** In the definition of `main()` above, the function body is surrounded by curly braces and contains two statements:

```
{
        printf( "Hello, World!\n" );

        return 0;
}
```

C uses curly braces in a variety of constructs that call for statements to be grouped. In the case of a function body, they surround a list of

```
Zero or more declarations
```

followed by

```
Zero or more other statements.
```

In our example, we have two 'simple' statements. The first is a function call followed by a semicolon. The function call is a legal expression (as in many languages). In C, any legal expression followed by a semicolon is a legal statement. In this way, functions serve as both functions and procedures. (In fact, `printf()` returns a value, which this program simply ignores.)

A function that returns no value at all should be declared to return `void`:

```
/*
 *     Do nothing.
 */
void
dummy( void )
{
       return;
}
```

or

```
/*
 *     Do nothing, differently.
 */
void
dummy( void )
{ }
```

The return statement causes the function to terminate and return control to the caller. It may also return a value. In the `Hello, World!` example, `main()` returns the value of the `int` constant 0 (integer zero). The return statement's form is

```
return optional-expression ;
```

The word *return* is a reserved word (keyword) in C and may not be used as a variable name or other programming symbol.

A function returning `void` may either return by a `return` statement or by "falling off the end" of the function, as in the second version of `dummy` above. A function returning any other type should return a value of that type using a `return` statement with an appropriate value. Not all current compilers check this properly, and some older compilers (from before the ANSI standard) don't check it at all.

A.1.1.5 `Hello, World!`: **printf().** The `printf()` is responsible for most of what the `Hello, World!` does:

```
printf( "Hello, World!\n" );
```

`printf()` is a very flexible function that can print many things in many ways. (And more general functions allow output to arbitrary files, rather than just to standard output.) `printf()` can take an arbitrary number of arguments. It examines the first argument and, based on what it finds there, then examines other arguments and prints them. For instance, we could have written

```
printf( "%s, %s!\n", "Hello", "World" );
```

The double-quoted strings are *string literals,* often just called `strings`, about which we will say more in Sec. A.2.3.6. Each `%s` in the first string literal directs `printf()` to look for another string literal. The `\n` is converted when the program is compiled into a newline character, which causes a new line to be begun in the output. (C output does not provide newlines automatically. The alternative seems to be to require 'carriage control,' which is probably a worse alternative.)

A.1.1.6 Variables and recursion. In C, all functions may be recursive, thus we could write a fibonnaci number function*:

```
/*
 *      Compute a fibonacci number naively.
 */
int
fib( int f )
{
        if( f <= 1 )
                return 1;

        return fib( f - 1 ) + fib( f - 2 );
}
```

Here we have declared a function `fib()` taking one parameter, an `int`. `int` is the 'most natural' integer data type on the machine at hand. It is guaranteed to be at least 16 bits long (–32768 to +32767) but on many machines will be 32 bits long (–2147483648 to 2147483647).

Fibonacci numbers grow large quickly. A 32-bit integer is the least we are likely to want. C provides a type called `long int` or just `long` that is guaranteed to be 32 bits long, and no shorter than `int`.

---

* The Fibonacci numbers are named for Leonardo de Fibonacci—Leonardo the Bonehead—who investigated their properties. This well-known series involves summing the previous two numbers in the series; there are Fibonacci series that sum the previous three, four, five, etc., numbers as well. (See Knuth, 1973, Vol. I.)

```
/*
 *      A fibonacci on longs
 */
long
lfib( long lf )
{
        if( lf <= 1)
                return 1;

        return lfib( lf - 1 ) + lfib( lf - 2 );
}
```

This will hold up for numbers up to `lfib( 45 )` for 32-bit `long ints`.

Notice that we can use a generalized expression in a `return` statement. This is characteristic of C: where an expression is asked for, any expression with the correct type will do. But if we wanted to separate the function calls into different statements, we could write

```
long
lfib( long lf )
{
        if( lf <= 1 )
                return 1;

        {
                int f1;         /* lfib( lf - 1 ) */
                int f2;         /* lfib( lf - 2 ) */
                f1 = lfib( lf - 1 );
                f2 = lfib( lf - 2 );

                return f1 + f2;
        }
}
```

Note that we've moved the new declarations into a brace-enclosed compound statement to limit their scope. This isn't necessary, but it can be helpful, especially in a larger function that handles many cases and subcases, each of which needs its own variables. Limiting the scope of variables makes it easier to be sure the reader understands what each variable is used for and what it means.

A.1.1.7 Types. Besides `int` and `long`, C supports a `short` integral type, which is guaranteed to be at least 16 bits long. On a given machine, any of these three integral types may be implemented as the same size, subject to the minimums. C guarantees that `int` is at least as wide as `short`, and `long` is at least as wide as `int`. Integral constants are written as one of

- A sequence of decimal digits (*not* beginning with zero) to indicate a decimal constant.
- A sequence of octal digits (0–7) *beginning* with a zero to indicate an octal (base eight) constant.
- 0x followed by a sequence of hexadecimal digits (0–9, a–f, A–F) to indicate a hexadecimal (base 16) constant.

Any of these may have a suffix of `l` or `L` to indicate that the constant is to be regarded as a `long`. (The author recommends against the lowercase 'ell' because it can be mistaken for a numeral-one in some typefaces.)

C also has three floating point types: `float`, `double`, and `long double`. C guarantees that `double` is no less precise than `float`, and `long double` no less precise than `double`. In particular, `long double` is generally implemented with the same machine representation as `double` except on machines whose architecture has special provisions for numerically sensitive or intensive work.

Floating point constants have several parts: an integral part, a decimal point, a fractional part, an `E` or an `e`, an exponent sign, an exponent, and a suffix.

```
iii . fff[Ee][+-]xxxS
```

All are optional, but not all can be omitted at once. The integral part, decimal point, and fractional part make up the significand. If the decimal point is present, the significand is a floating point significand and either the integral or fractional part may be missing (but not both), and the exponent part remains optional. If the decimal part is missing, the significand is just the integral part, and the exponent part must be present.

The exponent part of a floating point constant is the `E` or `e`, followed by the optional exponent sign, followed by one or more decimal digits to indicate the power-of-ten exponent.

So we have:

- A floating significand:

  ```
  456.123
  ```

- A floating significand with an exponent:

  ```
  456.123e-07
  ```

- An integral significand with an exponent:

  ```
  197e3
  ```

The floating point suffix can be added to indicate a `float` (`f` or `F`) or `long double` (`l` or `L`). As for the integral suffixes, the author recommends against using the lowercase 'ell.'

C's integer types are signed. A 16-bit `int` ranges from –32767 to +32768. For each type, there is a corresponding unsigned type: `unsigned short`, `unsigned int` (or just `unsigned`), and `unsigned short`. (All of these words are keywords and may not be used as variables, function names, etc.). Unsigned types are guaranteed to obey the laws of arithmetic-module-*N,* where *N* is $2^{(\text{number of bits in the type})}$. A sixteen-bit unsigned type ranges from 0 to 65536.

Unsigned constants are written like ordinary integer constants, except that they are suffixed by either `u` or `U`. Signed and unsigned integers may be freely converted. Converting from unsigned to signed may result in a negative value.

When `int`s or `unsigned`s of different widths appear together in an expression, C generally widens the narrower type to preserve the value during the computation. (There are some exceptions, e.g., assignment to a narrower type.) But when signed and unsigned types are mixed, things are more complicated. Pre-ANSI C had a simple rule: unsignedness prevailed. Under ANSI C, the wider type's signedness or unsignedness prevails if the resulting value can be stored in that type, otherwise unsignedness prevails. (These are called *value-preserving* semantics.)

C also supports character types in several flavors. They behave like very narrow integer types, may be freely mixed with integer types, and are often used as very short integers. The basic character type is `char`. `char` is the natural character type on the machine, which may be either signed or unsigned. Should signedness or unsignedness actually be required, there are `signed char` and `unsigned char`, which are distinct types from each other and from `char`.

C has character constants whose type is not `char` but `int`. Since character types behave like small integers, these constants may be used wherever any variety of `char` is needed. They are written like this:

```
printf( "%c%c%c%c%c, %c%c%c%c%c!\n", 'H', 'e', 'l', 'l', 'o',
                                     'W', 'o', 'r', 'l', 'd' );
```

Each quote-*character*-quote is a character constant whose value is that character. (`%c` is indication to `printf()` to look for a single character.) For hard-to-print characters, there are 'escape sequences':

`'\a'`	The bell or audible alert character
`'\b'`	Backspace
`'\f'`	Form feed
`'\v'`	Vertical tab
`'\r'`	Carriage return (without the line advance)

`'\t'`	Horizontal tab
`'\''`	Single quote
`'\?'`	Question mark (synonym for '?')
`'\\'`	Backslash
`'\n'`	(where *n* is an octal digit)
`'\nn'`	The character in the local native
`'\nnn'`	Character set represented by the octal digits *n*, *nn*, or *nnn*

`char`s are interpreted in the native character set on the machine at hand. Often, this will be some version of ASCII or of the ISO Latin character set. Sometimes, though, it will be EBCDIC.

This sets a trap. The following code will work for ASCII and the ISO Latin character sets, but not for EBCIDIC or various European national character sets:

```
int
for_ascii_only( char c )
{
        if( c >= 'A' )
        {
                if( c <= 'Z' )
                        return 1;
        }
        else
        if( c >= 'a' )
        {
                if( c <= 'z' )
                        return 1;
        }
        return 0;
}
```

(There are better and portable ways to accomplish this.)

Double-quoted string constants, such as those used with `printf()`, can only be explained in terms of pointers, and so will be deferred until Sec. A.2.3, except to note that the escape sequences for single-quoted character constants are also valid for double-quoted string constants, the escape for a single quote being replaced by an escape for a double quote:

```
printf( "\"Now THAT rings a bell\a,\" he chimed\n." );
printf( "\"%s,\" %s\n.",
        "I don't need all of this space     \b\b\b\b\b",
        "he backpedalled." );
```

These character sets are sufficient, more or less, for European languages. They do not serve for Asian character sets, nor for systems that must support multiple languages. There are several sixteen-bit and thirty-two-bit character sets being standardized. C provides for one expanded character set. A C implementation may provide a type called `wchar_t` ('wide char type') using a facility called the `typedef` (Sec. A.2.2.4). It will provide an implementation-dependent encoding of `wchar_t`s into a character constant written like this:

```
L'something'
```

Likewise, there is a 'string-of-wide-characters,' whose constants are written thus:

```
L"something"
```

A.1.1.8 Consts. ANSI C introduces the notion of 'constant variables' or *consts*. A const is declared with the keyword `const`, and must be initialized where it is defined. (See Sec. A.2.2 for the distinction between declaration and definition.)

Consts have several uses. A const can provide a 'manifest constant':

```
long
lfib( long lf )
{
        const int maxarg = 45;
        const int ret_NG = -1;
                ... ...
        if( lf > maxarg )
                return ret_NG;

        ... ...
}
```

This is more important in C++ than in C; in C, other mechanisms are commonly used (see App. C). `const` can also be used to indicate a 'variable' that is used for one and only one result:

```
... ...
{
        const double fu = fugacity( ... ...);

        ... lots of computations ...
        ... that use, not change ...
        ... fu ...
}
... ...
```

Finally, `const` is used with pointers to indicate that the pointer may not be used to change the object at which it points. (See Sec. A.2.3.6.)

A.1.1.9 `printf()`. `printf()` is C's basic formatted output function. It takes one or more arguments. The number of arguments expected is determined by the value of the first argument; if too few or too many arguments are provided, the program may fail catastrophically.

The first argument to `printf()` is taken as a format string. Its type must be `char*` or `const char*`. (The former is the type of the value of a double-quoted string; see Sec. A.2.3.6 for the full story.)

Most characters in `printf()`'s format string will be copied directly to the output (as in the simple version of the `Hello, World!` program). When a `%` (percent sign) is seen, special processing begins. Some number of characters following will be taken out of the output stream to indicate an output operation (called a *%-conversion*).

The general form is

% Opt-Ind O-W-Counts T-W-Ind Cv-Ind

Opt-Ind Option-Indicators:
  any of #, –, +, or space

O-W-Counts (Output width counts):
  $Field\text{-}Width_{opt}$ $Precision\text{-}Indicator_{opt}$

Field-Width: Decimal-Count-or-Star

Precision-Indicator: . $Precision_{opt}$

Precision: Decimal-Count-or-Star

T-W-Ind (Type-Width-Indicator):
  One of: l or L (for long)
  h or H (for short)
  nothing (for natural length)

Cv-Ind (Conversion-Indicator):
  One of: c, d, e, E, f, g, G, i, n, o, p, s, u, x, X

This is best understood by starting at the end. The conversion indicator gives the type expected and the format of the conversion. For example, `%c` indicates that a single character (signed, unsigned, or natural) is to be output. `%d` or `%i` indicates that an `int` (of some length) is to be output in decimal. `%o` and `%x` or `%X` indicate that an `int` is to be output in octal or hexadecimal, respectively. (The `X` indicates that the alphabetic hex digits—hexits?—are to be in uppercase, the `x` that they are to be in lowercase.) `%u` indicates that an `unsigned int` of some width is to be output as a decimal unsigned quantity (always positive).

`%e`, `%E`, `%f`, `%g`, and `%G` indicate conversions of floating point numbers of some width. The first two produce floating-point (exponential notation) with the `e` in lower- or uppercase. The second produces fixed-point notation. The third and fourth will produce fixed-point notation for exponents ≥ –4 and small enough not to discard the upper digits in the precision available, not printing trailing zeros or a trailing decimal point.

`%s` indicates a conversion of a character string identified by pointer-to-some-kind-of-char. (See Sec. A.2.3 for the full story on pointers.) Plain `char`, signed `char`, and unsigned `char` will all work. (Some values may lie outside the machine's printable character set if the signedness is wrong.) `printf()`'s arguments can't be type-checked, but it is safe to use a pointer-to-const-char (`const char*`) here as well. (Double-quoted strings should always be treated as pointer-to-const-char.)

`%p` indicates that a pointer of some sort is being passed, and it should be printed in an unambiguous but machine-dependent way.

`%n` indicates that a pointer-to-int is being passed, and that the number of characters generated *so far* by this call to `printf()` should be stored in the pointed-to `int`. No output is generated for this 'conversion.' (See Sec. A.2.3 on pointers.)

Preceding the conversion indicator there may be a type width indicator. If present, this will be `h` or `H` to indicate that a short object (a short int or unsigned or a float) is to be converted, or `l` or `L` to indicate that a long object (a long int or long unsigned or a long double) is to be converted. No indicator means that a 'natural length' object is to be converted (int, unsigned int, or double).

Before the type width indicator (if present) or the conversion indicator (if not), there may be one or two output width counts. This group of indicators may include a field width (before the decimal point, if there is a decimal point) and a precision (after the decimal point, which must be present if the precision is present). The precision indicates how much of the number to print. For an integral type, at least that many digits will be printed, and the output will be padded with leading zeros if necessary to make up the precision. For a string (`%s` conversion), at most that many characters will be printed. For the floating point conversions, it specifies the number of digits after the decimal point. For the `g` and `G` conversions, it also determines if the number should be printed in fixed or floating point format.

The field width indicator determines the minimum number of characters allotted for the output of the conversion. If fewer are needed, the output will be padded to bring it up to the minimum. The pad character is normally a space, but this can be changed for some conversions.

The field width and precision can each be replaced by a '*'. When a star is seen in these positions, `printf()` expects to find an extra argument, an `int`, to provide the value of the field width or precision. Since the arguments will be read right-to-left, the field width comes first, followed by the precision, followed by the actual argument to the conversion.

Before the output width counts (if present) or the type width indicator (if the former is absent and the latter present) or the conversion indicator (if neither is present), there may be one or more flags. These flags are recognized:

- `-`
  Left-adjustment: any pad characters needed to fill out the field width will be added after the converted characters.
- `+`
  Sign always: A numeric quantity will be converted with a sign, either - or +.
- (space)
  If no sign is to be printed, a space will be added instead.
- `0`
  For numeric conversion, pad to make up the field width with leading zeros.
- `#`
  Use an 'alternate form' in the conversion. Not all conversions have an alternate form. For `%o` (octal), the alternate form differs from the standard form in having a leading `0`. For `%x` and `%X`, the alternate form differs in having a leading `0x` or `0X` (respectively). For the floating point conversions, alternate form differs from the standard form in that there will always be a decimal point printed and, for the `%g` and `%G` conversions, trailing zeros will be kept (up to the precision count).

A.1.1.10 `putchar()` **and** `getchar()`. Besides `printf()`, C supports character-by-character I/O with the functions `putchar()` and `getchar()`:

```
int getchar();  // Returns the next character available on
                //  standard input; returns  EOF  on eof.
int putchar( char c );  // Places  c  on standard output.
                        //    Returns  c.
```

There are also versions called `putc()` and `getc()` which take an additional parameter representing an open file. See Sec. A.2.8.2 for the full story.

A.1.1.11 Keywords. Here are C's keywords, together with the section in which they are first described.

auto A.2.2.1.1	break A.1.2.6	case A.1.4	char A.1.1.7
const A.1.1.8	continue A.1.2.6	default A.1.4	do A.1.2.5
double A.1.1.7	else A.1.2.1	enum A.1.5	extern A.2.2.1.4

float A.1.1.7	for A.1.2.3	goto A.1.6	if A.1.2.1
int A.1.1.3	long A.1.1.6	register A.2.2.1.2	return A.1.1.4
short A.1.1.7	signed A.1.1.7	sizeof A.1.3.2	static A.2.2.1.3
struct A.2.5	switch A.1.4	typedef A.1.1.7	union A.2.6
unsigned A.1.1.7	void A.1.1.3	volatile A.2.9	while A.1.2.4

A.1.2 Basics for programming

Our Fibonacci function of A.1.1.6 is not very practical. The double recursion means that to compute `lfib( n )` we will need more than *lfib(n)* steps—in fact $2 \times lfib(n) - 1$ steps. (To compute *lfib(35)* on the author's 33 MHz 80486 machine takes almost 30 seconds for 29,860,703—almost thirty million—iterations.)

An iterative solution will be more practical. Here's one:

```
long
fib( long i )
{
        long f1 = 1;    /* f( n - 1 ) */
        long f2 = 1;    /* f( n - 2 ) */
        long f;
        long j;

        if( i <= 1 )
                return 1;

        for( j = 1 ; j < i ; j = j + 1 )
        {
                f = f2 + f1;

                f2 = f1;
                f1 = f;
        }

        return f;
}
```

(Note that we've dropped the "l-for-`long`" from `fib()`.)

Here we've declared not only the parameter `i` but variables `f1` and `f2` for the *(n–1)*th and *(n–2)*th Fibonacci number. These declarations are placed at the top of the brace-enclosed compound statement (block) that is the function body. For `f1` and `f2` we provide initial values by writing *initializers*—an equal sign followed by an integral expression. (We need these two initial values to start the computation.)

A.1.2.1 Conditional branches: the `if` and `if-else`. The first nondeclarative statement is an `if`-statement. This statement has two forms:

```
if( test-expression )
        statement
```

and

```
if( test-expression )
        statement
else
        statement
```

The `if()` statement evaluates the expression. If the expression evaluates to a nonzero value, the first statement within it (the 'then part') is executed; otherwise the second statement (the 'else part'), if present, is executed. In the `fib()` function's `if`, the expression is `i <= 1`, which evaluates to an `int` value of one if `i` is less than or equal to one, and to zero otherwise.

These can be nested:

```
if( test-expression )
        if( test-expression )
                statement
        else
                statement
else
        if( test-expression )
                statement
        else
                statement
```

Coding it like this is risky, especially if one of the intermediate statements is removed:

```
if( test-expression )       /* outer if */
        if( test-expression )    /* inner if */
                statement
        /* OOPS!!! */
else                                /* "outer" else ??? */
        if( test-expression )
                statement
        else
                statement
```

Here the first `else` is associated with the 'inner' `if`, not the outer one. The indentation doesn't match what is actually happening.

Whenever a statement governed by an `if` (or any other statement) governs other statements, it should be enclosed in a compound statement:

```
if( test-expression )
{
        if( test-expression )
                statement
}
else
{
        if( test-expression )
                statement
        else
                statement
}
```

This removes the ambiguities. There is one exception: when a more-or-less linear series of cases is tested for:

```
if( ... ... )
        ... ...
else
if( ... ... )
        ... ...
else
if( ... ... )
        ... ...
else
if( ... ... )
        ... ...
else
        ... ...
```

A.1.2.2 Conditional branches: comparison operators. C supports the usual set of equality and relational operators:

```
==    equal-to
!=    not-equal-to
<     less-than
>     greater-than
<=    less-than-or-equal-to
>=    greater-than-or-equal-to
```

There are a couple of subtleties. First, the equality test is ==, not =. Moreover, because assignment is an expression in C rather than a statement (see Sec. A.1.3.7), in many cases substituting the second for the first will result in code that is legal, but not what is meant.

The relational operators have a slightly higher precedence than the equality operators, so

```
a < b == c > d
```

evaluates to

```
( a < b ) == ( c > d )
```

And yes, this code is legal. These operators can take various types on their left- and right-hand-sides, but they all 'return' an `int`. That means we could write:

```
int
cmpfibs( long l, long r )
{
        return fib( l ) > fib( r );
}
```

or even, in a larger body of code,

```
int a;
int b;
...
{
        int r = a > b;
        ...
```

A.1.2.3 Looping: the `for` statement. Here's our iterative Fibonacci function again:

```
long
fib( long i )
{
        long f1 = 1;    /* f( n - 1 ) */
        long f2 = 1;    /* f( n - 2 ) */
        long f;
        long j;

        if( i <= 1 )
                return 1;

        for( j = 1 ; j < i ; j = j + 1 )
        {
                f = f2 + f1;
```

A.1.2.5 Test at the bottom: `do-while`. C provides a test-at-the-bottom loop, the `do-while` statement.

```
do
        statement
while( expression )
```

First the `statement` is executed, then the `expression` is evaluated. If it evaluates 'true' (nonzero) the sequence is repeated.

Test-at-the-bottom is rarely used; C's expression semantics and the loop control statements in the next section make test-at-the-top better for almost all uses.

A.1.2.6 Loop control: `break` and `continue`. C has two statements to control loops. The first, the `break` statement, exits the smallest enclosing loop statement or `switch` statement (Sec. A.1.4).

```
for(;;)
{
        ... some stuff ...
        if( expression )
                break;
        ... more stuff ...
}
```

The `break` is used like this to create a 'loop-and-a-half,' a loop whose test(s) cannot be expressed as a single expression. Multiple `break` statements are allowed:

```
for(;;)
{
        ... try to get ingredient 1 ...
        if( expression )
                break;
        ... try to get ingredient 2 ...
        if( expression )
                break;
        ... try to get ingredient 3 ...
        if( expression )
                break;
        ... try to get ingredient 4 ...
        if( expression )
                break;
        ... perform the recipe ...
}
```

The continue statement causes the smallest enclosing loop statement to skip the rest of the iteration and resume with the test or increment expression:

```
for( ...startup... ; ...more-to-do?... ; ...look-for-next... )
{
        if( ...simple case... )
        {
                ...simple, one-line case...
                continue;       -resumes with 'look-for-next'
        }

        ...long, thirty-line case...

}
```

A.1.2.7 Manifest constants and the preprocessor. Recall that our Fibonacci function is good for arguments up to 45 (on a machine with 32-bit longs). We can guard against excessive calls like this:

```
long
fib( long i )
{
        long f1 = 1;    /* f( n - 1 ) */
        long f2 = 1;    /* f( n - 2 ) */
        long f;
        long j;

        if( i <= 1 )
                return 1;

        /*
         *      fib( 45 ) fits in a long; fib( 46 ) does not.
         */
        if( i > 45 )
                return -1;

        ...
```

We have introduced not one but two constants. Even with the comment, this is undesirable. (For one thing, any caller that wants to conform to the computation limit must either have a copy of the constant or call fib() with successively larger values until it gets a -1—and how does it know that the error value is -1?)

C provides a *preprocessor* which can be used to substitute a value wherever a given name is seen:

```
#define MAX_FIB_ARG 45
#define FIB_RANGE_ERR -1

        ...

long
fib( long i )
{
            ...
        if( i <= 1 )
                return 1;

        if( i > MAX_FIB_ARG )
                return FIB_RANGE_ERR;

        ...
```

Now anything that calls `fib()` can use (*should* use) `FIB_RANGE_ERR` to check if the function has exceeded its range:

```
f = fib( n );
if( f == FIB_RANGE_ERR )
        ...
```

The preprocessor is capable of many other things wondrous and strange, and is described fully in Sec. A.3.

Because assignment is an expression in C, the example above can be written as

```
if( ( f = fib( n ) ) == FIB_RANGE_ERR )
        ...
```

The value of the assignment expression is the value of its left-hand side after the assignment is performed. Many find this excessively terse, but it is legal and it is a common C idiom: "try, and if you fail, then. . . ." The parentheses are needed; without them C would compare the return of `fib()` with `FIB_RANGE_ERR` and assign the result of the comparison (`1` or `0`) to `f` and test that value against zero.

A.1.3 C operators

C is known for its large set of operators, corresponding to the operations provided by most computer instruction sets. Some of the operators are used for pointer and structure operations and are described in Sec. A.2. The remaining operators will be described here.

A.1.3.1 ++ and −−. Let's look at the for(;;) loop in our fib() function:

```
for( j = 1 ; j < i ; j = j + 1 )
{
        f = f2 + f1;

        f2 = f1;
        f1 = f;
}
```

(Recall that j is declared as int.) The increment part of the for(;;) is j = j + 1. There are three more idiomatic ways to write this. The first is

```
for( j = 1 ; j < i ; j += 1 )
```

We'll consider this in Sec. A.1.3.7. The other ways use the 'increment' operator:

```
for( j = 1 ; j < i ; j++ )
```

The unary ++ operator increments its operand by one. ++ actually provides two operators. Here it has been written as a postfix operator. We can also use it as a prefix operator:

```
for( j = 1 ; j < i ; ++j )
```

Both forms increment j by one. The difference appears if we use their values as well as their side effects. The value of the prefix form is the value of the operand *after* the increment:

```
i = 0;
while( ++i < 2 )
{
        ...
}
```

Here the loop body will be executed once, with i equal to 1.

```
i = 0;
while( i ++ < 2 )
{
        ...
}
```

Here the loop body will be executed twice, with `i` equal first to 1, and then to 2. Only on the third pass, when `i` is equal to 2 *before* the test expression is evaluated, will the loop terminate. (After the loop terminates, the value of `i` will be 3.)

Besides ++, C has a decrement operator, --, which decrements its argument by one. It can be used as a prefix or postfix operator, just as the increment operator can.

In early versions of C, ++ and -- may only be applied to integral (character and integer) types, and to pointer types (Sec. A.2.3.4). In ANSI C, they may be applied to floating point types as well.

A.1.3.2 Arithmetic operators. Increment and decrement are unary operators. Unary operators have the highest priority in C and group right-to-left. Most unary operators are prefix operators. (The official grammar for C describes increment and decrement as *postfix* operators when they are used in postfix form.)

In general, arithmetic operators and bitwise operators return values of the same type and signedness as their operands. For binary operators, special rules apply when types are mixed. See Sec. A.1.1.6.

Other unary operators are - (unary negation), + (a no-op provided for symmetry with -), ~, !, and `sizeof`.

~ is a *bitwise* operator: it expects an integral argument which it treats as a set of bits, and it returns an integral argument of the same signedness and type (except that character arguments are converted to `int` of the same signedness as the character before the operator is applied).

In particular, ~ is the *bitwise complement* operator: its return value has every bit set that its argument has clear, and every bit clear which its argument has set.

! is the *logical not* operator: it returns an integer one or zero (true or false) as its argument is zero or nonzero.

`sizeof` accepts any expression, or any parenthesized type name, for its argument. It returns the size of the value generated by the expression, or the size of an instance of the type, in bytes. The notion of a byte is necessarily machine-dependent, but it is guaranteed that `sizeof ( char ) == 1`. The type of `sizeof`'s return value is given by a typedef (synonym for a type, Sec. A.2.2.4) called `size_t` and found in a standard include file called `stddef.h`.

Right after the unary operators in precedence are the binary *multiplicative operators,* which group from left to right:

```
* / %
```

These are (respectively) multiplication, division, and remaindering (modulo). Where signed types are concerned, the behavior of remaindering is machine-dependent; negative divisor or negative dividend can result in the value of an expression involving % being negative. The only guarantee is that (for an integral type)

```
( dvdend / dvsor ) * dvsor + ( dvdend % dvsor ) == dvdend
```

Unsigned types, of course, are never negative.

Next in order of precedence are the binary *additive operators,* which also group left-to-right:

```
+ -
```

When applied to arithmetic types, these evaluate to the sum or difference of their arguments. When types are mixed, the rules in Sec. A.1.1.6 apply. They also may be applied to pointer types or to combinations of arithmetic and pointer types. See Sec. A.2.3.4. Unsigned types are guaranteed to obey the laws of arithmetic modulo 2-to-the-power-of-the-type's-length; the response to overflow or underflow of a signed type is implementation-defined. (This implies that signed arithmetic, even on integral types, carries the possibility of an exception on overflow or underflow, if that is the behavior of the 'most natural' implementation of arithmetic on the machine at hand.)

A.1.3.3 Shift operators. Next in precedence after the arithmetic operators are the binary *shift operators,* which group left-to-right:

```
<< >>
```

The << operator is the *left-shift* operator; the >> operator is the *right-shift* operator. Their operands must be integral types, and their result is the type of the left-hand operand (promoted from character to integer if necessary). These operators interpret the left-hand operand as a bit pattern, and shift it bitwise left or right by the number given in the right-hand operand. The result is undefined if the right-hand operand is negative or larger than the length of the left-hand type. The right-shift operator, applied to a signed left-hand side, will propagate the sign bit instead of filling the upper bits with zero; this ensures that right-shifting by N bits is equivalent to division by 2^N.

A.1.3.4 Relational and equality operators. Next in precedence after the shift operators are the binary *relational operators,* and after them, the binary *equality operators.*

The relational operators are

```
>     greater than
<     less than
>=    greater than or equal to
<=    less than or equal to
```

These accept arguments of arithmetic types and return an `int` whose value is one or zero as the specified relationship is true or false. (They can also accept arguments of pointer types; see Sec. A.2.3.4.)

The `equality` operators have a precedence just below that of the relational operators.

```
==    is equal to
!=    is not equal to
```

Like the relational operators, they return one or zero as the relationship they specify is true or false.

Both the relational and equality operators group left-to-right.

Because the equality test is == and assignment =, there are opportunities both for typographic error and for the force of habit acquired from programming languages that perform assignment by statement rather than by operator. A = can look very like a == in a program listing.

Occasionally someone will ask if, in a statement such as this one,

```
if( i > 20 )
        ...
```

whether the compiler generates a comparison followed by branches and code that sets a temporary to one or zero, followed by more code to test the temporary. Officially, this is a 'quality of implementation' issue; the semantics are just as described and the compiler is free to generate any code that has the same overall effect (executes *as if* it were compiled that way). In fact, few compilers, or none, will actually generate code to evaluate the expression to one or zero; the code simply does the comparison and executes or skips the subordinate statement appropriately.

A.1.3.5 Binary bitwise operators. C provides three binary *bitwise* operators. These take arguments of integral type, and their return type is the integral type large enough to preserve the value of the result (Sec. A.1.1.6).

These operators have successively weaker precedences, and otherwise group left-to-right:

```
&    -- bitwise and
|    -- bitwise or
^    -- bitwise exclusive or
```

These operators result in the bit-by-bit *and, or,* or *exclusive or* of their operands.

A.1.3.6 Logical and conditional operators. Next in precedence are three operators with special properties. The first two are *short-circuit* logical operators:

```
&&    -- logical AND
||    -- logical OR
```

These operators return one or zero as their operands are both nonzero (for the *AND*) or not both zero (for the *OR*). They group and evaluate from right to left, and *they evaluate only as far as necessary.*

This latter property is called 'short-circuit evaluation' and it allows such code as

```
while( i < MAX
    && array[ i ] != END_OF_GROUP )
        ...
```

Here, the use of `i` as a subscript will not take place unless the test for `i < MAX` succeeds. Short-circuit evaluation has other good uses:

```
if( try_trivial_case()
 || try_easy_case()
 || try_difficult_case()
 || try_very_hard_case()
 || try_almost_impossible_case()
 || try_calling_in_the_marines()
 || try_pulling_a_rabbit_out_of_a_hat() )
        success();
else
        failure();
```

Here we will stop evaluating conditions (and trying the various cases) after the first function that returns 'true' (nonzero).

C has another operator that may or may not evaluate an operand. The ternary (3-argument) *conditional operator* comes right after the logical OR in precedence:

```
cond ? if-true-expr : if-false-expr
```

The first argument to the conditional expression is evaluated. If it evaluates to true (nonzero) the second expression is evaluated, otherwise the third expression is evaluated. The result of the expression is the result of evaluating the second or third expression. The second and third expressions must be compatible (as for addition) or must both be pointer expressions of the same type.

A.1.3.7 Assignops. In C, assignment is performed as a side effect of an expression:

```
lhs = rhs
```

Here *lhs* and *rhs* must have types which permit the value of *rhs* to be converted (if necessary) to the type of *lhs,* and the value of *lhs* set equal to the converted value. *lhs* must, in particular, name something to which an assignment of any kind is possible (e.g., a variable). Such a something is called an *l-value* (or *lvalue*), where the 'l' can be taken as a mnemonic for 'lhs.'* (Ordinary values are called *r-values,* by the same principle.) Some operators (e.g., subscripting) yield lvalues. *Parenthesizing an expression does not change its status as an lvalue,* so that we can write:

```
int i;
( i ) = 5;
```

(Parentheses in C may be inserted in many unexpected places. This expression is quite legal:

```
( printf ) ( ( "Hello, World\n" ) )
```

Both the function name and the argument to the function have been parenthesized, with no effect whatsoever.)

Assignment has a lower precedence than any operator except the comma operator. It groups from right to left and its value is the value of its left-hand side, so we can write

```
int i;
int j;

i = j = 5;
```

---

* In fact, the 'l' and 'r' stand for 'load' and 'read,' as in loading or reading a register.

Besides ordinary assignment, C has a group of combined assignment operators. They can shorten code, improve expression of simple ideas, and avoid the need for temporaries.

Wherever it is legal to write

```
x = x + y
```

it is also legal to write

```
x += y
```

The two forms have the same meaning, with one exception. If the left-hand expression has side effects, they will occur twice in the first expression, and only once in the second.

```
Using a temporary:

        temporary = somefunc( "Look me up" );

        /* Array expression on the LHS */

        x[ temporary ] = x[ temporary ] + n_used_here;

Using a combined assignment op:

        x[ somefunc( "Look me up" ) ] += n_used_here;
```

Most of C's binary operators have combined assignment forms. Here's the complete set:

```
*=  /=  %=  +=  -=  <<=  >>=  &=  |=  ^=
```

Like the simple assignment, these group from right to left. They have the same precedence as ordinary assignment, and their value is the value of the LHS after the assignment takes place.

A.1.3.8 Comma op. At the lowest priority, C has the comma operator. An expression such as

```
lhs-expr , rhs-expr
```

is evaluated by first evaluating the left-hand expression (including any side effect), then discarding its value and ignoring its type, and finally evaluating the right-hand expression and using its type and value as the type and value of the whole expression.

The comma operator is most often used in the controlling parts of `for(;;)` loops:

```
for( i = 0, j = start ; i < MAX ; i++, j++ )
        ...
```

The comma operator is also used heavily by some program generators.

The comma operator is illegal in places where commas already have meaning (e.g., in function argument lists). But the following is legal:

```
f( i, ( j += w( j ), t[ j + 3 ] ), 0 );
```

There are three arguments to the function. The middle argument is a parenthesized expression containing a comma operator.

A.1.3.9 Casts. C has a special unary operator called the *cast* (also sometimes called the 'typecast'). It has a high precedence, just like the other unary operators.

```
(typename) expression
```

The type of a cast is the type named in the parentheses. The value is the value of the right-hand-side expression converted, "as if by assignment," to the type named. Thus, these two are equivalent:

```
With assignment to a temporary:
        float f = ...

        {
                int temp = f;
                printf( "%d", temp );
        }

With a typecast:
        float f = ...

        printf( "%d", (int) f );
```

A.1.3.10 Arrays. C has arrays. The details of their semantics are tied up with the semantics of pointers, but their basics can be given here. Arrays are built up out of other types (integral and floating types, pointers, other arrays, etc.—almost anything except functions) and are declared like this:

```
int     five_ints[ 5 ];
double  da[ 22 ];
float   two_dimensional[ 4 ][ 15 ];
```

The last is a two-dimensional array. In C, a two-dimensional array is an array of arrays. We read such declarations from the inside out. `two_dimensional` is an array of four things, each of which is an array of fifteen `float`s.

Arrays are indexed by integral types, and array indices start at zero. Thus, the valid indices for `five_ints`, above, are 0, 1, 2, 3, and 4. In most C environments, array-indexing operations are not checked at runtime.

Whether an array can be initialized or not, and what it is initialized with by default, depends upon its *storage class* (Sec. A.2.2). For an array which can be explicitly initialized, the initializers are written like this:

```
int     five_ints[ 5 ] = { 5, 4, 3, 2, 1, };
double  da[ 22 ]
= {
           1.0,     1.0,      2.0,     3.0,     5.0,     8.0,
          13.0,    21.0,     34.0,    55.0,    89.0,   144.0,
         233.0,   377.0,    610.0    987.0,  1597.0,  2584.0,
        4181.0,  6765.0,  10946.0,  17711.0
};
float   two_dimensional[ 4 ][ 15 ]
={
        {       0., 0., 0., 0., 0., 4., 4., 4., 4., 4.,
                1., 1., 1., 1., 1., },
        {       1., 1., 1., 1., 1., 2., 2., 2., 2., 2.,
                3., 3., 3., 3., 3., },
        {       6., 6., 6., 6., 6., 3., 3., 3., 3., 3.,
                0., 0., 0., 0., 0., },
        {       2., 2., 2., 2., 2., 9., 9., 9., 9., 9.,
                8., 8., 8., 8., 8., }

};
```

Notice the brace-enclosed groups in the two-dimensional array initialization. Braces can be omitted if all the elements are written, but the rules can be complicated and it's generally simpler to write all the braces.

Trailing commas on the lists are optional; they may be present or absent without affecting the initializer's meaning. If there are fewer initializers than things to initialize, the remaining array elements receive default initialization.

Arrays of characters can be initialized by a double-quoted string:

```
char    notice[ 255 ] = "Used under license of The Nifty Co.";
```

This use of double-quoted strings is synonymous with

```
char    notice[ 255 ]
={
        'U',  's',  'e',  'd',  ' ',  'u',  'n',  'd',
        'e',  'r',  ' ',  'l',  'i',  'c',  'e',  'n',
        's',  'e',  ' ',  'o',  'f',  ' ',  'T',  'h',
        'e',  ' ',  'N',  'i',  'f',  't',  'y',  ' ',
        'C',  'o',  '.',
};
```

If there are array elements for which no initializing characters are specified, they will be initialized with zero. There is no requirement that a `'\0'` character appear at the end of an array that is initialized in this way in C (but there *is* in C++).

A.1.4 The `switch()`, `case`, and `default` statements

There is another structured control flow statement in C. It is the `switch()` statement, and it requires two other statements, the `case` and `default` statements. The `switch()` statement is a multiway branch on a single integral variable:

```
char command;
      ...

switch( command )
{
  default:
        offer_help();
        break;

  case 'a':
        do_append();
        break;

  case 'e':
  case 'x':
        if( ! changed
         || confirm_exit() )
              do_exit();
        break;
```

```
case 'g':
        if( ! changed
          || confirm_get() )
                do_get();
        break;
                ...
}
```

Upon entry, the switch compares its argument expression against all of the constants in the case statements within it. If any matches, control is transferred to the statement labeled by that case. If none match, control is passed to the statement labeled by the default statement, if there is one; otherwise, control is passed to the first statement after the switch(). (Note the use of the short-circuit operators in two of the cases, by the way.)

The case statements actually act like labels; if control reaches them from above, they 'fall through.' This permits multiple case statements to label one statement, but requires that the code for a single case exit the switch() with a break statement. More complicated fall-through cases should probably be commented:

```
switch( c_type )
{
    ...
        break;

  case 5:
    ...
        /* Fall-through */
  case 6:
    ...

        break;

  case 7:
    ...
}
```

A particularly exotic use of fall-through in a switch statement is Duff's Device, described in Sec. B.3.

A.1.5 enums

C has one more 'integral' type, the *enumerated type* or enum. An enum declares a small set of named integral constants, with values that may be specified or provided by default:

```
enum Compass_Point { North, South, East, West };

enum Compass_Point rough_heading = North;
```

`rough_heading` becomes a variable of type `enum Compass_Point`. `North` is a constant of that type. Enumeration values may be freely converted to integers, and each enumeration constant has an integer value.

The constants in an enumeration may be given values explicitly:

```
enum Grades { gA = 5, gB = 4, gC = 3, gD = 2, gF = 0, gW = -1 };
```

If no value is given, each enumerator is given a value one greater than the preceding enumerator, and the first enumerator is given value 0.

A.1.6 `goto` and labels

C provides a `goto` statement. Its use is not encouraged and it is rarely used, but it is available if needed:

```
goto label ;
        ...
label :
```

label must be a C identifier not otherwise used in the current scope. It must lie within the same function as the `goto` and may come either before or after the `goto`.

(Very early versions of C allowed a variable to be used to identify a label. This capability was dropped before publication of the first book on C programming.)

A.1.7 Some style guidelines

C can be used to write very clear code. It can also be used to write very obscure code. Here are some hints for the best use of C.

A.1.7.1 Don't code another language in C. The conventions of other languages do not always translate well into C. C's short-circuit operators and potent expression syntax make it easy to avoid circumlocutions needed in languages that lack such operators. In particular, C's powerful expression syntax, with assignment-as-expression, short-circuit operators, and the conditional expression can often replace convoluted branches and loop control flags. These features of C are good; *use them.*

A.1.7.2 Use the loop-and-a-half. When the 'try-it-and-test' part of a loop is still too big to fit in one C expression, don't use flags and a test-at-the-bottom loop. Use a 'forever' loop and a `break`. The flags obscure; the `break` clarifies, regardless of the conventional wisdom in other programming languages and doctrines.

A.1.7.3 Use function prototypes and prototype modules in their header files. This makes best use of ANSI C's typechecking and can spare you many errors.

A.1.7.4 Declare variables in the smallest enclosing scope. This will protect you against accidental misuse of the variable and help the reader understand the entire meaning of the variable.

A.1.7.5 Group functions in files by *Module.* Seldom is a single function a logical module by itself. Group your functions and the data for which they are responsible into modules.

A.1.7.6 Declare new functions as needed. C deliberately makes it easy to declare and use functions. Take advantage of this; use functions whenever you need to name a unit of code.

A.1.7.7 Avoid gotos. Very few situations in C actually call for a goto. Usually the problem is better expressed using expressions and the structured flow constructs (including `break` and `continue`). If you find large units of code being repeated inside a nest of conditional tests, try making them into functions, and invoke them in conditional or short-circuit expressions as needed.

A.2 Finishing Touches (Utmost C)

The material in Sec. A.1 allows us to use C in a variety of simple ways. It does not allow us to use the full power of C. This chapter completes our understanding of C, excluding the preprocessor, which is covered in Sec. A.3.

A.2.1 Function delimiters

We noted in Sec. A.1.1.1 that functions are defined slightly differently under ANSI and pre-ANSI C. Both support the old declarations; ANSI C supports the new ('prototyped') declarations and definitions.

First the old form:

```
double
gumflummit( s, f, l, d, i )
short s;
float f;
```

```
long l;
double d;
int i;
{
        return ( s + f * l + 1. ) / ( d + i ) ;
}
```

Let's say that something somewhere calls this function without declaring it (or seeing a declaration in a `#include`'d header file). C assumes that the return type is `int`, so the return value will be misinterpreted, and the bit pattern of a floating point value will be treated as integral value. This is a serious error; `gumflummit()` should be declared in a header file forthwith, and in a header file that will be `included` by both the code defining and the code using `gumflummit()`. (Having the code defining the function see the declaration allows the compiler to detect any discrepancy.)

```
    In flumgummery.h:
double gumflummit();

    In gumflummery.c:
double
gumflummit( s, f, l, d, i )
short s;
float f;
long l;
double d;
int i;
{
        return ( s + f * l + 1. ) / ( d + i ) ;
}

    In Gummed_N_Flummed.c:
float mumfgummf = gumflummit( 4, 45.0, 110, 3.14159 );
```

Whoops! We've made a boo-boo. `gumfummit()` expects five arguments. We've provided four, and we've got the types wrong, too. Functions written in the pre-ANSI form are not checked for type and number of arguments, so this won't be caught during compilation or linking.

For nonprototyped functions, `short`-length and `char`-length arguments are widened to an `int` of the appropriate signedness, and `float` arguments are widened to `double`, so the first and second arguments are correct. The third argument isn't, the fourth is, and the fifth is missing altogether. Here's a correct version:

```
In Gummed_N_Flummed.c:
   float mumfgummf = gumflummit( 4, 45.0F, 110L, 3.14159, 17 );
```

We've added the `F` to the second argument even though it's not needed.

Return values for nonprototyped functions are widened just as parameters are. This indulgent approach to parameters and return values reflects C's origins as a 'systems programming' language, in which most interesting things were expressed as the machine's most natural integral type. Fortunately, it is no longer necessary. We can write the function with ANSI-style prototypes:

```
    In flumgummery.h:
double gumflummit( short sozzled, float feeling_no_pain,
             long loaded, double drunk, int intoxicated );

    In gumflummery.c:
double
gumflummit( short sozzled, float feeling_no_pain,
             long loaded, double drunk, int intoxicated )
{
      return ( sozzled + feeling_no_pain * loaded + 1. ) /
                              ( drunk + intoxicated ) ;
}

In Gummed_N_Flummed.c:
      float mumfgummf = gumflummit( 4, 45.0, 110, 3.14159, 17 );
```

Now the incorrect arguments will automatically be converted (assuming that `Gummed_N_Flummed.c` actually includes `flumgummery.h`).

The prototype for a function with no arguments must be written thus:

```
void no_argument( void ):

void
no_argument( void )
{
      ... ...
}
```

Otherwise it will be compiled as an unprototyped function.

To specify variable trailing arguments (in the style of `printf()`) a special technique called `stdargs` must be used.

The function defined to accept unknown arguments must either use nonportable constructions or use `stdargs`, defined `stdargs.h`. (On some machines, especially RISC machines, `stdargs` is the only way, and it invokes special 'hooks' provided by the compiler.)

```
#include <stdargs.h>      /* Includes definitions for */
                          /* va_list, va_start(),     *
                           * va_arg(), and va_end()   */
```

A.2.2.3 Tentative and incomplete definitions. Finally, as a concession to older programs, C will allow a variable or array (but not a function) to be defined several times within a single compilation (source file with its `#include`'d files), so long as it is initialized no more than once. C treats each initializer-less external definition of a variable or array as "tentative," and does not actually deem it a definition until the end of the compilation. This behavior is meant to accommodate old programs, not to indulge new ones, and should not be used in new code. (Nor are tentative definitions allowed in C++.)

When an array is declared (but not defined) the first (innermost and slowest-to-vary) subscript may be omitted:

```
extern int ia[];
extern double idd[] [ 44 ];
```

These declarations are said to have *incomplete type.* There is enough information to generate code that uses these arrays, but not enough to fully define them.

A.2.2.4 `typedef`. There is a special 'storage class' that does not declare storage of any kind. This is the *typedef.* `typedef` is a keyword that introduces synonyms for a type:

```
typedef short Circ_deg;
```

This introduces `Circ_deg` as a synonym for `short`. Following this declaration, the declarations

```
Circ_deg alpha;
Circ_deg theta;
Circ_deg rho;
```

declare and define `short`s named `alpha`, `theta`, and `rho`.

Because `typedef` is syntactically a storage class, it is legal (but not recommended) to write

```
short typedef Circ_deg;
```

instead.

Typedefs are useful for parameterizing a program:

```
typedef int Temperature;
typedef double Distance;
```

```
typedef int Tm_v[ 12 ];
typedef int Tm_vx[];
```

Here, `Temperature` becomes a synonym for `int`, and `Distance` for `double`. What about the "`Tm_`" declarations?

```
Tm_v this_one;
int that_one[ 12 ];
```

`this_one` and `that_one` have exactly the same type, even though they are declared in radically different forms. And, if we write

```
Tm_v these_four[ 4 ];
int those_four[ 4 ][ 12 ];
```

`these_four` and `those_four` have exactly the same type. And in

```
Tm_vx hither;
int yon[];
```

both `hither` and `yon` have the same (incomplete) type.

A.2.3 Pointers

Pointers are an integral and inalienable part of C's model of the computation and of the machine. They are also the cause of distress among newcomers to C.

A.2.3.1 Addresses. To understand pointers, one must understand addresses. In C's model of the machine, every memory cell (and every variable, save only those declared `register`) has a unique address by which that memory cell or variable may be reached. In the world of real machines, the address may be 'featureless' or it may be composed of fields indicating segment or page, offset, access control, or whatever. C is deliberately vague (i.e., portable) in its description of what an address looks like.

A pointer is just an address with some type information. The type information describes what sort of thing the pointer points at. Pointer variables in C are declared with type information, so a given pointer variable may be a pointer to `float`, a pointer to `unsigned char`, a pointer to `enum Whichovem`, etc. The type of a pointer tells C the size of the object at which it points and how to interpret the bits in those memory locations.

Pointers introduce two new operators, *address-of* and *indirection*. These are inverses; address-of gives the address of an object (assuming it has an address) and indirection accesses the object at a given address.

The address-of operator is a prefix unary ampersand ("&"). Applied to an object (lvalue) of type **T,** it yields a value of type *pointer-to-***T:**

```
int aye;
float eff;
const unsigned char unkie;

&aye;   /* The address of aye--a pointer to int   */
&eff;   /* The address of eff--a pointer to float  */
&unkie; /* The address of unkie--a pointer to a
         * const unsigned char .
         */
```

What to do with these addresses? We can apply indirection to them to get back to the original lvalues:

```
*&aye;  /* Indirection on the address of aye--gets
         * us back to aye.
         */
*&aye = 4;      /* The same as  aye = 4  */

*&eff = 6.283185;       /* The same as  eff = TwoPi */

*&unkie = 'U';  /* The same as  unkie = 'U'  -- which is
                 * ILLEGAL because  unkie  is  const .
                 */
```

Applying indirection is also called 'dereferencing.'

A.2.3.2 Declaring pointers. This isn't very useful unless we can store the pointers, pass them as parameters, etc. We can declare pointer variables:

```
{
       int    aye;        /*  aye  is declared an  int .    */
       int    *ip;        /*  Since  *ip  is declared  int ,
                           *   ip  must be a  pointer-to-int .
                           */

       floata  eff;        /*  Likewise for  eff  and  fp .  */
       float   *fp = &eff; /*  We can initialize or assign
                            *  pointers like any other type.
                            */
```

```
const char uc = 'U'; /*  And likewise also for
const char *unkie;    *  uc and unkie .
                      */

ip = &aye;          /* So now ip points at aye . . . */

unkie = &uc;        /* . . . and unkie points at uc . */

*ip = 10;
printf( "aye = %d\n", *ip );
prints aye = 10 on standard output.

eff = 6.283185;
printf( "*fp = %f, *unkie = %c\n", *fp, *unkie );
prints *fp = 6.283185, *unkie = U
on standard output.
```

There are some important nuances around pointers and consts.

A.2.3.3 Pointer-to-const. We've declared a pointer-to-const in `unkie`, *not* a constant pointer. That means that we can assign to the pointer, but we cannot use it to assign to what it points at. If we take the address of a const, we cannot just assign it to a pointer-to-non-const, as this could allow "innocent" code to violate the const-ness:

```
void innocent( int * ); /* innocent() takes a pointer-to-int */

const int myconst = 66;

int *p = &myconst;       /* If it were legal … */

innocent( p );
        …now let's look at innocent()…

void
innocent( int *ip )
{
        *ip = ( *ip + 5 ) / ( 7 - *ip );    /* Oops! We are changing
                                             * a const whose
                                             * address was entrusted
                                             * to us!
                                             */
}
```

So implicit conversion of pointer-to-const into pointer-to-non-const must be forbidden. The reverse conversion is permitted:

```
void stringing( const char * );

char *cp = … …;

stringing( cp );        /* Quite legal. */
```

Explicit conversion (by casting) of a pointer-to-const into a pointer-to-non-const is permitted.

```
const int myconst = 66;

const int *p = &myconst;   /* Legal:
                            *  const int *  = const int *
                            */

innocent( p );          /* Error:
                         *  innocent() wants a  char*
                         */
innocent( (char*) p ); . /* Legal:
                          *   innocent() receives a  char*
                          */
```

There are four common uses for pointers: to provide a reference parameter, to manage dynamically allocated memory, to index and scan arrays, and to provide linked data structures. In `innocent()` we have an example of a pointer used as a parameter to provide a reference parameters. In Sec. A.2.4 we'll examine dynamically allocated memory, and in Sec. A.2.5 we'll examine linked structures.

A.2.3.4 Arithmetic, relational, and equality operators. C supports various operators on pointers or on pointers and integers. C's model of computation makes certain assumptions.

These are binary operators, and three values are involved: the LHS, the RHS, and the return value. In general, if one of these is a pointer-to-X, then a second must be pointer-to-X. Also, not all possible combinations are allowed, but only those described below.

When two pointers-to-X are involved in one of these expressions, C assumes that the memory region bounded by them is an array of X, either declared or dynamically allocated, so that the memory contains a sequence of objects of type X with no memory between them, save for that which the machine architecture may require for alignment.

Given a pointer-to-X, C allows you to add an integer N to that pointer. The result is another pointer-to-X, offset from the first by N instances of X (*not* by N bytes, unless `sizeof` (X) happens to equal 1).

The addition may be carried out by either the simple addition or by assignment addition:

```
{
    unsigned long  larry[ 135 ];
    unsigned long  *pa = &larry[ 0 ];

    unsigned long  *pb = pa + 10;  /* Now pb points at
                                    *   larry[ 10 ]
                                    */
    pa += 11;      /* And now pa points at larry[ 11 ] */
```

Subtraction of an integer is also allowed:

```
pb -= 10;      /* Now pb points back at larry[ 0 ] */
```

The ++ and -- (increment and decrement) operators can be applied to pointers; they are equivalent to " += 1 " and " -= 1 " respectively, and they can be applied as prefix (before) or postfix (after) operators, just as for integral types.

Two pointers to the same type may be subtracted:

```
larry[ 0 ] = pa - pb;
```

The type of the difference is an integral type represented by the typedef `ptr_diff` found in the standard header file `stddef.h`. (Prior to ANSI C, it was an "appropriate" integral type on the machine at hand.)

If two pointers can be subtracted, they can be compared for equality and relative value:

```
if( pa > pb )
    printf( "pa > pb\n" );

if( pa >= pb )
    printf( "pa >= pb\n" );

if( pa < pb )
    printf( "pa < pb\n" );

if( pa <= pb )
    printf( "pa <= pb\n" );

if( pa == pb )
    printf( "pa == pb\n" );

if( pa != pb )
    printf( "pa != pb\n" );
```

If the pointers do not actually point into the same array, neither the difference nor these comparisons have any real meaning. On any given machine with its own addressing structure, (e.g., with segments, rings, etc.) it may not be possible to make the comparison meaningful.

A.2.3.5 The null pointer. For any pointer type (pointer-to-*X*) there is a special, distinguished pointer value known as Null or "the null pointer." The null pointer does not point 'at' anything, and dereferencing it is an error that may cause an address fault (memory fault, bus error, Unrecoverable Application Error, etc.) or other strange behavior.

Some languages have a special keyword (e.g., `nil`) to represent the null pointer. In C, any integral constant that evaluates to zero can be converted to the null pointer. This does not mean that the null pointer's bit pattern is all zeros; all it means is that the null pointer is written using a particular sort of integral constant.

The null pointer can be distinguished from any other pointer. No matter what the segment, memory region, ring, etc., that a pointer may point into, a valid pointer will never compare equal to the null pointer:

```
int
checked_deref ( int *p )
{
        if( p == 0 )
                return -1;

        return *p;
}
```

The test for the null pointer can be made implicit:

```
int
checked_deref2( int *p )
{
        /*
         *      If p isn't null, use it ...
         */
        if( p )
                return *p;

        /*
         *      ... otherwise return -1.
         */
        return -1;
}
```

A.2.3.6 Pointers, arrays, and strings. The semantics of C arrays, C pointers, and C literal strings are inseparable.

A.2.3.6.1 Arrays and subscripting. When a variable name appears in a C program, it stands for its variable. But when an array name appears, the array name is handled differently.

C treats an array name as a constant pointer to the zeroeth element of the array:

```
{
        int    sundries[ 45 ];       /* An array of int . */

        if( sundries == &sundries[ 0 ] ) /* True by definition ... */
             ... ...
```

This means that arrays are never passed by value, but only by reference:

```
        forxnagle( sundries );
         ... ...
void
forxnagel( int *ip )
{
         ... ...
```

(However, when an array is a member of a struct and the struct is passed or assigned, the entire array is copied. See Sec. A.2.5.)

How is the array name treated when it appears in a subscripted expression?

```
        sundries[ 4 ]   /* "sundries" becomes a pointer to      */
                        /* the zeroeth element of sundries ...  */
```

In C, subscripting is performed by an operator (`[]`). By definition,

```
A[ B ]
```

is equivalent to

```
*( A + B )
```

(excluding such syntactic issues of operator precedence for the moment—the subscripting operator has a higher precedence than any unary operator).

This equivalence is oblivious to the types involved, so subscripting is a commutative operator; in the example at hand these two expressions are identical:

```
sundries[ 4 ]
4[ sundries ]   /* Please don't actually WRITE
                 * this in a real program!
                 */
```

This means, also, that the subscripting operator can be applied to any pointer at all.

```
{
       int *sunp = sundries + 22;      /* or ... =
                                        *   &sundries[ 22 ]
                                        */

       sunp[ 0 ];      /* sundries[ 22 ] */
       sunp[ 22 ];     /* sundries[ 44 ] */
       sunp[ -22 ];    /* sundries[ 0 ] -- and yes, this is
                        * perfectly legal, since the reference
                        * still lies within the  sundries  array.
                        */
       ( sunp + 23 ); /* Addressing one past the end of the
                        * array is legal ... but only to make
                        * the writing of loops easier; don't
                        * try to dereference this expression.
                        */
       sunp[ 23 ];     /* This is not legal, as we are
                        * actually addressing an element
                        * past the end of the original array.
                        */
       sunp[ -23 ];    /* Likewise here we are outside the
                        * boundaries of the original array.
                        */
}
```

A.2.3.6.2 Array parameters. We have seen that an array is never passed as a parameter; only a pointer to the array's zeroeth element is passed. C allows some 'syntactic sugar' in this, however:

```
int nimeue( int* a_row );
```

can also be declared as

```
int nimeue( int a_row[] );
```

and the function can be written

```
int
nimeue( int a_row[] )
{
        int i;

        for( i = 0 ; a_row[ i ] > 0 ; i++ )
        {
                ... ...
```

A.2.3.6.3 Multidimensional arrays. When an array name appears in an expression, the name is converted to a pointer to the zeroeth element of the array. This, however, is not the type of the array:

```
int     grommish[ 17 ];          /* The type of the array
                                  * is  int [ 17 ]
                                  */
int     *grp = grommish;         /* But the name evaluates
                                  * as an  int *  pointing
                                  * to  grommish[ 0 ] .
                                  */
```

It is possible, nevertheless, to name and use the type `int [ 17 ]`:

```
typedef int     Grommery[ 17 ];

Grommery        grubbish;        /* Now  grubbish
                                  * is  int [ 17 ]
                                  */
```

We can also declare an array of `Grommery`:

```
Grommery        gormtrees[ 3 ]; /* And  gormtrees  is
                                 *  Grommery [ 3 ] --
                                 *      which means
                                 *  int [ 3 ][ 17 ]
                                 */
```

We could get exactly the same effect with this declaration:

```
int     gormtrees[ 3 ][ 17 ];
```

Such declarations must be read from the inside out: `gormtrees` is an array (length 3) of arrays (length 17) of `int`.

This is how C creates a multidimensional array. It follows that the outermost (last, nearest-to-the-typename) dimension varies fastest when the array is laid out in memory.

To step through such an array with pointers requires some 'magic' in declarations and expressions:

```
int     (*seventeen_p) [ 17 ]; /* A pointer to an
                                * array of  int [ 17 ]
                                */

for( seventeen_p = gormtrees ;
        seventeen_p < &gormtrees[ 3 ] ; seventeen_p++ )
{
        int     *ip;

        for( ip = *seventeen_p ;
                ip < *(*seventeen_p) [ 17 ] ; ip++ )
        {
                ...do whatever with *ip...
        }
}
```

This is hardly clear! In practice, multidimensional arrays are little used in C, perhaps because most things for which multidimensional arrays are used are better coded as arrays of `struct`s containing arrays (see Sec. A.2.5) or as 'ragged arrays' in the style of `argv` (see Sec. A.2.3.7).

A.2.3.6.4 Walking pointers and strings. Usages such as this are common:

```
void
vadd( int *addend_1, int *addend_2, int *sum, int len )
{
        int *end_1;

        for( end_1 = addend_1 + len ; addend_1 < end_1 ;
                        addend_1++, addend_2++, sum++ )
                *sum = *addend_1 + *addend_2;
}
```

The pointers 'walk' along one or more parallel arrays, and the test for the end of the loop is performed using an 'out-of-bounds' pointer.

ANSI C explicitly allows a pointer to be created that lies 'one beyond' the end of an array. If a pointer is created that lies two (or more) beyond, the result is undefined. On most machines, it may work for most arrays, but a program that does this is not a valid program. (This accommodates machines with scrupulous addressing mechanisms.)

On early C implementations (most notably the PDP-11), walking pointers with the range check performed on the pointer made for very efficient code. This is no longer true, and such loops may actually run slower than those which maintain a count. Moreover, they may make it difficult or impossible for a vectorizing compiler to recognize vector operations. The moral? Use walking pointers if they make the code clearer; don't think of them as a portable efficiency hack.

Walking pointers do make sense when the end of an array is signaled by a sentinel (a distinguished value placed after the end of the data in the array). C idiom includes one important sentinel usage: character strings. Here's an implementation of the standard C library `strlen()` (string length) function:

```
int
strlen( const char *cp )
{
	int len;

	for( len = 0 ; *cp++ ; )
		len++;

	return len;
}
```

(This is an example of the 'delightful terseness' to which C pointers lend themselves. Once learned, the idioms read well.)

Here the sentinel is the character whose integer value is zero. In the ASCII character set, this is called `NUL` (one 'L') or "the null character." (Do not confuse this with the null pointer.) The length of the string is all the characters up to (but not including) the null character.

The `*cp++` is evaluated thus: first the pointer is dereferenced to obtain the character at which it points. Then the pointer is incremented. Finally, the character obtained is 'returned' to the enclosing context, which is a test against zero.

On some machines, under some circumstances, performing the increment unconditionally (as the post-increment does) permits the compiler to use special instructions or instruction sequences. For a library function like `strlen()` this could be important. (For short strings, the function call overhead may dwarf the time in the function, but a compiler is free to turn a standard library function into inline code, or even into a special instruction.)

Why this idiom of a null-terminated character array? C practically forces it on us. Recall that we can write double-quoted strings:

```
printf( "Hello, World!\n" );
```

A double-quoted string literal is compiled into a null-terminated, anonymous, static array of const chars, and its value is a pointer to the first character in that array:

```
#include <string.h>
#include <stdio.h>

int
main()
{
        const char *hello = "Hello, World!\n" ;

        printf( "strlen( %s ) = %d\n", hello, strlen( hello ) );

        return 0;
}
```

This program prints

```
strlen( Hello, World!
) = 14
```

(Remember that there is a newline after the exclamation point.) Notice that this use of a double-quoted string differs from its use as an initializer for an array of characters (Sec. A.1.3.10). There it is a synonym for a list of character constants. Here it means something else altogether.

Although the chars in a string literal must be treated as `const`, C does not enforce this. The pointer type returned is actually `char *` rather than `const char*`. This preserves compatibility for old (pre-ANSI) C programs—but only for those that don't actually modify the characters. (Some did.)

Because a string literal's value is a pointer to its first character, we can write code such as this:

```
*out++ = "01234567890"[ ( i >= 0 && i < 10 ) ? i : 10 ] ;
```

Whether this is "code as in 'cryptic' " or a terse way to write a minor and uninteresting computation depends on how skilled you are with the idiom. This example can be written more clearly as

```
*out++ = ( i >= 0 && i < 10 ) ? "0123456789"[ i ]
                               : '0' ;
```

A.2.3.7 `argc` **and** `argv`. We now have the tools to consider parameters to `main()`. The ANSI standard does not actually dictate the return type and parameter types for `main()`, but it recommends that these two forms be permitted:

```
int main();
int main( int arcg, char **argv );
```

It also recommends that if any other forms are allowed, the first and second parameters should be the same argc and argv.

What are argc and argv? These variable names are conventional names, and not part of C. Any other names would do. But what do they represent?

On many operating systems, the user who executes a program can provide the program with parameters of various sorts. These 'command line arguments' often look like this:

```
calendar -pretty march 1995
```

We might guess that the "-pretty" instructs calendar to change its output format, and the "march" and "1995" tell it for what month of what year to print a calendar.

In such an environment, the three 'strings' -pretty, march, and 1995 would be passed to the calendar program using the argc/argv mechanism.

argc stands for "argument count." It indicates the number of 'command line arguments' passed to the program *including the program name itself*. In this example, argc = 4.

argv stands for 'argument vector.' It is a pointer-to-pointer-to-char, and it points to an array of char *, each of which points to one of the argument strings.

```
argv[ 0 ] =>"calendar"
argv[ 1 ] =>"-pretty"
argv[ 2 ] =>"march"
argv[ 3 ] =>"1995"
argv[ argc ] == undefined
```

In many environments, argv[argc] will be equal to NULL. You shouldn't depend upon it.

Various environments have conventions about how command line arguments are written. In one, flag arguments may begin with a dash; in another with a slash. In one, flag arguments are individual letters which can occur together in a single word; in others, flag arguments must be in separate words. In one, the *from* argument occurs before the *to* argument; in another the order is reversed.

Some environments provide functions with names like getopt() and getsubopt() to parse command line arguments. These are 'standard' in the environment, but are not portable between environments. Nevertheless, they can help to ensure that a program meets the conventions of its environment.

A.2.3.8 String functions, mem functions, and `<ctype.h>`. The ANSI standard specifies a number of library functions and macros, including some to help with strings, characters, and so forth.

The standard header file `string.h(#include <string.h>)` contains *string* functions and `memory` functions.

A.2.3.8.1 String functions

```
char *strcpy( char *to, const char *from );
void* memcpy( void* to, const void* from, size_t n );
char *strncpy( char *to, const char *from, size_t count );

char *strcat( char *to, const char *from );
char *strncat( char *to, const char *from, size_t count );
```

`strcpy()` copies the characters pointed at by the `from` pointer into the area pointed at by the `to` pointer. Copying continues until a '\0' has been copied. `strncpy()` does the same, except that it will copy no more than `count` characters, whether or not a '\0' is encountered.

`strcat()` copies the characters pointed at by the `from` pointer *onto the end* of the string pointed at by the `to` pointer, stopping after a '\0' has been copied. (Thus `from[ 0 ]` overwrites the '\0' in the `to` string, etc.) `strncat()` does the same, except that no more than `count` characters are copied.

None of these functions allocates memory. Sufficient memory for copy operations must be allocated beforehand. (And note that `strlen()` does not count the '\0' in the length of the string; you must allocate at least *`strlen() + 1`* characters.)

```
int strcmp( const char *str1, const char *str2 );
int strncmp( const char* str1, const char* str2, size_t count );
```

`strcmp()` and `strncmp()` compare whether the string `str1` is 'lexographically' less than, equal to, or greater than the string `str2`, and returns an integer that is accordingly less than, equal to, or greater than zero. `strcmp()` continues the comparison until the strings differ or until a '\0' occurs. `strncmp()` will compare no more than `count` characters even if the strings are identical to that length, and longer.

```
char   *strchr( const char *str, int c );
char   *strrchr( const char *str, int c );
```

`strchr()` and `strrchr()` search the string named by `str` for an occurrence of the character given by c (which is converted to `char` internally). `strchr()` searches forward from the beginning for `str`;

strrchr() searches backward from the end of str. They return a pointer to the first or last such character in the string, or NULL if no instance was found. (Notice that these can violate the type system, since they return a pointer to char * which points to an array which was passed in as const char *.)

```
size_t strspn( const char* str,  const char* ch_list );
size_t strcspn( const char* str,  const char* ch_list );
```

These functions treat the second string as a set of characters, and examine the first string for a prefix that includes the characters in (strspn()) or not in (strcspn()) the second string. They return the length of the longest such prefix to the first string.

```
char    *strpbrk( const char* str,  const char* ch_list );
```

strpbrk() treats the second string as a set of characters. It scans the first string for the first character that is in the second string. It returns a pointer to that character, or NULL if no such character is found. Like strchr() and strrchr(), these can violate the C type system.

```
char    *strstr( const char* str,  const char* to_find );
```

strstr() searches the first argument string for an occurrence of the second argument. It returns a pointer to the first character of the substring, or NULL if there is none. Like other functions above, this can violate the type system.

```
size_t  strlen( const char* str );
```

strlen() returns the number of characters in the string, not counting the '\0' by which the string is ended.

```
char    *strerror( size_t n );
```

strerror() returns a pointer to an error message corresponding to error number n. The messages and the mapping of error numbers to messages is implementation-defined.

```
char    *strtok( char *s, const char *separators );
```

strtok() is used to divide a string s into substrings (or *tokens*). The interface is somewhat awkward.

strtok() is called once with the string to be tokenized as its first parameter. The second parameter is a string of characters which separate tokens (e.g., whitespace, punctuation, etc.) If it returns NULL, the entire string was whitespace. If it returns non-NULL, the pointer returned points to the first token substring, and the first separator character (if any) has been overwritten with '\0' so that the token appears as a string of its own.

`strtok()` has, at this point, maintained an internal, static pointer to the beginning of the rest of the string. Subsequent calls should pass NULL for the string `s`. So long as token substrings remain, `strtok()` will return a pointer to the next (i.e., 'first remaining') substring.

The separator character list may vary from call to call.

A.2.3.8.2 Memory functions

```
void *memcpy( void *to, const void *from, size_t n );
void *memmove( void *to, const void *from, size_t n );
```

These functions copy `n` characters from `from` to `to`, and return `to`. The operation of `memcpy()` is undefined if the arrays defined by `from` and `to` overlap; `memmove()` will work correctly even if they do (but may run more slowly in some or all cases).

(The type `void *` is used to point to memory without specifying an actual type for it. See Sec. A.2.4.)

Implicitly assumed is that any memory on the machine at hand may be represented as an array of characters (bytes) which completely tile the memory—that is, cover it with neither gaps nor overlap. A C implementation must find a way to guarantee this.

```
void   *memset( void* to, int fill, size_t n );
```

`memset()` fills the first `n` characters starting at the location to which `to` points with the value that results when `fill` is converted to `unsigned char`. `to` is returned.

```
int    memcmp( const void* s1, const void* s2, size_t n );
```

Compare memory, character-by-character (byte by byte) stopping at the first character that differs, or after `n` characters. Return less than zero, zero, or greater than zero as the first string is less than, equal to, or greater than the second.

```
void* memchr( const void* str, int c, size_t n );
```

Search the first `n` characters of `str` for the value of `c` converted to `unsigned char`. Return a pointer to the character found, or NULL if none are found.

A.2.3.8.3 `<ctype.h>`. The standard header file included by `#include <ctype.h>` contains a set of functions (possibly implemented as macros) which characterize characters in the machine's character set. Their parameter is `int` which they convert to `char`. Their return is `int`, nonzero or zero as the condition for which they test is true or false.

```
int isdigit( int c )    c is a decimal digit
int isxdigit( int c )   c is a hexadecimal digit
int isupper( int c )    c is an upper-case letter
int islower( int c )    c is a lower-case letter
int isalpha( int c )    c is a letter (either case)
int isalnum( int c )    c is a letter or a digit
int isprint( int c )    c is a printable character (including blank)
int ispunct( int c )    c is a printable character not space, letter, or digit
int isgraph( int c )    c is a printing character not space
int isspace( int c )    c is a space, formfeed, tab, newline,
                           carriage return, or vertical tab
```

Two more are provided to convert case:

```
int tolower( int c )    Return c converted to lower case
int toupper( int c )    Return c converted to upper case
```

If `c` cannot be converted (it is not a letter, or it is already in the specified case) it is returned unchanged.

A.2.3.8.4 `scanf()`. `printf()` (Sec. A.1.1.9) produces formatted output for a variety of types according to a form at specification. There is an analagous (but not quite complementary) input function called `scanf()`. There are two major differences between them. First, because values must be returned through the various parameters, pointers to variables must be passed instead of the variables. Second, `scanf()`'s interpretation of fields and characters in the format string reflects the need to parse input instead of simply producing output.

Specifically:

- Blanks and tabs in the format string are ignored.
- There is no field precision (but a maximum field width is respected).
- The "*" indicates *suppression of assignment.* The field will be read, but not assigned to variable and no parameter will be consumed.
- There is a `%i` which can accept integers as decimal, octal (with a leading zero), or hexadecimal (with a leading 0x or 0X) numbers.
- `%n` indicates that the number of characters read so far is to be assigned to the `int` variable at which the matching parameter points.

- `%[chars]` reads the longest possible string of characters matched by *chars*. *chars* may contain 'ordinary' characters, in which case it matches any of those characters. If the first character of `chars` is ^, it matches *all but* those characters. And if the first character (or first character after a leading ^) is `]`, the `]` is included in `chars`, and does not close the list. This conversion requires a `char *` argument that points to an array, and the string assigned will be terminated by '\0'.
- `%c` will read one or more characters (depending on the field width). `%c` and `%[]` will read whitespace; the other conversions will skip it.
- Other characters in the format string are expected to match literally.

`scanf()` returns the number of fields successfully accepted (converted) (not counting any `%n` fields). It returns EOF if end-of-file or error occurs before all the fields are read.

`scanf()` requires that input errors be handled very carefully. If `scanf()` refuses to accept any input characters, they remain there to be read by the next input operation. If that operation is the same call to `scanf()`, an infinite loop results.

A.2.4 Managing memory

A.2.4.1 `void *`. There is a special pointer type, `void *`. `void *` is used to represent memory to which no type has been assigned, or to talk about that memory without giving it a type. A pointer of any kind may be implicitly converted to `void *`, and a `void *` pointer may be converted to any pointer type. A `void *` may not be dereferenced until it is converted to a meaningful pointer type, and the conversion from a pointer type to `void *` and back again will restore the original pointer type faithfully.

A.2.4.2 Free store. C provides four functions to allocate and free memory dynamically. (Standard C provides no garbage collection.)

```
void *malloc( size_t n_bytes );
void *realloc( void *current_space, size_t new_n_bytes );
void *calloc( size_t n_objects, size_t object_size );
void free( void* space_to_free );
```

Their declarations are found in the header included by `#include <stdlib.h>`.

`malloc()` allocates `n_bytes` of contiguous memory. It returns a pointer to the first byte of memory, or NULL if the memory could not be allocated. The memory's contents are random.

`realloc()` attempts to either adjust the (previously allocated) memory region given by its first argument to the size given in its second argument, or to allocate a new area and copy the memory's contents to the new area (up to the minimum of the old and new sizes). In the latter case, the old memory is returned to the free space manager. `realloc()` returns NULL if it could not allocate the space requested, in which case the original memory is undisturbed.

`calloc()` attempts to allocate a region of memory large enough to hold `n_objects` of size `object_size`. It returns a pointer to that space, or to NULL if it cannot allocate the space requested. The memory will be initialized with a bit pattern of zeros.

`free()` returns the memory to the free space manager, the memory to which its argument points. It is a grievous error to `free()` a pointer that was not returned from `malloc()`, `realloc()`, or `calloc()`, or to `free()` a pointer twice (unless it was returned again from one of the allocation functions in between the two calls to `free()`). Such an error can cause corruption of the free store and of all the program's memory, depending on how much checking the implementation's free store system does.

A.2.5 Structures

Structs are C's 'record' type. For a FORTRAN or Basic programmer, they probably represent a hurdle to be cleared.

A.2.5.1 Declaring and using `struct`s. The *structure* (`struct`) is C's version of the record type. `struct`s are used to organize a program's data. Instead of writing (for example) parallel arrays:

```
short   coursenum[ MAX_SECTIONS ];      /* Internal course number */
short   section[ MAX_SECTIONS ];        /* Section               */
short   room_no[ MAX_SECTIONS ];        /* Room index            */
short   num_seat[ MAX_SECTIONS ];       /* Maximum # of students  */
short   avail_seat[ MAX_SECTIONS ];     /* Number of open places  */
char    **stud_info[ MAX_SECTIONS ];    /* Student list.          */
        ... ...

int course;
        ... ...

        gen_roster( coursenum[ course ], section[ course ],
                room_no[ course ], num_seat[ course ],
                avail_seat[ course ], stud_info[ course ] );
```

We write a structure representing one record, then declare an array of those records:

```
                                /* Declare a struct        */
struct  Course_section          /* called Course_section   */
{
        short   coursenum;
        short   section;
        short   room_no;
        short   num_seat;
        short   avail_seat;
        char    **stud_info;
};

/*
 * Now an array of Course_section structs .
 */
struct Course_section   sections[ MAX_SECTIONS ];

int     course;
        ... ...
        /*
         *      Now we can pass a pointer to an entire record for a
         *      course section.  (And we could just as well pass a
         *      copy of the section record ...)
         */
        gen_roster( &sections[ course ] );
```

The name Course_section is a *structure tag*. It describes the layout of variables within the struct. These variables are called *members*. Each tag has its own name space, which is to say that the coursenum in Course_section is distinct from a coursenum in any other struct, and also from any ordinary variable named coursenum. (In very early versions of C, in the prehistory before UNIX v6, all structs shared the same name space for members.)

The tag isn't actually necessary. A structure declaration looks like this:

```
struct struct-body variable_list ;
struct tag struct-body ;
struct tag struct-body variable_list ;
struct tag variable_list ;
```

A *struct-body* is a brace-enclosed list of data declarations. There must be at least one; they may not have initializers; they may not have storage classes. (Their storage class is "member of struct.")

A structure declaration with both a body and a tag introduces the tag; a structure declaration with a variable list introduces those variables as structs of the given type. (C's syntax also allows structure declarations that don't actually declare anything; most compilers will flag these as ineffective.)

A structure declaration may also be used within a typedef:

```
typedef struct middlin
{
        int     mediocre;
        char    median[ 17 ];
        short   mezzo_mezzo;
}                       Middlin;

Middlin average;
Middlin *mean;
Middlin more_or_less[ 129 ];
```

A.2.5.2 Structure initializers. `struct` objects can be initialized where they are defined. The syntax is the same as for array initialization:

```
Middlin piddlin
={
        4,
        "hardly 'tall",
        2,
};

Middlin muddlin[ 4 ]
={
        { 0,    "muddle", 2, },
        { 1,    "fuddle", 1, },
        { 2,    "puddle", 1, },
        { 3,    "befuddle", 1, },
};
```

The members of a given struct are laid out in memory one after the other, with such 'holes' between them as are needed for word/long-word/quadword/N-word alignment of the various types within. Thus, the `sizeof( struct Xyzzy )` is no less than the sum of the sizes of the members of `Xyzzy`.

To select a member out of a `struct`, use the `.` (dot) operator:

```
int i;

printf( "%hd: '%s' ( %hd )\n", piddlin.mediocre,
                piddlin.median, piddlin.mezzo_mezzo );
piddlin.mezzo_mezzo *= 2;

for( i = 0 ; i < 4 ; i++ )
{
```

```
        printf( "%hd: '%s' ( %hd )\n",
                muddlin[ i ].mediocre,
                muddlin[ i ].median,
                muddlin[ i ].mezzo_mezzo );
}
```

`struct`s can be assigned whole, passed whole as value parameters to functions, and returned from functions as the return value. (Function pass and return, while safe for recursion, might not be safe for reentrant programming because in some implementations pass/return uses non-reentrant mechanisms.)

Very old versions of C (from the 1970s) will not allow `struct` to be assigned, passed into a function or returned from a function.

A.2.5.3 Pointers to structures. Observe that array operations, and therefore pointer operations, are legal on structures.

```
Middlin *mudp = &muddlin[ i ];

printf( "%hd: '%s' ( %hd )\n", ( *mudp ).mediocre,
       ( *mudp ).median, ( *mudp ).mezzo_mezzo );
```

The parentheses on each expression are needed: the dot operator binds very tightly—just as tightly as subscripting does.

Expressions like `( *mudp ).`*`member`* are so common that a shorthand is provided for them: the operator `->` (sometimes pronounced 'pointing to'):

```
Middlin *mudp = &muddlin[ i ];

printf( "%hd: '%s' ( %hd )\n", mudp->mediocre,
       mudp->median, mudp->mezzo_mezzo );
```

This "structure arrow" operator binds just as tightly as the structure dot. Both group from left to right.

A.2.5.4 Implementing data structures with `structs`. A `struct` cannot contain an instance of itself, but it can contain an instance of another struct, and it can contain a pointer to itself. This is how C implements linked lists, trees, and all manner of other linked data structures. (Much of the 'cryptic' code in C has to do with these things.)

Here's a partial implementation of a linked list manager.

```
#include <stdlib.h>
```

```
struct  text_link
{
        struct text_link        *forw;
        struct text_link        *back;

        char *text;
};

/*
 *      Allocate a text link, and assign it its text.
 *      Protect against memory exhaustion.
 */
struct text_link *
mk_text_link( const char* txt )
{
        struct text_link        *tlp;

        tlp = malloc( sizeof( struct text_link ) );

        if( ! tlp )
                return 0;

        /*
         *      Initially not linked ...
         */
        tlp->forw = 0;
        tlp->back = 0;

        /*
         *      If there's no text to store, we're done.
         */
        if( ! txt )
        {
                tlp->txt = 0;
                return tlp;
        }

        /*
         *      Otherwise, can we get the memory to store it?
         */
        tlp->text = malloc( strlen( txt ) + 1 );

        if( ! tlp->text )
        {
                free( tlp );
                return 0;
        }
```

```
        strcpy( tlp->text, txt );
        return tlp;
}

struct text_link        txt_head = 0;
struct text_link        txt_tail = 0;

/*
 *      Put a text_link after another in the list.  If the 'other' is
 *      zero, we mean to put this link at the head of the list.
 */
void
ins_text_link( struct text_link *tl, struct text_link *after )
{
        struct text_link *prev;
        struct text_link *next;

        /*
         *      We can't put a link after itself.
         */
        if( tl == after )
                return;

        /*
         *      If the link is already linked, we have to unlink it.
         *      (If both pointers are zero, it could still be the only
         *      thing on the list.)
         */
        if( tl->next
         && tl->prev
         && txt_head == tl )
                unlink_text_link( tl );

        if( after )
        {
                prev = after->prev;
                next = after->next;
        }
        else
        {
                prev = 0;
                next = txt_head;
        }

        tl->prev = prev;
        tl->next = next;

        if( prev )
                prev->next = tl;
        else
                txt_head = tl;
```

```
        if( next )
                next->prev = tl;
        else
                txt_tail = tl;
        return;
}
```

A.2.6 Unions and bitfields

C has two features related to the `struct`. The first is the `union`. Whereas an object of a `struct` type contains one of each of its members, an object of a `union` type can contain any of its members, *but only one at a time.* A `struct` is a data aggregate which contains one or more members, one after the other. A `union` has one or more members, but they are overlaid, one on top of the other.

```
union   N_ptr
{
        struct Node     *np;
        struct Leaf     *lp;
        const char      *data;
};
```

Unlike a Pascal variant record, a `union` carries no information on which of its members is 'in use.' To add such information, enclose the union in a `struct`:

```
enum Subtree_t { subt_Node, subt_Leaf, subt_data };

struct  Subtree
{
        Subtree_t       type;
        union N_ptr     data;
};
```

The second special feature of structures (and of unions as well) is the *bitfield.* A member of a structure or union can be declared to be a specific number of bits wide:

```
struct  squeezem
{
        unsigned int cylinder : 9;
        unsigned int platter : 5;
};
```

Here the compiler is allowed (but not required) to pack two variables of 9 and 5 bits, respectively, into a single `unsigned int`. Any integral type may be used:

```
struct  squeezemore
{
        unsigned long unit : 4;
        unsigned long cylinder : 5;
        unsigned long platter : 9;
        unsigned long sector : 8:
};
```

This requests that four bitfields be packed into an `unsigned`.

Arithmetic may be performed on bitfields, in which case an `int` bitfield may be treated as unsigned; this is defined by the implementation. A bitfield of width zero, named or unnamed, instructs the compiler to begin the next bitfield at the next appropriate boundary (an `int` boundary for an `int`, a `long` boundary for a `long`).

The order in which bitfields are assigned (most significant first or least significant first) is implementation-defined. Using bitfields to map to external storage layouts is therefore implementation-dependent and should be avoided for code which is not inherently nonportable.

A.2.7 Pointer, function, and array operators

C's expression syntax exhibits a tight connection between the syntax and the underlying semantics. For instance, the syntax of multidimensional arrays is precisely that of arrays of arrays. And parentheses affect only the associativity of expressions, not their type:

```
int    x;
int    y;
int    myfun( int );

( x ) = y;              /* Legal */
( x ) = ( int ) y;      /* Legal */
x = myfun( y );         /* Legal */
( x ) = myfun( y );     /* Legal */
x = ( myfun )( y );     /* Legal */

( x ) = ( int )( y );     /* Legal--a cast! */
( x ) = ( myfun )( y ); /* Legal--a function call! */
```

In C, a function call with no arguments still requires the parenthesized argument list. This is because the parenthesized list is defined as the function call operator. That makes the following calls identical:

```
printf( "Hello, World\n" );                /* Call 1 */
( printf )( "Hello, World\n" );            /* Call 2 */

{
        int (*func_p)( const char*, ... );

        func_p = printf;

        ( *func_p )( "Hello, World\n" );           /* Call 3 */
}
```

When a function name is used alone, it is converted into a pointer to the function. The type of `printf` is "function returning `int` whose parameters are pointer to `const char` and 'unknown'." The type of `func_p` is "pointer to function returning `int` whose parameters are pointer to `const char` and 'unknown'," so the assignment is legal.

The 'extra' parentheses are needed. The function call operator binds very tightly, so without them we would have "function returning pointer to `int` . . . " instead of "pointer to function returning `int`."

ANSI C allows a shorthand for the Call 3 above:

```
( *func_p )( "Hello, World\n" );       /* Ordinary call */
func_p( "Hello, World\n" );            /* Shorthand */
```

Some find the shorthand confusing; ANSI C allows it because some popular compilers permitted it before the ANSI committee met.

Pointers to functions are ordinary variables and may be assigned and initialized like ordinary variables. They may also be compared to NULL (pointer 0), but they may not participate in any kind of arithmetic.

Declaring more complicated pointers can get confusing. Here is a declaration of a pointer to a function whose parameter and return value are pointers to functions whose parameters and return values are `int`s:

```
int (*(*fiiiiiip)( int (*)( int ) ) )( int );
```

If we wanted to initialize the pointer, we would need a function of the correct type:

```
int (*fiiiiii( int (*)( int ) ) )( int );

int (*(*fiiiiiip)( int (*)( int ) ) )( int ) = fiiiiii;
```

Here the price of applied generality is extracted: these are unreadable by anything except a compiler—and even some compilers may get into trouble. This is a job for `typedef`s:

```
typedef int (*Fiip)( int );     /* Now Fiip is
                                 *   int(*)( int )
                                 */

Fiip (*fFiFip)( Fiip ) = fiiiiii;
```

It's still difficult to understand. Making the names meaningful in the context of the problem and algorithm at hand will help. If things get much more complicated, however, the various pointers should be wrapped in named structures.

A.2.8 Input and output

C's input and output are conditional on the environment: if the language is "hosted" they must be provided. The facilities need not be provided if there is no underlying operating system, no file system, no monitor. This often occurs when C is used to program embedded systems, or to program the operating system itself.

Accordingly, C's I/O facilities are provided by standard libraries and standard `#include` files.

A.2.8.1 Standard input and output—the FILE struct. We have already seen `printf()` and `scanf()`. These send output to a predefined destination ("sink") and accept it from a predefined source. These are called *standard output* and *standard input*, respectively.

Another output sink is commonly provided. This is called *standard error*. Standard error is used for 'exceptional' output (e.g., error messages that might get lost in many lines of ordinary output, or in ordinary output that is sent to a file instead of to the terminal from which the program is invoked).

To access sources and sinks other than standard input and output, there must be a "file pointer" for the source or sink. This is a pointer to a FILE structure with the appropriate data provided in the appropriate ways.

```
#include <stdio.h>        /* Get the declarations
                           * for the FILE struct.
                           */

       /* FILE is a typedef for a struct that represents
        * stdio's  understanding of a file or I/O stream.
        *
        * The predefined streams are:
        *
        *  For standard input  -- stdin
        *  For standard output -- stdout
```

```
     * For standard error -- stderr
     */
    ... ...

    fprintf( stderr, "Fatal Error!\n" );
    fprintf( stderr, "Goodbye, Cruel World!\n" );
    exit( 1 );
}
```

fprintf() and fscanf() act just like printf() and scanf(), except that they act on output sinks and input sources named by FILE *. The first parameters to these two functions have type FILE *.

A.2.8.2 Input and output functions (and macros). Besides printf(), fprintf(), scanf(), and fscanf(), there are other functions (and macros) for formatted, character-by-character, and 'direct' I/O.

There are two more groups of formatted I/O functions, paralleling printf()/scanf() and fprintf()/fscanf(). The first group operates on strings (arrays of characters) instead of on FILE streams:

```
int sprintf( char *output, const char *format, ... );
int sscanf( const char *input, const char *format, ... );
```

The second group also operates on arrays of characters, but it expects its 'conversion' arguments in the form provided by the stdargs mechanism (Sec. 2.4.3). It provides output only for standard output, for output to FILE *, and for writing to a string:

```
#include <stdargs.h>
int vprintf( const char *format, va_list args );
int vfprintf( FILE *output, const char *format, va_list args );
int vsprintf( char *output, const char *format, va_list args );
```

The character-by-character functions and macros deal in characters and arrays of characters. The simplest are putchar() and getchar():

```
int getchar( void );    /* Read one character from standard
                         * input; return EOF (a value outside the
                         * standard character set) on end-of-file.
                         */
int putchar( int c );   /* Put  c  on standard output and return
                         * the value of  c.
                         */
```

Because these are macros, putchar() may evaluate its argument more than once, leading to errors if there are side effects in the evaluation. If there are such side effects, use the function version of the general-purpose macros:

```
int getc( FILE *in );     /* Like getchar() , but reads from in .
                           */
int putc( int c, FILE *out );   /* Like putchar() , but sends
                                 * output to out .
                                 */

int fgetc( FILE *in );  /* Function version of the macro getc() .
                         */
int fputc( int c, FILE *out );  /* Function version of putc() ,
                                 * but sends output to out .
                                 */
```

A similar group is provided for strings. Note that they are not quite symmetrical:

```
int puts( const char *s ); /* Writes the characters in s (up
                            * to the \0) to standard output.
                            */
int fputs( const char *s, FILE *stream );  /* Like puts() for any
                                            * any output stream.
                                            */
char *gets( char *to_string );  /* Writes the next input line to
                                 * to_string ; returns to_string
                                 * on success; NULL on EOF on error.
                                 * The string is terminated by a \0 .
                                 */
char *fgets( char *s, int max_read, FILE* in ); /* Like gets()
                                 * except that it reads from a
                                 * file, and it will read no
                                 * more than max_read - 1
                                 * characters before writing
                                 * the \0 .
                                 */
```

It is possible to push *one* character back onto a stream:

```
int ungetc( int c, FILE *in );
```

`ungetc()` returns the character pushed back, or EOF on error. EOF is not a character and may not be pushed back onto the input stream.

A.2.8.3 Direct input and output functions. Two functions provide binary input and output of arbitrary arrays of data without regard for their declared types or their content:

```
size_t fread( void *to, size_t obj_size, size_t n_obj,
                                  FILE *from );
size_t fwrite( const void* from, size_t obj_size, size_t n_obj,
                                  FILE *to );
```

These return the number of objects read or written, which may be less than the number requested. To determine why, use these functions/macros:

```
int feof( FILE *stream );        /* True if EOF has occurred
                                  * on the stream.
*/
int ferror( FILE *stream );      /* True if an error has
                                  * occurred on the stream.
                                  */
void clearerr( FILE *stream ); /* Clears the error and end-of-file
                                  * indicators for the stream.
                                  */
```

A.2.8.4 File operation functions. To attach a FILE structure to a stream, use fopen() or freopen():

```
FILE *fopen( const char *filename, const char *mode );
FILE *freopen( const char *filename, const char *mode,
                             FILE *use_me );
```

fopen() and freopen() attempt to associate a FILE struct with an external file. They return a pointer to the FILE if they succeed; NULL if they fail. fopen() chooses a FILE struct from those not in use; freopen uses the FILE struct given. (Typically, freopen() is used to change the file association of stdin, stdout, or stderr.)

The *mode* parameter is as follows:

```
"r" -- Open text file for reading.
"w" -- Open text file for writing.
"r" -- Open or create text file to append (to write at the end).
"r+" -- Open text file for update (reading and writing).
"w+" -- Create text file for update; discard any previous contents.
"a+" -- Open or create text file to append.
```

To disassociate a FILE from a file, use fclose():

```
int fclose( FILE *stream );
```

fclose() flushes any buffered I/O to the file and then closes the connection between the FILE struct and the file. It returns zero on success, EOF on error.

```
fflush( FILE *stream );
```

`fflush()` causes any buffered output to the file to be completed. On an input FILE the effect is undefined. Passing NULL to `fflush()` flushes all buffered output on all output streams.

These functions operate on the 'file pointer,' the place in the file where the next read or write operation will occur.

```
long ftell( FILE *stream );
```

`ftell()` returns the current file pointer position in the file. For a binary file, this is the number of characters from the beginning of the file. For a text file, vagaries of the local file system may make the number meaningless as anything but a parameter to `fseek()`. `ftell()` returns `-1L` on error.

```
int fseek( FILE *stream, long offset, int origin )
```

`fseek()` sets the file pointer position for the file to the value given by `offset` and `origin`. The origin is one of `SEEK_SET` (beginning of file), `SEEK_CUR` (present position), and `SEEK_END` (end of file). For a text file, legal combinations are an offset of zero with any origin, and an origin of `SEEK_SET` with an offset returned from `ftell()`. For a binary file, any combination which results in a non-negative position is legal.

```
void rewind( FILE *stream );
```

`rewind( my_file )` is synonymous with

```
fseek( my_file, OL, SEEK_SET ); clearerr( my_file );
```

There is an alternate mechanism to `fseek()` and `ftell()`:

```
int fgetpos( FILE *stream, fpos_t *pos );
int fsetpos( FILE *stream, const fpos_t *pos );
```

`fgetpos()` records the current position of the stream in the `fpos_t` identified by `*pos`. `fsetpos()` restores the stream to the position identified by `*post`. Both return zero on success, nonzero on error.

These functions manage the buffering of the stream:

```
int setvbuf( FILE *stream, char *buf, int mode, size_t size );
```

`setvbuf()` establishes or changes the buffering on the stream. It must be used before any I/O or file pointer movement operations on the stream. `mode` must be one of `_IOFBF` (full buffering), `_IOLBF` (line buffering—i.e., buffering up to a new line—on text files), or `_IONBF` (no buffering). If `buf` is `NULL`, `setvbuf()` will allocate a buffer of `size` (if needed), otherwise `setvbuf()` will assume that `buf` points to an area of at least `size` characters.

`setvbuf()` returns zero on success, nonzero on failure.

```
void setbuf( FILE *stream, char *buf );
```

`setbuf( myfile, my_buf )` is synonymous with

```
(void) setvbuf( myfile, mybuf, ( mybuf ? _IOFBF : _IONBF),
                                BUFSIZE );
```

These functions operate on files themselves:

```
int remove( const char *filename );
```

`remove()` removes the named file from the file system. It returns zero on success, nonzero on failure.

```
int rename( const char *oldfilename, const char *newfilename );
```

`rename()` changes the name of a file. It returns zero on success, nonzero on failure.

```
FILE *tmpfile( void );
```

`tmpfile()` creates and opens a temporary file with mode `"wb+"`. The file will be removed when it is `fclose()`'d or when the program terminates normally. If `tmpfile()` cannot create the file, it returns NULL.

```
char *tmpnam( char name[ L_tmpnam ] );
```

`tmpnam()` creates a name for a temporary file. At the time it is created, there will be no other file of that name on the system. It returns a pointer to the name string, and if the parameter to `tmpnam` is not `NULL`, it assumes that the pointer points to an array of at least `L_tmpnam` characters and stores the name there. Each call to `tmpnam` results in a different name string. There may be at most `TMP_MAX` files generated this way within a single program.

A.2.9 `setjmp()` and `longjmp()`: nonlocal goto

`setjmp()` and `longjmp()` provide a limited abort-and-recover capability. The processing model is this: some 'high-level' function (e.g., a command interpreter or event dispatcher) calls `setjmp( restore_buf )`.

```
#include <setjmp.h>

jump_buf restore_top_level;

void
top_level()
{
        ...

        ... setjmp( restore_top_level ) ...;

        while( readin() )
        {
                ... ...
                do_something();
                ... ...
        }
        ... ...
}
```

The same function calls another function, which sooner or later calls another, and so forth, until some low-level function finds it cannot continue.

```
int
do_something( void )
{
        ... ...
        anotherfun( args );
        ... ...
}
... ...
void
very_deep_fun( args )
{
        ... ...

        ...ghastly, irrecoverable error!...
        {
                fprintf( stderr, "Ghastly, irrecoverable error!\n" );
                longjmp( restore_top_level );
        }
        ... ...
}
```

It calls `long_jmp( restore_buf )`. `long_jmp()` does not return in the ordinary way. Instead, all of the functions between it and the function that made the corresponding call to `setjmp()` are abandoned. The call to setjmp() is reestablished, and returns to the same place from which it was originally called.

The essential specifics are these: either of these functions may be implemented as a macro rather than as a function. The jump_buf parameter is named directly; no address is taken in the call that appears. (jump_buf is typically a typedef for an array; if it is a typedef for a struct there must be a macro to insert the &.) setjmp() can only appear in very simple contexts: simple relational and equality expressions within the test of flow-of-control statements. On the original call, setjmp() returns zero; on the 'abnormal return' it returns nonzero:

```
void
top_level()
{
        ... ...

        if( setjmp( restore_top_level ) != 0 )
        {
                ...abnormal return; processing abandoned...
        }

        while( readin() )
        {
                ... ...
```

On abnormal return, variables had the value they had at the time of the call to longjump(). Local variables that must be preserved in the routine that calls setjmp() may have to be declared volatile.

A.3 ANSI C/C++ Preprocessor and Standard Headers

The preprocessor is a macro processor that is invoked on every C or C++ program as the first step in compilation. It provides token replacement, macro replacement, limited editing of tokens, substitution of 'trigraphs' to aid portability across character sets, file inclusion, and conditional compilation. It also has some extra facilities that support these features.

Historically the preprocessor was run as a separate phase on the compiler input, and was originally optional. The preprocessor need not be implemented this way; it may be integrated with the compiler proper. All the ANSI standard requires is that it behave 'as if' it were implemented as it is described.

A.3.1 The ANSI C and C++ preprocessor

The difference between the C and C++ preprocessors are very minor. The languages specify one major difference: the C++ preprocessor must recognize and strip out //-comments (Sec. 1.1.1).

The preprocessor performs its operations in a defined order. First trigraphs are expanded (Sec. A.3.1.1.3), and (if necessary) newline characters are inserted to terminate input 'records' (lines). Second, any line ending with a backslash is spliced into the next line by removing the backslash and the newline. Third, the program is tokenized. Fourth, the various "#-directives" (replacement, inclusion, conditional compilation, token pasting, and quoting) are carried out. Fifth, escape sequences are translated and adjacent string literals are catenated.

A.3.1.1 Token handling.

A programming language is parsed first into lexical units called 'tokens.' A token is the smallest unit that matters to the syntax of the language. The preprocessor does not know all of C's lexical conventions, and so has slightly different rules of its own for handling tokens.

A.3.1.1.1 Tokenizing vs. nontokenizing.

Some versions of the preprocessor treated input as a stream of characters; some treated it as a stream of tokens. This example illustrates the difference:

```
#define DO do
#define WHILE while

DO/* ... a comment in between ... */WHILE ( x ); while( z );
```

This could be expanded in one of two ways:

```
do while( x ); while( z );      /* A tokenizing preprocessor
                                 * gives a do-while around a
                                 * while:
                                 *   do { while( x ) {} } while( z );
                                 */
/* OR */

dowhile( x ); while( z );       /* A non-tokenizing preprocessor
                                 * gives a function call and a
                                 * while:
                                 *   dowhile( x ); while( z ) {}
                                 */
```

Nontokenizing was once considered a feature because it allowed the 'pasting' of tokens into other tokens. This allowed macros to combine prefixes and suffixes to create new names, etc.

ANSI C and C++ require a tokenizing preprocessor that provides explicit token pasting (Sec. A.3.1.1.4). When a program is tokenized, each comment is replaced by a single space, which becomes a token separator.

A.3.1.1.2 Alternate spellings. Because the # character does not exist in certain 'national character sets' (most notably the Danish seven-bit character set), the preprocessor recognizes %% and %%%% as synonyms for # and ##, respectively, *for C++ only.*

These alternate spellings were introduced in 1991 and 1992 by the ANSI/ISO standards committee for C++ (x3j16/WG21) and are not found in AT&T Release 3.0 or other compilers from that time. *Moreover, it is still possible, though unlikely, that that standards body will repent of these synonyms and delete them from the Working Paper or Draft Proposed Standard before it is submitted for acceptance.*

A.3.1.1.3 Trigraphs. The preprocessor's first step in reading a program is to replace certain *trigraphs* (sequences of three characters) with replacement characters. This replacement takes place even within quoted literals. The trigraph sequences and their replacements are

```
??=  #          ??(  [          ??<  {
??/  \          ??)  ]          ??>  }
??'  `          ??!  |          ??-  ~
```

Because the trigraphs all begin with two question marks, ANSI C and C++ permit an escaped question mark within a quoted constant or literal (Sec. A.1.1.6). Whenever multiple question marks occur together, at least every other one should be escaped. (Because trigraph replacement occurs before escape sequence processing, a *leading* backslash doesn't interrupt a trigraph; only backslashes *between* the question marks do.)

Trigraphs exist for the benefit of 'national character sets' other than ASCII. Many of these seven-bit sets replace the punctuation characters needed by C and C++ with characters needed for the national language (e.g., inflected vowels).

A.3.1.1.4 Line splicing. As explained above, a line ending with a backslash is joined to the next line. This is generally used only to extend a preprocessor directive across lines.

```
#define BOOJUM_decl (T1,T2)\
        struct BOOJ ## T1 ## t2 \
        {\
                T1* forw;\
                T1* back;\
        \
```

```
            T2* left;\
            T2* right;\
    \
            long serial_num;\
    };
```

This particular usage show grows less common as templates (Chap. 8) come into wider use.

Tokens will not be joined ('pasted') across spliced lines. The only exceptions are string literals, which can be continued across lines with the backslash:

```
const char* ever_deadly = "superplasmicauteroreverberating\
megamoleculozapperdingledangledonglehyperintensifiednewand\
improvedtimewarping complaint field generator";
```

This was needed before the ANSI version of C; with ANSI C and C++ it is not needed (see Sec. A.3.1.1.6).

A.3.1.1.5 Token pasting. The preprocessor provides an infix operator, ##, which catenates ('pastes') adjacent tokens, in effect removing the whitespace that separates them. It is applied to the text that replaces a `#define` (Sec. A.3.1.2.6). Whether the resulting token is legal C or C++ depends upon the tokens pasted:

```
alpha_ ## bravo_ ## charlie     /* Sensible     */
{ ## "ZzZzZ"                    /* Nonsensical. */
```

The preprocessor or compiler is entitled to complain about the second line.

Note that in C++ (but not C) `%%%%` is synonymous with ##; we could just as well have written this:

```
alpha_ %%%% bravo_ %%%% charlie     /* International */
```

A.3.1.1.6 Quoting. In addition to the token-pasting operator, the preprocessor provides a unary prefix # operator. This operator is only recognized when it occurs as part of the text that replaces a `#define` (Sec. A.3.1.2.6). The token immediately following it is surrounded by double-quotes, turning it into a string literal. Any double-quote or backslash inside that token is escaped with a backslash to keep the string literal legal.

Note that in C++ the token `%%` may be used instead of #.

A.3.1.1.7 Adjacent string literals. If two string literals appear adjacent to each other (no other token intervening) they are merged into a single string:

```
const char* ever_deadly = "superplasmicauteroreverberating"
"megamoleculozapperdingledangledonglehyperintensifiednew"
"andimprovedtimewarping complaint field generator" ;
```

A.3.1.2 Inclusion and replacement. The preprocessor is best known for its handling of `#include` and `#define` directives.

A.3.1.2.1 #-directives. Lines beginning with a # (or, in C++, with a %%) are taken to be *preprocessor directives.* White space may occur before and after the #:

```
#-rest-of-directive
/* A comment is white space. */ # /* It is, really. */-rest-of-directive
/* A comment is white space. */ %% /* In C++ */-rest-of-directive
```

This is useful when conditional directives are nested, since it allows them to be indented. (Conventionally, the # is left in the first column.)

A directive that contains a # (or, in C++, %%) and no other tokens is considered a *null* and has no effect.

A.3.1.2.2 `#include`. (In C++, the token %% may be substituted for the #.)

A preprocessor directive of the form

```
#include include-file
```

directs the preprocessor to replace the directive with the contents of the file indicated by *include-file.* There are two forms for *include-file:*

```
#include <system-supplied-header>

        /* e.g. */

#include <stddef.h>

    /* and */

#include "locally-supplied-header"

        /* e.g. */

#include "my_header.h"
```

The exact meaning of the *locally-supplied-header* name depends on the local compiler and file system conventions.

Typically, `#include`'d files contain shared declarations or lengthy initializations. Such files are often called "header files."

`#include`'d files may be nested.

If the text following the `include` preprocessor keyword does not begin with either the < (left angle bracket or 'open brocket') or the " (double quote), the preprocessor will attempt to apply its ordinary token replacement (Sec. A.3.1.2.6). The result must conform to either the 'angle bracket' or 'double quote' form.

A.3.1.2.3 `#define`—simple. (In C++, the token `%%` may be substituted for the `#`.)

A preprocessor directive of the form

```
#define macro-token replacement-text

        /* e.g. */

#define WORD_BUF_LEN ( MAX_WORDS * MAX_WORD_LEN + 1 )
```

instructs the preprocessor to replace the *macro-token* with the *replacement-text* whenever the *macro-token* occurs in subsequent text.

Note the parentheses used to ensure that the expression is evaluated properly if it is expanded in a context such as this:

```
char word_set[ WORD_BUF_LEN * 4 ];
```

The preprocessor knows nothing of expressions; it knows only of text, tokens, and replacement text.

If the *replacement-text* begins with a `(` it is especially important that the *macro-token* and the *replacement-text* be separated by whitespace.

A.3.1.2.4 `#define`—parameterized. (In C++, the token `%%` may be substituted for the `#`.)

The `#define` can also accept parameters:

```
#define SEEK( CYL, DRIVE ) \
       ( ( ( DRIV ) << 18 ) | ( ( CYL ) << 3 ) | 0x5 )
```

Here there may *not* be whitespace between the macro name and the parameter list. The preprocessor will attempt to expand any instance of the macro name; it must find a parameter list with the correct number of parameters:

```
out_command( SEEK( com->cyl, drive ) ); /* Ok */
```

```
confirm( SEEK( com->cyl ) );      /* No good; wrong */
                                  /* number of params */
```

Notice that every appearance of a parameter name in the replacement text is parenthesized. This is necessary in case of a 'call' like

```
out_command( SEEK( drive == -1 ? 0 : com->cyl, drive ) );
```

A.3.1.2.5 #undef. (In C++, the token %% may be substituted for the #.) The preprocessor directive #undef instructs the preprocessor to forget a name from a #define:

```
#undef DEBUG_LEVEL

#define DEBUG_LEVEL 0xF
```

A.3.1.2.6 Scanning rules. When text from a #define replaces a *macro-name* (with or without parameters), the ## (token pasting) and # (quoting) operators are applied if they appear in the replacement text.

If there are parameters, they are initially scanned for these operators. If none is found in a parameter, the parameter is rescanned looking for further *macro-names* to expand.

When the replacement text has been completely generated, it is rescanned repeatedly for more *macro-names* to expand. But once a given *macro-name* has been used in an expansion, it cannot be used again, ensuring that infinite expansion is not possible.

Because a parameter that already has a ## or # will not be scanned again for macro names, writing macros which can be nested may require two levels of macro:

```
/*
 *     Won't work right ...
 */

#define JOIN_NM( A, B ) A ## _ ## B

...JOIN_NM( tinker, date )...   /* Ok */

...JOIN_NM( JOIN_NM( tinker, date ), short )... /* No good   */
JOIN_NM( JOIN_NM( tinker, date ), short )     /* No good */
                    /* The outer JOIN_NM is carried,     */
                    /* out, yielding                     */
                    /*  JOIN_NM( tinker, date )_short    */
```

Making it work requires a two-level subterfuge that will allow the inner name to be expanded before the ## appears:

```
/*
 *     Better ...
 */

#define JOIN_NM( A, B ) JOIN_NM2( A, B )

#define JOIN_NM2( A, B ) A ## _ ## B

   JOIN_NM( JOIN_NM( tinker, date ), short )  /* Works now, */
/* This evaluates thus                              */
/* outer: JOIN_NM2( JOIN_NM( tinker, date ), short )   */
/* inner: JOIN_NM2( JOIN_NM2( tinker, date ), short )  */
/* inner: JOIN_NM2( tinker ## _ ## date, short )       */
/* outer: JOIN_NM2( tinker_date, short )               */
/* outer: tinker_date ## _ ## short )                  */
/*        tinker_date_short                            */
```

A.3.1.3 Conditional compilation. Another function of the preprocessor is control of what text gets compiled. This is called *conditional compilation.* Its uses include controlling machine-dependent versions of code, enabling program features (either user features or program instrumentation) in some compilations but not in others, and "commenting out" sections of code while debugging.

A.3.1.3.1 Conditional compilation directives. (In C++, the token `%%` may be substituted for the `#`.)

The directives which control conditional compilation are `#if`, `#else`, `#elif`, and `#endif`. There are also `#ifdef` and `#ifndef`, which are compound forms of `#if`. (See Sec. A.3.1.3.2.)

The general form of conditional compilation is

```
#if preprocessor-expression     /* Required */
     ... ...       /* Compiled if the              */
     ... ...       /* preprocessor-expression is true */
#elif preprocessor-expression/* Else-if part.  There    */
     ... ...       /* may be zero, one, or    */
     ... ...       /* many #elif directives.  */
#else preprocessor-expression/* Else-part.  Optional.   */
     ... ...       /* There may be zero or    */
     ... ...       /* one else-part.          */
#endif                           /* Required.  Terminates the */
                                 /* conditional compilation.  */
```

Only one of the code sections indicated by the ellipses will be compiled, and that will be the first one whose *preprocessor-expression* evaluates to *true,* or the `#else` section, if there is one and if none of the expressions evaluates to *true.*

Conditionals may contain other preprocessor directives, including other conditionals. The nested directives will not take effect if the code section containing them is not to be compiled; however, nested conditionals will be examined to parse the nesting.

A.3.1.3.2 Preprocessor arithmetic and functions. The *preprocessor-expression* needed for the conditional compilation directives is composed of integer or long integer constants, C operators that apply to rvalues of these types, and the preprocessor 'function' `defined`. In this directive:

```
#if defined XYZZY
```

the expression `defined XYZZY` evaluates to one `(1L)` if `XYZZY` is a macro name known to the preprocessor, and zero otherwise.

The alternative forms

```
#ifdef name
```

and

```
#ifndef name
```

are equivalent to

```
#if defined( name )
```

and

```
#if ! defined( name )
```

respectively.

A.3.1.3.3 Predefined symbols. The C and C++ preprocessors predefine certain macro names. These names begin with two underscores. (Names beginning with two underscores are reserved to the compilation environment.)

- `__STDC__` Defined to 1 in standard-conforming C environments; should not be defined in any other context.
- `__LINE__` The current line number in the file being compiled. (meant for use by error-reporting code).
- `__FILE__` A string literal containing the name of the current source or header file.
- `__DATE__` A string literal containing the date of the compilation, in the form `"Mon dd yyyy"`.

`__TIME__` A string literal containing the time of the compilation in the form `"hh:mm:ss"`.
`__cplusplus` Defined to `1` when compiling C++.

These macro names may not be `#undef`'d.

A.3.1.3.4 `#error`. The `#error` directive transmits an optional message to the standard error output of the compilation and creates a compile-time error:

```
#if SMALL_MEMORY && LARGE_PROBLEM

#  error "Cannot compile for LARGE problem with SMALL memory."

#endif
```

A.3.1.3.5 `#pragma`. The `#pragma` causes an implementation-defined action to be taken.

```
#pragma optional-token-sequence
```

An unknown `#pragma` will be ignored.

A.3.1.3.6 `#line`. (In C++, the token `%%` may be substituted for the `#`.) C is frequently used as the output language of program generators; it is expected that C++ may be used the same way. The `#line` directive allows the generated code to be mapped back to the original source code lines:

```
#line 44        /* Causes the preprocessor and compiler to */
                /* consider the current line 'line 44' for */
                /* error reporting, __LINE__, etc.         */

#line 46 "grunxn.W"    /* Causes the preprocessor and compiler */
                       /* to consider the current line 'line   */
                       /* 46' and the current file  grunxn.W   */
                       /* for error reporting, __LINE__ and    */
                       /* __FILE__, etc.                       */
```

A.3.1.3.7 Idempotence. It is often desirable, especially in C++, to ensure that a file may be included several times with the same effect as if it is included only once. This is called 'idempotence.' The preprocessor does not support idempotence directly. Instead, some method like this must be used:

```
/*
 *     header_ABC.h
```

```
*/

#if ! defined header_ABC_INC

#  define header_ABC_INC

        contents of header file
#endif  /* Nothing below this line! */
```

A.3.2 Standard header files

The C and C++ standard specify a variety of *standard header files.* These are included using the `#include <... ...>` syntax (Sec. A.3.1.2.2).

A.3.2.1 String and character handling. The standard header files `string.h` and `ctype.h` are discussed in Sec. A.2.3.8.1 and Sec. A.2.3.8.3, respectively. The first file declares functions to copy, scan, compare, and partition strings. The second file declares macros to identify character classes to which a character belongs.

A.3.2.2 Block memory moves. The standard header file `memory.h` declares functions for copying blocks of memory. They are described in Sec. A.2.3.8.2.

A.3.2.3 Math and other standard functions. The system header file `math.h` declares a variety of mathematical functions including square root, trig functions, hyperbolic functions, exponential and logarithmic functions, and functions to access and load the floating point representation.

The system header file `stdlib.h` declares a very wide variety of functions including character string-to-numeric conversions, random number generators, free store management (duplicating `malloc.h`), interacting with the program's environment, sorting, and searching.

A.3.2.4 Free store management. The system header file `malloc.h` declares the free store management functions `malloc()`, `calloc()`, `free()`, and `realloc()` described in Sec. A.2.4.2.

For C++, the file `new.h` declares the `new-handler` interface and other things necessary to use the advanced capabilities of `operator new`. (The basic uses do not need the header.)

A.3.2.5 Time. The system header `time.h` declares types, structures, and functions with which to obtain the current time, to convert time from the local internal representation into familiar calendric and horological formats, and to manipulate Universal (GM) Time, local time, and time differences.

A.3.2.6 Implementation dependencies. Several header files contain information about implementation dependencies. Dependencies which arise from numeric format are described by macros in `limits.h` and `float.h`, which give the ranges, precision limits, etc., for the built-in types.

`locale.h` provides information about character sets, collating sequences, currency and numeric formats, etc., for use by standard library and other programs in the local environment. (One example: in North America and Europe the conventions for using the comma and the period in numerals are reversed.)

`stddef.h` provides types and macros for `NULL`, `size_t` (Sec. A.1.3.2), `ptr_diff` (Sec. A.2.3.4), and `offsetof()`. The latter macro provides the distance, in characters (bytes), from the beginning of a `struct` to one of its members:

```
#include <stddef.h>
    ... ...
    ... ...
struct a_struct
{
        int member_1;
            ... ...
        char *member_N;
            ... ...
};

        ptr_diff offset;
            ... ...
        offset = offsetof( a_struct, member_N );
```

It turns out that this can be done in one way or another on any architecture that supports C, but it also turns out that the implementation cannot be portable, since no one implementation of the macro will work on every machine architecture. Using the compiler-provided macro *is* portable, since every standard C must provide a working version of the macro.

A.3.2.7 Input and output with standard I/O. Programs which are to perform input and output using the facilities of Standard I/O (Sec. A.2.8) should include the declarations for Standard I/O by `#include`'ing the system-provided header `stdio.h`.

stdio.h also declares perror(), a function used to assist in producing meaningful error messages. A code sequence such as

```
#include <stdio.h>
        ... ...
        FILE *myf = fopen( "AintNoSuchFile", "r" );
            ... ...
        if( ! myf )
        {
                perror( "AintNoSuchFile" );
                ... ...
        }
            ... ...
```

when run on the author's machine, and in the absence of a file called AintNoSuchFile, produces this message:

```
AintNoSuchFile: No such file or directory
```

perror()'s proper declaration is

```
void perror( const char *s );
```

perror() and the other I/O functions communicate among themselves using an external int variable named errno. errno may get set during the course of operations that do not result in failure; it and perror() may only be used correctly when the function in question has actually reported an error.

A.3.2.8 Variable argument lists: stdarg.h. The system-provided header stdarg.h contains the mechanisms by which variable-length argument lists are read (Sec. A.2.1). Note that on some compilers or some machine architectures these may require special 'magic' keywords for the compiler at hand. Such keywords will begin with an underscore so that they will not clash with any legitimate application-code identifiers (Sec. A.1.1.3).

A.3.2.9 Nonlocal 'Goto': setjmp.h. The system-provided header setjmp.h declares types and functions, and defines macros to support the setjmp()/longjmp() facility (Sec. A.2.9).

A.3.2.10 Signals and signal.h. *Signals* are software interrupts sent to a program by something in the environment (another program, a timer, the operating system in response to a change in the environment).

The core of the signal mechanism is specified by the ANSI C standard; many systems extend it considerably. The necessary declarations and definitions are found in the system-defined header file `signal.h`.

The principal functions in the standard interface are `signal()` and `raise()`:

```
void (*signal( int sig, void (*handler)(int)))(int);

int raise( int sig );
```

The declaration of `signal()` may be understood by thinking of an intermediate type:

```
typedef void (*Handler_t)(int);
Handler_t signal( int sig, Handler_t handler );
```

In this (nonstandard) formulation, `Handler_t` describes the type of a `signal handling function`. `signal()` takes a second argument of this type and stores it, returning the previous value stored.

The first argument to `signal()` is the signal number, obtained from a `#define` in `signal.h`. Valid signals include `SIGABRT` (abort), `SIGPFE` ('floating point exception,' i.e., arithmetic error), `SIGILL` (illegal instruction), `SIGINT` (user-generated interrupt), `SIGSEGV` ('segmentation violation,' i.e., addressing exception), and `SIGTERMV` (request for the program to terminate).

The second argument to `signal()` indicates the action to be taken upon receipt of the signal. Valid values include `SIGN_IGN` (ignore), `SIG_DFL` (default action) (implementation defined), and a pointer to any function whose signature is that of the hypothetical `Handler_t` type shown above. If such a function pointer is stored for a signal and the signal occurs, the function will be called, interrupting normal processing. When and if the function returns, normal processing will resume.

On some systems, if a signal handler function intends to call `longjmp()` (Secs. A.2.9 and A.3.2.9), it must take special action to restore the environment to the normal, 'out-of-signal' state. This is implementation-defined.

The `raise()` function allows a program to send a signal to itself. Other implementation-dependent methods are used to send signals between programs.

A.3.2.11 `assert.h`. The system-provided header file `assert.h` defines a set of macros which assist the writing of run-time checks:

```
#include <assert.h>
        ... ...
        ... ...
        assert( condition )
```

When execution passes to the assert() macro, the macro examines the condition expression, which is typically a range expression or a check against pointer NULL. If the expression is false (evaluates to zero) the macro prints a message on stderr to the effect that an assertion failed at such and such a line in such and such a file. The line and file are provided by __LINE__ and __FILE__.

The assert() macros can be disabled at compile time by #define'ing a macro named NDEBUG before any of the assert() macro invocations.

Appendix

B

Application Technologies

This appendix describes technology used for examples in the text but perhaps not familiar to all.

B.1 HeapSort exposed

The HeapSort algorithm is important in theory and in practice. It also illustrates an important point about sophisticated algorithms. And it provides an interesting scoping problem that is not well handled by most languages.

HeapSort is important theoretically because its running time is dominated by $O(N\log(N))$ (where N is the number of records to be sorted) no matter what the input. (With worst-case input, the various forms of QuickSort can degenerate to $O(N^2)$ or worse.)

It is important practically for the same reason. And it illustrates the point that a well-developed algorithm for a difficult problem may look nothing like any obvious way of solving the problem, and may thereby be unintelligible to the uninitiated.

HeapSort is built around a single data structure with a single key operation. The data structure is the Heap. (This Heap is not related to any data structures used to manage free store, which is also sometimes called 'The Heap.')

The HeapSort Heap is an array which can be interpreted as a binary tree. Each element of the array is also a node of the tree. For an array beginning at zero, the children of array element N lie at $2N + 1$ and $2N + 2$. Since we deal with finite arrays, some of the nodes will have no children, and one may have just one. In a properly arranged Heap, each node will be no smaller than either of its children.

The basic operation is the *sift*. Sifting is the process whereby a given array element is moved into the proper relationship with regard to its parent and children.

Sift: Given an element E at position N, determine if either of the children of N is greater than E; if so, exchange the larger of the child values with E and repeat the sift with that child. (Thus the sift works from wherever you start 'down' into the tree as far as it must to ensure that this subtree is properly ordered.)

HeapSort works by first converting an unsorted array into a Heap, and then converting the Heap into a sorted array.

To convert an unsorted array into a Heap, begin at the middle of the array (the last element that has a child), sifting that element into position. Then move towards the beginning of the array (root of the tree), sifting down at each element, including the element at the root of the tree.

In a properly arranged Heap, each element is no smaller than its children, and they are no smaller than their children, and so on. Thus the largest value appears at the zero position.

To convert the Heap into a sorted array, exchange the first element of the array with the last element, reduce the size of the Heap to exclude that last element, and sift the new root element down into the Heap. The Heap is now one shorter, and the largest and last element of the array is sorted. Repeat the operation with the revised Heap over and over, shortening the Heap by one each time until the entire Heap is reduced to one element. At this point, the entire array is sorted and no sift is necessary.

B.2 A brief introduction to complex numbers

Complex numbers are widely used in engineering and directly supported by programming languages such as FORTRAN and PL/1. They are also an excellent candidate for a class type with operator overloading, and (generally) simple enough that the operations on them can be understood at glance and represented by inlines.

Complex numbers are widely used in engineering problems involving the storage of energy, including oscillating systems, electromagnetic propagation (radio), and all branches of Communication Systems, Electrical Transmission Systems, Control Systems, and Filters.

This introduction may help those who have neither a mathematical nor engineering education.

A complex number is not a complicated number, but a number which is the sum of a real number and an *imaginary* number. An *imaginary* number is a real number multiplied by the principal square root of –1. That principal square root of –1 is commonly written as i (except in electrical engineering and related disciplines, where I and i represent current, and j is used for the principal square root of –1). (In Complex Number theory, there is a second square root of –1: $-i$, which is equal to $(-1)(i)$.

Thus, a complex number can be written as

$$w = u + vi$$

where u and v are real numbers, u is the *real* part of the complex number w, and v is the *imaginary* part. (If v is zero, the complex number w collapses to a real number.)

The right-hand expression above is sometimes written

$$(u,v)$$

This form is most commonly used for constants:

$$(0,-1) \qquad -i$$

$$(4.4,3.3) \qquad 4.4 + 3.3i$$

If w and p are complex numbers,

$$w = u + vi$$

$$p = q + ri$$

then their sum, difference, and product are given by

$$w + p = (u + q) + (v + r)i \qquad (u + q, v + r)$$

$$w - p = (u - q) + (v - r)i \qquad (u - q, v - r)$$

$$w \times p = (uq + vr) - (ur + qv)i$$

$$((uq + vr), (ur + qv))$$

It is also possible to take the quotient of two complex numbers. The simplest way to understand this is to recognize that the inverse of a complex number can be reexpressed with a real denominator, thus:

$$\frac{1}{(q + ri)} \frac{(q - ri)}{(q - ri)} = \frac{(q - ri)}{q^2 + r^2}$$

The division turns into a complex multiplication and a division by a real.

(This is a poor way to actually compute the inverse, since the squared terms are needlessly susceptible to overflow and underflow. Some careful algebra will yield two different formulas to use, one when the magnitude of the real part is greater and one when the magnitude of the imaginary part is greater.)

Complex numbers have other properties that may be unexpected. In complex analysis, infinity is considered to be 'projective': no matter in what direction you go towards infinity, whether on the positive or negative real or imaginary axes, or in any other direction, you are approaching the same infinity. Infinity and zero are duals, and in the problems for which engineers use complex variables, zero and infinity do behave like duals (as impedence goes to infinity, admittance goes to zero, and vice versa). Projective infinity is explicitly supported by the IEEE standard for floating point.

Complex numbers have other properties that confound the uninitiated. In complex space, exponential functions and circular (trigonometric) functions are also duals of each other: circular (trigonometric) functions in W are sums and differences of exponential functions of iW, and exponential functions in W are circular functions in iW.

The particular value of complex numbers in engineering is their use in 'transforms.' A transform allows you to convert a problem (e.g., a system described by linear differential or finite difference equations) into a problem that can be solved more easily (e.g., a system described by algebra without differentiation, integration, or finite difference methods). Engineers use Fourier, Laplace, and Z transforms for just this purpose. An engineer skilled in their use can approach a system with energy storage (and therefore time-dependent behavior) as a purely algebraic problem without ever writing the differential or difference equations. The disadvantage is that the variables of time or frequency are replaced by complex variables. It's a small price to pay.

More general than complex numbers are *quarternions* in which there are three different square roots of –1. Although rarely used by engineers, their properties underlie much of the three-dimensional vector mathematics that engineers use constantly. At one time they were heavily used; Oliver Heaviside (1850–1925) demonstrated that vector mathematics could represent Maxwell's Equations, which are a combined statement of the four basic laws of electromagnetic theory.

An introduction to the history of Laplace Transform analysis methods may be found in *Behind the Laplace Transform,* Paul J. Nahin, IEEE Spectrum, March 1991 (published by the *Institute of Electrical and Electronics Engineers*).

B.3 Duff's Device

Duff's Device was invented by Tom Duff (then at LucasFilm) on November 9, 1983. He was attempting to unroll a loop in the least costly way. The 'device' proved to be such an interesting, and sometimes useful, case of 'code bumming' that ANSIC was scrutinized to ensure that it remained legal.

Here is the original form:

```
send( to, from, count )
register short *to, *from;
register count;
{
        register n = ( count + 7 ) / 8;
        switch(count%8) {
        case 0: do{     *to = *from++;
        case 7:         *to = *from++;
        case 6:         *to = *from++;
        case 5:         *to = *from++;
        case 4:         *to = *from++;
        case 3:         *to = *from++;
        case 2:         *to = *from++;
        case 1:         *to = *from++;
          } while( -- n > 0 );
        }
}
```

Note the interlocking of the `switch` and the `do-while()`.

Tom Duff announced the discovery in electronic mail to several people, among them Dennis Ritchie (the inventor of C), on November 13, 1983.

Duff described his emotion at realizing that this was an original discovery as “a mixture of pride and revulsion.” When nobody else would claim (or admit) to having used it before, he made good a noble pledge to take the blame (“If no one's thought if it before, I think I'll name it after myself,”), and Duff's Device it is. (From a communication widely circulated on Netnews).

B.4 A brief description of Lempel-Ziv compression

Lempel-Ziv (LZ) compression is the basis of many widely used data compression algorithms. One variant, LZW compression (for ‘Lempel-Ziv-Welch’), uses an almost frighteningly compact data structure.

LZ compression, like many other compression techniques, identifies repeated substrings and codes them as shorter sequences. Decoding them requires the same dictionary that was used to encode them. LZ compression is distinguished by its approach to creating the dictionary and communicating it in the data stream: the dictionary is the body of text already sent (or some recent part thereof).

There are many ways of recording substrings and communicating what substrings have already been seen. The LZW algorithm turns text into a (conceptual) tree with an arbitrary number of leftward- and rightward-branching subtrees under each node. Leftward-branching subtrees have single characters associated with them; rightward-branching subtrees are references to other subtrees. A preorder traversal of the tree generates one or more 'new' text characters followed by a reference to some subtree that has already been seen; that reference is expanded recursively and the preorder traversal continues. (There are some subtleties when a subtree is to be expanded immediately after it has been created; they only crop up when you try to code the baffling thing.)

As the compression 'machine' builds the tree, it outputs what it adds as the compressed data, and the decoding machine builds an identical tree. The compression machine must determine, for each character, if that character has already been seen as an extension of the current substring (in which case it just moves down a node to the new substring) or if the character must be added (in which case the current node must be output and a new leftward node must be added). (There are some additional complications besides.)

The effectiveness of the compression algorithm depends on the size of tree that can be stored; once storage is filled, either no new substrings can be added or the tree must be flushed and a new one begun. *To conserve space, each node of the tree stores only an* upward *pointer.* Each node is stored as a character or a subtree reference along with the address of the parent subtree, and these records are stored in a large array. When a subtree must be sought, the character or reference is hashed and the hash value is used as a difference (hash chain) from the current record. The entire possible chain is searched and only those records that point to this parent node are actually considered. If no subtree node is found to match the character or subtree reference, one is added at the first open hash chain slot.

To maintain performance, the compression ratio is monitored; when it drops, the entire dictionary (tree) is abandoned and a new one begun. Likewise, if the entire table is filled, it is abandoned and a new one begun.

For a more complete description, see "A Technique for High Performance Data Compression," Terry A. Welch, IEEE Computer, vol. 17, no. 6 (June 1984), pp. 8–19.

Appendix

C

The Stream I/O System Interfaces

This appendix should be used along with Chap. 10.

The details of the stream I/O library are among the least uniform parts of pre-ANSI/ISO C++. The version presented here is drawn primarily from the documentation and code for the AT&T Release 3.0 version. 'Your mileage may vary.' This version is serving as the starting point for the ANSI/ISO effort. The final outcome of that effort is not in sight.

Figure 10.1 is repeated here as Figure C.1 to provide a roadmap of the stream I/O system's inheritance and ownership structures.

Should ANSI/ISO C++ include a namespace management facility, as the committee presently (as of fall 1992) hopes, the types and objects described below will probably be placed in either a general 'standard library' namespace or in a 'standard I/O library' namespace. (See Sec. 1.9.)

C.1 Stream and streambuf base classes

The stream base classes provide services to input, output, and bidirectional streams. `ios` is the base class of all; other base classes accommodate I/O to and from files and character arrays. `streambuf` is inherited by the special streambufs that serve the specialized stream classes.

C.1.1 `ios`

```
class   ios
{
  public:
      /*
       *    General public services for users of  ios -based objects.
       *
       *
```

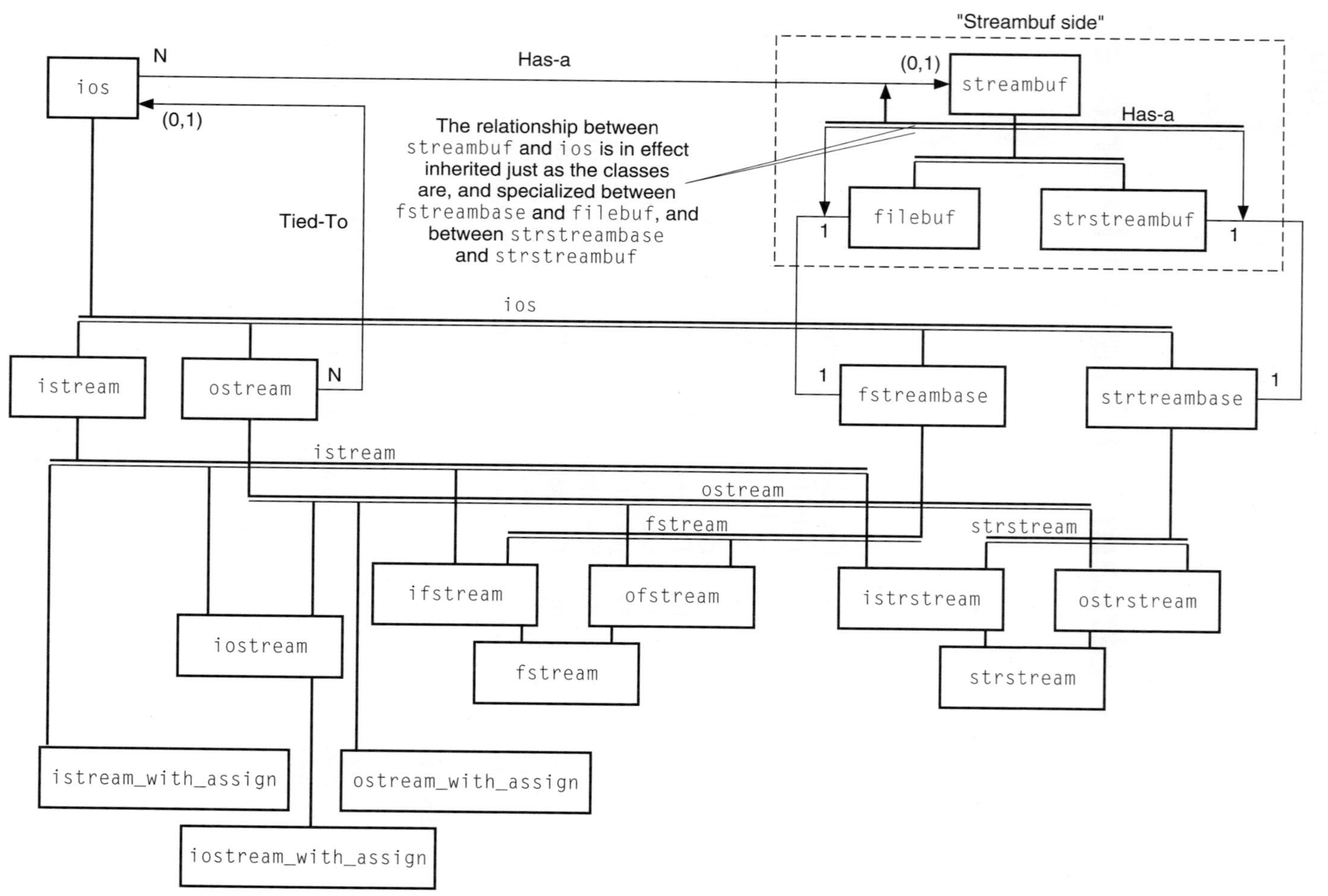

Figure C.1 (Repeat of Fig. 10.1)

```
 *    Types 'n stuff to use them.
 */
enum io_state
    { goodbit, eofbit, failbit, badbit, hardfail };
enum open_mode
    { in, out, ate, app, trunc, nocreate, noreplace };
enum seek_dir { beg, cur, end };

/*
 * Format control flags
 */
enum { skipws,                     // skip whitespace
                                   //      on input
       left,  right, internal,     // padding location
       dec, oct, hex,              // conversion base
       showbase, showpoint,
       uppercase, showpos,         // modifiers
       scientific, fixed           // floating point
                                   //      notation
};
static const long basefield;       // initialized to ( dec | oct
                                   //    | hex )
static const long adjustfield;     // initialized to ( left |
                                   //    right | internal )
static const long floatfield;      // initialized to
                                   //    ( scientific | fixed )


/*
 *      Constructors and destructor.
 */
ios( streambuf* );
virtual ~ios();

/*
 *      Formatting control.
 */
long flags();
long flags( long f );

long setf( long setbits, long field );
long setf( long );
long unsetf( long );

int width();
int width( int w );

char fill( char );
char fill();
```

```
        int precision( int );
        int precision();

        /*
         *      Manage I/O synchronization.
         */
        ostream* tie( ostream* s );
        ostream* tie();

        /*
         *      Read and set status.
         */
        int rdstate();
        operator void*();

        int operator!();
        int eof();
        int fail();
        int bad();
        int good();
        void clear( io_state i = 0 );
        streambuf* rdbuf();

        /*
         *      See Sec. 10.6.4 for the use of these 'extensible'
         *      services.
         */
        long &iword( int );
        void* &pword( int );
        static long bitalloc();
        static long xalloc();

        /*
         *      Engage lockstep with C standard I/O.
         */
        static void sync_with_stdio();

protected:
        /*
         *      Types, etc.  See Secs. 10.10.2 and 10.10.4 for a full
         *      description of these services.
         */
        enum { skipping, tied };

        streambuf* bp;

        void setstate( int b );
        int state;
```

```
        int ispecial;
        int ospecial;
        int isfx_special;
        int osfx_special;

        int delbuf;
        ostream* x_tie;
        long x_flags;
        short x_precision;
        char x_fill;
        short x_width;

        /*
         *      The constructors defer their work to  init()  so
         *      that an  Iostream_init()  can pre-construct things,
         *      allowing any functions in any file with an
         *      Iostream_init() to set up the standard streams
         *      before doing I/O.  See Sec. 2.1.13 for a description
         *      of the technique.
         *
         *      ios() doesn't much do anything except keep hold a
         *      constructor's place in the world of MI.
         */
        void init( streambuf* );
        ios();

        /*
         *      For the use of the 'with assign' derived classes.
         */
        int assign_private;

        /*
         *      In an odd way, two private functions are part of
         *      the public interface; the private declaration of
         *      the copy constructor and the assignment operator
         *      prevent non-sensible copying and assignment to an
         *      ios.
         */
    private:
        ios( ios& );
        void operator=( ios& );
};
```

C.1.2 `streambuf`. `streambuf` **provides the basic character buffering facilities; specialized buffers for files and arrays of characters are provided; others may be derived at need.**

```
class   streambuf
{
  public:
        /*
         *      Constructors and destructors.  They probably ought to
         *      be protected.
         */
        streambuf();
        streambuf( char* p, int l );

        virtual ~streambuf();

        /*
         *      These services are for the I/O client of the stream.
         *      See Secs. 10.10.1 and 10.10.3.
         */
        virtual int overflow( int c = EOF );
        virtual int underflow();
        virtual int pbackfail( int c );
        virtual int sync();
        virtual streampos seekoff( streamoff, seek_dir,
                                   open_mode = ios::in | ios::out );
        virtual streampos seekpos( streampos,
                                   open_mode = ios::in | ios::out );

        int in_avail();
        int out_waiting();

        int sgetc();
        int snextc();
        int sbumpc();
        void stossc();

        int sputbackc( char c );
        int sputc( int c );
        int sputn( const char* s,int n );
        int sgetn( char* s, int n );

        virtual streambuf* setbuf( char* p, int len );
        streambuf* setbuf( unsigned char* p, int len );

        /*
         *      Debugging print
         */
        void dbp();

        /*
         *      The protected parts are for the use of derived class
```

```
         *      clients.  See Secs. 10.10.2 and 10.10.4.
         */
  protected:
        char* base();
        char* pbase();
        char* pptr();
        char* epptr();
        char* gptr();
        char* egptr();
        char* eback();
        char* ebuf();
        int blen();
        void setp( char* p, char* ep );
        void setg( char* eb, char* g, char* eg );
        void pbump( int n );
        void gbump( int n );
        void setb(char* b, char* eb, int a = 0 );
        int unbuffered();
        void unbuffered( int unb );
        int allocate();
        virtual int doallocate();
};
```

C.1.3 istream. `istream` **adds the basic input capabilities (formatted and unformatted) to** `ios`.

```
class   istream
  : virtual public ios
{
  public:
        /*
         *      Constructor and destructor.
         */
        istream( streambuf* );
        virtual ~istream();

        /*
         *      Formatted input.  See Sec. 10.5.2
         */
        istream& operator>>( ios& (*f) (ios&) );
        istream& operator>>( char* );
        istream& operator>>( unsigned char* );
        istream& operator>>( unsigned char& c );
        istream& operator>>( char& c );
        istream& operator>>( short& );
        istream& operator>>( int& );
        istream& operator>>( long& );
        istream& operator>>( unsigned short& );
```

```
istream& operator>>( unsigned int& );
istream& operator>>( unsigned long& );
istream& operator>>( float& );
istream& operator>>( double& );
istream& operator>>( streambuf* );

/*
 *      This extractor accepts and activates a manipulator.
 *      Formatted input.  See Sec. 10.5.4
 */
istream& operator>>( istream& (*f)( istream& ) );

/*
 *      Unformatted and raw-byte operations.  See Sec. 10.7.1.
 */
istream& seekg( streampos p );
istream& seekg( streamoff o, seek_dir d );
streampos tellg();

istream& get( char*, int lim, char delim = '\n' );
istream& get( unsigned char* b, int lim,
                         char delim = '\n' );
istream& getline( char* b, int lim,
                         char delim = '\n' );
istream& getline( unsigned char* b, int lim,
                         char delim = '\n' );
istream& get( streambuf& sb, char delim = '\n' );
istream& get( unsigned char& c );
istream& get( char& c );

/*
 *      Input format services.  See Sec. 10.8.2.2.
 */
int ipfx( int noskipws = 0 );
int get();
int peek();
istream& ignore( int n = 1, int delim = EOF );
istream& read( char* s,int n );
istream& read( unsigned char* s, int n );
int gcount();
istream& putback( char c );

/*
 *      Force the stream to synchronize across the buffer with
 *      the ultimate character source.
 */
int sync();
```

```
        /*
         *   Services to derived classes.
         */
    protected:
        istream();

        int do_ipfx( int noskipws );
        void eatwhite();
};
```

C.1.4 `ostream`. `ostream` **adds the basic input capabilities (formatted and unformatted) to** `ios`.

```
class   ostream
  : virtual public ios
{
  public:
        /*
         *      Constructor and destructor
         */
        ostream( streambuf* );
        virtual ~ostream();

        /*
         *      Formatted output.  See Sec. 10.5.1.
         */
        ostream& operator<<( char c );
        ostream& operator<<( unsigned char c );
        ostream& operator<<( const char* );
        ostream& operator<<( int a );
        ostream& operator<<( long );
        ostream& operator<<( double );
        ostream& operator<<( float );
        ostream& operator<<( unsigned int a );
        ostream& operator<<( unsigned long );
        ostream& operator<<( void* );
        ostream& operator<<( streambuf* );
        ostream& operator<<( short i );
        ostream& operator<<( unsigned short i );
        ostream& operator<<( ostream& (*f)( ostream& ) );

        /*
         *      Accept and activate a manipulator.
         *      See Sec. 10.5.3.
         */
        ostream& operator<<( ios& (*f) ( ios& ) );
```

```
        /*
         *      Unformatted and raw-byte toperations.  See Sec. 10.7.2.
         */
        ostream& seekp( streampos p );
        ostream& seekp( streamoff o, seek_dir d );
        streampos tellp();
        ostream& put( char c );
        ostream& write( const char* s, int n );
        ostream& write( const unsigned char* s, int n );
        /*
         *      Output formatting services.  See Sec. 10.8.2.2.
         */
        int opfx();

        /*
         *      A one-way sync().
         */
        ostream& flush();

  protected:    /* More ostream members */
        int do_opfx();
        ostream();
};
```

C.1.5 `iostream`. `iostream` combines the facilities of `istream` and `ostream`. Only the "with-assign" input-and-output stream derives from it, but it sets a pattern for the specialized streams: an input stream, an output stream, and a two-way stream derived from both.

```
/*
 *      iostream  adds little to what  istream  and  ostream
 *      already provide.
 */
class   iostream
  : public istream, public ostream
{
  public:
        iostream( streambuf* );
        virtual ~iostream();

  protected:
        iostream();
};
```

C.2 "with assign" base classes

The "with assign" base classes use the technique described in Sec. 7.9 to delegate their actual operation to any other extant stream. In effect, they provide assignable aliases for streams (which normally do not allow assignment).

```
class   istream_withassign
  : public istream
{
  public:
        istream_withassign();
        virtual ~istream_withassign();
        istream_withassign& operator=( istream& );
        istream_withassign& operator=( streambuf* );
};

class   ostream_withassign
  : public ostream
}
  public:
        ostream_withassign();
        virtual ~ostream_withassign();
        ostream_withassign& operator=( ostream& );
        ostream_withassign& operator=( streambuf* );
};

class   iostream_withassign
  : public iostream
{
  public:
        iostream_withassign();
        virtual ~iostream_withassign();
        iostream_withassign& operator=( ios& );
        iostream_withassign& operator=( streambuf* );
};
```

The predefined streams cin, cout, and cerr are "with-assign" streams, and are set up by the Iostream_init(). The operation of Iostream_init() is described in Sec. 2.1.13.

```
static class   Iostream_init
{
        static int stdstatus; /* see cstreams.c */
        static int initcount;
        friend ios;
  public:
        Iostream_init();
        ~Iostream_init();
} iostream_init;
```

Notice that anything that includes the file containing the class declaration (<iostream.h>) automatically—or 'automagically'—gets a static Iostream_init object to ensure that the predefined streams are ready for use.

C.3 Specialized stream bases and streambufs

Specialized stream bases and streambufs allow I/O to and from arbitrary sinks and sources of characters. The standard library includes versions for files and for arrays of text ('strings').

C.3.1 File streambuf and file stream base. `filebuf` and `filebase` specialize the I/O system to files. Exactly what a file is depends upon the environment; in general it's a collection of characters which may be read or written to, once a connection has been established to it ('the file has been opened') and which is identified in the environment by a name consisting of a sequence of characters.

```
/*
 *      Streambuf specialized to files.
 */
class   filebuf
   : public streambuf
{
  public:
        /*
         *      Constructors to create, to create and open a file,
         *      and to create and open a file and attach a buffer.
         */
        filebuf();
        filebuf( int fd );
        filebuf( int fd, char* p, int l );
        ~filebuf();

        /*
         *      Determine if the file is open and obtain the 'descriptor'
         *      by which the open file is known.
         */
        int is_open();
        int fd();

        /*
         *      Open a file (for use when we have none open), attach to
         *      already open file (known by the file descriptor), or
         *      close an open file.
         */
        filebuf* open( const char *name, open_mode om,
                                        int prot = 0664 );
        filebuf* attach( int fd );
        filebuf* close();

        /*
         *      File-specific versions of stream interface functions.
         */
```

```
        virtual int overflow( int = EOF );
        virtual int underflow();
        virtual int sync();
        virtual streampos seekoff( streamoff, seek_dir,
                                                  open_mode );
        virtual streambuf* setbuf( char* p, int len );

        /*
         *      Stuff that derived classes may need to handle.
         */
  protected:
        int xfd;
        open_mode mode;
        char opened;
        streampos last_seek;
        char* in_start;
        int last_op();
        char lahead[ 2 ];
};

/*
 *      The  ios  specialized to files.  Much of the specialization
 *      reflects the extra activity the filebuf needs (compared to
 *      the vanilla streambuf).
 */
class   fstreambase
  : virtual public ios
{
public:
        fstreambase();

        fstreambase( const char* name, open_mode mode,
                                         int prot = 0664 );
        fstreambase( int fd );
        fstreambase( int fd, char* p, int l );
        ~fstreambase();
        void open( const char* name, open_mode mode,
                                         int prot = 0664 );
        void attach( int fd );
        void close();
        void setbuf( char* p, int l );
        filebuf* rdbuf();
};
```

C.3.2 Character array ('string') streambuf and streambase. The 'string' streambase and streambuf are specialized to use arrays of characters as their source and sink. They can provide the array buffers themselves dynamically, or can use buffers provided by their clients.

```
/*
 *      Streambuf specialized to character arrays ('strings').
 */
class   strstreambuf
  : public streambuf
{
  public:
        /*
         *      Create a strstreambuf, allocating memory
         *      dynamically. The second constructor pre-
         *      allocates a fixed space, and the third one
         *      accepts pointers to the allocate and free
         *      functions it is to use.
         */
        strstreambuf();
        strstreambuf( int );
        strstreambuf( void* (*a) ( long ), void (*f) ( void* ) );

        /*
         *      Create a strstreambuf using a client-supplied
         *      buffer.
         */
        strstreambuf( char* b, int size, char* pstart = 0 );
        strstreambuf( unsigned char* b, int size,
                                        unsigned char* pstart = 0 );
        ~strstreambuf();

        /*
         *      When a dynamic buffer is frozen, the strstreambuf
         *      relinquishes responsibility for freeing it; the
         *      client which brought the strstreambuf into
         *      existance should accept that responsibility.  The
         *      parameter is non-zero to freeze, zero to thaw.
         */
        void freeze( int n = 1 );

        /*
         *      Return the address of the current string buffer
         *      array.
         */
        char* str();

        /*
         *      Specialized versions of the stream interface
         *      functions.
         */
        virtual int doallocate();
        virtual int overflow( int );
```

```
        virtual int underflow();
        virtual streambuf* setbuf( char* p, int 1 );
        virtual streampos seekoff( streamoff, seek_dir, open_mode );
};

/*
 *      ios specialized to character strings (and to the use of the
 *      strstreambuf).
 */
class   strstreambase
  : public virtual ios
{
  public:
        strstreambuf* rdbuf();

  protected:
        /*
         *      The first constructor uses a usr-provided buffer;
         *      the second allocates dynamically.
         */
        strstreambase( char* start_buf, int size, char* start_chars );
        strstreambase();
        ~strstreambase();
};
```

C.4 Specialized derived streams

Derived streams follow a pattern: input and output streams are each derived from both the streambase and the basic input or output stream, then the two-way stream is derived from both the input and the output stream.

C.4.1 File streams. `ifstream`, `ofstream`, and `fstream` are the derived file streams.

```
class   ifstream
  : public fstreambase, public istream
{
  public:
        ifstream();
        ifstream( const char* name, int mode = ios::in,
                                        int prot = filebuf::openprot );
        ifstream( int fd );
        ifstream( int fd, char* p, int file_mode );
        ~ifstream();
```

```
        filebuf* rdbuf();
        void open( const char* name, int mode = ios::in,
                                 int prot = filebuf::openprot );
};

class   ofstream
  : public fstreambase, public ostream
{
  public:
        ofstream();
        ofstream( const char* name, int mode = ios::out,
                                 int prot = filebuf::openprot );
        ofstream( int fd );
        ofstream( int fd, char* p, int file_mode );
        ~ofstream();

        filebuf* rdbuf();
        void open( const char* name, int mode = ios::out,
                                 int prot = filebuf::openprot );
};

class   fstream
  : public fstreambase, public iostream
{
  public:
        fstream();
        fstream( const char* name, int mode, int prot =
                                 filebuf::openprot );
        fstream( int fd );
        fstream( int fd, char* p, int file_mode );
        ~fstream();
        filebuf* rdbuf();
        void open( const char* name, int mode,
                                 int prot = filebuf::openprot );
};
```

C.4.2 String streams. The derived string streams are `istrstream`, `ostrstream`, and `strstream`.

```
class   istrstream
  : public strstreambase, public istream
{
  public:
        istrstream( char* str );
        istrstream( char* str, int size );
        istrstream( const char* str );
        istrstream( const char* str, int size );
        ~istrstream();
};
```

```
class   ostrstream
  : public strstreambase, public ostream
{
public:
        ostrstream( char* str, int size, int=ios::out );
        ostrstream();
        ~ostrstream();
        char* str();
        int pcount();
};

class   strstream
 : public strstreambase, public iostream
{
  public:
        strstream();
        strstream( char* str, int size, int mode );
        ~strstream();
        char* str();
};
```

C.5 Manipulators

A manipulator is an object, or an expression which yields an object, which, when inserted into a stream, affects that stream in some manner other than generating input and output.

C.5.1 Predefined manipulators. For more information on the predefined manipulators, see Secs. 10.9.1 and 10.9.4.

The predefined manipulators are:

```
ios& dec( ios& );                // Set base 10
ios& hex( ios& );                // Set base 16
ios& oct( ios& );                // Set base 8

ostream& endl( ostream& i );     // Insert a newline and flush
ostream& ends( ostream& i );     // Insert a null and flush
ostream& flush( ostream& );      // Force output to ultimate sink

istream& ws( istream& );         // Consume whitespace from input

SMANIP(int)     setbase( int b );        /* 10, 8, 16 or 0--0 on input
                                          * means 'guess from the input
                                          * stream.'
                                          */
SMANIP(long)  setiosflags( long b );  // Set and clear format flags in
SMANIP(long)  resetiosflags( long b );// the ios.
SMANIP(int)   setfill( int f );       // Set the fill character
```

```
SMANIP(int)   setprecision( int p );  // Set the precision
SMANIP(int)   setw( int w );          // Set a fixed field width--this
                                      //   setting is good for one
                                      //   output operation only.
```

C.5.2 Facilities for building manipulators. The full story on these can be found in Secs. 10.9.3 and 10.9.4.

```
/*
 *      Given a type T, create the names for manipulator and applier:
 */
SMANIP(T)     // General IOS manipulator   (This is a #define macro !)
SAPP(T)       //    "     IOS applier      (This is a #define macro !)
IMANIP(T      // istream manipulator       (This is a #define macro !)
OMANIP(T)     //    "     applier          (This is a #define macro !)
IOMANIP(T)    // ostream manipulato        (This is a #define macro !)
IAPP(T)       //    "     applier          (This is a #define macro !)
OAPP(T)       // iostream manipulato       (This is a #define macro !)
IOAPP(T       //    "     applier          (This is a #define macro !)

/*
 *      It's not enough to create the name; the class declarations
 *      must be generated; this generates the class declarations for
 *      a manipulator type.
 *
 *      After IOMANIPdeclare(int), declarations involving
 *      SMANIP(int), IMANIP(int), OMANIP(int), SAPP(int), IAPP(int),
 *      OAPP(int), and IOAPP(int) are legal.
 */

IOMANIPdeclare(T);        // A gadawful #define macro that declares the
                          //   classes named by the various MANIP and
                          //   APP macros.

/*
 *      Predeclared I/O manipulator names.
 */
IOMANIPdeclare( int );
IOMANIPdeclare( long );
```

Appendix

D

C++ Operators

This appendix summarizes the C++ operator syntax and semantics. For the full story, refer to the appropriate sections in the main text.

D.1 Uses of operators

Besides their role in expressions, operators are used in declarations in a 'declare-by-example' fashion:

```
type operator name ;
```

means that an expression of the form *operator name* has the type *type,* and the type of *name* is such as to make this so. For example,

```
int *ip;
```

means that `*ip` has the type `int` and `ip` must therefore have the type *pointer-to-*`int`. Functions are declared with declarations for their entire argument list; such a declaration is called a *prototype* and the ordered list of argument types is called the function's *signature*. (The forms in the first column of the following table shouldn't be read as strict grammar productions; they are simplified.)

Operators are also used for miscellaneous purposes:

~class-name	the destructor for the class *class-name*.
`operator` *operator* (*e.g.,* `operator +`)	the function which represents the overloaded operator *operator*.
`~const`	proposed declaration qualifier to indicate that a member of class, struct, or union is 'never-`const`,' even when the enclosing object is `const`.

`mutable`	alternate proposal's version of `~const`.
type declarator = expression *type declarator (expression-list)* *type declarator = { expression-list optional-comma }*	initialize the variable named in *declarator* using the value(s) of the expression(s).
type function-declarator = 0;	indicate that the member function declared by *function-declarator* is a pure virtual function.
`enum` *Ename* { *Enumerator-name, Enumerator-name = expression,* … … }	the = introduces a value that is assigned by the programmer for the enumerator's value.
`new [ ]` `delete [ ]`	indicates the array form of the operator.
`4.0e-3, 1.0e+12`	indicates the sign of the exponent part of the floating point constant.

D.2 Precedence and associativity

Here is a complete list of the C++ operators in order of decreasing precedence, and with their associativities. The number indicates the precedence and the letter the associativity. Higher numbers indicate higher precedence (tighter binding) and the numbers correspond to the grammar production key numbers in Sec. D.3.

Those operators which cannot be overloaded are so noted; so are the operators whose overloading is somehow 'special.'

Operator	Precedence and associativity	Built-in meaning	Notes
`::`	20 Left	Class scope qualifier *(when used as a binary operator)*	Cannot be overloaded
`::`	20	Global scope qualifier *(when used as a unary operator)*	Cannot be overloaded
`()`	20	Parentheses for grouping	Unary; cannot be overloaded
`[]`	19 Left	Subscripting	Binary; overloads as member functions only.
`()`	19 Left	Function call	Binary; RHS is the *list* of arguments. Overloads as member functions only.
`()`	19 Left	Type conversion in functional form ('value builder')	Binary; LHS is the type; RHS is the *list* of arguments. Constructors provide overloads; other member overloads are allowed.
`.`	19 Left	Member selection from object	Cannot be overloaded. (There are proposals for overloading `operator.`

			but they probably won't be accepted.)
`->`	19 Left	Member selection from pointed-at object.	Overloadable as member member function only.
`++`	19	Postfix increment (postincrement).	Unary; overload takes an 'unnecessary' argument.
`--`	19	Postfix decrement (postdecrement).	Unary; overload takes an 'unnecessary' argument.
`new`	18	New (memory allocator)	Unary or binary; nonassociative. First argument is type; second is list of argument expressions. When overloaded as a member, represented by a static member function.
`delete`	18	Delete (memory deallocator)	Unary; When overloaded as a member, represented by a static member function. Type is always `void`.
`sizeof`	17	Size of type or object	Unary; returns `size_t`. Cannot be overloaded.
`++`	17	Pre-increment	Unary
`--`	17	Pre-decrement	Unary
`~`	17	Bitwise complement	Unary
`!`	17	Logical NOT	Unary
`-`	17	Negative	Unary
`+`	17		Unary, + for symmetry with `-`. Built-in operator requires operand of arithmetic type; returns value and type of its operand.
`*`	17	Indirection (Unary)	Built-in operator requires pointer type. Complement of `&`.
`&`	17	Address-of (Unary)	Overloads hide the built-in operator for class, struct, or union types. Members can get pointer as `this`. If overloaded on an enum, the built-in operand is permanently hidden.
`()`	16	Type conversion by cast (prefix)	Binary. First operand is type; second is expression to be converted. Can be overloaded when the equivalent functional form conversion can be.
`.*`	15 Left	Selection of member from object using pointer-to-member on the RHS.	Cannot be overloaded. Should a proposal for overloading `.` be accepted, overloads of `.*` will probably be accepted as well.
`->*`	15 Left	Member selection from pointed-to object using pointer-to-member on the RHS.	Overloadable as a member function only.
`*`	14 Left	Multiplication (Binary)	

/	14 Left	Division	
%	14 Left	Remainder	
+	13 Left	Addition (Binary)	
-	13 Left	Subtraction (Binary)	
<<	12 Left	Left shift	LHS shifted left bitwise by RHS. Undefined if RHS is negative. (The stream I/O system overloads this operator heavily.)
>>	12 Left	Right shift	RHS shifted right bitwise by RHS. Undefined if RHS is negative. Shift is arithmetic for signed types, logical for unsigned. (The stream I/O system overloads this operator heavily.)
>	11 Left	Greater-than	
<	11 Left	Less-than	
>=	11 Left	Greater-than or equal to	
<=	11 Left	Less-than or equal to	
==	10 Left	Equality	Compares the operands; returns 1 if they are equal, zero otherwise.
!=	10 Left	Inequality	Compares the operands; returns zero if they are equal, 1 otherwise.
&	9 Left	Bitwise AND (Binary)	Built-in requires integral types; returns bit-by-bit AND of operands.
^	8 Left	Bitwise XOR	Built-in requires integral types; returns bit-by-bit exclusive-or of operands.
|	7 Left	Bitwise OR	Built-in requires integral types; returns bit-by-bit inclusive-or of operands.
&&	6 Left	Logical (short-circuit) AND	Short-circuit properties do not apply to overloads.
||	5 Left	Logical (short-circuit) OR	Short-circuit properties do not apply to overloads.
? :	4 Left	Conditional Expression (Ternary)	Cannot be overloaded. C++ permits a conditional to return an lvalue (C does not) and the grammar permits an assignment in both the 'then' and 'else' expressions (C's grammar does not).
throw	3 Right	Throw an exception	Unary or nonary. Cannot be overloaded. Optional expression provides the object to be thrown. Right-associative in the grammar, but returns void, so the associativity cannot actually be used.

<table>
<tr><td>=</td><td>2 Right</td><td>Assignment</td><td>Can be overloaded as a member only. The built-in assignment operators return a non-const lvalue (in C assignment returns a const rvalue).</td></tr>
<tr><td>/=</td><td>2 Right</td><td>Compound assignment: division</td><td>Can be overloaded only as a member only.</td></tr>
<tr><td>%=</td><td>2 Right</td><td>Compound assignment: remainder</td><td>Can be overloaded only as a member.</td></tr>
<tr><td>*=</td><td>2 Right</td><td>Compound assignment: multiplication</td><td>Can be overloaded only as a member.</td></tr>
<tr><td>+=</td><td>2 Right</td><td>Compound assignment: addition</td><td>Can be overloaded only as a member.</td></tr>
<tr><td>-=</td><td>2 Right</td><td>Compound assignment: subtraction</td><td>Can be overloaded only as a member.</td></tr>
<tr><td><<=</td><td>2 Right</td><td>Compound assignment: left shift</td><td>Can be overloaded only as a member.</td></tr>
<tr><td>>>=</td><td>2 Right</td><td>Compound assignment: right shift</td><td>Can be overloaded only as a member.</td></tr>
<tr><td>&=</td><td>2 Right</td><td>Compound assignment: bitwise AND</td><td>Can be overloaded only as a member.</td></tr>
<tr><td>|=</td><td>2 Right</td><td>Compound assignment: bitwise OR</td><td>Can be overloaded only as a member.</td></tr>
<tr><td>^=</td><td>2 Right</td><td>Compound assignment: bitwise XOR</td><td>Can be overloaded only as a member.</td></tr>
<tr><td>,</td><td>1 Left</td><td>Comma or voiding operator.</td><td>When overloaded, the strict left-to-right evaluation property is lost.</td></tr>
</table>

D.3 Expression grammar

This grammar is based on one of the grammars being used by ANSI x3j16/ISO WG21. That grammar is under consideration to describe the language in the ultimate Standard. The other grammar in use by that body contains excruciating disambiguation and is used to study the syntax of the language from the point of view of a parser.

The grammar is expressed in a form similar to the input language of the YACC parser-generator. The numbers in parentheses are the precedence numbers given in the previous section. The grammar is incomplete; the intention is to illustrate the operator syntax, and especially precedence and associativity, not to present a grammar suited for machine parsing.

literal:
  integer-literal
  character-literal
  floating-literal
  string-literal

id-expr:
identifier
operator-function-id
conversion-function-id
~class-name
qualified-id

qualified-id:
(20) nested-class-specifier : : id-expr

primary-expr:
literal
`this`
(20) : : identifier
(20) : : operator-function-id
(20) : : qualified-id
(20) (expression)
id-expr

expression-list:
assignment-expr
expression-list , assignment-expr

optional-expression-list:
empty
expression-list

postfix-expr:
primary-expr
(19) postfix-expr [expression]
(19) postfix-expr (optional-expression-list)
(19) simple-type-specifier (optional-expression-list)
(19) postfix-expr . id-expr
(19) postfix-expr -> id-expr
(19) postfix-expr ++
(19) postfix-expr --

delete-expr:
(18) delete cast-expr
(18) : : delete cast-expr
(18) delete [] cast-expr
(18) :: delete [] cast-expr

new-expr:
(18) `new` optional-placement new-type-id new-initializer*opt*
(18) : : `new` optional-placement new-type-id new-initializer*opt*
(18) `new` optional-placement (type-id) optional-new-initializer
(18) : : `new` optional-placement (type-id) optional-new-initializer

optional-placement:
null
(expression-list)

unary-expr:
postfix-expr
(17) ++ unary-expr
(17) -- unary-expr
(17) * cast-expr
(17) & cast-expr
(17) + cast-expr
(17) - cast-expr
(17) ! cast-expr
(17) ~ cast-expr
(17) `sizeof` unary-expr
(17) `sizeof` (type-id)
new-expr
delete-expr

cast-expr:
unary-expr
(16) (type-id) cast-expr

memptr-expr:
cast-expr
(15) memptr-expr .* cast-expr
(15) memptr-expr ->* cast-expr

multiplicative-expr:
memptr-expr
(14) multiplicative-expr * memptr-expr
(14) multiplicative-expr / memptr-expr
(14) multiplicative-expr % memptr-expr

additive-expr:
multiplicative-expr
(13) additive-expr + multiplicative-expr
(13) additive-expr - multiplicative-expr

shift-expr:
additive-expr
(12) shift-expr << additive-expr
(12) shift-expr >> additive-expr

relational-expr:
shift-expr
(11) relational-expr < shift-expr
(11) relational-expr > shift-expr

(11) relational-expr <= shift-expr
(11) relational-expr >= shift-expr

equality-expr:
relational-expr
(10) equality-expr == relational-expr
(10) equality-expr != relational-expr

and-expr:
equality-expr
(9) and-expr & equality-expr

exclusive-or-expr:
and-expr
(8) exclusive-or-expr ^ and-expr

inclusive-or-expr:
exclusive-or-expr
(7) inclusive-or-expr | exclusive-or-expr

logical-and-expr:
inclusive-or-expr
(6) logical-and-expr && inclusive-or-expr

logical-or-expr:
logical-and-expr
(5) logical-or-expr || logical-and-expr

conditional-expr:
logical-or-expr
(4) logical-or-expr ? expression : assignment-expr

throw-expr:
(3) `throw` assignment-expr
(3) `throw`

assignment-expr:
conditional-expr
(2) unary-expr = assignment-expr
(2) unary-expr *= assignment-expr
(2) unary-expr /= assignment-expr
(2) unary-expr %= assignment-expr
(2) unary-expr += assignment-expr
(2) unary-expr -= assignment-expr
(2) unary-expr >>= assignment-expr
(2) unary-expr <<= assignment-expr
(2) unary-expr &= assignment-expr
(2) unary-expr ^= assignment-expr
(2) unary-expr |= assignment-expr
throw-expr

expression:
assignment-expr
(1) expression , assignment-expr

D.4 A pocket guide for overloaders

Note that overloading per-enum is an anticipated feature of ANSI/ISO C++, but is not yet incorporated in the documents of x3j16/WG21 as of fall 1992.

20	::	Global scope (Unary) (Sec. 2.6.1)
20 Right	::	Class scope (Binary) (Sec. 1.5.1)

These operators are evaluated entirely at compile time; they identify the scope to which a name belongs. They cannot be overloaded. (C++ only)

20	( )	Parentheses for grouping

Parentheses are used as an infix 'grouping' operator as in most programming languages. *The presence of parentheses does not affect whether an expression is an lvalue:*

```
int i;

( i ) = 5;        /* Legal C, legal C++ */
```

Parentheses for grouping cannot be overloaded.

19 Left	.	Member selection (Binary) (Sec. A2.5.2)

Takes a class, struct, or union object on the left and a member name on the right. It cannot be overloaded. (C and C++) (There are incompatible proposals to permit it to be overloaded; see Sec. 5.3.1.)

19 Light	->	Member selection (Binary) (Sec. A2.5.2)

Takes a pointer-to-class object on the left and a member name on the right. (C and C++)

It can be overloaded, taking a class object on the left. The overload operator function must be a member of no arguments returning a pointer to another class type. The member on the right if then a member of that other class type. Just one overload is permitted per class, except that the operator may be overloaded on `const`:

```
class   C
{
        D* operator->();
        const D* operator->() const;
        ... ...
};
```

The operator can also be "chained"; if `Chaos` has a `Pandemonium operator->()`, we can write

```
Perdition      z;      // Has a  Chaos* operator->()

z->member_of_Chaos();

z->member_of_Pandemonium();    // z.(Chaos* Perdition::operator->)()->

                               // (Pandemonium* Chaos::operator->())
```

19 Left	`[]`	Subscripting (Binary) (Sec. A1.3.10, Sec. 5.1.3)

Left-hand argument is a pointer-to-X; inner argument is an integer; identically equivalent to

```
*(ptr_to_X + subscript)
```

Can be overloaded for a class on the LHS and an arbitrary type inside; must be a member function taking one argument of that arbitrary type. It may be repeatedly overloaded per class. (C and C++)

If unary `*` and `&` are provided for the class, the consistency of C++'s "address arithmetic" should probably be retained.

19 Left	`()`	Function call (N-ary where $N >= 1$) (Sec. A2.7, Sec. 5.1.1)

Takes a function as the LHS and an argument list of arbitrary length inside the parentheses as the RHS.

Can be overloaded for a class type as a member function, and can be repeatedly overloaded with arbitrary argument lists of arbitrary length.

(`operator()()`) Best used for a class with a single purpose, or to provide a functional syntax within expressions (e.g., substring specifiers on strings). (C and C++)

19 Left	( )	Type conversion (Constructor Value Building and functional form conversions.) (*N*-ary family, where *N* >= 1) (Sec. 3.3)

Invokes conversions which may be built-in or provided by constructors or member conversion operator functions. The latter may be considered an overload. (C++ only)

When `operator void*()` is used to provide a true-false value on the state of an object, common usage is to return `this` for true and 0 for false. See the note on !.

19 Right	++ –	Increment, decrement (Unary) (Sec. A1.3.1, Sec. 5.3.2)

These operators may be applied postfix or prefix. As postfix operators, they are overloaded with an 'extra' parameter of type `int`:

```
class   Arithmetick:
{
        ... ...
        const Arithmetick& operator++( int );    /* Postfix */
        const Arithmetick& operator--( int );    /* Postfix */
        const Arithmetick& operator++();         /* Prefix */
        const Arithmetick& operator--();         /* Prefix */
        ... ...
};
```

For each class, struct, union, or enum type there may be one prefix and one postfix overload of each operator. Prior to Release 3.0, there is no separate form for the postfix operator and the same operator function will be applied for either the prefix or postfix operator (but it will be applied before or after the value of the expression is taken, preserving the pre- or postcharacter of the operator). (C and C++)

18	`new`	Memory allocator (unary or binary) (Sec. 3.1.2, Sec. 5.5)
18	`new[]`	Memory allocator (unary, binary, or ternary) (Sec. 3.1.2, Sec. 5.5)
18	`delete`	Memory deallocator (unary) (Sec. 3.1.2, Sec. 5.5)
18	`delete[]`	Memory deallocator (unary) (Sec. 3.1.2, Sec. 5.5)

`new` allocates memory of a given type. It may also be given a list of arguments (*placement syntax,* Sec. 5.5.8) and a count of objects to be allocated (invoking `new []` instead of `new`). The `delete` operators delete memory; they are invoked explicitly. C++ makes a subtle distinction between "the new operator" and "operator new," and between "the delete operator" and "operator delete." The former in each pair is the operator invoked in code; the letter is a special function invoked to implement the operator. See Sec. 6.4.6 for implications of this distinction.

Separate versions of each of these operators may be provided for global scope and for each class. Moreover, each of the `new` operators may be overloaded in each of its scopes. The per-class operators are static members, but interact with virtualization (Sec. 6.4.6, Sec. 6.4.7). The separate forms for arrays are anticipated as part of the ANSI/ISO C++ standard, but are not yet approved as of fall 1992. (C++ only)

17	~	Bitwise complement (Unary)

May be applied to any integral type to get one's complement of the bit pattern as an integer/unsigned/char of the same type. The result is not an lvalue. May be overloaded once per class, struct, union, or enum type by a unary nonmember or a nonary member. (C and C++)

17	!	Logical NOT (Unary)

Yields an integer that is zero if the integral or floating type operand is nonzero, 1 otherwise. May be overloaded once per class type as a unary nonmember or a nonary member. For most purposes (i.e., whenever used to check the "truth" or usability of an object) it should return the effective complement of the `operator void*()` or `operator int()` that provides the primary true-false value. (C and C++)

17	+ -	Unary + and – (Unary)

May be applied to integral and floating types; the type of the result is the type of the operand. (Unsigned types are allowed.) Overloading (nonary member function or unary nonmember function) are allowed. (C and C++; unary + not in pre-ANSI C nor very early releases of C++.)

17	* &	Indirection and Address-Of (Unary) (Sec. 5.3.4) (Sec. A2.3)

Complementary operations; `<cp>` takes *pointer-to-X* and provides *X*; `<cp>` takes *X* and yields *pointer-to-X*. The address of an overloaded function may only be taken in a context (initialization or assignment) that uniquely determines which overload is taken. (See Sec. 5.3.4 for considerations when overloading.) (C and C++)

16	`()`	Type conversion (type casting) (Sec. A1.3.9, Sec. 3.3.4) (Unary) (Prefix)

Conversions can be defined for class, struct, and union types. See also Sec. 5.3.5. (C and C++)

15 Left	`->*` `.*`	Member selection-by-pointer (Binary) (Sec. 2.7.1) (Sec. 3.1)

The right-hand operand must be pointer-to-member for a class, an object of which type (for `.*`) or a pointer to which type (for `->*`) must be the left-hand operand. `->*` may be overloaded in the same way as `->`. If `->` is overloaded, it may be wise to overload `->*` as well. `.*` may not be overloaded, however some of the proposals for overloading `operator.()` would also permit overloading `operator.*()` as well. (C++ only; not available in very early releases.)

14 Left	`*` `/` `%`	Multiplicative ops (Binary) (Sec. A1.3.2)

May be applied to integral or floating point operands (`%` may be applied to integral types only). The result is promoted or converted to retain range and precision. They may be overloaded as unary members or binary nonmembers. (C and C++)

13 Left	`*` `-`	Additive ops (Binary) (Sec. A1.3.2)

May be applied to integral or floating point operands. The result is promoted or converted to retain range and precision. They may be overloaded as unary member or binary nonmembers. (C and C++)

12 Left	`<<` `>>`	Shift ops (Binary) (Sec. A1.3.3) (Chap. 10)

May be applied to integral types. The result has the type of the LHS after promotion. The left-shift zero-fills; the right-shift zero-fills if the

Appendix

F

C++ Field Guide (Statement Syntax Summary)

Here is a rough-and-ready summary of C++'s statement syntax. It has a short index, shared with Appendix D, listing keywords, operators, and other symbols with the Appendix entries describing their use.

This field guide is provided in preference to a full grammar: grammars for C++ tend to be extremely large and unwieldly, less usable to the ordinary programmer as they are more nearly complete. Also, this format allows the reader to identify an unfamiliar construct with just a keyword or symbol.

F.1 Statement types

C++ statements can be divided loosely into

Object Declaration Statements—which introduce new objects into the program

Expression Statements—which contain an expression whose side effects (function call, assignment, etc.) are the effects of the statement

Flow-Control Statements—including grouping, empty statement, conditional (alternation), looping, multiway branch, three ways of stopping what you are doing, and general branching

Type Declaration Statements—whereby new type names and new types are introduced into the program

Function Definitions—which provide the program's executable code

Templates—which provide generic types and generic functions

Preprocessor Directives—not statements proper, but seen with them

Namespace Management—a new feature whose description is tentative, it divides a program's namespace along boundaries of module, library, or whatever, to prevent accidental name clashes and to provide flexibility in interchanging parts

Constants—Part of expression syntax, but convenient to summarize here

Linkage Directives—which allow the linking of C++ code with C code (and potentially with code in other programming languages as well)

F.2 Object declaration statements

C and C++ permit the declaration of objects (variables and 'constant objects' that resemble unchangeable variables), functions, types, and templates. The declaration of types is discussed in Sec. F.5, of templates in Sec. F.7.

An object or function is declared to have a given *type*. Some types have names; these may be built-in (`int, char`) or defined by the program.

F.2.1 Basic declarations. An object whose type has a name is declared in a statement that begins with the type and that lists one or more objects:

```
int i;
char seperator, end_mark;
double sum_squared, sum_of_squares;
dyn_array< unsigned > ua;
```

The last of these forms uses a *template* (`dyn_array`) with a parameter (`unsigned`) as the type name. Templates are described in Sec. F.7.

F.2.2 Built-in types. These are the names of the built-in types:

```
int             char                 float
long int        signed char          double
short int       unsigned char        long double
unsigned int    unsigned long int    unsigned short int
```

When the word `int` occurs with another word, the `int` may be omitted. For these types names, the words may appear in any order, thus `unsigned long` and `long unsigned` mean the same.

These types are not 'built-in' but are nevertheless predefined in Standard C and Standard C++:

```
size_t  wchar_t
```

In C they are simply synonyms for other types (`size_t`: Sec. A.3.2, `wchar_t`: Sec. A.1.1.6). In Standard C++, it is possible to overload on the difference between `wchar_t` and the type for which it is a 'synonym.'

Other words may appear with the type names; see Sec. F2.8 on storage classes and Secs. A.1.1.7, A.2.3.3 A.2.7 on `const` and `volatile`.

F.2.3 Nonbasic types. Not all types have names. Many types can be 'derived' from other types. For a type *X* there might be *arrays* of *X*, *pointers* to *X*, *functions* whose type includes *X*, and others.

C and C++ declare these 'nameless' types 'by example.' If `ip` is a pointer-to-`int`, then `*ip` is the `int` at which it points ('*' is the indirection or 'points-at' operator). `ip` would be declared like this:

```
int* ip;  // *ip is an int , so ip must be a pointer-to-int.
```

Likewise, an array of `double` is declared like this:

```
double coefficients[ 15 ];     // An array-of-double named
                               //   coefficients whose valid
                               //   indices are 0 through
                               //   ( 15 - 1 ), inclusive
```

The syntax allows one declaration to declare multiple variables:

```
int * ip, ** jp, *** kp;      // Pointer-to-int, pointer-to-
                              //  pointer-to-int, and pointer-
                              //  to-pointer-to-pointer-to-int.
```

The syntax of a declaration calls for type and storage class to be followed by a list of 'declarators.' Here, `*ip`, `***kp`, and `coefficients[ 15 ]` are declarators. See the caution in Sec. 1.1.8 about this construction!

F.2.4 References. *References* are nameless types whose declarator is marked by an ampersand:

```
int i;
int& ir = i;
```

A reference variable is not accessed using the ampersand. Instead, the name declared becomes an alias for its initializer (here, `i`). References are often used as function parameters (Sec. 1.2.4).

F.2.5 Initializers. An object (e.g., variable) declaration may initialize the variable. There are three syntaxes:

The expression assigns the value of the constant to `d`, then assigns the value of `d` to `j`, converting it to `int` in the process. Then it assigns the value of `j` (2) to `i`.

(In C, the type of the LHS is qualified by 'const,' so that you cannot twice assign to one variable in a single assignment expression.)

For user-defined types, assignment may be overloaded and many of its properties can be changed (Sec. 4.5).

F.3.3 Assignment, compound. C++ and C support 10 'compound' assignment operators; these combine assignment with some other operation. In general, a token made up of an equal sign followed by a binary arithmetic, shift, or bitwise operator is a compound assignment operator.

These two expression statements have the same effect:

```
int i = 0;

i = i + 5;
i += 5;
```

Each of the two assignments adds five to `i` and returns `i` as its result.

If the evaluation of the common LHS expression has a side effect, the two expressions will differ in how often it occurs:

```
int ai[ 24 ];
int f();
... ...

ai[ f() ] = ai[ f() ] + 5;      // f() is invoked twice.
ai[ f() ] += 5;  // f() is invoked only once.
```

The full set of compound assignment operators is

```
+=  -=      *=  /=  %=
<<=  >>=     &=  |=  ^=
```

Compound assignment operators are used both for notational power and for their control of LHS side effects. Where they are the 'right thing for the job' they may also help a naive compiler in generating code. For increment and decrement by one, see also Sec. F.3.4.

F.3.4 Increment and decrement operators. The ++ and -- operators are *increment* and *decrement* operators, respectively. They may be applied to integral and pointer types, and to such class types for which they have been defined (Sec. 5.3.2). They may be applied as prefix operators representing *pre*increment/*pre*decrement, or as postfix operators representing *post*increment/*post*decrement:

```
++1;    // Preincrement
--j;    // Predecrement
j = i++;      // Postincrement i; the value used in the
              //   assignment is the value before the increment.
i = j--;      // Postdecrement j; the value used in the
              //   assignment is the value before the increment.
```

F.3.5 Function call. C and C++ do not distinguish between functions and 'procedures' or 'subroutines.' Any function may be called for its side effects in an expression statement. Functions which have no useful return value should return void (Sec. A.1.1.4).

```
int
main()
{
        do_init();
        do_setup();
        do_part0();
        do_part1();
        do_part2();
        do_output();
        do_cleanup();

        return 0;
}
```

F.3.6 `throw`. An exception is thrown using the `throw` operator, which accepts an argument of any type and returns `void`:

```
if( n_states == 0 )
        throw Dfd_err( "Empty machine" );
```

The `throw` expression terminates the flow of control at this location and resumes it somewhere else, or nowhere. (It is just possible that future versions of C++ will support 'resumable' exceptions, in which instance control will flow through the `throw` expression.)

If the expression is omitted from the `throw`, the most recently caught expression will be rethrown.

F.3.7 Using conditional and short-circuit operators. Sec. A.1.3.6 describes three C++ operators that affect flow of control: the binary `&&` and `||` and the ternary (3-operand) conditional operator `? :` . These too may be used in expression statements. Often, another idiom will be better, but sometimes not:

```
   beeper->coax( "'Scuse me" )
|| beeper->cajole( "Hello there?" )
|| beeper->bug( "Earth to Object ..." )
|| beeper->nag( "Wake uuuuu-uup!" )
|| beeper->badger( "You got ears, there?" )
|| beeper->pester( "Hey, lissenup!" )
|| beeper->get_seriously_on_my_case( "Yo! Jack!" );
```

F.4 Flow-of-control

C++ and C provide the basic primitives for flow-of-control and additional controls for 'natural' structure. With C++'s expression syntax, they can reduce the depth of nesting in loops and eliminate loop control flags.

F.4.1 Grouping. An arbitrary set of statements may be gathered together and treated (from the outside) as one; this is called a *compound statement* (if it does not contain declarations) or a *block* (if it does):

```
{
        /*
         *      A brace-enclosed ...
         */
        ...list of arbitrary statements ...
}
```

The list may be empty, providing an alternate form of null statement (Sec. A.1.2.3):

```
{ }
```

A block is also a scope; declarations that appear within it go out of scope at its end, and hide declarations of the same name that lie without it.

F.4.2 Branching. C and C++ provide an `if` statement and an optional `else` part for it.

```
if( expression )
        statement

if( expression )
        statement-1
```

```
else
        statement-2
```

If the *expression* evaluates to 'true' (nonzero or nonnull), the (first) *statement* is executed; otherwise the *statement* belonging to the `else` (if any) is executed.

F.4.3 Looping. C++ and C provide two 'test-at-the-top' loops and one 'test-at-the-bottom' loop (Sec. A.1.2).

```
while( expression )      // Evaluate the expression, and if it
        statement        //   is true, execute the statement
                         //   and try the expression again.
for( init_stmt test_expression ; increment_expr )
        statement
```

In the `for(;;)` statement, the *init_stmt* is executed. Then the *test_expression* is evaluated; if true, the subordinate *statement* is executed and the *increment_expr* evaluated. Then the *test_expression* is tried again. See Sec. A.1.2 for restrictions on *init_sttmt.*

```
do                       // Test-at-the-bottom:
        statement        //   Execute the statement, then
while( expression )      //   evaluate the expression.  If
                         //   it evaluates true, go back to
                         //   the statement again.
```

The subordinate statement may be a compound statement or block.

F.4.4 The semicolon-as-null statement. A semicolon is a valid statement; it is the *null* statement (Sec. A.1.2.3), which has no effect but is useful as a placeholder.

F.4.5 Selection: the `switch/case-default`. The `switch` statement (Sec. A.1.4) performs a multiway branch on a single expression of integral or enumerated type:

```
switch( integral or enum expression )
{
  … A (compound) statement containing case & default labels …
        case constant-expression:
                … statements …
        case constant-expression:
                … statements …
        default:
                … statements …
}
```

There may be at most one `default:` label; there need not be any and it may be placed anywhere in the body of the `switch`. See Secs. F.4.6 and F.4.8.

`case` and `default` act like labels; control falls through them from above. (They can be grouped within inner blocks; see Sec. B.3 on Duff's Device.)

F.4.6 Loop and switch control: `break` **and** `continue`. The *break statement* immediately exits the smallest enclosing loop statement or `switch`. The *continue statement* terminates the body of the smallest enclosing loop and restarts the loop's increment (`for(;;)`) or test (`while()` and `do-while()`).

```
break;
... ...
continue;
```

F.4.7 Labels and `goto`. An identifier followed by a colon is a label statement, and declares the identifier as a label. Any label in the current function may be used as the target of a `goto` statement (subject to restrictions in Sec. F.4.8):

```
void
f()
{
        goto lab2;
  lab1:
          ... ...
        goto lab1;
  lab2:
}
```

F.4.8 Branches into scope. C++ disallows any branch *into* an object's scope. This affects `case` and `default` labels, as well as ordinary labels.

F.4.9 `return` **statement.** The `return` statement returns from the current function and provides the function's return value. In a function returning `void`, the *expression* is omitted:

```
return expression ;     // In a non- void function
return;                 // In a function returning void .
```

A function may have multiple `return` statements. A function returning `void` may return by 'falling off the end.'

F.4.10 `try` **and** `catch`. An exception within the `try`'s compound statement causes that statement to be abandoned. The exception is compared with the types in the *handlers* ('catch' clauses) of the try. If one of them matches the exception, it is executed; execution then resumes after the try-catch statement. See Chap. 9.

```
try
{
        ... statements ...
}
  catch( exception type )
  {
        ... statements ...
  }
catch( exception type )
  {
        ... statements ...
  }
```

F.5 Type declarations

Type declarations introduce enumerations, classes, structs, unions, and synonyms (by typedef).

F.5.1 typedef. The typedef (Sec. A.2.2.4) declares a synonym for a type. An otherwise ordinary declaration is written, then prefixed with typedef. Instead of declaring variables of the type, pointers to the type, etc., the statement declares synonyms for those types:

```
typedef int int_type, *ptr_to_int_type;
typedef double array_3_type[ 3 ], fn_returning_dbl();
```

F.5.2 enum. The enum declares a type with a set of named constants that behave like an integral type (Sec. A.1.5):

```
enum thataway { north, south, east, west, no_way = -1 };
```

the "= -1" overrides the value assigned by default.

F.5.3 struct, class, **and** union. struct (Sec. A.2.5), class (Sec. 1.5), and union (Sec. A.2.6) types gather named *members* into one unit. Members may be either data (Sec. A.2.5) or functions (Sec. 1.5.2):

```
struct  A_struct
{
        int i;
        A_struct* a_function();
};
```

```
class  A_class
{
  public:
       A_class* a_function();
       A_class( const A_class& );
       ~A_class();

  private:
       int i;
};

union A_union      // The type name may sometimes be
{                  //   omitted; see the text.
       int i;
       double d;
       void* vp ~const; // ~const may be renamed mutable
};
```

A member function whose name is the name of the struct, class, or union is a *constructor* (Sec. 2.1); a member function whose name is a tilde (~) followed by the name of class, struct, or union is a *destructor* (Sec. 2.1).

The labels `public`, `private`, and `protected` determine what code may access the members (Secs. 1.5.3 and 6.2.3.2).

A declaration within a class, struct, or union may begin with `friend` (Sec. 3.6) or `static` (Sec. 2.6.2).

The `~const` indicates that this member is not to be `const` even when it belongs to an object declared `const` (Sec. 3.1.4.5).

The tokens `::*` , `.*` , and `->*` are used with *pointer-to-member* (Sec. 2.7.1).

It is possible to declare objects of a class, struct, or union type in the same declaration as the type:

```
class  B_class       // class, or struct, or union ...
{
       ... ...
}  one_b, two_b, *ptr_to_b;
```

Under some circumstances, a union may be declared without either a type name or an object name; see Sec. 2.3.4 on *anonymous unions*.

F.5.4 Derived `class`es and `struct`s. A class or struct may be *derived* from an existing struct or class (Sec. 6.2):

```
class  Derived       // 'derived' class or struct
  : public Base      // existing 'base' class or struct
{
       ... ...
```

```
        virtual int abc( int );          // Virtual function
        virtual void def() = 0;          // Pure virtual function
        ... ...
};
```

The derived class *inherits* the members of its base class and adds its own (Sec. 6.3). When inheritance is used, either the derived or base class may declare functions `virtual` (Sec. 6.4) and *pure virtual* (Sec. 6.4.3).

The base class name is preceded (optionally) by one of `public`, `private`, or `protected` (Sec. 6.2.3).

Multiple base classes are allowed in a comma-separated list (Sec. 7.1.1):

```
class   Mult_derived
   : public Base1, private Base2, public virtual Base3
{
        ... ...
};
```

In this case the derived class inherits from all the base classes. Each base class is qualified separately. A base class may be designated "`virtual`" (Sec. 7.2).

F.6 Function definitions

In C and C++, all executable code belongs to one function or another. There is no separate construct for subroutine or procedure; a function can be called out of an expression statement and may return void.

F.6.1 Basic functions. A function is 'ordinarily' written in external scope. It has a header and a body. The body is a compound statement or block (Sec. 1.1.6). For the passing of parameters, see Secs. 1.1.7 and 1.2.4.

```
int                                     // Type of value returned
my_func( int i1, int i2, int* i3p )    // Parameters and their types
{                                       // Function body
        i1 += i2;
        if( i3p )
                i1 *= *i3p;

        return i1;                     // Return statement returns value.
}
```

F.6.2 Refinements to functions. A function may be declared *inline,* either by preceding its return type with the keyword `inline` or as described in Sec. F.6.3. This asks the compiler to expand it inline instead of calling it Sec. 2.4.4. The keyword '`inline`' is syntactically a *storage class,* like `static` (Sec. A.2.2.1.3).

A parameter that will be accepted but not used should be written as a type without a variable (Sec. 2.4.2).

A trailing parameter may be allowed to *default;* when the function is called it need not be written; the default value will be used instead (Sec. 2.4.1).

```
inline int                                  // Request to expand the
                                            // function inline
your_func( char, int i1, int i2 = 1 )       // First argument will
                                            // not be used,
{                                           // third argument
                                            // defaults to 1
        return ( i1 - 1 ) * ( i2 + 1 );
}
```

When a variable argument list must be used, at least the first argument must have a known type; trailing arguments are declared using the ellipsis ('...') (Sec. 2.4.3) and accessed using the `stdargs` mechanism (Sec. A.2.1).

C++ functions may be *overloaded* (Sec. 4.1, Sec. 4.2). In very old versions of C++, overloaded functions must be distinguished by the obsolete `overload` keyword.

An *exception specification* using the keyword `throw` declares the exceptions which the function may be expected to throw (Sec. 9.3):

```
Oomph&
biff_pow() throw( Bam, Wham, Socko )    // May throw Bam, Wham, Socko
{ ... ... }

void
innocuous() throw()                     // Mayn't throw anything at all
{ ... ... }

void
abandoned( int, void* )                 // May throw anything at all
{ ... ... }
```

F.6.3 Member functions and class header inlines. The name of a class member includes the name of the class, using a syntax called *qualification* (Sec. 1.5.1):

```
int
John::johns_func( int i1, int i2 )
{
        ... ...
```

The full type of a member function is also qualified (Sec. 1.5.1); in this example,

```
int John:: ( int, int ).
```

A member function may be made inline by writing it inside the class declaration (*class header*) (Sec. 2.4.1):

```
class  John
{
  public:
      void johns_other_func( char c ) const
      {
              ... ...
      }
      ... ...
};
```

See Sec. 1.5.2.4 for the meaning of the trailing `const` on the member function declaration or definition.

A friend function of a class may be written inline in the same way (Sec. 3.6.2).

A class defines a *scope* within which its member functions lie (Sec. 1.5.2.1); within that scope `this` is the name of a predefined pointer to the class object itself (Sec. 1.5.2.3).

F.6.4 Constructors and destructors. When a class object is created, a *constructor* for the class is invoked (if the class has any) to initialize the class object; when a class object is deleted, the class's destructor (if there is one) is called to dismantle it.

Constructors and destructors are named after the class:

```
class  Lively
{
       ... ...
       Lively();                  // A default constructor
       Lively( int );
       Lively( const Lively& );   // A copy constructor
       ~Lively();                 // The destructor.
       ... ...
       int mem;
       char ber;
};
  ... ...
Lively::Lively()                  // No return type on a
                                  // constructor or destructor
```

```
    : mem( 0 ), ber( '=' )          // syntax for initializing
                                    // member data
  {                                 // (Sec. 2.1.6) and base
                                    // classes (Sec. 6.2.4.1)
      ... ...
```

C++ can create default and copy constructors automatically (Secs. 2.1.7, 2.1.8, and 6.4.5). The copy constructor is invoked implicitly (Sec. 2.1.3).

Parameters to constructors are written in declarations (Sec. 2.1.2) and new expressions (Sec. 3.1.2):

```
Lively el( 17 );
Lively* elpea = new Lively( el );
```

Constructors of one argument can be invoked implicitly as conversions (Sec. 3.3.3).

F.6.5 Operator functions. The keyword `operator` followed by a C++ operator is a synonym for that operator and can be used to declare and define overloads for that operator (Sec. 4.4):

```
complex operator+( const complex&, const complex& );

Square_peg::operator Round_class() const
{
      ... ...
```

The second form declares an *operator conversion* which may be invoked explicitly or implicitly (Sec. 3.3.5).

F.7 Templates

A *template* (Chap. 8) is a parameterized type (*class template*) or function (*function template*). A *template specialization* (*template class* or *template function*) is created by combining the templates with the appropriate parameters. Template functions interact with overloading (Chaps. 4 and 5). The new conversion operators use template syntax, and so are discussed here.

F.7.1 Template syntax. A template declaration consists of the keyword `template`, an argument list, and a class or function declaration:

```
template< template parameter list >
class-or-function-definition
```

```
template< class T, size_t array_len >  //  'class T' makes T a typename
class  Flex_array                      //  within the Flex_array class
{                                      //  template; it can be a class
       ... ...                         //  or a built-in type.  array_len
                                       //  names a constant within the
                                       //  Flex_array class template; it
                                       //  may take on a new value for
                                       //  each instance created.

template< class M >                    //  M is a typename within the
const M&                               //  function template  max()
max( const M& m1, const M& m2 )
{
       return m1 >= m2 ? m1 : m2;
}
```

The member functions of a class template are function templates (Sec. 8.2.4):

```
template< class T, size_t array_len >
Flex_array::Flex_array()
{
       ... ...
```

For a nonmember function template, all parameters must affect the parameter list of the function, since the parameter list of the function provides the types by which parameters are inferred when a specialization of the template is chosen.

F.7.2 Template specialization. A template class (class template specialization) is created explicitly by writing the parameter list after the template name:

```
typedef Flex_array< int, 10 > a10_int;
Flex_array< const char*, 600 > names;
```

Template functions may be specialized explicitly or implicitly (Sec. 8.2.6).

A 'special version' of any template function may be created explicitly, instead of allowing the template function to be specialized:

```
Flex_array< void*, 64 >::Flex_array()   //  Bypass the template expansion
  : ... ...                             //  and define the < void*, 64 >
{                                       //  version of Flex_array .
```

Static member data may be initialized by default or by creating "initializer templates" for them:

```
size_t Flex_array< void*, 64 >::count = BIAS;
```

F.7.3 New conversion operators. C-style casts can have different semantics depending on details of the types (Sec. 3.4.2); this is dangerous. C++ borrows template syntax to provide more specific conversions:

```
/*
 *      T_A and T_B are defined as types
 */
T_B b;
static_cast< T_A >( b )           // Convert using the static type system;
                                  //   an error if no static conversion
                                  //   is possible.
dynamic_cast< T_A& >( b )         // Convert using RTTI (Sec. 7.1.4) if
                                  //   possible, run-time error (Sec. 7.1.4)
                                  //   otherwise.
reinterpret_cast< void* >( &b )   // Reinterpret the bit-pattern of &b as
                                  //   a void* value
const T_B cb = ... ... ;
const_cast< T_B& >( cb )          // Provide a reference-to-non-const
                                  //   that refers to  cb .
```

F.8 Preprocessor directives

The full story on the preprocessor may be found in App. A, Sec. A.3. The directives are written like this:

```
#define X 1                     // Define a symbol.
#define XX( Y ) ( (Y) + 1 )     // Define a macro.
#include "my_header"            // Include a file in the text stream ...
                                //   ... using a 'local' name
#include <official_header>      //   ... using a file from a 'standard place'

#if X                           // Conditional compilation; ignore following
                                //   text if  X  doesn't evaluate non-zero.
#else                           // Begin optional else-part of #if
#endif                          // End conditional compilation.

#ifdef X                        // Synonym for #if defined( X )

#error "This little piggy ..." // Emit the string and fail the compile.

        #S      Unary 'stringizing' operator -- becomes "S" .
        T ## U  Binary catenation operator -- becomes TU .

        %%      Alternate symbol for # to the preprocessor
        %%%%    Alternate symbol for ## to the preprocessor
```

F.9 Namespace management

(This section is based on a preliminary proposal for Namespace Management, current as of 6/93. *This description is tentative.* Consult your language reference manual for the exact story.)

Namespace management is designed to fend off name conflicts when assembling systems from separately designed and coded parts, and especially from libraries received from various, independent sources.

F.9.1 Namespaces. A program may declare *namespaces:*

```
namespace Joes_Lib
{
        … external declarations and definitions for Joe's library …
}

namespace Nances_Lib
{
        … external declarations and definitions for Nance's library …
}

namespace Joes_Lib
{
        … MORE external decls and defins for Joe's library …
}
```

Each namespace has access automatically to itself and to the global namespace. Anything which could be written externally can be written in one of these namespaces.

Code anywhere can access any type, template, or object defined in another namespace by qualifying the name with the namespace's name:

```
typedef Nances_Lib::Final_template< Joes_Lib::First_class >
                                        Final_first;
```

F.9.2 `using` **declaration.** Code anywhere can gain *un*qualified access to any type, template, or object defined in another namespace with a `using` *declaration:*

```
using Joes_Lib::First_class;
using Nances_Lib::Final_template;

typedef Final_template< First_class > Final_first;
```

F.9.3 `using` **directive.** Code anywhere can make the contents of another namespace visible with a `using` *directive:*

```
using Joes_Lib;
using Nances_Lib;

typedef Final_template< First_class > Final_first;
```

It is possible for a given name to appear in several namespaces; if they are all made visible by `using` directives, the version of the name in the current namespace, if any, is preferred. Otherwise the name is ambiguous. The ambiguity may be overridden with an explicit, specific `using` declaration for the name.

The `using` declaration and directive work differently. The declaration places an alias for the name among the symbols currently available in the current scope. The directive adds the namespace to the list of places to look for symbols if they are not found in the current scope.

F.9.4 Namespace renaming. A namespace may be given an alias (typically a short alias for a long one) by *namespace renaming:*

```
namespace USLT = James_Whittaker_Theobald_Throckmorton_ ##
                 Anderson_Bakersfields_Universal_ ##
                 Great_Jones_Street_Software_Library_and_Toolbox;
```

This can serve two purposes: as a kind of 'typedef' on implementations of the same library and to shorten long names, which may incorporate trademarks, company names, etc., to reduce the likelihood of clashes. (A name which must be split to keep it between the margins, then spliced by preprocessor catenation, is too long to write often in a program!)

F.9.5 Classes and inheritance. Under one version of the namespace proposal, the properties of namespaces would be implicit in classes. Inheritance would, by definition, have the effect of a `using` directive, and ambiguities or overrides of inherited names could be effected by a `using` declaration of those names.

F.10 Constants

Constants are expression syntax, not statement syntax, but this is a convenient place to list them. A full explanation can be found in Sec. A.1.1.7.

F.10.1 Integral constants

	Signed	Unsigned	Long	Unsigned Long
Decimal	10	10U 10u	10L 10l	10UL 10LU 10ul 10lu 10Ul 10Lu, etc.
Octal	012	012U 012u	012L 012l	012UL 012LU 012ul 012lu 012Ul 012Lu, etc.
Hexadecimal	0xa 0xA 0Xa 0XA	0xaU 0xAU 0XaU 0XAU	0xal 0xAL etc.	0xaUL 0xaLU

F.10.2 Character constants. Note that in C, these have either signed or unsigned integral type; in C++ their type is `char`.

Character constant	`'a'`
Character constants with an escape sequence	`'\n' '\a' '\\'`
Octal character constant	`'\012' (up to three 'octal digits' (octits?))`
Hexadecimal character constant	`'\x00a' (up to three 'hex digits' (hexits?))`

F.10.3 Floating point constants

Double	Float	Long Double
1.	1.f 1.F	1.l 1.L
1.0	1.0f 1.0F	1.0l 1.0L
.10	.10f .10F	.10l .10L
1e0	1e0f 1e0F	1e0l 1e0L
1e+0	1e+0f 1e+0F	1e+0l 1e+0L
1e-0	1e-0f 1e-0F	1e-0l 1e-0L
1e+03	1e+03f 1e+03F	1e+03l 1e+03L
1.e0	1.e0f 1.e0F	1.e0l 1.e0L
1.e+0	1.e+0f 1.e+0F	1.e+0l 1.e+0L
1.e-0	1.e-0f 1.e-0F	1.e-0l 1.e-0L
1.e+03	1.e+03f 1.e+03F	1.e+03l 1.e+03L
	etc.	

F.10.4 String (literal) constants. These have type `const char*`.

```
"abcde"          // String literal
"abcde\n"        // String literal with escape for newline
"abcde\012"      // String literal with octal escape
"abcde\x0A"      // String literal with hexadecimal escape
```

F.10.5 Wide chars and strings. These deal with `wchar_t` instead of `char`, and `const wchar_t*` instead of `const char*`.

```
L'a'   L'\n'    // Escape sequences, etc., are defined by
L"abcde\xA0B"   // the implementation and the environment.
```

F.11 Linkage specification

A C++ program can be linked with functions written in C and compiled in the local environment (Sec. 4.2.2). Such functions must be marked for C linkage conventions:

```
extern "C" int printf( const char*, ... );

extern "C" {
#include "local_clib.h"
}
```

Linkage declarations can be nested, and C++ linkage can be declared:

```
extern "C" {
        ... ...
  extern "C++" {
        ... ...
  }
        ... ...
}
```

An implementation may support linkage with other languages; the language's name should be spelled in its 'preferred' spelling, thus `"Pascal"` but `"LISP"`.

F.12 Short index to Apps. A and F C++'s various keywords, operators, and symbols are listed with the sections in Apps. A and F in which their uses are described or illustrated.

`!`	Logical NOT (Unary) (Sec. A.1.3.2)
`!=`	Inequality (Binary) (Sec. A.1.3.2)
`"`	And Include of Local File (Sec. F.8)
`"`	And String Constants (Sec. F.10.4)
`"`	In Linkage Specification (Sec. F.11)
`#`	Preprocessor Unary 'Stringizing' Operator (Sec. F.8)
`##`	Preprocessor Catenation Operator (Sec. F.8)
`#define`	Of Macro (Sec. F.8)
`#define`	Of Symbol (Sec. F.8)
`#else`	Conditional Compilation (Sec. F.8)
`#endif`	Conditional Compilation (Sec. F.8)
`#error`	(Sec. F.8)
`#if`	Conditional Compilation (Sec. F.8)
`#ifdef`	Conditional Compilation (Sec. F.8)
`#include`	Of File From 'Standard Place' (Sec. F.8)
`#include`	Of Local File (Sec. F.8)
`%`	Multiplicative ops (Binary) (Sec. A.1.3.2)
`%%`	Preprocessor Unary 'Stringizing' Operator—Alternate Form (Sec. F.8)
`%%%%`	Preprocessor Catenation Operator—Alternate Form (Sec. F.8)
`%=`	Assignment operators (Binary) (Sec. A.1.3.7, Sec. 4.5)
`&`	Address-Of (Unary) (Sec. A.2.3, Sec. 5.3.4)

&	Bitwise AND (Binary) (Sec. A.1.3.5)
&	Declaring references (Sec. F.2.4)
&&	Conditional and Short-Circuit Operators in Expression Statement (Sec. F.3.7)
&=	Assignment operators (Binary) (Sec. A.1.3.7, Sec. 4.5)
'	And Character Constants (Sec. F.10.2)
( )	Function call (N-ary where N ≥ 1) (Sec. A.2.7, Sec. 5.1.1)
( )	Parentheses for grouping
( )	Type conversion (functional form) (Sec. 3.3.1)
( )	Type conversion (type casting) (Sec. A.1.3.9, Sec. 3.3.4) (Unary) (Prefix)
)	( ) Function call (*N*-ary where *N* ≥ 1) (Sec. A.2.7, Sec. 5.1.1)
)	( ) Parentheses for grouping
)	( ) Type conversion (functional form) (Sec. 3.3.4)
)	( ) Type conversion (type casting) (Sec. A.1.3.9, Sec. 3.3.4) (Unary) (Prefix)
*	Declaring pointers (Sec. F.2.3)
*	Indirection (Unary) (Sec. A.2.3, Sec. 5.3.4)
*	Multiplicative ops (Binary) (Sec. A.1.3.2)
*=	Assignment operators (Binary) (Sec. A.1.3.7, Sec. 4.5)
+	Addition ops (Binary) (Sec. A.1.3.2)
+	In Floating Point Constants (Sec. F.10.3)
+	Unary + (Unary) (Sec. A.1.3.2)
++	Increment (Unary) (Sec. A.1.3.1, Sec. 5.3.2)
+=	Assignment operators (Binary) (Sec. A.1.3.7, Sec. 4.5)
,	Comma (voiding) operator (Binary) (Sec. A.1.3.8)
−	In Floating Point Constants (Sec. F.10.3)
−	Subtraction ops (Binary) (Sec. A.1.3.2)
−	Unary – (Unary) (Sec. A.1.3.2)
−−	Decrement (Unary) (Sec. A.1.3.1, Sec. 5.3.2)
-=	Assignment operators (Binary) (Sec. A.1.3.7, Sec. 4.5)
->	Member selection (Binary) (Sec. A.2.5.2)
->*	And pointer-to-member (Sec. F.5.3)
.	Member selection (Binary) (Sec. A.2.5.2)
.*	And pointer-to-member (Sec. F.5.3)
...	And Variable Parameter Lists (Sec. F.6.2)
/	Multiplicative ops (Binary) (Sec. A.1.3.2)

/=	Assignment operators (Binary) (Sec. A.1.3.7, Sec. 4.5)
0-9	Constants (Sec. F.10)
:	And Label for Goto Statement (Sec. F.4.7)
:	And Member/Base Initializer List in Constructors (Sec. F.6.4)
:	In Access Declarations (Sec. F.5.3)
:	In case or default label in switch() Statement (Sec. F.4.5)
:	In Declaring Derived Classes and Structs (Sec. F.5.4)
::	Class scope (Binary) (Sec. 1.5.1)
::	Global scope (Unary) (Sec. 2.6.1)
::	In Defining Member Functions (Sec. F.6.3)
::	Static Class Member Initializers (Sec. F.2.7)
::*	And pointer-to-member (Sec. F.5.3)
;	As Null Statement (Sec. F.4.4)
;	In Expression Statement (Sec. F.3)
<	Less-than (Binary) (Sec. A.1.3.4)
< >	Include of File From 'Standard Place' (Sec. F.8)
< >	New Conversion Type Parameter (Sec. F.7.3)
< >	Template Parameter List (Sec. F.7)
<<	Shift ops (Binary) (Sec. A.1.3.3)
<<=	Assignment operators (Binary) (Sec. A.1.3.7, Sec. 4.5)
<=	Less-than-or-equal-to (Binary) (Sec. A.1.3.4)
=	Assigning Value to Enumerator (Sec. F.5.2)
=	Assignment operators (Binary) (Sec. A.1.3.7, Sec. 4.5)
=	Initialiers (Sec. F.2.5)
=	Pure Virtual Member Functions (Sec. F.5.4)
=	Static Class Member Initializers (Sec. F.2.7)
=	= { } Array and Aggregate initializers (Sec. F.2.6)
=0	Pure Virtual Member Functions (Sec. F.5.4)
==	Equality (Binary) (Sec. A.1.3.4)
={ }	Array and Aggregate initializers (Sec. F.2.6)
>	< > And Include of File From 'Standard Place' (Sec. F.8)
>	< > And New Conversion Type Parameter (Sec. F.7.3)
>	< > And Template Parameter List (Sec. F.7)
>	Greater-than (Binary) (Sec. A.1.3.4)
>=	Greater-than-or-equal-to (Binary) (Sec. A.1.3.4)
>>	Shift ops (Binary) (Sec. A.1.3.3)

`defined()`	And Conditional Compilation (Sec. F.8)
`delete`	Memory deallocator (unary) (Sec. 3.1.2, Sec. 5.5)
derived classes	Derived Classes and Structs (Sec. F.5.4)
destructor	Constructors and Destructors (Sec. F.6.4)
`do`	`do-while()` Statement (Sec. F.4.3)
`double`	Built-in types (Sec. F.2.2)
`dynamic_cast`	New Conversion Operators and Template Syntax (Sec. F.7.3)
`E`	Floating Point Constants (Sec. F.10.3)
`e`	Floating Point Constants (Sec. F.10.3)
`enum`	enum Declaration (Sec. F.5.2)
`enum`	Enumerated Type (Sec. F.5.2)
exception specification	Exception Specification (Sec. F.6.2)
expression	Expression Statement (Sec. F.3)
`extern`	Storage Class (Sec. A.2.2.1.4)
`extern "C"`	Linkage Specification (Sec. F.11)
`extern "C++"`	Linkage Specification (Sec. F.11)
`extern static`	Storage Class (Sec. A.2.2.1.5)
`F`	Floating Point Constants (Sec. F.10.3)
`f`	Floating Point Constants (Sec. F.10.3)
`float`	Built-in types (Sec. F.2.2)
`for`	`for(;;)` Statement (Sec. F.4.3)
Foreign Language Linkage	(Sec. F.11)
`friend`	`friend` Declaration (Sec. F.5.3)
function body	Function Body (Sec. F.6.1)
function call	In Expression Statement (Sec. F.3.5)
function header	Function Header (Sec. F.6.1)
function template	Templates (Sec. F.7.2)
`goto`	Goto Statement (Sec. F.4.7)
Handler	For Exception Handling (Sec. F.4.10)
header	Function Header (Sec. F.6.1)
`if`	`if(), if()-else` Statement (Sec. F.4.2)
inheritance	Derived Classes and Structs (Sec. F.5.4)
`inline`	Inline Functions (Sec. F.6.2)
`inline`	Inline Functions in Class Headers (Sec. F.6.3)
`int`	Built-in types (Sec. F.2.2)

]	[] new, Memory allocator (unary, binary, or ternary) (Sec. 3.1.2, Sec. 5.5)
^	Bitwise XOR (Binary) (Sec. A.1.3.2)
^=	Assignment operators (Binary) (Sec. A.1.3.7, Sec. 4.5)
}	= { } Array and Aggregate initializers (Sec. F.2.6)
{ }	Alternate Null Statement (Sec. F.4.1)
{ }	Compound Statement or Block (Sec. F.4.1)
{ }	Declaring Enumerators (Sec. F.5.2)
|	Bitwise OR (Binary) (Sec. A.1.3.2)
|=	Assignment operators (Binary) (Sec. A.1.3.7, Sec. 4.5)
||	Conditional and Short-Circuit Operators in Expression Statement (Sec. A.1.3.6, Sec. F.3.7)
}	= { } Array and Aggregate initializers (Sec. F.2.6)
}	{ } Alternate Null Statement (Sec. F.4.1)
}	{ } Compound Statement or Block (Sec. F.4.1)
}	{ } Declaring Enumerators (Sec. F.5.2)
~	Bitwise complement (Unary) (Sec. A.1.3.1)
~	~const—Never-const member (Sec. F.5.3)
~const	Never-const member (Sec. F.5.3)

Bibliography

(In Order of Appearance)

A. Aho, R. Sethi, and J. D. Ullman, 1986. *Compilers: Principles, Techniques, and Tools.* Reading, MA: Addison-Wesley.

N. Wirth, 1975. *Algorithms + Data Structures = Programs.* Englewood Cliffs, NJ: Prentice-Hall.

D. E. Knuth, 1973. *The Art of Computer Programming (Vols. I and III).* Reading, MA: Addison-Wesley.

B. W. Kernighan and P. J. Plauge, 1978. *The Elements of Programming Style* (2nd Edition). New York, NY: McGraw-Hill.

M. Ellis and B. Stroustrup, 1990 (Reprinted with corrections, 1991). *The Annotated C++ Reference Manual.* Reading, MA: Addison-Wesley. (This book is often called "the ARM.")

M. Page-Jones, 1980. *The Practical Guide to Structured Systems.* New York, NY: Yourdon Press.

R. S. Pressman, 1992. *Software Engineering: A Practitioner's Approach.* New York, NY: McGraw-Hill.

J. Rumbaugh, et al., 1991. *Object-Oriented Modelling and Design.* Englewood Cliffs, NJ: Prentice-Hall.

S. Schlaer and S. J. Mellor, 1988. *Object-Oriented Systems Analysis: Modelling the World in Data.* New York, NY: Yourdon Press.

Index

ABOUT THE AUTHOR

Mark Terribile is currently affiliated with AT&T and has over eight years' experience working with UNIX, C, and C++. Among other projects, he has been involved in the C++ software design and testing of a telephone network, UNIX software development for a medical imaging system, reverse engineering, and enhancing a midrange PBX system.